NATIONALISM IN CANADA

by the UNIVERSITY LEAGUE FOR SOCIAL REFORM

edited by PETER RUSSELL

with a foreword by FRANK UNDERHILL

McGRAW-HILL COMPANY OF CANADA LIMITED

TORONTO NEW YORK LONDON SYDNEY

NATIONALISM IN CANADA

Library of Congress Catalog Card Number 66-26842

94745

1 2 3 4 5 6 7 8 9 0   D - 6 6 - 9 8 7 6 6

Printed and bound in Canada.

the authors

CARL BERGER   Department of History, University of Toronto

CRAIG BROWN   Department of History, University of Toronto

MICHEL BRUNET   Département d'Histoire, Université de Montréal

MAURICE CARELESS   Department of History, University of Toronto

STEPHEN CLARKSON   Department of Political Economy, University of Toronto

JOHN DALES   Department of Political Economy, University of Toronto

ALFRED DUBUC   Département des Sciences Economiques, Université de Montréal

JAMES GUILLET   Department of Chemistry, University of Toronto

CHARLES HANLY   Department of Philosophy, University of Toronto

COLE HARRIS   Department of Geography, University of Toronto

GEORGE HEIMAN	Department of Political Economy, University of Toronto
JOHN HOLMES	Canadian Institute of International Affairs
STEPHEN HYMER	Department of Economics, Yale University
IAN MACDONALD	Chief Economist, Province of Ontario (formerly member of the Department of Political Economy, University of Toronto)
KENNETH McNAUGHT	Department of History, University of Toronto
FRANK PEERS	Department of Political Economy, University of Toronto (formerly Supervisor of Public Affairs, Canadian Broadcasting Corporation)
ABRAHAM ROTSTEIN	Department of Political Economy, University of Toronto
PETER RUSSELL	Department of Political Economy, University of Toronto
DONALD SMILEY	Department of Economics and Political Science, University of British Columbia
ELIZABETH WANGENHEIM	Graduate Student in Sociology, University of Toronto
MELVILLE WATKINS	Department of Political Economy, University of Toronto
FRANK WATT	Department of English, University College, University of Toronto

preface

This is the second volume produced under the auspices of the University League for Social Reform. The first volume, entitled *The Prospect of Change,* was edited by Abraham Rotstein and published by McGraw-Hill of Canada early in 1965. In the Preface to that volume the editor described the history and nature of the U.L.S.R., and the events which led up to the publication of its first book. Here we need only explain the developments which have taken place since then and form the background of the present volume.

As was the case with *Prospect,* this book has grown out of a series of monthly meetings which constituted the U.L.S.R.'s programme for the academic year 1964-65. Approximately half the essays were read and discussed at these meetings. Although the others were assembled after the programme of meetings had been completed, most of them have been circulated, usually in draft form, among the various contributors and U.L.S.R. members. Throughout, an effort was made to insure that authors who were working on related topics were kept in touch with the development of one another's ideas.

It should be noted that the roster of authors for this volume, unlike *Prospect's,* includes the names of four professors from universities outside the Toronto area. We should explain that in soliciting papers from Alfred Dubuc and Michel Brunet, both of whom are French-speaking professors at the University of Montreal, Professor Donald Smiley of the University of British Columbia and Professor Stephen Hymer of Yale University, our intention has not been to achieve anything that might be called "regional representation", let alone ethnic or national representation. Rather we believed that all four, as individuals, had interesting and distinctive things to say about important phases of our theme, Nationalism in Canada.

Beyond these contributions we remain a Toronto-based group—a fact of which we are neither proud nor ashamed. Although, as editor, I have come to doubt whether it is a very significant fact; the difficulty experienced in establishing points of agreement among the authors suggests that if their locale has been a major determinant of their thought, it is an influence which has not had uniform effects.

It may, at first glance, seem odd that a group such as the U.L.S.R. which, ostensibly, is devoted to the development of reform ideas in Canada should organize a collection of papers focusing on the theme of nationalism. After all, nationalism as a body of political attitudes, whatever it is, does not seem to be the stuff of which hard-headed, well-researched reform programmes are made. As political thought, nationalism conforms much more to the type which Georges Sorel characterized as "myth", in contrast to what he called "utopia". The "utopia" is the normal product of scholarly criticism and advocacy, based on systematic diagnosis of a social ill and the deliberate construction of its appropriate remedy, whereas the "myth"—and this is surely true of a deeply felt sense of nationalism—is above all an expression of faith, a call for action, a plea for collective solidarity which depends for its validity not on the truth or logic of its contention but on its ability to inspire its adherents with a belief in its historical destiny.

Certainly the U.L.S.R.'s choice of nationalism as the unifying theme for its most recent programme did not stem from a shared feeling of ardent nationalism. Readers should not expect to find in this book a cohesive manifesto of Canadian nationalism. The common denominator of our contributors' concerns has been not an affinity for nationalism, but a recognition of its great importance in the contemporary world. For in an age of mass politics, however empirical and logical the would-be reformer might wish to be, his work, if it is to be politically relevant, must take into account those sentiments which move large groups of politically active people. Today, on both the Canadian and the international scene, it is nationalist sentiment of one kind or another which appears most frequently as an ingredient of popular political ferment.

The same newspapers which have been reporting the intensification of nationalist opinion in Quebec and the nationalist reaction to that opinion in the rest of Canada are also constantly informing Canadians of explosive nationalist agitations in Asia, Africa, Latin America, the Middle East, and throughout much of the Communist world. It is for this reason that Canadians, confronting the challenge to the future of their nation-state posed by the centrifugal forces of co-operative federalism and the Quiet Revolution in Quebec or by the supranational pull of North American continentalism, should see their situation as part of a larger global pattern in which the future of the nation-state as the basic unit of political organization is the most important single issue. It is for this reason that an organization such as the U.L.S.R., determined as many of its members may be to be cool and careful in their approach to social problems, finds it imperative to plunge into the passionate and elusive world of nationalism.

To torture an old adage: "nationalism is too important to be left to the nationalists". Nationalism is too rich a vein of our experience to be irrelevant to the shape of our future. We cannot, if we wish to act intelligently on that future, afford to leave the character and cultivation of nationalism as the exclusive preserve of the romantic rhetorician or the jingoistic politician. Canadian scholarship has at its disposal now both a large body of historical knowledge as well as many new methods of social and historical analysis which should make it possible to gain a much firmer mental grasp of our nationalist energies. It is to the prospect of achieving such an enlarged understanding and communicating it to a larger public that this volume is dedicated.

It has been far easier to agree on nationalism as our central theme than to define and assess it. Nationalism has meant and now means so many different things to so many different people. It is a political sentiment which can be experienced at quite different levels: for some it is simply a deep sense of loyalty to, or pride in, one's native land, whereas for others it takes the form of a well-articulated political philosophy, encompassing the overriding goals and policies of the nation-state. Both of these conceptions of nationalism and modifications of them are represented in the volume. It might have been tidier to have had all the contributors agree on a conception and definition of nationalism, but then we would have had a much smaller book, if a book at all. While we have not achieved uniformity in the treatment of nationalism, our hope is that each author has clearly identified the distinctive terms of his own approach to the subject.

In planning our exploration of nationalism in Canada we identified three major dimensions of the subject and invited contributors to address themselves to any or all of these aspects. The first two dimensions were essentially historical or descriptive, involving an inquiry into the peculiar shape of nationalist thought in Canada and the role which it has played in Canadian life. We wanted some papers to portray the substantive content—the concrete beliefs—which have sustained Canadian nationalists in the past, and attempt some explanation of the determinants of these beliefs. Others have been directed more towards examining the effect which nationalist attitudes have had, generally, on the main course of Canadian history, or more particularly, on specific areas of policy or culture. Finally, all those who have participated in the programme have been urged to address themselves to the normative question of what kind and degree of nationalism is appropriate or desirable for Canada.

While these three dimensions are all present to some degree in most of the essays, there is a rough distinction in emphasis among the various divisions into which the book is organized. The opening sections on *The Land* and *The People* are, in the main, devoted to identifying elements which have entered into Canadian nationalist thought. A later section on *New Perspectives* endeavours to illuminate some of these nationalist sentiments and anxieties—their past and their future—in terms of categories of explanation stimulated by recent developments in the social sciences. The papers in the sections on *Policy* and *Culture* have concentrated primarily on the interaction between discrete phases of national life and nationalist sentiments or aspirations. In the section on *The Federation*, although the papers all have an explanatory or historical phase, they tend to be more concerned with the prescription of guidelines for the development of the Canadian nation-state. The broader question of nationalism as a governing political philosophy both for Canada and for the world community is taken up in the final section on *Ideology*.

In shaping the general style of discussion, our editorial goal throughout has been to encourage our authors to strike a level which lies somewhere between the scholarly journal and the mass circulation newspaper or magazine. This, indeed, is the publishing ideal of the U. L. S. R.: to provide a medium in which Canadian scholars in a variety of fields can share their ideas on public affairs with a wider audience than they normally reach in their more esoteric and specialized publications. We continue to believe that this is a worthwhile ideal, although this editor, for one, is under no illusion that it is an easy ideal to achieve nor one that should be pressed too far.

No doubt it is important, some would say essential, that the knowledge and convinctions of academics should be communicated more broadly to the general public. But it is equally essential to sustain a division of labour between the journalistic and scholarly treatment of subjects. The journalist provides the instantaneous and intuitive portrayal of public events, clearly identifying the most immediate problems and possibilities in the various dimensions of community life. The academic usually sees events in a broader perspective and is at once more cautious and more theoretical in his attempts to explain them; his analysis of problems is more complex, and if he proposes any solutions, his endorsement of them will be more restrained and qualified. Perhaps there are a gifted few who move easily between these two modes of communication, but most do not. The popular commentator and the scholarly analyst both lose if they fail to respect the distinctive merits of one another's work. The community loses, in terms of the vitality and depth of its cultural life, if either forsakes his own idiom for the other's.

Perhaps the measure of our success in this volume will be the extent to which the journalists accuse us of being too academic and the academic purists charge us with being too journalistic!

It would be impossible to acknowledge all those who have assisted in the production of this volume. In both its conception and execution it has been a thoroughly collective enterprise. However, we would like to record our very special gratitude for the constant support and encouragement which we received from Abraham Rotstein, not to mention the guidance we derived from his own editorship of *The Prospect of Change*. Of the others whose names stand out among those who helped with the editing of papers and the direction of the general programme, we should mention Trevor Lloyd and Jack McLeod, who are now organizing yet another collection of U. L. S. R. essays, this time on the theme of Big

Government, Ronald Blair, Stephen Clarkson, Melville Watkins, Ramsay Cook, Kenneth McNaught, John Dales, Harry Eastman and Gerald Helleiner. Finally, our very deep thanks are due to the secretaries in the University of Toronto's Department of Political Economy, Miss Gloria Draper, Mrs. E. McCulloch, Miss Elaine Pyatt and Miss Dianne Kislashko for their patience and skill in typing the numerous drafts of all the papers.

P. H. R.
May, 1966

table of contents

THE FEDERATION

POLICY

CULTURE

NEW PERSPECTIVES

IDEOLOGY

foreword •   frank underhill

We shall all officially be nationalists in our centenary year of 1967—well, nearly all. But the twenty-two contributors to this book make clear how many varieties of nationalist sentiment there are in our country. This diversity is all to the good, within limits. There is not the slightest likelihood of the national state disappearing in our day like some obsolete dinosaur. It is the natural framework into which peoples will continue to group themselves. But nationalism has become the dominant twentieth century form of religion. And all organized religions are dangerous unless they include a strong element of Laodiceans, sceptics, heretics and plain unbelievers among their membership.

Our authors here have passed beyond two of the forms of Canadian nationalism that have flourished in the past century. They abandon the myth of the Canadian as the strong silent he-man of the North, deriving his un-American and anti-American virtues from his mystic communion with the northern lights of the Arctic. (As for his silence, he was silent not because he was strong but because he had nothing to say.) We can now all recognize that this once popular national hero was striding about the southern fringes of the Pre-Cambrian Shield with false hair on his chest. They also abandon the concept of *British* North America as defining the Canadian identity, a concept which, of course, was always rejected by the French-Canadian part of the community. Our new Maple Leaf flag will, one hopes, be taken by future generations as the epoch-making symbol marking the end of the era of the Wasp domination of Canadian society. At any rate, our authors are all post-Wasp in their outlook.

On the other hand, they do not quite come to grips with the two major problems that have always confronted us as Canadian nationalists: the relations between the English-speaking majority and the French-speaking minority; and the relations between Canadians and Americans. I suspect that this is because they are all a little bit romantic about how social reform is going to unite the French and English citizens of the Left as no other force has succeeded in doing, and is also at last going to give all Canadians something about which they can genuinely feel that they are superior to the private-enterprise Americans. I was romantic in this way myself in the 1930's; but since then the world has had great opportunities to learn about some of the more sinister potentialities of both nationalism and socialism. The innocence of the radicals of the 1930's is not permissible to those of the 1960's.

First, as to English-French relations. The Fathers in 1867 announced "a new nationality". It was to be a pan-Canadian nationality. It was to be that of a composite, heterogeneous, plural society, transcending differences of ethnic origin and religion among its citizens. It was also to be an open society, recruiting its population through large-scale immigration. This conception of the term "nation" was, of course, the American conception. Nationalism was to be a great constructive uniting force, overcoming the particularisms of ethnic, religious and regional groups. The Fathers of Confederation were not quite aware that this wider, more liberal conception of nationality was being replaced in the Europe of their day by a narrower, more exclusive one. The nation was coming to be thought of as an organic folk group, separated off by biological descent from other groups, deriving its reason for separateness from the mystical distinctive qualities of its original folk founders. This narrow tribal nationalism has become steadily more attractive to the French Canadians as they have discovered that the Calhoun-Cartier gospel of concurrent majorities in a pluralistic society doesn't work as they had hoped it would in 1867.

On this question of the meaning of the concept "nation" in Canada, Messrs. Brunet and McNaught collide head-on in this volume. I wish that some of Mr. McNaught's English-speaking colleagues had been as frank and outspoken as he is.

If a pan-Canadian nation is to become a reality in our country we must find some great enterprises in which French and English Canadians will agree to cooperate under the leadership of the national government. (At present, we do not even dare to call that government national.) It is the program-content of our nationalism that matters; everything else, such as the ideal paper constitution, is mere housekeeping. Before 1914, we seemed to have discovered such enterprises in the Pacific railway, the National Policy, and the immigration programme designed to fill up our empty spaces. Since World War I we have failed to find anything to take their place.

In the 1930's it seemed to those of us on the political left in English-speaking Canada that the economic-planning, social-welfare state would provide the moral equivalent of the C.P.R., and that the C.C.F. might prove to be the political instrument which would lead the Canadian people into the next era of a constructive nationalism. But we could not convert enough of our fellow English Canadians to this vision, while the French Canadians still accepted the *anti-étatisme* of their church and still remembered what English-Canadian majority rule had meant in World War I. Today, so one would guess, the majority of both French and English are coming to accept the concept of the economic-planning, social-welfare state. But the vital question has become: which state is to be entrusted with these planning and welfare functions, the pan-Canadian state whose capital is in Ottawa, or the French-Canadian state whose capital is in Quebec?

What makes this problem of "which state?" the more difficult is the fact that, in the new realm of world power-politics into which we have entered, the French-Canadian and the English-Canadian outlooks are equally far apart. We did not agree back in the thirties when the leaders of Quebec hankered after the corporatism of Mussolini and Franco. We do not agree today; for, just as we English Canadians have at last got rid of our Mother Country, the French Canadians, who have stood on their own feet for two centuries, are discovering that they too have a Mother Country. We have failed to synchronize our watches. All that can be hoped for is that it will not take them as long as it took us to get rid of our Mother Country complex. In the meantime, they join the Gaullist side in European and Nato matters, as against the special Anglo-American relationship which we English Canadians have found so attractive in our North Atlantic Triangle.

Continentalism is the second difficult problem about which I find our authors insufficiently realistic. "Continentalism" has, alas, become a four-letter word in our Canadian political vocabulary, and seems as a rule to be used as such in this book. We cannot at present discuss our relations with the United States in a cool, rational frame of mind. Note how easily some of the cool, rational intellectuals of this volume accept assumptions about the Americans which are the precise twentieth century equivalents of those nineteenth century assumptions about our Canadian moral superiority at which we all now smile in genial irony. I mean assumptions such as that our Canadian "mosaic" differs in some fundamental and profoundly healthy way from the American "melting-pot", or that we have at our disposal some international policy which is better fitted for the needs of the contemporary world—it is certainly cheaper—than the "imperialistic" power politics of Washington.

On this subject of continentalism, may it not be that our ordinary rank-and-file Canadians have shown a deeper instinctive wisdom than most of their intellectual leaders? The leaders have been busy with the high mission of saving the northern half of the continent from Americanism, while thousands, millions of ordinary Canadians, French as well as English, have quietly emigrated and become American citizens. The leaders of 1867 were proud of setting up a national community which was not a populist democracy like the United States—all the Fathers disapproved of manhood suffrage—which was monarchical rather than republican, which retained the sober agrarian virtues and had not fallen victim to the flashy urban vices. And steadily since then, while obediently saying yes yes to their leaders, the Canadian people have been adopting the American way of life.

What I am suggesting is that the mass of ordinary Canadians, without in any sense being in danger of losing their Canadian identity, are subconsciously experimenting with some new form of international relationship, while our social scientists have not yet discovered the new categories of thought into which this emerging new relationship may be fitted. Our alarmist intellectuals—and not all of the authors in this book are in the alarmist ranks—are archaists suffering from hardening of the categories. It is the mean, sensual Canadians who are in the avant garde.

In addition to the delightful literary essays of Frank Watt and Carl Berger, I was especially attracted by the essays of Abraham Rotstein and Melville Watkins on the effects of the developing twentieth century technology on the spirit of nationalism. One of them seemed to take comfort in the reflection that the collectivism which is the essential result of modern technology is something that nationalists find congenial, while the other concluded that we are moving toward a great complex of collectivities, many of which transcend national boundaries. My archaist nineteenth century liberal sympathies make me worry about what happens to individual liberties in the midst of all these collectivities, national or supranational.

But I have succumbed too completely to the temptation to tell my younger contemporaries what they should have written. This is a most ungracious way to respond to the invitation to write a foreword to their book. I was really only trying to let them know how stimulating I have found their twenty-two contributions.

THE LAND •

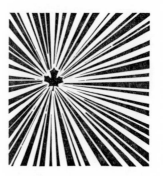

the true north

strong and free •

carl berger

Hail! Rugged monarch, Northern Winter, hail!
Come! Great Physician, vitalize the gale;
Dispense the ozone thou has purified,
With Frost and Fire, where Health and age reside,—
Where Northern Lights electrify the soul
Of Mother Earth, whose throne is near the Pole.

Why should the children of the North deny
The sanitary virtues of the sky?
Why should they fear the cold, or dread the snow,
When ruddier blood thro' their hot pulses flow?

. . .

We have the Viking blood, and Celtic bone,
The Saxons' muscled flesh, and scorn to groan,
Because we do not bask in Ceylon's Isle,
Where Heber said, that "only man is vile".

3

. . .

But we, as laymen, must get down to earth,
And praise the clime which gave our nation birth.
Kind Winter is our theme.

> William Henry Taylor,
> *Canadian Seasons. Spring: Summer: Autumn:*
> *Winter: with a Medley of Reveries in Verse*
> *and Prose and Other Curios,*
> Toronto, 1913, pp. 63-64.

Everybody talks about the weather and the climate: seldom have these been exalted as major attributes of nationality. Yet from the days of the French explorers, who often remarked that the future inhabitants of northern America must necessarily be as hardy as their environment, to John Diefenbaker's invocation of the northern destiny of the nation, detached observers and patriotic spokesmen alike have fixed upon the northern character of Canada as one of the chief attributes of her nationality. Canadian national feeling, like the nationalist impulse in other countries, has expressed itself in myths and legends about the past and anticipations of noble mission in the future, as well as in distinctive economic and international policies. Such myths and symbols nourish and sustain the emotional taproot of nationalism, and impart to it an intellectual content which itself has an attractive power. The purpose of this paper is to describe the elements and savour the texture of one such recurrent theme in Canadian nationalist thought which flowered in the half century after Confederation and which is, in muted form, still with us—the idea that Canada's unique character derived from her northern location, her severe winters and her heritage of 'northern races'.

THE TRUE NORTH, STRONG AND FREE

In the rhetoric of the day, Canada was the "Britain of the North", "this northern kingdom", the "True North" in Tennyson's phrase, the "Lady of the Snows" in Kipling's. "Canada is a young, fair and stalwart maiden of the north."[1] "The very atmosphere of her northern latitude, the breath of life that rose from lake and forest, prairie and mountain, was fast developing a race of men with bodies enduring as iron and minds as highly tempered as steel."[2] Canada was the "Young giant nation of the North", the "Young scion of the northern zone"; her people, "Our hardy northern race"; her location, those "Stern latitudes".[3] These images denote not merely geographical location or climatic condition but the combination of both, moulding racial character. The result of life in the northern latitudes was the creation and sustenance of self-reliance, strength, hardness—in short, all the attributes of a dominant race. "Northern nations always excel southern ones in energy and stamina, which accounts for their prevailing power."[4] In the north "the race is compelled by nature to maintain its robust attributes, mental and physical, whereas in more sunny countries like Africa and Australia the tendency of the climate is toward deterioration."[5] "A constitution nursed upon the oxygen of our bright winter atmosphere", exclaimed Governor General Dufferin, "makes its owner feel as though he could toss about the pine trees in his glee . . ."[6] Just as "northern" was synonymous with strength and self-reliance, so "southern" was equated with degeneration, decay and effeminacy. Our "bracing northern winters," declared the Globe in 1869, "will preserve us from the effeminacy which naturally steals over the most vigorous races when long under the relaxing influence of tropical or even generally mild and genial skies."[7] Moreover, it was believed that liberty originated among the tribes of northern Europe and was dependent upon those very characteristics which the northern environment called forth. Canada, then, was not only the true north, but also strong and free.

In origin, ideas about the relationship between climate and the character of "races" and their institutions were rooted in myths and stereotypes in classical, medieval and renaissance Europe, most of which viewed the southern Mediterranean peoples as gay, lively and individualistic, and the northerners as stupid and dull barbarians.[8] The first coherent Canadian statement of the idea of the northern race came from an associate of the Canada First Movement who was also a Fellow of the Royal Society of Northern Antiquaries of Copenhagen, Robert Grant Haliburton. Lamenting the fact that Confederation had been created with as little excitement among the masses as if a joint-stock company had been formed, he asked, "Can the generous flame of national spirit be kindled and blaze in the icy bosom of the frozen north?" Convinced that the indispensable attribute of a nation, a "national spirit", was the product of slow growth unless stimulated by a violent struggle, the memory of a glorious past, or the anticipation of a bright future, Haliburton added to the Canada First spirit the contention that Canada's future as a dominant nation was secure because of its northern character. *"We are the Northmen of the New World"*, his lecture to the Montreal Literary Club in 1869 on the men of the north and their place in history was the seedbed of the northern race idea. Ironically, Haliburton's poor health compelled him to spend his winters in tropical climates, where he devoted himself to ethnological and anthropological investigations. In 1887 he discovered the existence of a race of pigmies in North Africa.

Haliburton's declaration that Canadians were a northern race was expressed in the language of science and the rich imagery of romantic history. "Our corn fields, rich though they are, cannot compare with the fertile prairies of the West, and our long winters are a drain on the profits of business, but may not our snow and frost give us what is of more value than gold or silver, a healthy, hardy, virtuous, dominant race?" The peculiar characteristic of the new dominion, he asserted, "must ever be that it is a Northern country inhabited by the descendants of Northern races." This claim to dominance rested on two assumptions: firstly, the hardy northern races of Europe are attracted to Canada. The British people themselves are "but a fusion of many northern elements which are here again meeting and mingling, and blending together to form a new nationality." This new nationality must comprise at once "the Celtic, the Teutonic, and the Scandinavian elements, and embrace the Celt, the Norman French, the Saxon and the Swede." Secondly, to Haliburton, the climate itself was a creative force. "Is it climate that produces varieties in our race or must we adopt the views of some eminent authorities of science, who hold that the striking diversities now apparent in the languages, temperament, and capacities of nations, must have existed *ab initio*? The Mosaic chronology must be rejected and the period of man's life on earth must be extended to millions of years." "If climate has not had the effect of moulding races, how is it that southern nations have almost invariably been inferior to and subjugated by the men of the north?"

The stern climate would preserve in their pristine vigour the characteristics of the northern races and ensure that Canada would share the destiny of the northmen of the old world, who destroyed Rome after it "had become essentially Southern in its characteristics." Those northmen were not barbarians but the carriers of the germ of liberty. "On investigating the history of our laws and of the rise of civil and political liberty in Europe," Haliburton found them rooted in the elemental institutions of the northmen. "Almost all the Northern nations had similar systems of regulating the rights of property and the remedies of wrongs. Their laws were traditions called by them their *customs,* an unwritten code which still exists in England where it is known as the Common law, ... (and) it is a remarkable fact that wherever these unwritten laws have been preserved, civil and political liberty has also survived." In Canada, "the cold north wind that rocked the cradle of our race, still blows through our forests, and breathes the spirit of liberty into our hearts."[9] Thus, because of the climate and because Canadians are sprung from these men of the north—the "Aryan" family, Canada must be a pre-eminent power, the home of a superior race, the heir of both the historical destiny of the ancient Scandinavians and their spirit of liberty.

In the exuberant optimism of Canada First nationalism, Haliburton took the Canadian climate—since the days of Voltaire's famous disparagement, the symbol of sterility, inhospitality and worthlessness—and turned it into the dynamic element of national greatness. Though he was to break with Haliburton over the issue of Canadian independence, to the end of his days the irrepressible Colonel Denison could boast that "We are the Northmen of the new world."[10] Charles Mair, too, thought that "whilst the south is in a great measure a region of effeminacy and disease, the north-west is a decided recuperator of decayed function and wasted tissue."[11] And William Foster, in his address on the new nationality in 1871, said that "The old Norse mythology, with its Thor hammers and Thor hammerings, appeals to us,—for we are a Northern people,—as the true out-crop of human nature, more manly, more real, than the weak marrow-bones superstition of an effeminate South."[12] It is no accident that members of this youthful and intellectual nationalist group should appeal to what Mair, in his poem on Foster's death, called "the unconquered North", that they should extol Alexander Morris' vision of "the Great Britannic Empire of the North", or that they should be remembered a generation later as exponents of the northern destiny of Canada. Their most practical achievement in politics was the agitation for Canadian acquisition of the north-west territory, the importance of which they contended had been obscured by tales of ice and snow falsely broadcast by Hudson Bay Company officials to protect their fur domain from settlement.

CLIMATIC OR RACIAL DETERMINISM?

While Haliburton's address included much that was to receive progressive elaboration by others, such as the notion that both French and English were, in racial terms, one people, it contained an ambivalence that was to become more obvious as the idea of the northern race became enmeshed in a popularized Darwinism. This dichotomy was simply between an optimistic, idealistic meliorism which took climate as moulding desirable qualities irrespective of the racial origins of the people, and a scientific determinism which saw racial capacities as fixed, or changeable only to a limited degree. Haliburton avoided such subtleties by implying that all future immigration into Canada would consist of those races already inured and adapted to the northern environment. Later, more pessimistic writers were to see the climate as a "barrier" to certain kinds of immigrants, rather than as an agency for totally transforming them. This dualism can be best illustrated by considering two different versions of the idea.

A most forceful statement of the view that assumed the complete malleability of character was made in 1877 by another Nova Scotian, Charles R. Tuttle. A self-educated school teacher who later made a career of journalism in Winnipeg and the United States, Tuttle produced a large number of now forgotten books including an imposing two-volume history of Canada. In this history he expressed the optimistic opinion that the institutions, soil and climate of Canada would determine the character of the people. The immigrants, he wrote, come from the monarchical countries of Europe, "ignorant, rude, and unmannerly", but their character is transformed, they become self-reliant, and exhibit a "manly independence," under the influence of British institutions and the "broad rivers, boundless prairies, high mountains, and pathless woods."[13]

In Tuttle, a romantic ruralism was mixed with the conviction that man's capacity for improvement was infinite and, in a favourable environment, inevitable. Where he saw the "ignorant, rude, and unmannerly" being formed into independent and hardy yeomen by the natural features of the country and British institutions, more pessimistic observers, while not denying the potent influence of environment, nevertheless emphasized rather the inherent and unchangeable aptitudes of the "northern races." That the northern climate constituted a national blessing because it excluded "weaker" races was the persistent theme of the writings and orations of the Canadian imperialist George Parkin. A native of New Brunswick, Parkin was one of the most forceful and idealistic spokesmen of the Imperial Federation League, Principal of Upper Canada College during the late 1890's, and subsequently one of the organizers of the Cecil Rhodes scholarship trust. Heavily influenced by the social Darwinism of the time, and acknowledging his debt to the historian Buckle for the idea of climatic influence upon the life of nations, Parkin called the Canadian climate "one of our greatest blessings." The "severe winter climate of Canada," he said, "is perhaps the most valuable asset that the country has." A temperature of twenty degrees below zero which he found at Winnipeg "seemed to give an added activity to peoples' steps and a buoyancy to their spirits." The climate necessitates vigorous effort; "it teaches foresight; it cures or kills the shiftless and improvident; history shows that in the long run it has made strong races."

Where Tuttle viewed the capacity for self-government as the product of the environment, Parkin contended that fitness for self-government was itself the inherent function of the northern races. Without race vanity, he asserted, we may attribute to the Anglo-Saxon race a unique aptitude for self-government. The special importance of the Canadian climate, therefore, was not merely that it sustained the hardy character of the stronger races, but that it also constituted, in Darwinian terms, "a persistent process of natural selection." The northern winters ensured that Canada would have no negro problem, "which weighs like a troublesome nightmare upon the civilization of the United States"; and it seemed that nature itself had decreed that Canada would have no cities "like New York, St. Louis, Cincinnati, or New Orleans which attract even the vagrant population of Italy and other countries of Southern Europe." "Canada," Parkin emphasized, "will belong to the sturdy races of the North-Saxon, and Celt, Scandinavian, Dane and Northern German, fighting their way under conditions sometimes rather more severe than those to which they have been accustomed in their old homes." The climate "is certain, in short, to secure for the Dominion and perpetuate there the vigour of the best northern races."[14]

THE ADVANTAGES OF NORTHERNNESS

To recapitulate and detail the elements of this concept is to indicate the basis of its credibility and the nature of its appeal. First of all, the very fact of northernness connoted strength and hardihood, vigour and purity. "Strength and power," ran the familiar refrain, "have ever been with the Northern peoples."[15] In the struggle for existence, the northern conditions called forth the virtues of self-reliance and strength: only the fittest survived. On the other hand, the "south" conjured up the image of enervation, of abundance stifling the Victorian values of self-help, work and thrift, of effeminacy, of voluptuous living and consequently of the decay and degeneration of character.

A whole series of desirable national characteristics were derived from Canada's northern location. It was implied that northern peoples expressed their hard individualism in an individualistic religion, stripped of the gorgeous luxuries congenial to southern Catholicism. The climate, said Parkin, imparts "a Puritan turn of mind which gives moral strenuousness."[16] A Methodist clergyman and editor, who attended the American centennial exhibition in 1876 and saw a representative collection of European paintings, reported his disgust with the Catholic art of the south, a reaction he attributed to the lax morals of the "Latin" races. "I must," he wrote, "record my protest against the sensuous character of many of the foreign paintings, especially of France, Austria, and Spain. In this respect they are in striking contrast with the almost universal chaste and modest character of the English and American pictures, and those of Rothern (sic, Northern) Europe. I attribute this difference partly to the only partial moral restraints of the Roman Catholic religion, and partly to a survival, in the old Latin races, of the ancient pagan characteristics which created the odious art and literature, and social corruptions of the effete and dying Roman Empire."[17] These impurities, of course, were due to much else besides climate, but the clear, cold and frosty air itself seemed an insulation against lax morality. Another clergyman found in the Canadian winter the impulse to cultural and mental improvement. The winter "is prophetic . . . of a race, in mind and body and moral culture, of the highest type." Applying to Canada the remarks that Sir Charles Dilke had made in reference to Scotland, Reverend Wightman cited with approval the opinion that the " 'long winters cultivate thrift, energy and fore-thought, without which civilization would perish, and at the same time give leisure for reading and study. So the Scottish, the Icelanders, the Swedes, and the northern races generally, are much better educated than the Latin and southern races.' "[18]

The Canadian winter was not only considered to be conducive to mental improvement: in maintaining physical health and stimulating robustness, according to one of the foremost Canadian physicians of the day, it was unsurpassed. A belief in the healthful qualities of the climate was expressed in much of the literature on the northern theme, but it was left to a surgeon at the Hôtel-Dieu in Montreal to impart to this idea the authority of medical knowledge and statistical proof. William Hales Hingston had studied medicine at McGill and Edinburgh, as well as Berlin, Heidelberg and Vienna; in 1854 he began practice in Montreal and was for many years surgeon at the largest hospital in Canada and a professor of clinical surgery at the Montreal School of Medicine. In 1884 Hingston published a series of papers under the title, *The Climate of Canada and its relation to Life and Health.* Employing statistics provided by the surgeons at British and American army stations, he ascertained that as one passed northward the salubrity of the climate increased, that the ratios of mortality from digestive, respiratory and nervous disorders decreased in a northward progression. After considering practically every known malady from diarrhoea to dysentery, consumption to cataract, he emphasized that there are no diseases indigenous to the country. The dry air and cold winter, moreover, are decided recuperators of disease. "Indeed," he concluded, "in considering the few diseases which here afflict humanity relatively to elsewhere, we have great reason to be thankful to the All-powerful Controller of the seasons as of our fate, . . . He keeps us in health, comfort and safety." If only such pernicious social habits as intemperance could be avoided, the climate was most "favourable to the highest development of a hardy, long-lived, intelligent people"; the tendency "is unmistakably in favour of increased muscular development"; "the future occupants of the soil will be taller, straighter, leaner people—hair darker and drier and coarser; muscles more tendinous and prominent and less cushioned . . ." These future occupants of the soil will be, emphatically, a "*Canadian* people", for the distinct nationalities of Europe will blend here into a homogeneous race, the predominating characteristics of which will be determined "after the fashion described by Darwin as the struggle for existence." To this people "will belong the privilege, the great privilege, of aiding in erecting, in what was so lately a wilderness, a monument of liberty and civilization, broader, deeper, firmer, than has ever yet been raised by the hand of man."[19] There was much in Hingston's book—a description of the variety of the climate, reflections on social habits, and the straight-faced observation that those frozen to death display on their visages a look of contentment achieved only by successful religious mystics —but its central burden was that the northern location will breed a distinctive, superior and healthy people.

It seemed that scarcely any advantages accruing to Canada from the winter season went unnoticed or unsung. The winter snow covers and protects fall crops; the frost acts as a solvent on the soil, ploughing the ground and leaving it in springtime "completely pulverized"; the cold freezes newly-killed livestock and preserves them for market. It makes possible the commercial activity of lumbering for the "frost makes bridges without a cent of cost; the snow provides the best roads", "the whole face of the country being literally Macadamized by nature." Winter makes possible sleighing, tobogganing, snowshoeing and skating. "Jack Frost effectually and gratuitously guards us on three thousand miles of our northern coast, and in this he does us a distinct service, greatly relieving national expenditure and contributing much to our sense of security."[20]

A BASIS FOR RACIAL UNITY

While Canada's northernness implied these desirable national advantages, in its second aspect it underlined the fundamental unity of the French and British Canadians. According to most definitions of nationality offered in the late nineteenth century, a nation was held together by the ties of race, religion and language, as well as by a general similarity in political and social institutions. The very existence of the French Canadians, however, and the "racial conflict" and disunity their distinctive social and religious institutions helped to engender, seemed to belie the contention that Canada was a nation.

But the French Canadians, by the very facts of their colonization, settlement and multiplication, had demonstrated their fitness to cope with the inhospitable, northern environment. The stern climate and the winds of winter were uniform on both sides of the Ottawa River. The "geographical contour of our Country," said F. B. Cumberland, Vice-President of the National Club of Toronto, "assists by creating a Unity of Race. Living throughout in a region wherein winter is everywhere a distinct season of the year, inuring the body and stimulating to exertion, we are by nature led to be a provident, a thrifty, and a hardy people; no weakling can thrive among us, we must be as vigorous as our climate." Through the "natural selection" of immigration, only the northern races, including the "Norman

French", have settled here, and what selective immigration has effected "nature is welding together into Unity and by this very similarity of climate creating in Canada a homogeneous Race, sturdy in frame, stable in character, which will be to America what their forefathers, the North-men of old, were to the continent of Europe."[21]

It was argued, moreover, that "there is no real or vital difference in the origin of these two races; back beyond the foreground of history they were one."[22] This identification of the common racial origin of both the British and French Canadians rested on the results of the research of genealogists, like Benjamin Sulte and Cyprien Tanguay, who had inquired into the origins of the original immigrants to New France. Between 1871 and 1890 Tanguay compiled no less than seven volumes of his *Dictionnaire généol-ogique des familles Canadiennes* and demonstrated that the majority of French Canadians were descended from immigrants who had come from Brittany and Normandy. The "French Canadian type," declared Sulte, "is Norman, whether its origin be pure Norman, mixed Norman, Gascon or French-English."[23] Since the Normans themselves were descendants of the Scandinavian invaders of the ninth and tenth centuries who had gone to conquer Britain, it could be claimed that both British and French were a northern race, or at least that both contained elements of the northern strains. It is an interesting fact, asserted the historian William Wood, "that many of the French-Canadians are descended from the Norman-Franks, who conquered England seven hundred years before the English conquered La Nouvelle France, and that, however diverse they are now, the French and British peoples both have some Norman stock in com-mon."[24]

That the "Norman blood" was a positive unifying force in Canada was emphasized by George Bourinot in his constitutional histories, and, in 1925, G. M. Wrong, Professor of History in the University of Toronto, told the Canadian Historical Association that "There is in reality no barrier of race to keep the English and French apart in Canada: the two peoples are identical in racial origins."[25] As late as 1944, Abbé Arthur Maheux, Professor of History at Laval University, after condemning those "people who think along the lines of blood, so being Hitlerites without knowing it," pointed out that "the Norman blood, at least, is a real link between our two groups." The French people, the Abbé explained, "is a mixture of different bloods; the Gaul, the Briton, the Romans, the Norman each gave their share. The same is true with the English people, the Celt, the Briton, the Roman, the Saxon, the Dane, the Norman each gave their share of blood. It is easy to see that the elements are about the same and in about the same proportions in each of these two nations. Both are close relatives by blood from the very beginning of their national existences. And both Canadian groups have the same close kinship."[26]

A RATIONALE FOR ANTI-AMERICANISM

The Canadian people were thus not only collectively a superior race, but their "northernness" was constantly compared to the "southernness" of the United States. The third use of the idea was a vigorous statement of the separateness of the two countries. When the annexationists asked "why should the schism which divided our race on this continent 100 years ago, be perpetuated? ... What do we gain by remaining apart?" and answered their own question by saying that "Union would be the means of ultimately cementing the Anglo-Saxon race throughout the world,"[27] the usual retort was to deny that the Republic was an Anglo-Saxon country and to elaborate Canadian virtues derived from its northernness against the degeneration of "the south". While the northern climate of Canada was both moulding the northern elements and rejecting weaker, southern immigration, thus creating a homogeneous race, the southern climate of the United States was sapping the energies of even those descendants of vigorous races at the same time that it was attracting multitudes of the weaker races from Southern Europe, in addition to providing a hospitable home to the large negro element. This destruction of the homogeneity of the Republic was regarded as "diluting" its strength, as a species of "deterioration". This was because the southern immigrants were neither formed by a hardy climate in their homeland nor forced to adapt to one in the States. In Canada, Principal Falconer of the University of Toronto reassured his readers, "the rigour of the northern climate has been, and will continue to be, a deterrent for the peoples of Southern Europe."[28] Our climate, contended Parkin, excludes the lower races, "squeezed out by that 30 or 40 degrees below zero." Canada attracts "the stronger people of the northern lands. That is the tendency to squeeze out the undesirable and pump in, as Kipling says, . . . the strong and desirable." "We have an advantage, this northern race, of a stern nature which makes us struggle for existence." The "submerged tenth", the weaker members of even the stronger races, are also excluded, and hence

Canada does not suffer from the American labour troubles. Labour problems are unknown in Canada partly because of the abundance of land and partly because the "Canadian winter exercises upon the tramp a silent but well-nigh irresistible persuasion to shift to a warmer latitude." The United States itself thus serves as a "safety-valve" for labour questions in the Dominion. The climate "is a fundamental political and social advantage which the Dominion enjoys over the United States." It ensures stability and ordered development as well as superiority.[29]

NORTHERNNESS AND LIBERTY

The notion of strength and superiority inhering in the quality of northernness included a fourth, and perhaps the most important, element of the general idea. Expressed in the words of Emerson, it was that "Wherever snow falls, there is usually civil freedom."[30] Not only did the northern climate foster exactly those characteristics without which self-government could not work, but it was held that, historically, the "germs" of the institutions of liberty originated among the northern peoples and that northern races, inured by centuries of struggles with the elements and acquaintance with these institutions of self-government, enjoyed a superior capacity for governing themselves. Liberty itself depended upon self-reliance, a rugged independence, instilled by the struggle for existence. Thus to the equation of "northern" with strength and the strenuous virtues, against "southern" with degeneration and effeminacy, was added the identification of the former with liberty and the latter with tyranny.

Because "liberty" was itself somehow the major stimulant to "progress", the comparison was often made in terms of progress and regression. In a book review, the editor of the *Canadian Methodist Magazine* contrasted the result of Anglo-Saxon development in North America with that of the Latin races in South America. "On the one side," he wrote, "a forward motion of society and the greatest development of agriculture, commerce and industry; on the other, society thrown backward and plunged to grovel in a morass of idle, unproductive town life, and given up to officialism and political revolutions. In the North we have the rising of the future, in the South the crumbling and decaying past."[31] Wherein, asked a pamphleteer, lies the secret of such marvellous progress? "It springs largely from the fact that the country was peopled by the Anglo-Saxon race, . . . When Rome was overshadowing the nations of Southern and Central Europe with its greatness, in the cheerless, uninviting north, a people was undergoing hardy discipline, on land and sea, in constant strife and endless foray, which produced a nobler type of manhood than Rome. . . It is from these fearless freemen of North Germany, England is indebted in a large measure for her political liberties."[32]

The idea that it was in the north "that the liberties of the world had their birth" was sustained by the political science of the day. Influenced by the "comparative politics" of E. A. Freeman in England and H. B. Adams in the United States, the constitutional and political writings of George Bourinot detailed the operations of the Teutonic germ theory in Canada. In biological analogy, freedom was a "seed", a "germ", which originated in the tribal assemblies of the ancient Scandinavians, was transplanted to England and subsequently to New England and then to Canada by the migration of descendants of these Teutonic races. Wherever the favoured race appeared, its early institutional life was repeated and amplified because "freedom" was in "the blood". Conversely, southern non-Teutonic peoples were either "untutored" in self-government but were educable, or were incapable of governing themselves altogether. In the bracing climate of the north, so resembling freedom's original home, liberty, it was thought, would flourish in a purer form.[33]

It was this identification of liberty with northernness that gave such force to the anti-American emotion that Canadian, or "British", liberty, was far superior to the uproarious democracy of the United States. It was a charge taken directly from pessimistic American racists. The "new immigration" coming from southern and south-eastern Europe became the object of concern and then dread in the late 1880's, partly because it coincided with political and social disturbances arising from the transition from an agrarian to an industrial civilization. It was thought that this immigration not only destroyed the homogeneity of the American people, but also threatened the very existence of Anglo-Saxon leadership and Anglo-Saxon values. Commenting editorially on an article by Henry Cabot Lodge, the chief immigration restrictionist in the Senate, the *Empire* agreed that the old-stock families in the United States were losing their hold, that immigration and the multiplication of "the dregs of the old world population" were increasing too rapidly for assimilation. "The Anglo-Saxon element, the real strength of the nation, is not proportionally as influential now as it once was."[34] Even earlier, Goldwin Smith feared that "the Anglo-American race is declining in numbers; . . .

The question is whether its remaining stock of vitality is sufficient to enable it, before it loses its tutelary ascendancy, to complete the political education of the other races."[35] What Smith viewed with apprehension, others relished in the conviction that Canada was preserved from such a fate. "Take the fact that one million two hundred thousand people passed through Ellis Island into the port of New York last year. Who were they," asked Parkin, "Italians, Greeks, Armenians, Bulgarians, the Latin races of the South. People unaccustomed to political freedom, unaccustomed to self-government, pouring in. . . They did not come to Canada."[36] In Canada, because of the climate, there were no Haymarket riots, no lynchings, no assassinations of public men. "The United States", declared the *Dominion Illustrated* in 1891, "are welcome to the Hungarians, Poles, Italians and others of that class; they are, as a rule, wretchedly poor, make very poor settlers, and bring with them many of the vices and socialistic tendencies which have caused much trouble to their hosts already. Renewed efforts should . . . be made by our government to induce more of of the hardy German and Norwegian races to remain here."[37]

THE IMPERIALISM OF THE NORTHERN RACE

For the imperialist the idea of the northern race had an importance which transcended its purely Canadian application. It supported the notion of the tutelary role of the stronger races in extending order and liberty to southern peoples who, either because of their climate alone, or, because of their inherent weakness, could neither generate progress unassisted nor erect the institutions of self-government. Imperialists like Parkin had an immense pride in their native Canada: it alone, of all the Dominions, lay above the forty-fifth parallel. Because of the vigour implied in its northernness, Canada could exercise within the imperial framework a dynamic influence on the future, perhaps even exceeding that of the homeland. Because of the inevitable deterioration that was creeping over the urbanized and industrialized Englishman, cut off from the land, Canada was to be a kind of rejuvenator of the imperial blood. For all their rhetoric about the citizens of Canada regarding South Africa or Australia as their own country, this notion of northernness bolstered their feeling of a unique connection between Canada and Britain.

The imperial role of Canada depended on the character of the race, and it was with "character" that imperialists like Parkin and Kipling were most concerned. Their apprehensions that the character of the imperial race had deteriorated, that the instinct of adventure and self-sacrifice which had been the motive force of imperial expansion had decayed, were coupled with the pervasive fear that the race was becoming "soft", that it no longer manifested "hardness"—hardness meaning not callousness but the stoical acceptance of the strenuous life and the performance of duty irrespective of rewards. It was this concern that lay at the bottom of their advocacy of a manly athleticism, their praise for what seemed to some a martial arrogance, and their exhortations to uplift the weaker races, not so much because they believed that the weaker races could be transformed but because the imperial race's assumption of the burden was in itself a test and an exaltation of their race's "character". The motive was as much self-regeneration as altruism. The northern race idea is subtly related to this concern, at least psychologically. In Canada, said Kipling, "there is a fine, hard, bracing climate, the climate that puts iron and grit into men's bones."[38] In moulding character this climate was a permanent fixture, unlike an abundance of free land. It instilled exactly those characteristics upon which the imperialists themselves placed the most value—hardness, strenuousness, endurance—so vital to dominance.

The aspect of northernness was associated with the historic imperialism of the northern races. The British Isles were conquered by the northmen, who transmitted to the Anglo-Saxons their love of the sea as well as their genius for self-government. "The English came to America," wrote the secretary of the Navy League in Quebec, "in obedience to the same racial sea-faring instincts that led their ancestors to England itself."[39] One of the reasons for British primacy, explained another historian, was that "our northern climate has produced a race of sailors and adventurers from the days of the Vikings to the present, inured to all the perils of the sea and the rigours of climate." The Icelandic sagas, he continued, "are an interesting part of the native literature of our race, which owes much of its hardihood and enterprise to the admixture of northern blood."[40] The celebrations in 1892 and 1897 of the voyages of Columbus and Cabot deepened interest in the Norsemen who had preceded both of them, an interest sometimes associated with the arguments of the navalists in the Navy League. Like liberty, the "seafaring instincts" were racial properties. Parkin said that imperial expansion was not haphazard but the inevitable result of "racial instincts" as well as national necessities. The mind which viewed expansive and hardy racial character as northern products saw the Norse voyages as something more than interesting details at the beginning of Canadian history books. "Though nothing came of these Norse discoveries," wrote Charles G. D. Roberts, "they are interesting as the first recorded contact of our race with these lands which we now occupy. They are significant, because they were a direct result of that spirit of determined independence which dwells in our blood."[41]

Moreover, this northerness of the imperial race was connected with the notion of the tendency of world power to shift northward as the phases of evolution proceeded. Parkin, who confessed finding confirmation and amplification of his own beliefs in Benjamin Kidd's *Social Evolution*, must have read with approval Kidd's prediction that northward the march of Empire makes its way:

> The successful peoples have moved west-wards for physical reasons; the seat of power has moved continuously northwards for reasons connected with the evolution in character which the race is undergoing. Man, originally a creature of a warm climate and still multiplying most easily and rapidly there, has not attained his highest development where the conditions of existence have been easiest. Throughout history the centre of power has moved gradually but surely to the north into those stern regions where men have been trained for the rivalry of life in the strenuous conflict with nature in which they have acquired energy, courage, integrity, and those characteristic qualitites which contribute to raise them to a high state of social efficiency. . .[42]

Especially after 1890, the northern race concept was frequently explained in the language of a popularized social Darwinism which imparted to it a scientific credibility surpassing in authority either vague rhetoric or poetic allusions. Parkin often employed the terminology of evolutionary science when expressing the notion, but it was left to an obscure writer in a university magazine to place the idea in the general context of "The Theory of Evolution". Beginning with a curt dismissal of the Mosaic account of creation as "a mixture of Hebrew folk-lore and Christian teaching", he stated that "man himself does not stand apart from the rest of living things as a separate creation, but has had a common origin with them and is governed by the same laws." One of these laws is the progressive evolution of man which accompanied his migration from the tropical to the northern zones. "The most primitive type of man at present existing is the Negro, who, like the Apes most nearly allied to Man, is essentially a tropical animal, and does not flourish in cold countries." "As the negro race, however, spread, it gradually reached the temperate regions, and here the struggle with Nature became fiercer and the whole civilization underwent development and a higher type of man— the yellow or Mongolian race was evolved." This race, which included the Red Indians, Peruvians, Chinese and Japanese, also came into contact with a more vigorous climate, either by expanding northward, or meeting the Ice Age as it moved southward. The result was progressive evolution: "the struggle for the necessities of life, the need for bravery, endurance, and all the manly virtues, reached its climax, and the highest type of man was evolved—the Nordic type or white man, whose original home was on the fringe of the ice-sheet." Subsequently, from Scandinavia and Russia, the Nordic race conquered Britain and temperate Europe. From this capsule history, "as determined by zoological methods", the writer drew several "comforting conclusions as to the future of Canada." For one thing, the Canadian must be "the conquering type of man", and this included the "French-speaking fellow countrymen who, so far as they are of Norman descent, belong to the same race." Moreover, the "Nordic man is essentially an arctic animal and only flourishes in a cold climate— whilst in a warmer region he gradually loses virility and vitality. So that from a zoological point of view the outlook is bright for Canada."[43]

THE NORTHERN MYTH IN CANADIAN ART

The image of Canada as a northern country with a strenuous and masterful people was reinforced and sustained in the novels, travelogues, and works of scientific exploration that abounded in the period. The adventure stories centering on life in the isolated Hudson Bay posts and the exploits of the lonely trapper had long been the staple themes of the novels of Robert M. Ballantyne and the boys' books of J. Macdonald Oxley. But after 1896, when the north-west became the locus of im- migration and investment, imaginative writers found in that region not only a picturesque setting and indigenous historical incidents and themes; but also an area which a large number of their readers had never exper- ienced. Certainly it is significant that a number of the best-selling writers in the decade before the first world war, Ralph Connor, Robert Service and William Fraser, not only set their works in the northerly setting but also lived there.

The very titles of these books are indicative of their focus: Agnes Laut's story of the fur trader, *Lords of the North* (1900), and her history, *—Canada, Empire of the North* (1909); Gilbert Parker's *An Adventure of the North* (1905); H. A. Cody's life of Bishop Bompas, *An Apostle of the North* (1905); Ralph Connor's many manly novels set in the northwest, like *Corporal Cameron* (1912) with its inevitable blizzard; travelogues like Agnes D. Cameron's description of her journey through the Athabaska and Mackenzie River region to the Arctic, *The New North* (1909); chronicles of exploration, J. W. Tyrell's *Across the Sub-Arctic of Canada* (1897), and Vilhjalmur Stefansson's *My Life with the Eskimo* (1913). In 1926, a literary critic complained that the "whole of Canada has come to be identified with her northernmost reaches", and in "modern folk-geography Canada means the North."[44]

This image was strengthened by the paintings of the "national movement" in Canadian art, the Group of Seven. While some of the most characteristic work of men like A. Y. Jackson and J. E. H. Macdonald was done in the post-war decades, it was during the years before 1913 that their group was formed, their nationalism inspired, and their determination made to express the essence of Canada through her landscape. Some of them were directly influenced by a Scandinavian art exhibition in 1912 which "impressed them as an example of what other northern countries could do in art." A member of the group admitted that in their minds Canada was "a long, thin strip of civilization on the southern fringe of a vast expanse of immensely varied, virgin land reaching into the remote north. Our whole country is cleansed by the pristine and replenishing air which sweeps out of that great hinterland. It was the discovery of this great northern area as a field of art which enticed and inspired these painters." But the north—with its sparkling clear air and sharp outlines which could never be apprehended with the techniques of Old World art—was much more than a field of art: it was the mirror of national character. After a trip into the Arctic with A. Y. Jackson, Lawren Harris reported that "We came to know that it is only through the deep and vital experience of its total environment that a people identifies itself with its land and gradually a deep and satisfying awareness develops. We were convinced that no virile people could remain subservient to, and dependent upon the creations in art of other peoples . . . To us there was also the strange brooding sense of another nature fostering a new race and a new age." Though they displayed a variety of personal styles and attitudes, the group was united in the effort to portray the rugged terrain of the Canadian shield and the changing seasons in the northern woods. While present in J. E. H. Macdonald's *The Solemn Land* (1921) and other early works, the theme of northernness culminated in A. Y. Jackson's *The North Shore of Baffin Island* (c. 1929) and Lawren Harris' *Bylot Island* (1930) both of which literally exude the crystalline cold and seem themselves to be a part of the stark northern wastes.[45]

THE NORTHERN THEME IN RETROSPECT

In retrospect, the northern theme, as it was expressed in the first half century after Confederation, must be regarded as a myth, for not only did the observations it exalted conflict with objective appraisal, but its primary, intellectual assumptions became suspect. While it rested on the truism, confirmed by modern human geography, that certain climates are stimulating to human exertion, it too frequently glossed over the variety of climatic regions within Canada, and it tended to identify the whole country with that region of it which contained the fewest of her people. It was related and sustained, moreover, by the ebullient faith in the progress of the north-west, in the lusty but mistaken hopes of the wheat-boom years that the northern zone would become the home of millions of happy yeomen. The northern theme also assumed a racist aspect, holding that the capacity for freedom and progress were inherent in the blood of northern races. Not only was this belief progressively undermined by modern anthropological scholarship, but the identification of the Teutonic race with the spirit of liberty appeared especially specious after the first world war. In addition, the appeal of the northern race idea was limited in the post-war period because its main usefulness had been to underline the differences between Canada and the United States. In the 1920's the focus of nationalist thought shifted, and one of its dominant preoccupations came to be the definition of Canadian character in terms of North American experience, to emphasize the similarities between Canada and the United States.

Intellectual styles change but the permanent facts they seek to interpret and render meaningful do not. As long as there exists a nationalist impulse in Canada the imagination of men will be challenged by the very existence of the fascinating north. Though racism and crude environmentalism have now largely been discredited, the effort to explain Canadian uniqueness in terms of the north has not. As late as 1948, Vincent Massey found several differences between the United States and Canada, such as "the air of moderation in Canadian habits" to be derived from climate and race:

> Climate plays a great part in giving us our special character, different from that of our southern neighbours. Quite apart from the huge annual bill our winter imposes on us in terms of building construction and clothing and fuel, it influences our mentality, produces a sober temperament. Our racial composition—and this is partly because of our climate—is different, too. A small percentage of our people comes from central or southern Europe. The vast majority springs either from the British Isles or Northern France, a good many, too, from Scandinavia and Germany, and it is in northwestern Europe that one finds the elements of human stability highly developed. Nothing is more characteristic of Canadians than the inclination to be moderate.[46]

Apart from the muted tone, these observations do not really differ in substance from the remarks made in ringing rhetoric and with scientific certainty in the late nineteenth century by George Parkin, who was, incidentally, Massey's father-in-law.

Very different, however, and of high political potency, was the emotional appeal to the Canadian northern mission evoked by John Diefenbaker in the election of 1958. Seizing upon a theme which his native northwest had inspired in poets and nationalists since Confederation, he declared, suitably enough at Winnipeg, that "I see a new Canada"—not orientated east and west, but looking northward, responding to the challenges of that hinterland, its energies focused on the exploration and exploitation of the Arctic—"A CANADA OF THE NORTH!" To this compelling theme, which runs so persistently through Canadian nationalist thought since the days of D'Arcy McGee, Canadians responded eagerly and with conviction.[47]

On a more sober and scholarly plane, but not less pungent and appealing, is another recent exposition of the northern theme articulated by a president of the Canadian Historical Association, W. L. Morton, also a native of the north-west. In an address delivered in 1960, Professor Morton fixed upon Canada's "northern character", her origins in the expansion of a northern, maritime frontier, and her possession of a distinctive, staple economy, as factors which explained a substantial aspect of her development, her historical dependence upon Britain and the

United States, the character of her literature, even the seasonal rhythm of Canadian life.[48]

The concept of Canada as a northern nation, like the idea that the unique character of the United States was shaped by the westward movement, is as important for understanding the intellectual content and emotional appeal of nationalism as it is for explaining the objective determinants of historical development. From the time of Benjamin Franklin, Americans saw 'the west' not so much as a geographical fact but as a symbol, around which they grouped the leading tenets of their nationalist faith—that its movement westward was carrying the American further and further away from effete Europe, that 'the garden' would become the home of an independent yeomanry in which alone reposed true Republican virtue, that the frontier was a safety valve which kept social conditions in the new world from ever approximating those in decadent, classridden Europe. Like the American symbol of the west, the Canadian symbol of the north subsumed a whole series of beliefs about the exalted past, the national character and the certain future. Unlike the American frontier of free land, however, the north itself was inexhaustible: as A. R. M. Lower has recently reminded us, it is a perpetual breath of fresh air.

If Canadian nationalism is to be understood, its meaning must be sought and apprehended not simply in the sphere of political decisions, but also in myths, legends and symbols like these. For while some might think that Canadians have happily been immune to the wilder manifestations of the nationalist impulse and rhetoric, it seems that they too have had their utopian dreamers, and that they are not totally innocent of a tradition of racism and a falsified but glorious past, tendencies which have always been the invariable by-products of nationalism. For by its very nature, nationalism must seize upon objective dissimilarities and tendencies and invest them in the language of religion, mission and destiny.

NOTES

1. William Pitman Lett, *Annexation and British Connection, Address to Brother Jonathan*, Ottawa, 1889, p. 10.
2. Walter R. Nursey, *The Story of Isaac Brock*, Toronto, 1909, p. 173.
3. Joseph Pope, *The Tour of Their Royal Highnesses the Duke and Duchess of Cornwall and York through the Dominion of Canada in the Year 1901*, Ottawa, 1903, p. 259; Hon. George W. Ross, *The Historical Significance of the Plains of*

Abraham, Address Delivered Before the Canadian Club of Hamilton, April 27th, 1908 (n.p., n.d.) p. 18; *The Canadian Military Gazette* XV (January 2, 1900) p. 15; Silas Alward, *An Anglo-American Alliance,* St. John, N.B., 1911.

4. G. D. Griffin, *Canada Past, Present, Future, and New System of Government* (n.p.) 1884, p. ii.

5. George Parkin, address to the Canadian Club and Board of Trade in St. John, N.B., reported in *The Daily Telegraph,* St. John, N.B., March 6, 1907. Clipping in *Parkin Papers,* Vol. 82 (Public Archives of Canada, hereinafter P.A.C.)

6. William Leggo, *History of the Administration of the Earl of Dufferin in Canada* Toronto, 1878, p. 599.

7. *Weekly Globe,* April 2, 1869.

8. For a fascinating sketch of these myths see J. W. Johnson, " 'Of Differing Ages and Climes' ", *Journal of the History of Ideas* XXI (Oct.–Dec., 1960) pp. 465-480.

9. R. G. Haliburton, *The Men of the North and their place in history. A Lecture delivered before the Montreal Literary Club, March 31st, 1869,* Montreal, 1869, pp. 2, 8, 16.

10. Clipping from *The Globe,* December 8, 1904 in *Denison Scrapbook 1897-1915,* p. 167. *Denison Papers* (P.A.C.)

11. Charles Mair, "The New Canada: its natural features and climate," *Canadian Monthly Magazine* VIII (July, 1875) p. 5.

12. *Canada First: A Memorial of the late William A. Foster,* Toronto 1890, p. 25.

13. Charles R. Tuttle, *Popular History of the Dominion of Canada,* 2 vols., Boston, 1877 and 1879, vol. 1, p. 28.

14. G. R. Parkin, *The Great Dominion, Studies of Canada,* London, 1895, pp. 25, 211-215; "The Railway Development of Canada", *The Scottish Geographical Magazine* (May, 1909) p. 249, reprint in *Parkin Papers* vol. 66 (P.A.C.), address to Canadian Club and Board of Trade in St. John, New Brunswick, reported in *The Daily Telegraph,* March 6, 1907. Clipping in *Parkin Papers,* vol. 82 (P.A.C.)

15. Edward Harris, *Canada, The Making of a Nation,* (n.p., ca. 1907) p. 7.

16. G. R. Parkin, *The Great Dominion,* p. 216.

17. W. H. Withrow, "Notes of a Visit to the Centennial Exhibition", *Canadian Methodist Magazine* IV (December, 1876) p. 530.

18. Rev. F. A. Wightman, *Our Canadian Heritage, Its Resources and Possibilities,* Toronto, 1905, p. 46.

19. W. H. Hingston, *The Climate of Canada and its Relation to Life and Health* Montreal, 1884, pp. xviii, 94, 126-27, 260, 263, 265-66.

20. Wightman, *Our Canadian Heritage,* pp. 280, 44-45; J. Sheridan Hogan, *Canada, An Essay: to which was awarded the first prize by the Paris Exhibition Committee of Canada,* Montreal, 1855, pp. 53-54.

21. F. B. Cumberland, "Introduction", *Maple Leaves: being the papers read before the National Club of Toronto at the "National Evenings", during the Winter 1890-1891,* Toronto, 1891, pp. vii-viii.

22. Wightman, as cited, p. 221.

23. Benjamin Sulte, *Origin of the French Canadian. Read before the British Association, Toronto, August, 1897,* Ottawa, 1897, p. 14. See also his essay of 1897, "Défense de nos Origines" in *Mélanges Historiques,* compiled by Gérard Malchelosse, vol. 17, Montreal, 1930.

24. *The Storied Province of Quebec, Past and Present,* W. Wood, (ed.) vol. 1, Toronto, 1931, p. 3.

25. G. M. Wrong, *The Two Races in Canada, a Lecture delivered before the Canadian Historical Association, Montreal, May 21st, 1925,* Montreal, 1925, pp. 4-5.

26 · the land

26. Abbé Arthur Maheux, *Canadian Unity: What Keeps Us Apart*, Quebec, 1944, pp. 22, 23, 25.
27. *Canada's Future! Political Union With the U.S. Desirable*, 1891, pp. 2-3.
28. Principal R. A. Falconer, "The Unification of Canada", *University Magazine* VII (February, 1908) pp. 4-5.
29. George Parkin, "Canada and the United States on the American Continent", reported in *Yarmouth Herald*, March 3, 1908. Clipping in *Parkin Papers*, vol 84, (P.A.C.) ; *The Great Dominion*, p. 214.
30. Cited in Charles and Mary Beard, *The American Spirit, A Study of the Civilization in the United States*, New York, 1962, p. 173.
31. *Canadian Methodist Magazine*, LXVIII (December, 1898) pp. 566-567.
32. Silas Alward, as cited, pp. 8-10.
33. See especially, J. G. Bourinot, *Canadian Studies in Comparative Politics*, Montreal, 1890.
34. *The Empire*, January 24, 1891.
35. *The Week*, January 1, 1885.
36. G. Parkin, in *Yarmouth Herald*, March 3, 1908.
37. *Dominion Illustrated* VI (April 11, 1891) .
38. Cited in *Canadian Methodist Magazine* XLIX (June, 1899) p. 536.
39. William Wood, *The Fight for Canada*, Boston, 1906, p. 33.
40. Rev. W. P. Creswell, *History of the Dominion of Canada*, Oxford, 1890, pp. 11, 15.
41. Charles G. D. Roberts, *A History of Canada*, Boston, 1897, p. 3.
42. Benjamin Kidd, *Social Evolution*, London, 1895, pp. 61-62.
43. E. W. MacBride, "The Theory of Evolution", *The McGill University Magazine* I (April, 1902) pp. 244-262.
44. Lionel Stevenson, *Appraisals of Canadian Literature*, Toronto, 1926, pp. 245-253.
45. R. H. Hubbard, *The Development of Canadian Art*, Ottawa, 1964, p. 88; L. Harris, "The Group of Seven in Canadian History" *Canadian Historical Association Report* (1948) pp. 30, 36-37.
46. Vincent Massey, *On Being Canadian*, Toronto, 1948, pp. 29-30.
47. Peter Newman, *Renegade in Power: The Diefenbaker Years*, Toronto, 1964, p. 218.
48. W. L. Morton, "The Relevance of Canadian History" in *The Canadian Indentity*, Toronto, 1961, pp. 88-114.

the myth of the land

in canadian nationalism · cole harris

When people weigh the nature and basis of their nationalism they usually dwell on aspects of their culture, history, or race; but English-speaking Canadians tend to explain themselves in terms of land and location. Some Canadians, as Mr. Berger points out,[1] considered their countrymen to have been shaped and strengthened by a hard northern realm, while others have envisaged a Canadian nation forged by the development of northern resources. An appeal to our northern destiny was one of the responsive notes struck by Diefenbaker in 1957 and 1958, and that appeal was probably strengthened by the Canadian apprehension that geographically we are North American, a fringe of regions on top of the United States. These two conflicting geographical propositions are central to many discussions about the nature of Canada: Canada exists because it is a distinctive northern land; Canada is North American, its southern boundary is geographically illogical and therefore fragile and probably temporary.

In print these geographical poles are clearest in the historical literature, for Canadian historians, along with some Canadian novelists,[2] have most frequently turned to the land to explain the character of Canada. The Laurentian theme running through the writings of Harold Innis, Donald Creighton, William Morton, and other Canadian historians, is the theme of the fur trade—the transcontinental enterprise based on the resources

27

of the north, and anchored to the towns which provided manpower, capital, and skills for northern development. In extreme form the theme becomes an incantation to the north:

> Canadian history began when the Vikings carried the frontier of fish, fur, and farm across the North Atlantic to Iceland and Greenland. . . From that obscure beginning Canada had a distinct, a unique, a northern destiny. Its modern beginnings are not Columbian but Cabotan. And when the French followed Cartier up the St. Lawrence, they were at once committed by the development of the fur trade to the exploitations of the Canadian Shield. . . The Canadian or Precambrian Shield is as central in Canadian history as it is to Canadian geography, and to all understanding of Canada. . . And this alternate penetration of the wilderness and return to civilization is the basic rhythm of Canadian life, and forms the basic elements of Canadian character.[3]

At the other pole are the continentalists: A. S. Morton, Fred Landon and, to a degree, A. R. M. Lower, Frank Underhill and A. L. Burt. Their studies have tended to emphasize "the mingling of the Canadian and American People",[4] and have agreed with J. B. Brebner who opened his history of Canada with the sentence, "Perhaps the most striking thing about Canada is that it is not part of the United States."[5]

Geographers, who have often been more hesitant than others to propose sweeping geographical generalizations, have stood aside from this debate. Yet there may be some value in considering, from a geographical vantage point, the past validity, and present relevance and utility of these two propositions about Canada. What follows is an essay directed towards these ends.

THE NORTHERN BASIS OF CANADIAN IDENTITY

The concept of the northern character and destiny of Canada has usually been bound up with the Precambrian Shield. Its landscape of rock, water, and stunted spruce, its thin, acidic podzols and glacially disrupted drainage form an environment with which few Americans have had to contend. As the boundary of this environment is close to the southern boundary of eastern Canada, it is not surprising that the resources of the Shield, furs, timber and minerals, the centres which provided the capital and some of the skills for the development of the Shield, as well as the enterprises which emerged in the Shields, have been considered to be the mainspring of Canada. Nor, in view of the size of the Shield and its proximity to settled Canada, is it surprising that the Shield has been part of the Canadian consciousness. No one objected that the Group of Seven should be considered the most Canadian of our painters because they painted a part of the country with which few Canadians were familiar. Harold Innis probably argued correctly that the boundaries of the Canadian state were laid in the fur trade;[6] and today, if railways, radio and television networks could be considered to have inherited the route of the fur trade, then the Shield is also indirectly responsible for any sense of territoriality "from sea to sea" that has emerged in Canada.

And yet, however important the Shield has been in the development of Canada, only a handful of Canadians have lived there, or anywhere in our non-agricultural north. A relatively small percentage of Montrealers or Torontonians have been the employees of firms developing the resources of the north. Rather, Canadians have been a people living in pockets between the non-agricultural north and the United States. From the early years of Canada until well into the present century, farming was the principal Canadian occupation, and thus the character of French- or English-speaking Canadians has been drawn more from this agricultural background than from contacts with the Shield.

In New France, distance from the mother country, a largely illiterate population and the life which some had found in the fur trade made a drift from French ways inevitable, but the most enduring impetus for change came from the agricultural lands along the St. Lawrence where most of the population lived. These lands were conceded under a French system of seigneurial tenure which, in spite of many Canadian modifications, remained French in legal structure until long after the British conquest. However, a landed gentry could not be established as long as there was no population pressure on the land; similarly, a legal structure designed to protect scarce land was irrelevant and at first was bypassed consistently. Seigneurs neglected their land because it was not profitable. The habitants, rarely disturbed by their seigneurs or royal officials, or visited by curés, went their own way. After the initial fertility of virgin fields declined, yields per acre were low, but yields per man were generally higher than those in France. None of the habitants were wealthy, but by the early eighteenth century many lived in stone farm houses, occasionally bought French luxury items and could hire a girl to assist with the housework and the children or a hand to help work the farm. The habitants' standard of living was higher than that of their counterparts in Europe; their lives were less trammelled by traditional or formal obligations. French officials frequently described the *canadiens* as an independent, unmanageable lot, characteristics usually associated with the *coureurs de bois*, but also those of the habitants who for many years had lived almost as they chose on the agricultural lands along the lower St. Lawrence.[7]

Although the ratio of rural to urban *canadiens* changed very little in the century after the conquest, most of the independence and modest prosperity, which had once characterized farm life along the lower St. Lawrence, vanished by the middle of the 19th century. In part the change can be attributed to wheat blights and to outmoded methods of farming and milling, which made wheat and flour from Lower Canada particularly vulnerable to competition from Upper Canada and the American middle west. In part it was also related to the fact that some seigneurs had increased their rents and were enforcing obligations which had once been allowed to lapse. But the basic change was the enormous increase in the rural population (by some twenty fold in one hundred years) in an area with a scarcity of agricultural land. Most of the cultivable lowland had been settled by 1800, and by the late 1820's French Canadians were beginning to displace Irish Protestants who had taken over the land along the southern margin of the Shield a few years before. As seigneuries filled with settlers, the potential seigneurial revenue rose and the seigneur, or an agent appointed by him, began to supervise the seigneurie closely. As new farmland became scarce, old farms were subdivided, but the semi-extensive agricultural methods, which provided an adequate living only when there was ample land, were continued. The features of French customary law designed to protect land from ill-considered alienations— the *légitimes*, *douaires*, and *retraits*—were checks on commerce when land was scarce and made it even more difficult for the enterprising habitant to prosper.[8]

Midway through the nineteenth century the prospects for French Canada were bleak. The merchant class and many of the seigneurs were English. Some of the religious orders and a very few *canadiens* were wealthy, but most capital was in English hands; the *canadiens* had become an impoverished rural people who had no more land for agricultural expansion. Attempts to save nation and faith by settling the Shield compounded the problem of poverty and delayed the adjustment to urban life.

When for want of alternative opportunities, French Canadians moved to the cities, they came, much as Lord Durham foretold, as the unskilled peons of English Canadian capitalism. With them came and lingered many rural characteristics—a distrust of education (the wife was usually the literate member of the habitant family), a simple and powerful Catholicism, strong family ties, and an open, unsophisticated friendliness. Today this rural background is fading, but it is still impossible to understand contemporary French Canada without knowing its deep roots in the countryside of the lower St. Lawrence.

The roots of English-speaking Canada are less dependent on agriculture. New England merchants came to Montreal in the wake of the Conquest and the first English-speaking farmers arrived more than twenty years later. In the Ottawa Valley farming began on loggers' clearings and was sustained at first by the markets in the logging camps. Well before the end of the 19th century, furniture plants, knitting mills, and a score of other small industries were established in many Ontario towns. Kingston and Toronto were metropolitan centres in the 1820's, and by the 1880's Toronto had 100,000 people. The livelihood of most Newfoundlanders, and of many others in the coastal settlements of Nova Scotia, depended on the sea, while lumbering was as important as agriculture in the early days of New Brunswick. In British Columbia lumbering and mining have both been more important than agriculture to the economy of the province.

Still, since English-speaking Canadians have become an urban people, the importance of their agricultural background often has been forgotten. Until nearly the middle of the 19th century most Upper Canadians were beginning or had just completed the backbreaking work of clearing the forest, uprooting stumps, and moving stones. In the 1850's, when railways could provide nearly every largely subsistent backwoods' farm with a market, wheat became a staple. Hundreds of villages and hamlets, many of which are now deserted, emerged as rural service centres. But by the 1880's in the northern counties, and earlier in the southern, wheat had given way to mixed commercial agriculture. Creameries were scattered across southern Ontario. The area devoted to orchards in 1900 was several times greater than at present. Beef, pork, and mutton were marketed in the towns and abroad. The prosperity of the period is still reflected in the substantial, and even stately farmhouses which dot rural southern Ontario, and in the main streets and residences of many small

Ontario towns. Their air of solid prosperity is now at least sixty years old and reflects the agricultural success of the last decades of the 19th century. All the cities, including Toronto which was growing rapidly during these years, owed much to a prosperous agricultural hinterland. Farmers and tradesmen who served them were a majority in the province until the present century.

On the eve of the First World War, the rural population in the Maritimes (excluding Newfoundland) twice exceeded the urban. Many of those enumerated as rural were not actual farmers, and many Maritime farmers found alternative employment each year in the forests or fishery; but, with the exception of Newfoundland, the Maritimes have been predominantly agricultural provinces until almost the present generation. The fact that far too many Maritimers are continuing to farm is one of the region's chronic problems. By contrast, the agricultural origins of the prairie provinces need no emphasis; the key prairie issue in the 1965 election, "Who sold the wheat?", reveals how little this has changed. British Columbia has not been an agricultural province. Nevertheless, fifteen per cent of its population were farmers in 1931, and many more British Columbians or their parents had come from the farms and small towns of Ontario and the Maritimes.

It is clear, therefore, that much of the Canadian past is bound up with life on the farm and in small farm service centres. The question to be considered here is whether there is a geographical basis for differentiating Canadian from American agricultural societies. Canadian farming societies have been relatively little studied, possibly because their analysis was thought to lead towards frontierism and a continental interpretation of Canada. However, it does not necessarily follow that because Canadian agriculture has been practised close to the United States, there has been no geographical basis for the emergence of distinctive Canadian agricultural societies. Canadians have always struggled to farm on the cold fringe of North American agricultural land, and until recently Canadian farmers were isolated from the mainstream of American life.

January isotherms on a map of North America are widely spaced towards the northern and southern extremities of the continent and are bunched in the middle. The north is cold, the south is warm, and the temperature gradient between is steep. This pattern, modified in the West by the Cordillera, is extremely clear in central and eastern North America. The January mean temperature in Ottawa is approximately

11° F., while in Cincinnati, which is only 400 miles closer to the equator, it is over 30° F. The frost-free season increases from just over 130 days at Ottawa to 180 in Cincinnati. Along the southern border of Manitoba the frost-free period is under 120 days; in Minneapolis it is almost a month longer. Thus the southern boundary of Canada lies in a band where the climate is changing rapidly. Mid-summer temperatures in Canadian agricultural lands are only slightly cooler than those in the northern United States, but our winters are colder and considerably longer.

The Canadian winter and the shortness of the Canadian summer have been a constant threat to Canadian agriculture. In the Okanagan valley the 1965 soft fruit crop and many of the trees were destroyed by an out-pouring of continental polar air in the previous winter. Some orchards will be replanted; others will be converted to hardier species by farmers who have found too much risk in the commercial growing of peaches, apricots, and cherries at the northern limit of their range. Spring wheat farming is uncertain everywhere on the central plains, but particularly on the Canadian prairie, where to the danger of drought, hail and wind is added that of early frost. Corn, the backbone of agriculture in the American middle west, usually matures near Windsor or Toronto, but seldom near Ottawa; on the Ile de Montréal, but not on the Ile d'Orléans. The northern limit of tobacco and soft fruits is in Southern Ontario. Wheat, the agricultural staple along the lower St. Lawrence until the 19th century, was reported seldom to mature perfectly there, and its cultivation on Cape Breton Island and in much of the Nova Scotian peninsula was even more precarious.

Because of the climate and the Canadian Shield there is a lack of good farmland in Canada. Our farmers, living on the edge of North American agriculture, too frequently have had to be content with thin soils and rocks as well as with winter. The fertile pockets of the Maritimes—Prince Edward Island, the Saint John and the Annapolis valleys —have supported prosperous farmers, but more Maritimers have scratched out near-subsistence livelihoods on the stony hills of New Brunswick and Nova Scotia. Through most of the nineteenth and in the first decades of the twentieth century, habitants were settling in the Shield and in un-productive parts of the Appalachian Highlands. Even between Quebec and Montreal on the St. Lawrence lowland there is a scarcity of good agricultural land. In Ontario, plans to colonize the Shield led to years of misery for those who settled there. Southwestern Ontario contains some excellent farmland, but, by American standards, not very much of it. The rest of Southern Ontario, interrupted by the Frontenac axis of the Shield and by limestone plains and mantled with glacial sands and gravels on which thin soils have often developed, is not particularly productive agricultural land. On the prairie, where there is far more farming land than in the rest of Canada, the climate has made farming precarious.

It is evident that Canadian farmers have struggled with the land. Some have prospered, but many more have just got by or have given up. In the United States, while there exists rural poverty and cultivated land that would have been better left in forest, there can be found the world's most prosperous farmers and great stretches of unsurpassed agricultural land. East of the 100th meridian in the United States and in a few areas to the west, the landscape is overwhelmingly lush. The feeling that "We belong to the land, and the land we belong to is grand" is part of the American experience. Until the *Saturday Evening Post* was restyled for readers who were judged to have become more urbane and sophisticated, the hero of the *Post* short story was the one who won the girl, a spread of prime agricultural land, and fifty head of herefords. This myth of the garden, as Henry Nash Smith has called it,[9] has much validity in a country where, notwithstanding share croppers and dust bowls, agriculture has generally been successful. Particularly when the middle west was being settled, pioneers prospered, in part because northern American farmers were an inventive and energetic lot, but principally because the land was rich. In Canada the garden myth is inappropriate except perhaps in Southern Ontario, a region which is a poor fringe area of the agricultural heartland of the United States. If there is a myth about Canadian agriculture, it is about the toil and uncertainty of farming in a harsh environment, and this is a very different myth from any in the United States.

Whatever emphasis is given to unsuccessful Shield agriculture and the short frost-free season in the Upper Ottawa valley and around Georgian Bay, this myth can hardly fit Ontario. Most of those who came to the province from New England or upstate New York found an easier agricultural environment where, eventually, a prosperous agricultural society developed. Until well into the present century this society was the backbone of the dominant English-speaking province, and when people from Ontario began to move westward they formed one of the few Canadian links in the early years of the western provinces. This stable and restrained society of Ontario developed in an environment which has been less a challenge than a neutral backdrop.[10] Ontario farmers argued about clergy reserves and the family compact, but these disputes, however heated they became, never had the life or death quality of the prairie farmers' struggle with the land. Whether or not one agrees with George Grant that "our stodginess has made us a people of greater simplicity, formality, and perhaps even innocence than the people to the south",[11] English Canadian solidarity has come largely from the farms and small towns of Ontario. There it developed partly because of the conservative mood of the loyalists and the early governors who attempted "to create and strengthen an Aristocracy of which the best use may be made on this Continent where all Governments are feeble and the general condition of things tends to a wild democracy",[12] but also because the land did not create tensions.

THE ISOLATION OF CANADIAN SOCIETY

Although Southern Ontario could partake of the myth of the garden with the states of the American middle west, it and other parts of Eastern Canada were usually isolated from influences from the United States. Marcus Lee Hansen's concept of the westward advance of Canadian and American settlement as an integral rather than a parallel movement, while useful in considering the earliest years of settlement in rural Canada,[13] does not describe the societies which emerged out of the labours of the pioneers. Prior to the war of 1812, Upper Canada was in the line of American westward advance and was accurately described by a pair of discouraged farmers as "a damned wild country full of Yankees and agues".[14] To the west, where a flood of miners and adventurers, most of them from the United States, were working the gravel bars of the Fraser River, the *British Colonist* in Victoria reported in 1867 that nine-tenths of the people "are bound in their expression of preference for the stars and stripes".[15] These were the first years of settlement during which people were on the move and society and loyalties were in a state of flux. The immigrant deposited on a dock in Montreal or New York often knew nothing of North America and went where a land agent directed him. Others came with the clear intention of settling in British North America or of staying away from it. Whatever their reasons for coming to the New World, when immigrants settled on the land, a political boundary and distance isolated British North Americans, particularly rural British North Americans, from the society of the United States.

The first wave of immigration to Upper Canada came from the south, the second from the British Isles, and beginning in the 1840's a backwash from Ontario flowed into the United States. Although Americans bound for Michigan trekked along Dundas Street, and others eventually built summer houses along the Canadian shore of Lake Ontario, relatively few Americans crossed the Great Lakes to settle in British North America after the war of 1812, and in many rural counties in Upper Canada an American became an unusual sight. A lively trade in timber, wheat and American manufactures was carried on across the Lakes, and American inventions—farm machinery for example—came quickly to Canada. However, the Great Lakes, reinforced by a political boundary, were enough, when communications were poor, to isolate Canadians who read their own newspapers, argued their own politics, and knew little of the outside world.[16] American legislatures, scoffed a typically ignorant and prejudiced writer in a Barrie newspaper, abound with "demagogues, prizefighters, and other specimens of the genus vagabond, who can handle a bowie knife much better than a pen."[17] In Upper Canada the forms of government were British; the men in control of governmental, ecclesiastical, educational, and financial institutions were predominantly British in origin as, in the middle of the 19th century, was the great bulk of the population. The American ways which had come with the first settlers were being modified. American initiative had launched Methodism in Canada, but British Wesleyans arrived shortly after the War of 1812, and in 1824 the Canadian Methodists became an autonomous conference.[18] This pattern was frequently repeated. When visitors wrote of their travels in the United States and Canada they were wont to comment that the difference between Americans and Canadians "is not a matter of reasoning, of reference, of opinion; it is instantly felt, as much as in going out of a warm room into a cold atmosphere."[19] The Nova Scotians were more isolated from the Americans than the Canadians; the New Brunswickers somewhat less. On the prairies and in British Columbia settlement began when communications were improving rapidly, so that the western provinces were never as isolated from the south as those to the east had been.

In many respects, however, the isolation of British North America
from the United States in the middle of the 19th century was less than
the isolation of regions within the United States, or of the British North
American colonies, from each other. Between North and South, between
New England and the Ohio Valley, or even between the tidewater and
backwoods of Virginia there were few personal contacts to break down
enormous differences in tradition and outlook. The Wisconsin farmer
was far more ignorant of the Georgian planter than was the Upper
Canadian of the mid-western American. Nevertheless, common denomin-
ators of government and politics, and of education, were slowly breaking
down regional isolation in the United States. North of the American
border, distinctive institutions and the predominantly British cast of
the English-speaking population reinforced the isolation of British
North Americans. The British colonies held in common their British
colonial status and a deep suspicion of the United States, but the
same difficulties of communication which enabled British North
Americans to develop differently from the Americans meant that the
bonds among British North Americans would be slight. There was no
carriage road from the lower St. Lawrence to the Bay of Fundy until
the 1840's and no railway for another thirty years. When the Canadian
delegates to Charlottetown arrived in the Maritimes they were curiosities
from a distant land. Along the lower St. Lawrence and the Great Lakes,
where there was a measure of commercial integration, there were two
different peoples. Some of the seigneurs and their agents were bilingual.
In Montreal and Quebec, French and English societies overlapped
slightly. However, the habitant could not speak English, nor the English-
speaking farmer French. This alone insured that two adjacent agricultural peoples would live in virtually complete isolation from each
other.

Finally, it may be that the most important by-product of Canada's
northern climate and early isolation from the United States has been
American indifference to us. For all the declarations about "manifest
destiny" by politicians who envisaged the stars and stripes flying over a
continent north of the Rio Grande, the wave of American expansion
which moved westward with inexorable force did not turn northward.
British North Americans often feared American invasion, but Americans were not very interested in their northern neighbours. The invasion during the Revolution was directed against a supposedly soft point

in the British armour. The half-hearted attacks during the War of 1812
stemmed more from dissatisfaction with British mercantile policy than
from territorial ambitions.[20] The cry "fifty-four forty or fight" was bluster.
The "war" in the San Juan islands involved several families and a pig.
While American sallies northward are emphasized in Canadian history,
they are virtually absent in American, not because the Americans are
trying to hide anything, but because northern objectives occupied little
American attention. Had there been more agricultural land in Canada,
or had the resources of the Shield been better known, American interest
would undoubtedly have been greater; but, as it was, for most Americans
19th century Canada was a remote wasteland. When Americans accepted
the 49th parallel as the boundary across the prairie, they were still
hesitating to settle in southern Wisconsin, where the winters were judged
too severe for agriculture. Canadians who are exasperated when American
friends remark that they had not realized there was "anything up there
in Canada", should consider the degree to which this American conception of Canada permitted Canada to exist.

THE EROSION OF THE OLD BASES OF CANADIAN IDENTITY

Until recently the continuing British connection and the sense of
having developed in a northern environment have been the only points
of attachment for English-speaking Canadian nationalists. British
forms of government, the predominantly British ancestry of English-
speaking Canadians and the British sense of fair play and social order
were contrasted with American forms and values. As long as British
capital was required to finance the development of northern staples and
English Canadians felt that they had been part of a movement from a
northern environment in Britain to another in Canada, the themes of the
British connection and the northern environment were interconnected.
Now the British connection is fading from Canadian life and the theme
of the northern environment is standing shakily alone. The Royal Commission on Bilingualism and Biculturalism reported that:

> Attachment to the land itself was undoubtedly an element of importance for
> both groups [French and English-speaking Canadians]. Many English-speak-
> ing Canadians looked back to a pioneering era which in the Maritimes began
> in the mid-eighteenth century and in Ontario and the eastern townships of
> Quebec in the late eighteenth and early nineteenth centuries. In the

Prairie Provinces there was much pride expressed in the settling of a vast
territory by people from older parts of Canada, including some from Quebec
at an early stage; from the United States; and from many parts of Europe. . .
We were conscious, then, of a love of country based on settlement which all
Canadians shared.[21]

Had the commissioners pointed out that Americans looked back to a
similar pioneer era, they would probably have had the reply from most
parts of Canada that Canadian pioneers had contended with a more
difficult land. However, the pioneer days, even the agricultural days,
are distant memories for most Canadians, and the northern theme has
not filled the gap left by the weakening of the British connection because it no longer fits in a man-made environment of cities and central
heating.

In the summer of 1965 Japanese exchange students at the University
of British Columbia stated in an interview with the press that Vancouver
looked just like Tokyo. While these students were perhaps not particularly observant, they were pointing correctly to the rapid standardiza-
tion of the urban scene. The majority of Canadians now live in the
same environment as most Americans—the same shopping plazas, re-
juvenated central business districts, suburban sprawl, high-rise apart-
ments, amid turn-of-the-century housing, traffic jams and throughways.
The climate forces Canadians to put on storm windows, to spend more
than Americans for snow removal or heating, and to stay away longer
from the balcony or garden, but requires no further basic adjustments.
Cottages include the automatic paraphernalia of mid-twentieth century
life; canoes have been replaced by outboards and water skis. Canadian
farmers remain more sensitive to the northern environment, but attempt
as much as urbanites to equip their homes in the comfortable mode of
twentieth century technology.

The other basic and closely related geographical change in twentieth
century Canada has been the loss of isolation from the United States.
The tendency towards spatial coherence within language units which
was a by-product of the printing press[22] has been strengthened by radio,
movies and television, each of which, along with the automobile, has
opened the United States to Canadians. These advances in communications eventually produced Canadian responses—C.B.C. radio and television, the National Film Board, the trans-Canada highway—which
enormously strengthened the possiblities of interregional exchanges in

Canada only after American connections had been established. On the eve of the Second World War a drive from Vancouver to Seattle, Winnipeg to Minneapolis, or Montreal to New York was relatively easy; while in Canada the same venture from Montreal to Winnipeg was still impossible. In 1930, when some 60% of Canadian radio owners could tune in to Canadian programmes on a regular basis, virtually 100% were within range of American stations.[23] Much the same was true in the early days of television. East-west links in Canada of road, radio and television all emerged as alternatives to established north-south connections which had given Canada a more continental position than ever before.

TOWARDS A NEW PROGRAMME FOR THE CANADIAN LAND

A sense of being a northern people, a consciousness of the Shield and of the rest of the empty north, and an assumption that the unsettled north is a reserve of riches, have been important ingredients for Canadian nationalism. Once the state and regular east-west connections were established, a weak Canadian sense of territoriality may have developed gradually. Moreover, as this paper has argued, in contending with a harsh environment Canadian farmers have created a myth about farming which is different from the American; the Canadian sense of the northern character of Canada undoubtedly has much to do with this agricultural myth. Until recently the geographical support for these and other aspects of Canadian nationalism has been the partial isolation of Canadian society from Americans and from American ideas.

The fact that this support has vanished and that assumptions about the influence of the land on the Canadian identity are increasingly irrelevant in an urban and technological society have undoubtedly contributed to the present crisis of Canadian nationalism. Nor are the former geographical bases of Canadian nationalism likely to be reestablished. The rural myth about the land will virtually disappear in an urban age. To strengthen interregional connections in Canada is to increase the disparity between Canadian and American incomes and to isolate Canadians from the mainstream of 20th century ideas. These prices are high. Further development of the resources of the unsettled north will attract more American attention partly because Canadians, through a cautiousness born of their agricultural traditions, have hesitated to invest risk capital. However, the nature of Canada's northern

resources has always been misunderstood, for further development of
water power and minerals can add only more specks of settlement in a
wilderness. From an economic point of view, there are few more worth-
less areas, square mile for square mile, than the unsettled Canadian
north.

This fact suggests an approach to the north which conceivably could
heighten the northern awareness of Canadians. Because of the preponderance of agriculturally unproductive land, Canada is largely an empty
space which is likely to remain empty for a long time. As the urban
population of North America and individual leisure time increase, and as
transportation into the wilderness improves, much of this empty space
will become recreation land. Already the unproductive land within easy
driving range of the cities is occupied in summer, and the push into the
wilderness can only accelerate. If Canadians recognized that the outstanding Canadian resource is vast areas with no other potential than
recreational use, this resource could be protected by carefully planned
development. Present policy concerning parks, which is based on the
assumption that land which is not in a park can be despoiled, could give
way to a broader concept of the "park of Canada". Such a policy would
not exclude non-recreational land uses. Under present parks policy, for
example, logging in Banff National Park would be a tragedy, but if the
entire Canadian Cordillera were being developed for recreation, carefully
supervised logging within the confines of the present park could be developed. The planned development of the Canadian wilderness lands
could ensure that the deterioration or alienation of recreational land,
which is taking place within easy driving range of every Canadian city,
would end. It could ensure that much land would be zoned for the
preserve of canoeists, hikers, and all those for whom unpeopled space
is occasionally important. Clusters of cottages could be interspersed
with wilderness so that nearby water would not be the only attraction
of cottage summers. Animal populations could be kept high for hunters,
fishermen and nature lovers. Tours could be conducted into the far
north, and, as well, many of the recreational uses of the Canadian
wilderness could be provided closer to the cities.

Canadian/who have canoed, hiked or built cottages in the wilderness
have often missed the land more than their countrymen, when away
from Canada. Until recently this group of Canadians has been small, for
loggers, miners and farmers, contending day by day with the land,

have tended to leave it on their holidays. This pattern is reversed for urban Canadians who, paradoxically, are the first large group of Canadians to spend ample time in the wilderness lands. Of course, as their economic resources have attracted American attention, so have their recreational opportunities. Americans rather than Canadians are hunting grizzlies and sheep in the Mackenzie Mountains; American cottagers are more numerous than Canadian around some parts of the Shield fringe; and if the recreational development of the unsettled north were planned, more Americans than Canadians would probably frequent this land. However, Canadian contact with the wild lands would be proportionately greater than American, and in a destructive age Canadians could take pride in the great achievement of having preserved their wilderness.

Whether the recreational development of the unsettled north will heighten a sense of Canadian identity is probably no more certain than the future of nations in the western world. Yet, if nations are desirable, steps which may lead to their preservation need to be taken. In Canada these will involve working out a mutually enriching relationship between French and English-speaking Canadians and, perhaps, a treatment of ethnic minorities within French-or English-speaking areas which does not lead to an American melting pot. They could also involve the recreational development of the north. Whereas a bicultural concept of Canada must develop in the face of a British tradition which has been anti-French and a rural tradition which has been unsophisticated, the Canadian imagination has often turned to the north. A programme for the recreational development of the north could seize the Canadian imagination and in so doing might perpetuate an awareness of the land which, in various ways, has been a part of Canadian nationalism for a long time.

NOTES

1. See above, Carl Berger, "The True North Strong and Free", p. 3ff.
2. See below, Frank Watt, "Nationalism in Canadian Literature", pp. 238-246.
3. William Morton, *The Canadian Identity*, Madison and Toronto, 1961, pp. 4-5.
4. M. L. Hansen, *The Mingling of the Canadian and American Peoples*, New Haven and Toronto, 1940.
5. J. B. Brebner, *Canada*, Ann Arbor, 1960, p. ix.
6. Harold Innis, *The Fur Trade in Canada*, New Haven, 1930.
7. The points in this paragraph are developed at much greater length in R. C. Harris, *The Seigneurial System in Early Canada: A Geographical Study*, University of Wisconsin Press, Madison, 1966.

8. Some of the points in this paragraph are developed more fully in Fernand Ouellet, *Lower Canada, 1792-1841*, now being published for the Canadian Centenary Series. Others depend on my present research into the seigneurial geography of Canada after the conquest.
9. Henry Nash Smith, *Virgin Land: The American West as Symbol and Myth*, Cambridge, 1950.
10. John Warkentin, "Southern Ontario", paper read at the Canadian Association of Geographers' Annual Meeting in Vancouver, June, 1965.
11. George Grant, *Lament for a Nation: The Defeat of Canadian Nationalism*, Toronto, 1965, p. 70.
12. Dorchester to Sydney, Québec, 13 juin, 1787, APC, Q. 27-2: 985-988; cited in André Lefort, "Le Point de Vue de Lord Dorchester sur les Problèmes Canadiens, entre 1786 et 1791," unpublished M. A. thesis at the University of Ottawa, 1964.
13. M. L. Hansen, *The Mingling of the Canadian and American Peoples*, New Haven and Toronto, 1940.
14. John Palmer, *Journal of Travels in the United States*, p. 231; cited in Edwin C. Guillet, *The Great Migration*, 2nd ed., Toronto, 1963, p. 216.
15. *Weekly British Colonist*, April 30, 1867; cited in P. B. Waite, *The Life and Times of Confederation, 1864-1867*, Toronto, 1962, p. 317.
16. The indifference of the early Canadian press to international news is discussed by H. F. Angus in *Canada and Her Great Neighbour*, Toronto, 1938, p. 61.
17. Barrie, *Northern Advance*, April 4, 1867; cited in Waite, *The Life and Times of Confederation*, Toronto, 1962, p. 13.
18. G. M. Craig, *Upper Canada; The Formative Years, 1784-1841*, Toronto, 1963, p. 167.
19. James Dixon, *Personal Narrative of a Tour Through a Part of the United States and Canada*, pp. 121-124; cited in G. M. Craig, *Early Travellers in the Canadas*, Toronto, 1955, p. 166.
20. Reginald Horsman, *The Causes of the War of 1812*, New York, 1962.
21. *A Preliminary Report of the Royal Commission on Bilingualism and Biculturalism*, Ottawa, 1965, p. 121.
22. See below, Melville Watkins, "Technology and Nationalism", pp. 284-291.
23. Margaret Prang, "The Origins of Public Broadcasting in Canada", *Canadian Historical Review* XLVI (March, 1965) p. 3.

THE PEOPLE •

the french canadians'

search for a fatherland • michel brunet

What is nationalism? It is simply the manifestation of the natural and spontaneous solidarity that exists among members of a human group sharing a historical and cultural tradition from which the group derives its distinctive identity. This manifestation of solidarity is more or less conscious and more or less complete, according to the peculiar circumstances which have influenced and continue to condition the development of each collectivity.

Nationalism is not an artificial feeling or movement. It is the consequence of the necessity which compels human beings to live together. Obliged to associate together for the achievement of common goals, the members of the group gradually become accustomed to acting and thinking collectively. Inspired by leaders who have the responsibility of maintaining their cohesion, heirs to a culture which is different—at least partly—from other cultural traditions, having ideals and objectives of their own, they assert themselves as a distinctive collectivity.

This essay may surprise those who believe or have been told that nationalism, and especially French-Canadian nationalism, is first an ideology. There is no doubt that men have always felt the necessity to explain their conduct by attributing to it lofty and unselfish aims. They like to embellish all their actions—chiefly their most egoistic ones. It is another proof that they are not mere animals. The social scientist, especially the historian, must never forget that ideologies need men to exist, and that they are the product of men engaged in historical evolution. This evolution has to be studied, if one wants to understand the ideologies it engendered. Such is the purpose of this essay.

There has been and there is a French-Canadian nationalism for the simple reason that there are men and women who call themselves French Canadians.

The story began more than three and a half centuries ago when Champlain founded Quebec in 1608. The French who had decided to establish themselves in the St. Lawrence Valley soon realized that they were not mere French travellers or explorers visiting the region or French officials on duty in the colony. New France was their country. They wanted it to be the fatherland of their children. To show their intention of identifying themselves with the new land, they took the name of *habitants*. The word then meant that they were here to stay as residents, to inhabit. The generations born in the colony preferred to be known as the *Canadiens*. The new country called Canada had given birth to a collectivity, *canadienne*. The word *habitants* was then used to designate the Canadian farmers who did not think of themselves as European peasants.

The collectivity *canadienne* and its leaders fought hard to establish their fatherland in the St. Lawrence Valley. They had to convince the French government that New France had a future. With the help of the Indian tribes, they managed to take control of the hinterland on which the colony depended for its commercial prosperity. The *Canadiens* waged war against the Iroquois and the British colonists to maintain their monopoly of the fur trade and to protect the very existence of the colony. The story of New France is that of a weak colony whose population was too small to keep for herself four-fifths of North America. The courage, the imagination and the diplomacy of its leaders delayed for a while a real showdown with the British colonies.

When the last encounter came during the French and Indian War (1754-1763), the British won. Victory always belongs—in the end—to those who are the stronger. Canada was conquered. The fatherland the *Canadiens* had wanted to establish in the St. Lawrence Valley had become a Province of the British Empire.

Did the *Canadiens* of 1763 conclude that they had failed and had to renounce their collective goals? Not at all. A majority among them kept the conviction that, even if they now owed allegiance to a new king, the St. Lawrence Valley was still their fatherland. Were they not the overwhelming majority of the population in the colony? It never entered their minds that a new Canada would be built on the ruins of the first one. They had no special objection—even if they were not over-enthusiastic—to proclaiming their loyalty toward the king of Great Britain, as long as this symbolic act did not challenge their substantive existence as a distinctive collectivity in the St. Lawrence Valley. In fact, they still aimed at building a fatherland of their own in North America. Now, they sincerely believed, it would be under the protection of George III instead of Louis XV.

Many factors tended to strengthen this belief. Only a few dozen British settlers came during the first ten years after the Conquest. This slight immigration and the agitation of the American colonies compelled Murray, Carleton and the British government to put aside the Royal Proclamation, whose programme was utterly unrealistic, and to give some recognition to the fact that the new colony was peopled with *Canadiens*. The nomination of Bishop Briand (1766), the consecration of his coadjutor (1772) and the Quebec Act (1774) helped to confirm the *Canadiens* in their illusion that the St. Lawrence Valley would remain "their" fatherland. In their numerous petitions to the king and to the British authorities, they would state with pride and confidence that they constituted more than ninety-five per cent of the population.

The arrival of a few thousand Loyalists from 1778 to 1785 somewhat disturbed the leaders of the *Canadiens*. The hopes this British immigration brought forth among the English minority which aspired to build a British American nation in the St. Lawrence Valley appeared as a threat to the *Canadiens*' own national ends. But the Constitutional Act of 1791 and the division of the colony into Lower and Upper Canada calmed the *Canadiens*' alarm. Lower Canada was the new name of their fatherland.

Thanks to the representative system, the *Canadiens* gave themselves new and more responsible leaders. The former military and seignorial class had vanished. The electoral process and the House of Assembly bred a new political class closer to the mass of the people. Papineau became the first and only true national leader of the *Canadiens*. He kept repeating that Lower Canada was the fatherland of the *nation ca-nadienne* and that the British immigrants who had chosen to settle in the colony were bound to accept the leadership of the majority. He invoked democratic principles to bolster his viewpoint. These principles served his national ends and those of his compatriots.

The English-speaking minority of Lower Canada had no intention of being assimilated by the *nation canadienne*. On the contrary, its ambition had always been to see the *Canadiens* melting away into a powerful British American nation. One can easily understand their angry reaction and their stubborn opposition to the division of the colony in 1791. From 1818 to 1837 the leaders of Lower Canada's English minority had the economic and political power—thanks to the undemocratic composition of the Legislative and Executive Councils—to check Papineau's and the *parti canadien's* programme. They persisted in demanding the union of the two colonies in order to put the *Canadiens'* representatives in a minority in the Lower House. Two collectivities were fighting for opposed national ends in Lower Canada. They were both in search of a fatherland, a country where they could freely exert the powers of a majority.

The armed revolt of 1837-1838 gave to the Imperial government the opportunity of correcting the error committed in 1791. Lower and Upper Canada were united. The *Canadiens* protested against what they called an act of despotism. The fact is that Lower Canada was treated as a conquered land—which it was in spite of all the pious declarations to the contrary. The British American nation had triumphed over the *nation canadienne*. Canada would be a British and English-speaking country. Some leaders of the British American nation were even so naïve as to believe that the *Canadiens'* complete assimilation was still possible eighty years after the Conquest.

Papineau being absent, the younger leaders of the *parti canadien* concluded an alliance with Baldwin's and Hincks' Reformers of Upper Canada. The union of the colonies had completely modified the former political equilibrium. Even some clearsighted British Montrealers were favourable to this alliance whose main objective was the establishment of responsible government. The *Canadiens* had been unable to democratize the political institutions of Lower Canada because this democratization was contrary to the interests of the British American nation. On the other hand, from 1842 to 1848, the *Canadiens'* representatives in the Assembly of United Canada helped the British American nation obtain responsible government. Is it not an ironic aspect of history that the French-Canadian politicians of the 1840's were told that they had contributed to the building of the second British Empire? They might perhaps have satisfied themselves with the founding of a fatherland for the *Canadiens,* but now they could say to their constituency that in the cabinet there was an attorney-general for Lower Canada and that the French language had become official. The Church enjoyed more freedom than formerly and the influence of the priesthood had begun to become greater than that of the politicians. With the help of British capital, the British American entrepreneurs had given a new impetus to the economic development of the St. Lawrence Valley. The French Canadians' standard of living had somewhat improved; when their political leaders, who enjoyed for the first time the benefits of being associated as junior partners with the party in power, were repeating to them that they had nothing to complain about, they almost unanimously agreed.

THE GREAT COMPROMISE OF CONFEDERATION

In 1854 MacNab's Tories and Morin's former Reformers were united to form the Liberal-Conservative party. One of the last survivors of the Family Compact, who had led a regiment against the rebels of Upper Canada, had become the political ally of a *Canadien* agitator accused of high treason in 1837. A new equilibrium of material and ideological forces had imposed this alliance. The principal leaders of the French-Canadian collectivity were, on the whole, satisfied with the situation. Realizing that they could not challenge it, they had come to accept the British American nation's leadership in all fields of collective action. There was a tacit agreement between the Church, the politicians—both French- and English-speaking—and the economic leaders of St. James and Bay Streets. This alliance can be called the Great Compromise of Canadian history. It lasted till the second half of the twentieth century.

Part of the Great Compromise was the creation of the province of Quebec in 1867. Having come to the conclusion that they could not completely assimilate the *Canadiens,* the British Americans had granted them a provincial government whose powers were originally very limited. It was mainly entrusted with the responsibility of preserving Civil Law and of promoting agriculture. The Church, whose authority and prestige had

been much enlarged since Papineau's failure, was, thanks to the action
of dynamic ecclesiastical leaders, free to organize the religious, educational and charitable institutions it needed to keep and increase the
confidence and obedience of the faithful. Most of the French-Canadian
politicians soon understood that it was wiser to renounce the liberal-
democratic ideals of Papineau's time which were cursed both by the
Church and by the privileged, conservative-minded, English-speaking
bourgeoisie of Montreal. They did not dare, for almost three generations, to challenge the bishops' and St. James Street's power. On the
other hand, the most perceptive leaders of Quebec's English-speaking
minority had conceded that they could not indefinitely prevent the establishment of a provincial government and legislature based on a French-
Canadian majority. The British North America Act granted special
rights to the British Americans living in Quebec. Moreover, they relied
on the "national" government and on their economic power to maintain
their peculiar status which was almost that of a dominant group in a
colonial territory. St. James Street had efficient means to teach the French-
Canadians' politicians how to behave.

Confederation could be hailed in 1867 as a great achievement by the
British Americans. Had they not succeeded in securing for themselves
the northern part of the continent as a fatherland? They could now
freely harness their energies and resources to build a continental nation.
They sincerely believed that they had solved for ever the French-Canadian problem, and the attitude of both French Canada's lay and
clerical leaders encouraged them in this way of thinking.

The fact is that Confederation gave satisfaction to most of the French
Canadians. The Church had no reason to think that the new political
framework was contrary to its vested interests. The Quebec lawyer-
politicians were convinced that they had obtained all the guarantees
they then deemed essential for the protection of French Canada's cultural
values. The new Constitution had many features which greatly impressed
the French Canadians of 1867. It created a local administration which
would take care of the immediate needs of the population. The French
language was official in the province of Quebec and in the federal administration, and the school rights of the religious minorities were recognized in
all the provinces. Moreover, the new country was called CANADA, a name
that stirred the imagination of the first white inhabitants of the St.
Lawrence Valley.

The *Canadiens* wanted to convince themselves that this second Canada would be the fatherland they had been longing for since the seventeenth century, a continental fatherland which they were ready to build in close collaboration with their English-speaking fellow-countrymen. The Manitoba Act (1870), which gave to the new province a bilingual status, reinforced this belief. The New Brunswick school crisis (1873), the Riel Affair (1885) and the Ontario Orangemen's agitation somewhat cooled off their enthusiasm toward Confederation. However, most of their lay and clerical leaders endeavoured to persuade them that they should forget these incidents and keep their faith in the future of a Canada which could be the fatherland of all Canadians.

Laurier's accession to the premiership of Canada was a unique moment in French Canada's history and nationalism. The *Canadiens*, forgetting the Manitoba school crisis and deaf to their Bishops' appeals, had spontaneously given their full confidence to the man who, they thought, would accelerate the building of the fatherland which they had always sought. One can hardly imagine today what Laurier's victory meant for the French Canadians of the last decade of the nineteenth century. They reacted with the feeling that one hundred and thirty-six years of British domination were completely over and that they had reconquered Canada from *les Anglais*. The less emotive had no doubt that with Laurier at the head of the central government a new Canada was in the making, a Canada which the *Canadiens* would spontaneously recognize as their fatherland.

CANADA'S EMERGENCE AS THE BRITISH-AMERICAN FATHERLAND

Once more the French Canadians' hopes were disappointed. Laurier could not change the fact that Canada was a British Dominion inhabited by a majority of English-speaking Canadians who considered the country as "their" fatherland and who had no intention of changing their national ends to please the French Canadians. The Anglo-Canadians knew who had actually built the second Kingdom of Canada, and they liked to repeat that, "it is not the tail that wags the dog." They suspected that the French Canadians had the secret ambition of establishing a "Popish and French domination" over Canada, and they were ready to crush this priest-inspired plot. The unsatisfactory compromise Laurier was compelled to accept on the Manitoba school problem; Canada's intervention in the South African War, which fostered and gave vent to the pan-British nationalism of the English-speaking Canadians; Laurier's retreat on the school rights of the Catholic minority when the provinces of Saskatchewan and Albert were created; the slow progress of bilingualism outside of Quebec; the imperialistic propaganda and the frequent violent outbursts of francophobia and anti-catholicism of the Anglo-Canadians—even among those who lived in the province of Quebec—reminded the French Canadians that the country in which they lived could not yet be considered as their fatherland.

Henri Bourassa and a small but influential group of young politicians, journalists and teachers—both lay and clerical—became the interpreters of a new generation of French Canadians. They questioned Laurier's leadership and began to re-examine critically the true nature of the relations between the two cultural groups that formed the Canadian union. They realized that there was no partnership between the English-speaking majority and the French-speaking minority except that of the rider with his horse. Canada's autonomy within the British Empire was one of their primary concerns. They became very critical of the traditional leaders of French Canada who, while claiming rights for Catholic and French schools in the other provinces, had not even been able to secure the linguistic rights of the French-speaking majority in the province of Quebec itself. They denounced what they called their lack of courage and their submissiveness to the English hegemony. Their pressure could not be ignored because they represented a powerful new trend in the French-Canadian society. The Gouin government, after much hesitation caused by the Quebec Prime Minister's fears of the stubborn opposition of the English-speaking business community, enacted a law establishing compulsory bilingualism in the public service of Quebec. When Thomas Shaughnessy, President of the Canadian Pacific Railway, announced that his company would not appeal to the courts to fight the measure, the Grand Trunk, the Montreal Light, Heat and Power, the Bell Telephone, and other large English-owned companies also decided to comply with the law. This legislation (1910) can be considered as an important landmark in French Canada's contemporary history. The French-Canadian collectivity, inspired by a new generation of leaders who had on some occasions the courage to challenge the former undisputed domination of the English-speaking minority in Quebec, realized that it had the electoral power to use the provincial government for promoting its national ends. The lesson was not to be forgotten.

The First World War, the Conscription Crisis and the struggles of the Ontario French-speaking minority to keep its parochial schools had a profound impact on the minds of the French Canadians. They had the proof that the English Canadians—at least a noisy and powerful group among them—did not accept French Canada as an equal partner. The fatherland they had dreamed of since 1867 had not yet materialized. Moreover, with the coming of the industrial and urban civilization, the economic rivalry between the two cultural groups coexisting in Quebec became more acute. As long as the vast majority of the French Canadians earned their living as peasants, day-labourers, servants, shop-keepers, small contractors, family doctors, lawyers and priests, the English-speaking Quebeckers had been free to organize on their own terms and for their own profit the economic development of the province. French-Canadian university graduates—whose number largely increased after the First World War—desiring to make a career as business executives, brokers, engineers, chemists, accountants and architects, discovered that they faced an unfair competition. They could not look for jobs in the other parts of Canada, and the English-owned large companies in Quebec had little place for them in their offices. The few who were hired had to work in English and knew that no matter how competent they were they would rarely get to the top. The Quebec English-speaking business community formed a select private club into which only a few assimilated former French Canadians were admitted. Another objective of the traditional leaders of French Canada was shown to be mere wishful thinking. The young French Canadians had been told for years—it began in the 1840's—that if they studied sciences, mathematics, economics and accounting instead of theology, philosophy, medicine and law they would improve their own lot and contribute to the economic prosperity of the province and of their own cultural group. The result was that there were now more educated French Canadians unemployed or doing menial work. Nevertheless, at the same time, the university graduates of the other Canadian provinces obtained jobs in Quebec companies. This fact did not go unnoticed.

During the depression of the 1930's, the economic and social problems of Quebec came to the forefront. The action of the new, most dynamic representatives of the French-Canadian collectivity was no longer limited to linguistic questions. Canada now had bilingual stamps and bank-notes, but the acrimonious debates these two minor measures had provoked on Parliament Hill and throughout the country had once more demonstrated that the English-speaking majority still anticipated that the French Canadians would one day be completely assimilated and that it had never intended to accept them as its fellow-countrymen. English Canada refused to listen to the French Canadians when, elated by the Statute of Westminster, they proposed a Canadian flag and a national anthem to foster Canada's nationhood. English Canadians had not changed their mind: they wanted Canada to be an English-speaking country and to remain a British Kingdom. They were always convinced that Canada's prosperity and future were exclusively entrusted to their care. As a majority, it was their right to think so.

THE RETURN TO QUEBEC AS THE FRENCH-CANADIAN FATHERLAND

It was at this time that many French Canadians began to ask themselves if it would not be more realistic to promote the economic and cultural progress of their community inside the borders of Quebec instead of waging exhausting and fruitless fights to establish bilingualism throughout Canada and to secure the collaboration of their English-speaking fellow citizens in building a Canadian nation. Was it not more important to remedy the economic and social ills of Quebec? The domination of the Anglo-American capitalists and their alliance with the Quebec politicians were severely denounced. The inhuman working conditions which prevailed in manufacturing and retailing were publicly exposed. The wretched situation of the unemployed in the cities and of the settlers in the colonization regions condemned the economic system and the men who defended it because it benefited them. The economic crisis compelled the French Canadians to realize that they were a people of proletarians.

The Second World War put an end to the unemployment and delayed for a while the great debate about the economic and social reforms needed to improve the lot of the French Canadians in Quebec. Old questions and problems attracted the voters' attention. One must never forget that the French Canadians' opposition to the South African War and to the First and Second World Wars was a kind of passive resistance to the English Canadians' domination. A subjugated collectivity always takes advantage of situations of this kind to express its discontent. Participation in the war was finally accepted mainly because it created jobs, but French Canada's rejection of conscription was always adamant. All the French-Canadian Liberal leaders, who were in power both in Quebec and in Ottawa, solemnly promised that there would be no compulsory military service overseas. Many leaders of the Quebec Liberal Party had even foolishly repeated since 1917 that Canada would never support Great Britain in another war! When the plebiscite of 1942 was held, the French Canadians were not surprised by the result. They now knew that there were two Canadas. In 1944 they elected the Union Nationale with the mandate of protecting the autonomy of the only government they could hope to control through their electoral power as a majority.

When Mr. Louis Saint-Laurent became the leader of the federal Liberal party and Prime Minister of Canada in 1948, the French-Canadian voters gave him a cheer. However, their reaction was quite different from that of the French Canadians of the last decade of the nineteenth century when Laurier came to power in Ottawa. Gone were the illusions of former generations. At the end of the 1940's a majority of French-Canadians had concluded, most of them with reluctance, that Canada was not their fatherland, and they knew that Mr. Saint-Laurent could not change this fact. Mr. Saint-Laurent himself, when he tried to influence the vote of his Quebec compatriots in provincial matters, learned that he was not the leader of the *Québécois*. The 1954 debate over the provincial income tax issue proved beyond any doubt that Duplessis alone had the full confidence of Quebec French-Canadian voters. In this crisis, he appeared as a true national leader reminiscent of Papineau and Mercier. After all the humiliations and rebuffs they had suffered during the depression and war years, the French Canadians had come to consider Duplessis—in spite of his many shortcomings, to which they were not blind—as the uncompromising defender of Quebec rights and autonomy, the primary goals of French Canada's collective consciousness. Duplessis himself was surprised by the reaction of his compatriots, whose national aspirations he had hardly shared a few years earlier. He had long thought of simply using them for his own political advancement—as all the French-Canadian politicians had done before him—but now he had been overcome by events. New social and psychological forces had radically changed the traditional pattern of Quebec political life. The "Quiet Revolution" had already begun.

When Duplessis died in 1959, a new French-Canadian man was born, and the Union Nationale had contributed much to his birth. For fifteen years, that political party, founded by conservatives, liberals, nationalists and independents, succeeded in identifying itself with the collectivity. In 1948, under the pressure of the nationalist groups and of the rank and file of his own party, who were very close to the mass of the people, Duplessis acknowledged that he could no longer delay the adoption of a provincial flag. The *fleur-de-lis* became the emblem of the French-Canadian nation and of its fatherland, Quebec. Duplessis' stand on the fiscal autonomy of the provincial government and his stubborn opposition to federal centralization gradually taught the French-Canadian voters that good government by Ottawa is no substitute for self-government. At the precise moment when the French Canadians, abandoning the *laissez-faire* teachings of their traditional leaders, were beginning to realize that the urban and industrial age required the direct and constant intervention of government in the educational, social and economic fields, they were also discovering that their electoral power as a majority of the voters in Quebec gave them the means of assuring their individual and collective progress. The democratic process has transformed the province of Quebec into the State of Quebec.

The federal elections of 1957 and 1958 reminded the *Québécois*—at least those who had forgotten it since the Conscription Crisis of 1917—that the English-speaking citizens of the country always have the power to choose alone, if they want, the Canadian government. Already, the census of 1951 and 1956 had revealed how foolishly sanguine had been the French Canadians who had thought, after the 1941 census, that the French-speaking citizens would one day constitute the majority of the Canadian population and how unrealistic had been the English Canadians who had for a while seriously feared a "revenge of the cradles" in favour of the *Canadiens*. A lower birth rate of the French-Canadian urbanized families, a decrease in the emigration of English-speaking Canadians to the United States and the arrival of thousands of immigrants had turned the scale. The unbecoming haste with which the English-Canadian Liberals removed Mr. Saint-Laurent from his leadership (September 1957) also made a profound impression on the *Québécois*. All these facts and events plus the poor communications between the Diefenbaker government and French Canada did much to accelerate what can be called the "nationalization" of the Quebec government.

In 1960 the provincial Liberal Party, whose leaders and organizers—having broken the former spell of the federal Liberal politicians—now understood better the new political mood of Quebec, was elected on a progressive platform which proposed to the French Canadians a positive

State with policies that would take into account their national ends. For the past six years the Lesage government has been under constant pressure to implement an educational, economic, social and labour policy that is supposed to enable the *Québécois* to be "Masters in Our Own House", according to the slogan of the general election of 1962, which was called on the issue of nationalizing the private hydro-electric companies.

. . .

Thus we have returned to Papineau's days. Following the Rebellion of 1837, the *Canadiens* went through an agonizing reappraisal. The intervention of the British army against the *Patriotes*, the arbitrary abrogation of the constitution of 1791 which had fostered the *Canadiens*' belief that the Imperial government was in sympathy with their national objectives, Colborne's ruthless repression, Durham's Report, the racial hatred openly displayed by Lower Canada's British minority, the manner in which the union of Lower and Upper Canada was achieved in order to annex them as a minority to British Canada, the various plans devised to assimilate them completely, were harsh blows to their former self-confidence. They were forced to revise their collective aims and they became much more modest in their practical expectations.

The French Canadians' ideology then became that of a minority group on the defensive, aspiring to nothing more than survival. Their politicians had accepted British Canada's economic and political leadership. In return for their collaboration, they participated in the administration of the country and in the advantages which the exercise of power gives. Their role in decision-making and their share of patronage were always very limited. On the other hand, the priesthood, whose prestige and influence greatly increased after the 1850's, began to preach that the French Canadians had received from God the mission of promoting the Catholic faith in North America and of defending traditional values, which the Protestant and materialistic English-speaking North Americans were supposed to have abandoned. This messianic nationalism—typical among all the downtrodden ethnic groups that are powerless to change their fate—was well received by most of the French-Canadian *intelligentsia*, who found real solace in it. At the same time, it gave good conscience to French Canada's lay leaders, who knew that their actual influence on the political and economic development of the country was very weak and did not endanger English Canada's hegemony. This ideology helped to maintain the Great Compromise upon which the Canadian union rested from the 1850's to the 1950's.

French Canadians now understand the full possibilities of the democratic process. They no longer consider themselves a minority. In Quebec they are experiencing the power that derives from numbers in the age of the Welfare State. They have the will to organize inside Quebec's borders a new society for all the members of the French-Canadian nation and for all those who have chosen or will choose to associate themselves with it.

The new generations in Quebec have come to regret the former messianic nationalism. They have renounced their forefathers' illusions. Their approach to French Canada's contemporary problems is a realistic one. They are eager to enter into and master the twentieth century. They have the knowledge and the will to shape the future of a distinctive collectivity to which they have no choice but to belong and which has kept its identity on the same territory since the seventeenth century. Their first objective is a new Quebec, and they know that their undertaking will give birth to a new Canadian union and a new Canada.

The French Canadians' long search for a fatherland is ended.

the national outlook of english-speaking canadians • kenneth mcnaught

TWO FOUNDING RACES?

Probably because the alternative is so clumsy, the terms "English-Canadian" or "English" are used interchangeably in Quebec to signify those people in the rest of Canada who do not speak French or who are not of French descent. Yet these terms are wildly misleading. They imply the existence in Canada of only two races, and thus that any revision of Confederation must be based upon a dialogue or bargaining process between these two races. Each term also carries the suggestion that the words "Canada" and "Canadian" have come to mean "English Canada" and "English Canadian". Thus the problem in Quebec eyes concerns the relations between the "two nations"; and it is a striking fact that "nation" and "race'" are virtually interchangeable terms in Quebec.

Under the hammer-blows of *nationaliste* theoreticians and the preconceptions of the Bilingualism and Biculturalism Royal Commission, these notions have become widely accepted in journalistic and intellectual circles outside Quebec. Professor Charles Taylor, for example, began a discussion of co-operative federalism in the influential Quiet Revolutionist journal, *Cité Libre*,[1] with the words, "Les Canadiens et les Québécois. . . ." Such usage is now common in the French-Canadian press and few spokesmen for the New Wave pause to reflect that the whole

61

concept of two nations is false. Certainly they have not dwelt upon the startling internal contradiction which more often than not pervades the Quebec argument.

Having established that Canada is composed of two races (or nations, or cultures), the argument goes on to say that only the French nation is really conscious of its own identity and destiny and that without Quebec Canada would become balkanized. The "English" race or culture is so amorphous that it depends upon the French-Canadian nation to keep it from falling into the arms of the United States or from breaking up into regional fragments. At the same time, it is this enfeebled English-Canadian race which has triumphantly imposed its image on Canada and made necessary the French-Canadian revolution. Strange argument.

The illogic springs from a failure to understand the meaning attached to nationality by English-speaking Canadians. And the confusion is deepened by the fascination with which English-speaking Canadian intellectuals, journalists and politicians regard the sophisticated theorizing of French-Canadian spokesmen. In Quebec the battle of ideas and refinement of logic are more highly valued than is generally the case elsewhere in the country. English-speaking Canadian intellectuals, impressed by the progress of the Quiet Revolution's ideological conquest of Quebec, are strongly tempted to reply in kind with counter ideologies of English-Canadian nationalism.

This is a dangerous exercise, as may be seen from a brilliant example of it in a recent issue of *Canadian Dimension*.[2] There, a young political scientist from McGill, Gad Horowitz, pleads for the creation of a specifically English-Canadian nationalism as a necessary counterpoise to the new, extreme French-Canadian nationalism. "There must," he writes, "be an English-Canadian nation (not a mere collection of English-speaking provinces) in partnership with the French-Canadian nation. . . . It is time to dignify French Canada's demands, to recognize them as normal human demands, by making the same demands for ourselves. Harmonious interpersonal relations can exist only among fully developed persons. The same applies, not metaphorically but strictly, to nations, whether they are within a single state or not."

It is time, writes Horowitz, to work out a new constitution in which Quebec will have its parliament, the English-Canadian nation will have its parliament, and to adjust the new international relations between the two there could be a third body to look after matters of common interest.

Impeccable logic—if one grants the major premise: that it is desirable, even necessary, to create an idealogical, constitutional English-Canadian nation.

To grant this premise is to accede to the demand, which is implicit (and sometimes explicit) in the course which was set by the Quiet Revolution, for a Canada composed of two "associate states". Not only would such a federation of associate states be clumsy and purposeless, it would be a shattering refutation of the concept of Canada entertained by generations of Canadians—both French- and English-speaking. It would make a fact out of what has so far been carefully-woven propagandist theory. Horowitz is right when he calls for a careful consideration of English-speaking concepts of nationalism in this country. He is dead wrong when he follows out the logic of the French Canadian *nationaliste* view of two racial nations. And this matter of the English-speaking view of Confederation is now of crucial importance.

The most striking facts about the English-speaking view of Canada are that it rejects racial nationalism and is the product of a deep commitment to slowly evolved historical tradition. There are good reasons why both these aspects of the English-speaking view are less well publicized and less widely discussed than the racial nationalism of French-Canadian spokesmen. There are even better reasons why the English-speaking view should be much more precisely understood at the present time. For that view, in the developing crisis of Confederation, will assert itself with increasing vigour.

I have said that English-speaking Canadians take a non-racial view of nationality. This will astonish the spokesmen of French-Canadian nationalism, and may surprise some others who have unreflectively accepted the French-Canadian version. Fingers will point to such historical expressions of English-Canadian racialism as the United Empire Loyalist tradition, the Imperial Federation movement, the Protestant Protective Association, the Ontario and Manitoba schools questions and the conscription crises of two world wars. Specialists in this argument will even resurrect Louis Riel. In each of these instances (with the probable exception of Riel) there was undoubtedly, on the part of Canadians of British descent, a feeling of racial identification. But one would have to be blind not to recognize that the racial component in the English-speaking view has steadily grown less significant. Not only that, the English-speaking view has always anticipated a Canadian nationality in which the significance of racial origin will diminish rather than increase.

At the time of Confederation, indeed, all the supporters of the movement, French- and English-speaking alike, talked of the founding of a new
nationality. No amount of quibbling about the different meanings attached by "English" and "French" to the word "nation" can obscure
the fact that in the 1860's a political nationality was being founded. The
debate and conferences leave absolutely no room for doubt on the matter.
Nor is there room to doubt that English-speaking Canadians, then and
even more now, thought of Canadian nationality as something that included people of French, British and other origins and which would move
steadily toward its own sense of identity. That identity was not to be
homogeneous in the American sense, but diverse. It would, and has
guaranteed to various minorities (especially the French-speaking minority) particular rights with respect to language, religion, land-holding,
military service, hunting and fishing.

Yet, while local differences of culture and law were to be guaranteed
(especially in Quebec), there was never any question of an "equality of
two founding races." The "races" were, in fact, not equal. A central
purpose of Confederation was to recognize this fact and to avoid the
frictions which the "two nations" idea had created during the unhappy
political evolution under the 1841 Act of Union.

In order to maintain minority rights within Quebec and the other
provinces, without at the same time permitting Quebec to become a
state within a state, the predominance of Ottawa and the rights of the
Canadian majority there (however it might be composed) had to be
accepted. As *Le Canadien* of Quebec put it in 1864: "Il faut que nous
nous résignions à n'être dans le congrès fédéral qu'une minorité comme il
faut que de son côté la population anglaise du Bas-Canada se résigne
à n'être qu'une minorité dans le législature provinciale."[3]

Any survey of Canadian political history reveals that the idea of two
"founding races" (each with the expectation of its own developing
nationality) has been and must be destructive of the idea of Canada.
Moreover, even if one wishes to call the political settlement of 1867 a
"compact" or "entente", it is still crystal clear that the "entente" is being
broken today by the leaders of the Quiet Revolution and not by any
"English-Canadian" view of Confederation. Strange, because of all
Canadians the Quebeckers refer most frequently to history as their
master.

PRAGMATISM AND "THE COMPACT"

A large part of contemporary Quebec's distrust of "English Canadians" stems from a fixed belief that they are inveterate centralizers. In fact, of course, centralization has never been a fixed goal of English-speaking Canadians. At the time of Confederation Macdonald encountered stiff opposition to an overblown central government from the Maritime Provinces and, in some respects, from the Grit elements within the coalition government of the united province of Canada. Indeed, it was one measure of his pragmatism and of his faith in the idea of a political nationality that he abandoned his preferred goal of legislative union as opposed to a federal pattern of government. Again, the great political-legal battles of the 1880's and '90's between Mowat and Macdonald, the "better terms" campaign in the Maritimes with its peak in the secession resolutions presented by W. S. Fielding in Nova Scotia, and the near-rebellion in Manitoba over the C.P.R. monopoly, all attest to a jealous regard for provincial rights on the part of a majority of English-speaking Canadians.

It is certainly true that English-speaking Canadians have also frequently turned to the central government for the fulfillment of some of their aspirations. But very often this has been for the protection of regional rights or opportunities. In the struggle over Manitoba Schools, for example, the division of Canadian opinion was not simply Quebec against the rest. A very large number of English-speaking Canadians believed that the remedial power of the federal government should be used to sustain minority rights within a province. Furthermore, in many of the instances of apparent English-speaking Canadian support for centralization, a major purpose has been that of using the economic powers of Ottawa to equalize provincial opportunities—not for the purpose of producing a bland national conformity but for the purpose of preserving viable provincial or regional differences of culture. This has been illustrated particularly in the various phases of the Maritimes Rights movement and in the western Progressive movement.

The point is that English-speaking Canadians have always seen the Canadian political state as one in which there is a necessarily shifting balance between the central and provincial powers. Their willingness today to undertake a major redressing of that balance is simply one of many historical examples of a continuing process. Nor is the process always dictated by reasons of ideology or politics. Frequently it has had a strong material basis. In the 1880's, the 1920's and the 1960's, the almost independent prosperity of Ontario and British Columbia has been a considerable factor in these provinces' ready acceptance of "co-operative federalism".

Yet despite the cyclical provincial-rightism of English-speaking Canadians, there is an equally consistent reassertion of the validity of the nation, and it is this that seems most to irritate the *nationalistes* of Quebec. It does so because they vastly underrate the complexity and change in the idea itself. Perhaps the most telling failure in Quebec's assessment is in the area of immigration. A classical sore point in Quebec is "Ottawa's immigration policy", which has not infrequently been regarded as a devious Orange plot to swamp the French. In fact, the history of immigration simply underlines the pragmatism and increasingly *non*-ideological English-speaking approach. The surge of immigration following World War II has been viewed by most English-speaking Canadians as a desirable means of enriching the nation. Pressures for "assimilation" have been markedly less than was the case in the massive population influx of the Wheat Boom years. Much of the reason for this change—an acceptance of multi-racialism, or multi-culturalism—is to be found in the confidence produced by the simple fact of Canadian survival. And since that survival has clearly depended upon a flexible response to regionalism, racial feeling and religious differences, tradition has planted firmly in the minds of English-speaking Canadians the idea that their national loyalty is to national diversity. Unhappily this seems trite only to English-speaking Canadians.

Quebec, despite these facts of the English-speaking Canadian development, still charges that in the past English-speaking Canadians have broken "the compact"—by refusing to honour the guarantees to the French language in Manitoba, by refusing to extend language privileges to French Canadian minorities in other provinces, by imposing conscription for overseas service in the interests of British imperialism and by excluding French Canadians from a fair share of the senior positions in the federal civil service. Less convincingly, but with even greater heat, Quebec charges that the English-speaking power élite has used its combined political-economic domination to exclude Quebeckers from managerial and ownership status in the province's industry. The result of this arrogant domination, argue the Quebeckers, was to render their province a "reservation" or "colony" to be exploited by English-Canadian and American capital, which adroitly financed such unsavoury politicians as Maurice Duplessis and used demagogic pseudo-nationalism as a blind behind which to extend their economic control. The answer to such colonialism was, of course, revolution.

Again we find inconsistency in the Quebec argument—inconsistency with which many English-speaking Canadians have found it either difficult or distasteful to grapple. From declaring that the Quiet Revolution is justified because "English Canada" broke the compact, the ideological directors of Quebec pass to the assertion that the original agreement never was good enough. Now it is not enough merely to undo the grievances within the original framework. It is necessary to break the structure altogether and establish two racial states. Even the most moderate spokesmen of the revolution (as can be seen by a glance at *Le Devoir* or *Cité Libre*) find it agreeable to talk of the "states" or the "provincial states" rather than the presently consituted "provinces".

In dealing with this nimble logic English-speaking Canadians are both baffled and resentful. But to say that they have not drawn up any thin red line of verbal battle, that they have generally preferred the familiar paths of compromise and conciliation, is not to say that they have no convictions. I have already noted that the English-speaking Canadians have a very definite concept of Canada—an historic amalgam of the original and undoubted purposes of Confederation plus modifications enjoined by the facts of immigration and growth. Reluctance to contend directly with the ever more extreme racial nationalism of Quebec (except by way of concession) is also explained by a compound of causes.

First, strangely, is acceptance of much of the case put forward by Quebec. Most English-speaking Canadians agree that there has been injustice along the way. In the Manitoba schools question that injustice was a specific and unconstitutional denial to French Canadians of rights and expectations spelled out in 1867 and 1870. In the case of conscription in 1917 there was extremely bad political management of the policy itself, and Quebec opinion was still further inflamed by the contemporaneous and deliberate prohibition by Manitoba and Ontario of teaching in the French language in public schools. There has also been admitted injustice in the appointments policy in the federal civil service—not unconstitutional injustice, but human and political injustice. On all these counts English-speaking Canadians feel guilty. Indeed, many of them who are Liberals have a positive guilt complex which has led them into a position which might be called the counterpart of those French Canadians who are called *vendus*.

THE PRESENT CONDITION

Beyond the English-speaking *vendu* (perhaps "sold out" is the accurate translation) most Canadians sympathize entirely with the feeling of exclusion which is the basis of the Quiet Revolution's triumph. Indeed, most English-speaking Canadians who have followed Quebec affairs (and there are many more such people than Quebeckers care to admit) admire the new and forthright willingness to use the government of Quebec to achieve collective purposes: to broaden the base of social welfare and to halt the takeover by American capital. But these are purposes which are agreeable to most Canadians, and they are repelled by the new Quebec insistence that such goals can be achieved only through virtually independent "provincial states". That insistence is bound to render difficult or impossible the achievement of similar goals at the national level since it will rob Ottawa of the essential powers of economic planning—indeed it has already placed grave impediments in the path of such planning.

But guilt-feelings and admiration for the new positive approach to the use of government are only half of the explanation of the English-speaking Canadian reluctance to spell out its mounting resistance to racial nationalism and to a new straightjacket constitution. The non-French Canadians know that they have attained a genuine sense of Canadian independence and that the growth of this feeling is not the result of logic-chopping and perpetual rewriting of constitutional formulae. It is the result of deep belief in growth by precedent and the converse suspicion that it is dangerous to commit to words the inner nature of human or social relationships. Since these two facts of feeling and philosophy lie at the heart of the matter, they are worth a further word.

First, independence. Since the enunciation in the 1860's of a new nationality, and despite the chronic outcropping of British loyalties, English-speaking Canadians have moved steadily towards independence. From one precedent to another down to the separate declaration of war in 1939 and the notably "un-British" stand taken at the time of the Suez crisis they gradually severed the constitutional and, to a considerable extent, the emotional ties with the "mother country". Not infrequently, as the career of Mackenzie King amply demonstrates, this process was hastened by an almost too sensitive recognition of Quebec's anti-British creed. Even with respect to the Commonwealth, as opposed to specifically British interest, it would take exceptional daring to assert that the English-speaking majority does not place its primary loyalty with the United Nations or with Canada itself before its concern for things British. The plain fact is that non-French Canada has experienced a sense of independence extending much further beyond the constitutional aspect than has Quebec. It is not without reason that some English-speaking Canadians begin to suspect Quebec of frailty in its protestations of independent goals.

In contrast to English-speaking Canada's deepening sense of independence, Quebec gives every evidence of a kind of psychological neo-colonialism. Far from feeling secure in its proclamation of Laurentian nationalism, it seeks security and identity by closer integration in French or Latin civilization. At the very time when the rest of Canada moves toward genuine internationalism (for which genuine political nationality is a prerequisite), Quebec seeks to tighten her "cultural contacts" with her mother country. She appears to have discovered that the legendary alienation of Quebec from France, based on a rejection of its rationalist revolution, was after all only legend. Now the prodigal daughter returns to the maternal fold. One almost has the feeling that *la gloire* of Gaullist France is necessary to the *amour propre* of Quebec.

Canadians of British descent have always regarded the political process as essentially pragmatic-experimental. They have shied away from detailed and comprehensive definitions of political and social relationships, preferring to see change come by the establishment of precedents which then become the justification of future decisions. That is why they have continued to hold to the English common law, and that is why civil liberties in English-speaking Canada have been more carefully cherished than they have in Quebec. That is why, too, they adjust more easily to multi-racial nationality than does Quebec. A broadening of rights by precedent—such as the instituting of simultaneous translation in Parliament, the proliferation of dominion-provincial consultations, revision of the appointments policy in the federal civil service and crown corporations, or such other possibilities as special Supreme Court panels of judges trained in the Quebec Civil Code to hear cases arising under that Code —it is this method of change that appeals to English-speaking Canadians.

By contrast, French Canadians prefer to systematize and codify the law, the constitution and, indeed, a broad range of social relationships. Because of these philosophic characteristics and a natural proclivity to verbalization, French Canadians mistake the nearly silent and the usually flexible English-speaking attitude as an absence of conviction or determination. No misunderstanding could have more disastrous and predictable consequences. The point has been well taken by some of the very originators of the Quiet Revolution—by those, in particular, who saw that revolution not only as a movement for social justice but also for the liberalization of Quebec. Of these, Pierre-Elliott Trudeau is perhaps the outstanding example.

Four years after the unseating of the Union Nationale, Trudeau began to deplore the wave of racial nationalism (whether the outright *separatiste* variety or that which held up the doctrinal veil of associate state) that rolled up in the wake of the Lesage victory. Discerning in the new extreme nationalism a threat of neofascism, he saw, in 1964, the clear possibility that the new anti-clericalism in Quebec could mean merely the substitution of "national sectarianism" for "religious sectarianism".[4] Having helped to prepare his province for its release from the Duplessis bondage, Trudeau was appalled to see the direction being taken by a steadily growing number of his compatriots—a direction which he felt compelled to dub a "counter-revolution". It was to stem the now common habit of looking upon and treating Ottawa as a foreign power that this brilliant and essentially non-political sophisticate plunged into the icy waters of federal politics in Quebec. For his pains he has been smeared as a *vendu*, and there is little doubt that he shares what I have called the English-speaking view of Canada. His political fate will likely be the political fate of Canada. Nor should anyone question the agony of his decision, for it involved further crippling the struggling Quebec wing of the NDP, which is the party that best represents Trudeau's social thought. His decision that the Liberal party—the party which flirts most openly with American continentalism—is yet the party which alone might avert the imminent culmination of racial nationalism was the measure of his fears for Canada. It also represents, one imagines, his firm (and occasionally amused) perception of the differences of philosophic assumption between French- and English-speaking Canadians.

For Trudeau, as for many Quebeckers who have felt the sting of *nationaliste* reprobation, to contemplate a separate or virtually separate

Quebec is to contemplate an introverted racial totalitarianism in which the purpose of individual liberty and social justice would be certainly subverted. It would be too great a sacrifice—a nearly inevitable sacrifice if Quebec much longer misunderstands English-speaking Canada and takes seriously Daniel Johnson's election promises.

NOTES

1. No. 76, April, 1965. (Montreal)
2. Vol. 2, No. 5, July-August, 1965. (Winnipeg)
3. September, 1864.
4. P. E. Trudeau, "Quebec Neo-Fascism?", *Canadian Forum*, vol. XLIV, No. 522, July, 1964. (Toronto)

the ukrainians:

a case study of

the "third force" • elizabeth wangenheim

A great deal has been written and spoken in the last few years about the problem of Canadian nationalism. This problem is generally considered as one of reconciling two conflicting nationalisms—French-Canadian nationalism and English-Canadian nationalism. Even if such a formula were found, however, it might prove to be inadequate to solve the more general problem of Canadian nationalism: the problem of developing a national identity, a complex of common goals, common values and common symbols acceptable to all segments of the population. Recent events, especially those connected with the Royal Commission on Bilingualism and Biculturalism and with preparations for Canada's Centennial Celebrations, have demonstrated that a third element, hitherto fairly submerged and reticent, is becoming increasingly important and must be taken into account.

Senator Paul Yuzyk, Manitoba-born of Ukrainian origin, in his maiden speech in the Canadian Senate on May 3, 1964, discussed the emergence of a "Third Force" made up of all those Canadians of non-English and non-French origin. Senator Yuzyk cited 1961 Census figures to show that this Third Force now constitutes 26% of the population of Canada, but its proportion in the three Prairie Provinces ranges from 48% to 53%. Senator Yuzyk suggested that the ethnic groups which constitute this Third Force have, because of their minority status, much in common and that as a united group they can hold the balance of power between the English and the French. Although this idea has since been subjected to much critical analysis[1] and has met with mixed reception by individuals and organizations of some other ethnic groups, it has been enthusiastically supported in public by the majority of Ukrainian organizations.

The publication of the terms of reference of the Royal Commission on Bilingualism and Biculturalism produced immediate and continuing protests from individuals and groups of non-English and non-French origin. The main complaint was against the concept of the "two founding races" which, it was claimed, relegated all other residents of Canada —especially those groups which started arriving in Canada after 1867—to the status of second-class citizens. Further objections were raised, including a protest against the idea that "bilingualism" must mean English and French ("Why not English and Ukrainian? or English and Icelandic?"). In addition it was constantly claimed that Canada is a "multi-cultural" nation. These public protests were raised preponderantly but not exclusively by persons of Ukrainian origin, many of them second or third generation Canadians.

Despite the common characteristics which all non-French and non-English ethnic groups in the Canadian population possess as a result of their "minority status", there are striking differences among them, such as, period of first immigration, degree of similarity of language and culture to those of the "founding races", and relationship to the country or region of origin, all of which tend to weaken the possibility of their uniting in any solid Third Force. Therefore it is dangerous to choose any one ethnic group as representative of all the "New Canadians". However, as the above items suggest, the Ukrainians themselves show a growing tendency to "speak for" all these groups, while pursuing the goals which they see as important for their own separate continued existence within Canadian society.

Ukrainians have been chosen for this paper because they are an example of a people whose own lately burgeoning nationalist spirit is fairly typical of the genre "Eastern European Nationalism". They also provide an extreme example of the effects which "nationalism without autonomy" can have upon the integration of immigrants into a society such as Canada's.

We shall examine the growth of this particular example of Eastern European Nationalism in the lands of the Ukraine, after which we shall describe the history of Ukrainian immigration and settlement in Canada. Finally, we shall attempt to analyze some of the factors contributing to the rather special role being played by Ukrainian Canadians in the present-day crisis in Canada's effort to evolve her own sense of national identity.

THE EMERGENCE OF UKRAINIAN NATIONALISM

For the purpose of this paper, nationalism will be considered as chiefly related to a consciousness, however strong or weak, of a national identity —the awareness by a reasonably large group of common values, traditions and commonly accepted patterns of behaviour. This consciousness need not cover all areas of individual actions—but it must be sufficiently embracing that members of the group can recognize their differences from members of other national groups.

While in many cases this sense of national identity is linked with the occupation of a specific geographic area and possession of political autonomy, these are by no means necessarily correlated. There have been many instances, especially in Eastern Europe, of people subject to the political domination of one or even several other states and perhaps scattered into geographically separated enclaves, who nevertheless possessed or developed a sense of national identity. On the other hand, there are today several instances of countries with clear-cut geographic boundaries and political autonomy which, nevertheless, because of the widely differing cultural patterns of the sub-groups brought together (often by outside decisions) within their boundaries, do not possess any strong awareness of national identity. In considering the nationalism of Ukrainians in Canada, these two general problems converge. For Ukrainian emigration to Canada provides an extraordinary example of a people, who came to possess a lively sense of their national identity without securing a national territory or state, moving to a territorial state whose inhabitants lack a clear sense of their own common identity as a national people.

In Western Europe in the eighteenth and nineteenth centuries the growing trend towards cultural nationalism contributed to the process whereby groups with a similar language and culture, but belonging to separate political units, were brought together to form the basis of new nation states. The creation of the German nation and the uniting of the Italian principalities were prime examples of this process. In Central and Eastern

Europe, however, similar forces led to tne rise of many self-conscious
minorities within the larger political units, each of these sub-groups
pressing for self-determination and political as well as cultural autonomy.
Some of these cultural groupings had at some remote period been independent states; others had not. Over the centuries they had been
subjected to military invasions and political domination by a variety of
powers. They had been constantly deprived of leaders, either through
physical annihilation or by integration into the "foreign" ruling elite.
What had remained more or less constant over the centuries was the
broad mass of peasants occupying a certain geographic area, speaking
closely related dialects and following similar customs, though with slight
variations from village to village and region to region. Because of the
general immobility of land-bound peasants, they had little notion of the
geographic range of their own language and culture and, except in border
areas, little contact with other languages and cultures except as embodied
in the military agents of the dominant state and the economic agents of
the local landowner. Being mainly illiterate, their sense of continuity
with their own past was a function of the operation of the oral tradition
—folk songs and dances, epic poems, etc.—passed on from generation to
generation.

The stimulus to weld these large masses of generally illiterate peasants
into a self-conscious nationality came in most instances from small groups
of educated people whose hitherto reluctant or complacent acceptance
of the political and cultural dominance of the ruling political power had
been shaken by their contact with the ideals of liberal romanticism and
cultural nationalism. The challenge of German and Russian integral
nationalism which, no longer content merely to rule over a variety of
peoples, threatened to impose on them the German—or Russian—language
and culture, provided a further impetus to quickening the sense of national identity among these ethnic minorities. As Professor Trevor-Roper
has described these attempts to create self-conscious groups as a prerequisite to the struggle for freedom, they would

> declare that they, too, were historic nations and to prove it would discover
> their ancient history, find the continuity of their ancient traditions, recreate
> their half-forgotten language, remember their old literature and, with the aid
> of ingenious statistics, retrace on the map the generous if not always strictly
> accurate frontiers of the past.[2]

The Ukrainians had a particular difficulty in establishing their claim to be a separate nation because of counterpressures from the militarily and politically stronger Russians. Not only do the two groups have closely related languages which can be traced back to a common origin in "Old Slavonic" and common religious traditions, but also the Kievan Rus', the highly developed orthodox Christian Kingdom of the 10th-12th centuries to which the Ukraine traces its political origins was until very recently claimed by Russia for itself alone and has traditionally been designated as Russian by most histories of Eastern Europe. But the Ukrainians faced yet a further difficulty in that sovereignty over the lands with a strong concentration of ethnic Ukrainians was divided between several states, notably Russia and Austro-Hungary—the latter's control being mainly taken over after World War I by the Poles (a cultural group who had worked actively for their own autonomy but were unwilling to grant this to others).

But none of these difficulties could stem the growing agitation for cultural autonomy among the Ukrainian people. At first the movement found its main inspiration in the work of literary figures among whom the poet Taras Shevchenko was the outstanding person. The early nationalists concentrated mainly on educating the broad mass of the peasants in order to develop among them the needed sense of national identity. But by the early twentieth century the Ukrainians had begun to organize along political and para-military lines. In the confusion resulting from the Russian Revolution and the defeat of the Central Powers, they were able to establish an independent Ukrainian regime. Short-lived as this emergent Ukrainian State was, its brief existence meant that for the first time in their modern history the majority of Ukrainians from all regions were united—fighting in all-Ukrainian army units for common goals, acknowledging the legitimacy of a Ukrainian governmental hierarchy and possessing common national symbols.

Despite the inevitable collapse of this regime and the re-division of the territory among several states, the Ukrainian national spirit, far from being crushed, was now reinforced by the memory of the brief experience of political autonomy. In the Western Ukraine there was a strong reaction among Ukrainians to attempts by the Poles to wipe out all traces of Ukrainian separatism. Ukrainian organizations were driven underground, with the result that nationalist ideology became more formalized and authoritarian in character.[3] Similarly in the Eastern Ukraine, while the Ukrainian nationalists were at first encouraged by the Soviet stress on the self-determination of nationalities, later Soviet attempts to counteract what they perceived to be the divisive effects of this nationalities policy led to great unrest. Many of those condemned during the purges in the 1930's were Ukrainian Communists who accepted the political ideology of the U.S.S.R. but who wanted an independent *Ukrainian* Communist State. A further source of nationalist reaction was the Great Famine of 1934—a famine artificially induced to break the backs of the Kulaks, the great majority of whom (because of historical differences in Ukrainian and Russian village structures and land tenure systems) "happened" to be Ukrainians.

After the Second World War nearly all of the ethnologically Ukrainian territories were incorporated into the Ukrainian Soviet Socialist Republic, which according to the Constitution has a considerable amount of regional autonomy and even has its own representative in the United Nations. It is a bilingual country having two school systems—the Russian system where Ukrainian is taught as a second language, and the Ukrainian system where Russian takes second place. The proportion of Russians in the population is constantly increasing. Though Russian, as the lingua franca of the U.S.S.R., has high prestige and is much used both for administrative and social purposes, Ukrainian still predominates in rural areas, while creative writing in Ukrainian is to some extent encouraged (though subject to considerable restrictions as to subject and manner of expression).

While the official Ukrainian Soviet attitude conflicts violently with that of the displaced nationalists, large numbers of whom emigrated during and after World War II, as to the heroes and villains of modern Ukrainian history, there is considerable agreement as to the choice of significant figures and events in the earlier periods. Soviet Ukraine, too, pays homage to Taras Shevchenko and to other nineteenth century writers, though Ukrainians outside the country complain that these and other heroes are distorted to fit the U.S.S.R.'s own purposes. Nationalists who are convinced that Soviet Russia is continuing the Czarist Russian policy of complete Russification of the Ukraine and Ukrainians consider all signs of Ukrainian autonomy as an illusion. They tend to see even the encouragement of creative writing and the honours paid to the earlier heroes as part of a plot to weaken the resistance of nationalists both within and outside the Ukraine.

UKRAINIAN IMMIGRATION AND SETTLEMENT IN CANADA

In some ways Ukrainians were fairly typical of the immigration which first came to Canada after Confederation when official encouragement of large-scale immigration to settle the vacant Prairies and to keep the Americans out was seen as in the new nation's best interest. The offer of free land brought great numbers of land-hungry, semi-literate peasants to the Prairie Provinces between 1891, the year the first two Ukrainians arrived, and 1914.[4] They settled in clusters, often on fairly marginal land (because it had trees and resembled the land they grew up on), roughly on a line from south-eastern Manitoba to north-western Alberta. Applying their traditional farming techniques, they opened up new land and also brought into production land abandoned by less skillful settlers. Incidentally, legend has it that grains brought by early Ukrainian settlers were responsible for the development of Marquis hard wheat, the foundation of the Prairies' later wealth. To supplement their earnings many Ukrainian men worked long months of each year on the construction of the railways. Very few of these early immigrants settled in the cities and towns of eastern Canada. Indeed government and railway officials co-operated to ensure that Eastern European peasant colonists were transported almost without a pause to Winnipeg or further west.

The second wave of immigrants in the 1920's was more mixed in composition. It included a number of teachers, journalists and others who had participated in the Ukrainians' long struggle for and short-lived enjoyment of independence. These considered themselves as essentially political emigrés. Greater numbers of these new immigrants settled in urban areas of both central and western Canada, though the trend was still towards the Prairies. In addition, during the period of the 20's and 30's, there was a growing secondary migration to the cities of those born in Canada, with the consequent development of highly organized Ukrainian community enclaves. World War II increased the geographic and social mobility of Ukrainians in Canada, many moving to man large defence production plants in eastern Canada, other thousands enlisting in the Armed Forces, where in the course of their training they came in contact with people from many regions and of varied ethnic origins. Only a minority of these people were content to settle back after the war into the old isolated rural communities; the movement of the Prairie-born to the cities, especially those of Ontario, accelerated, while the numbers with higher education and professional skills increased rapidly. As a by-product of World War II, a further large influx of Ukrainian immigrants came via Displaced Persons Camps to Canada in the period between 1947 and 1953, settling mainly in the cities of Eastern Canada (predominantly in Toronto and Montreal). This wave differed significantly in social characteristics from the previous waves in that it included a large proportion of urban middle-class individuals, with higher education and often professional skills.

It might be mentioned here that, except for the Jews, no immigrant groups other than British and French had previously contained more than a sprinkling of urban and middle-class people. Under reasonably stable social and political conditions, the urban middle-class in most countries has very little motivation to emigrate. However, the political and military upheavals and destruction of the 1940's displaced many from their own countries and convinced many others that Europe was "sitting on a powderkeg". Consequently the character of immigration to North and South America and Australia changed significantly. Not only among refugees from political oppression such as Jews, Poles, Ukrainians, Estonians, Hungarians, but also among "regular immigrants" such as the Dutch, Germans, Austrians, large numbers of highly educated professionals and businessmen, as well as highly skilled craftsmen, have been appearing. Indeed the only groups which now approximate closely to the "traditional" pattern of immigration, so thoroughly documented in the prewar literature, are those from the Mediterranean countries, Italy, Portugal, Greece, which still contribute large proportions of the poorly-educated and minimally-skilled.

This influx of a 'new type' of immigrant has, in most cases, had a marked effect upon the structure of existing ethnic communities. Control of ethnic organizations has in many cases been seized from the hands of the usually poorly educated peasant founders and their at least partly acculturated descendants; political ideologies and sectarian conflicts bred in the European cauldron have been forced into the local ethnic community's consciousness; new norms, new standards of dress and behaviour have been imported to dominate the social life of the ethnic community. The presence of this new type of immigrant has also had repercussions within the economic and, to a lesser extent, social structures of the larger society. While some of these immigrants, especially among the refugees, have been prevented or hindered by age, lack of proper language skills or resistance by professional societies from re-establishing themselves in their former occupations, others have been able by devious or straightforward methods to overcome or circumvent these difficulties. Indeed, often where a need for their skills was obvious, their employment has been welcomed and facilitated by both governmental and private groups. The significant fact for this discussion is that for the very first time considerable numbers of immigrants of non-English and non-French origin have been entering the economic structure at the middle or upper levels. This has not been accompanied by a proportionate integration into the middle- and upper-class social networks of the dominant society, nor, up until now, have many of them participated actively in the community power structure. Nevertheless the growing incidence of equal-status contacts, the publicity given to immigrants who are financiers or company managers, the contributions by immigrant academics to scientific and humanistic research—all these factors have tended to diminish the force of the stereotyped image of the immigrant as an uneducated, uncivilized peasant with or without a sheep-skin coat. Contacts with these new immigrants have not always been amicable because of their frequent attempts (at least in the beginning) to introduce European methods of doing things and their sometimes ill-concealed evaluation of Canada and Canadians as "completely without culture".

Almost from the beginning of their immigration, Ukrainians have been among the most highly "visible" of Canada's minority groups. In the early era, however, they were not visible as "Ukrainians" because most peasants had not yet acquired that strong consciousness of their own common identity which we have described as developing among their intelligentsia. They saw themselves as, and were called by others, Galicians, Bukovinans (according to their region of origin) or, more generally, as Ruthenians (a label derived from the old kingdom of Kievan Rus'). It remained for later immigrants, the veterans of the Ukrainian National Armies of the short-lived Ukrainian Republic and the political emigrés fleeing from Polish and Soviet oppression, to develop in a large majority a sense of their common Ukrainian identity.[5]

The Ukrainians were the prototype of "Sifton's peasant in a sheep-skin coat"[6], which became the general image of the type of immigrant flooding into the Prairies in the early years of this century. Early colonization officers' reports were full of complaints about the difficulties encountered in settling "The Galicians", "The Bukovinans", "The Ruthenians", . . . etc. Such complaints may have stemmed merely from the numerical preponderance of such people. However when it came to establishing and administering public school systems in the newly created Prairie Provinces, the Ukrainians certainly were perceived by the authorities as presenting a special problem. For a long time they resisted or sabotaged all attempts to establish local schools, refused non-Ukrainian teachers, and forced the establishment of special institutions to train "Ruthenians" as school teachers, who then often turned round and taught classes in the Ukrainian language.[7] Paul Yuzyk explains this early opposition by Ukrainians to English-language schools and teachers as stemming from their resistance to

> instruments of assimilation employed to wipe out their nationality, and culture. *Mistakenly* they considered the situation analogous to the one in Galicia where the ascendant Poles forced Polish schools on the Ukrainians and denied the Ukrainian people a separate existence.[8]

We have italicized Yuzyk's use of the word "mistakenly" because it would appear from government records that, on the contrary, in the early period the school systems of the Prairies were seen as the one possible tool for producing some degree of homogeneity out of the wide variety of peoples. During these early years Ukrainians were the victims of a considerable amount of discrimination, being called "Bohunks", "Hunkies" and even "white negroes".[9] In addition to the problems faced by individuals, Ukrainians as a group were denounced in the public press as an inferior and undesirable element and were the objects of scornful remarks by some Anglo-Saxon leaders.

These outside pressures, coupled with memories of persecutions suffered in the Western Ukraine, caused the Ukrainians in self-defence to take an increasingly active part in public affairs. Because of their patterns of settlement, they were provided with a strong weapon—namely the bloc vote. Ukrainians were not slow to learn about the political system and its advantages. Already in 1908 a Ukrainian was elected reeve of the municipality of Stuartburn, Manitoba. By 1912 there was a Ukrainian alderman in Winnipeg. In 1913 and 1915 Ukrainians were elected to the Alberta and Manitoba legislatures respectively and by 1926 they had a member in the House of Commons at Ottawa. We say "they had" intentionally, because one of the consequences of bloc voting is that the politician elected through the support of one particular ethnic group, predominant in his riding, is often expected to sit as the representative of that group. The politician is most likely to succumb to this pressure if he is himself of the same ethnic origin, but it can also happen when he is not. The effects of this special group loyalty need not be particularly damaging but they can lead a politician to advocate and even to force through measures in the domestic or international spheres which may encourage the growth of internal disunity or be otherwise against the best interests of Canada as a whole.

The success of the bloc vote should not, however be taken as an indication of internal Ukrainian unity but only as a preference for Ukrainian representatives over those of any other origin. Ukrainians were from the beginning of their immigration beset by violent internal conflicts. The early conflicts were of a religious nature and probably impinged but little on outsiders other than religious leaders. However, in the interwar period coincident with the trend towards the cities, fundamental political disputes developed which certainly affected the relations of Ukrainians with other Canadians. Two large organizations sprang up —the one Communist in ideology and positively oriented towards the U.S.S.R., the other with a right-wing trend, favouring Ukrainian nationalism and opposed to both Polish and Russian influences. There is considerable evidence to suggest that the majority of the members of both groups were politically quite unsophisticated and joined one or other organization—the choice often a matter of sheer chance—because of the cultural and social facilities offered by each group. Nonetheless, the conflict between them raged openly in prairie cities and in Ontario communities and led to a public image of Ukrainians as "just a bunch of extremists—half Communists and the others Fascists".[10] In actuality, the image did not fit the facts, for there were several Ukrainian organizations and many individuals who rejected the ideologies and the methods of both political extremes and were seeking to establish the satisfactory integration of Ukrainians into Canadian life. During the war, government intervention of various sorts tamed down the extremists of both varieties and brought about a degree of unification of all major Ukrainian organizations, except the left-wing group, through the creation of the Ukrainian Canadian Committee. External pressure gave an opportunity to the middle-of-the-road organizations and, in general, to the Canadian-born, to gain some control and to promulgate values and goals more oriented to integration into the fabric of Canadian society.

This unity and pro-Canadian orientation was badly threatened in the post-war period by the large-scale influx of political emigrés. These veterans of the underground armies or nationalist political struggles endeavoured with varying degrees of success to force Ukrainian organizations to repudiate or tone down their pro-Canada orientation; they also introduced new ideological conflicts based on European political schisms. By acquiring control of the majority of existing Ukrainian-language publications and developing a wide range of new journals and radio programmes, these newcomers have disseminated the ideas and goals of Ukrainian nationalism far beyond the range of active organizational participants. By constantly claiming that the U.S.S.R.'s Russification tactics pose a threat to the continued existence of a Ukrainian language and culture, they have created within many of the younger generation, born or educated here, a sense of commitment—an obligation to fight for the perpetuation of the Ukrainian language, the glorification of Ukrainian history and culture, its myths and symbols. This appeal tends to be more powerful than all the pressures working towards a dissolution of close in-groups ties—both the pressures of intergenerational cross-cultural conflict and the monetary and social attractions of the larger society. While this appeal probably has the greatest impact on post-war immigrants and their children, it also finds a response among many of the Canadian-born Ukrainians who have been baffled in their attempts to be "just Canadian" by their failure to perceive any solid content in Canadian identity. Similar, though perhaps not so extreme, effects are being reported in other ethnic communities—such as Polish, Hungarian and Chinese—as a result of large influxes of political emigrés. Thus, the post-war immigration which aided in raising the image of "the immigrant" in the eyes of the host society also created a counter-pressure diminishing the likelihood of the early cultural and structural assimilation of minority ethnic groups into a more homogeneous society.

UKRAINIAN NATIONALISM AND THE CANADIAN MOSAIC

Many writers have pointed out the contrast between the American "melting pot" philosophy and the Canadian government's espousal of the concept of "cultural pluralism". Some American writers have recently pointed out the incompleteness of the melting process,[11] while, on the other hand, Canadian newspapers are constantly offering evidence that not all Canadians agree with their government's avowed preference for a mosaic. This need not concern us here. What we are interested in is the effect of the Canadian pluralistic policy upon the various ethnic groups and, by extension, upon the state of Canadian nationalism.

The Canadian Government, through the Citizenship Branch of the Department of Citizenship and Immigration, encourages ethnic groups to retain their own institutions, as experience has shown such institutions perform valuable functions for the entire society in cushioning the "culture shock" experienced by all new immigrants.[12] However, as is usual with organizations, they tend to be self-perpetuating long after immigration has ceased. Ethnic community leaders, such as priests, editors and organization executives, who find gratification in their high in-group status, are largely instrumental in attempting to keep the members of their groups facing inward—and backward—towards the homeland, thus perpetuating divisions and a sense of strangeness among the groups who constitute the Canadian population.

They constantly find acceptable justifications for their actions: Ukrainians continue to quote Lord Tweedsmuir's statement in an address to a Ukrainian group in 1936, "You will be better Canadians for being Ukrainians." And leaders of many ethnic communities have developed a litany:

> Canada has no culture of its own. Only by assuring the perpetuation of our own culture, by continuing our own traditions, can we make our contribution to the Canadian mosaic.

Government support and constant repetition have developed this into a sacred theme which, as with all things sacred, protects it from challenge. However, when one observes the process in practice, one comes to question the amount of effective action being taken to place all the stones in the mosaic in such a way as to create an identifiable picture.

Most ethnic groups seem concerned to teach the language and folk arts of their people only to members of their own group. Even those organizations which are not by policy "closed" to outsiders do not usually make special efforts to attract outsiders and make them welcome. Most ethnic groups provide an active cultural life for their members. For example, Ukrainians in Metropolitan Toronto are offered a varied diet of concerts, plays, lectures, art exhibits, religious festivals, and mass meetings in celebration of historic events—solemn gatherings to honour the heroes and martyrs of the Ukrainian struggles for independence. Other ethnic groups enjoy a similar variety of activities. However, each of these sets of activities is separated from the others by an opaque curtain partially but not wholly caused by language problems. Certainly very few "out-siders" are aware of this great variety of activity going on constantly in the metropolitan area. When the various folk cultures are displayed in public at exhibitions, as service club entertainment, or in folk festivals, interest on the part of the general public would seem to be in the per-formances as entertainment, as illustrations of exotic customs from "over there", rather than as an integrated part of Canadian culture. Further-more, members of each ethnic group display little interest in any but their own groups. This is one instance where everyone is interested in giving and no one in receiving. Surely no mosaic can present an identifi-able picture or image if the stones of various colours are not significantly related to one another!

Ukrainians and other "new" groups rebel against being expected to adopt as Canadian those symbols arising out of French or British tra-ditions. One might ask how much, even disregarding the language problem, Canadians of other origins could incorporate from the content of Ukrainian folk songs and literature. Much of this material extols the beauties of the Ukraine (a land as to whose exact location many Canadians have only hazy ideas); there is much talk of the bravery and stirring deeds of the Cossacks (whose names few Canadians would link with Ukrainians and whose image is generally that of "blood-thirsty barbarians"); and there are many stories of Ukrainians who suffered under oppression from the Tartars, Poles, Russians and Germans, in struggles of which most Canadians have little knowledge and, so far as one can judge, less interest. Ukrainians have tried to impress upon other groups the symbol of their leading poet, Taras Shevchenko, as a world figure. He has been compared with Robert Burns and Shakespeare, and has been put forward as a leader in the general world struggle against oppression. As a result of Ukrainian efforts, statues of Shevchenko have been erected in the grounds of the Legislature in Winnipeg and in Washington, D.C. (a third statue to Shevchenko exists at the summer camp of the Association of United Ukrainian Canadians at Palermo, Ontario). Nevertheless, there would seem to be widespread ignorance among most Canadians (other than politicians!) not only as to what Shevchenko wrote but even that he ever existed.

Some ethnic groups are content to carry on their cultural and social activities, including the education of the younger generation, completely within their own organizational facilities, relying exclusively on their own financial resources. Others, and here the Ukrainians are an outstanding example, are not. Ukrainian organizations and politicians have for many years urged that the Ukrainian language be taught in the public school system *wherever there is a certain concentration of students of Ukrainian origin*. While they do not exclude the possibility of other students also studying the language, they are essentially requesting that public funds be used to satisfy the interests of a particular group. Their aim has been achieved in the Alberta and Saskatchewan school systems, and the extension of this privilege to other provinces was one of the main recommendations contained in the majority of briefs submitted by Ukrainian organizations to the Royal Commission on Bilingualism and Biculturalism. Other submissions to the same Commission suggested that the charter of the Canadian Broadcasting Corporation should be changed to allow programmes in other languages besides French and English, while one wanted special recognition given to the Ukrainian language by considering Ukrainian-Canadian writing when selecting the Governor General's awards for literature.[13]

Ukrainian organizations have for some time been using other public facilities for their own purposes. Two examples will suffice: municipal authorities in Toronto and other cities have been prevailed upon to fly the Ukrainian (Nationalist) flag on city hall flag staffs during celebration of the Ukraine's short-lived independence; at the request of Ukrainian organizations, Dominion Government Post Office franking machines in various cities carry announcements of the anniversaries of Ukrainian poets and other heroes. Most people would probably ignore or be indifferent to these activities, which in all probability harm no one. Nevertheless, as examples of claims for special privileges, they do represent a trend.

The submissions of Ukrainian groups to the Royal Commission on Bilingualism and Biculturalism demonstrate an increasing tendency for minority ethnic groups to echo the complaints and claims of French Canadians. One submission seuggested that the next Governor General should be a Ukrainian, while others complained that Ukrainians were the victims of discrimination in the higher echelons of business and the public service. This type of complaint has also, of course, been prominent in recent agitations of French Canadians. Many people willing to concede the unfairness of excluding a French Canadian from a particular post just because he is French may, however, be unwilling to have a French-Canadian appointed to a post just because of his ethnic origins. If ethnic claims were extended to the point where each group (including French and English) must receive its "fair share" of top honours according to its proportion of the population, then Canada might become so "balkanized" that the development of effective national agencies and a unified national spirit would be well-nigh impossible.

As it happens, Ukrainians who represent approximately 2.6% of the population of Canada, are not completely ignored in the distribution of public honours. They were one of only two minority groups to be represented on the Royal Commission on Bilingualism and Biculturalism; they and the Jews are the only minorities to have representatives on the Canada Council (when one Ukrainian's term expired, another was appointed). There are also two Ukrainians in the Canadian Senate: this might be considered a normal part of the political process to be compared with the appointment of the first Ukrainian cabinet minister, except for the fact that, when one Ukrainian Senator died, another Ukrainian was appointed. Many Ukrainians, including many living far from the provinces from which these men were appointed, exult over "our Senators" and are pleased by the fact that, as one is of the Ukrainian Catholic and the other of the Ukrainian Orthodox faith, both of the large Ukrainian national churches are represented in the Canadian Senate.

The position of Ukrainians in Canada today must be considered as important in yet another way. Like the majority of the Third Force, Ukrainians have identified with the English rather than with the French. When a Ukrainian asserts (hiding all his uncertainty and ambivalences), "I am a Canadian," he means, "I am an English-speaking Canadian." Even in Montreal, immigrants tend to learn English rather than French.[14] Many immigrants who deliberately choose to settle in Montreal because they are already French-speaking soon make great efforts to learn English and some of them relocate when possible in other parts of Canada.

French Canadians have long been bitterly hostile to immigrants and to minority groups in general. They long feared that a great influx of English-oriented immigrants would prevent the French Canadians from achieving their goal of balancing the forces through "la revanche des berceaux". Now that the French Canadians have gained a more secure control over the Province of Quebec, the activities of minorities within that province probably are regarded as mere irritations. However, the attitudes of Ukrainians and other groups in other regions, especially in the Prairie Provinces, are still resented by many French Canadians. News reports and editorials in the French-language press, covering the Royal Commission on Bilingualism and Biculturalism meetings, have given almost as much attention to the briefs and comments of Third Force organizations and individuals as to all others. The general complaint is against the Third Force's stress on multi-culturalism rather than bi-culturalism and the pressure of some ethnic groups "surtout les Ukrainiens" for special treatment.

> They won't acknowledge our special status. They want to reduce us to being just a minority group like they are.

This apparent threat is particularly troublesome to those French Canadians whose horizon is not limited to the borders of the Province of Quebec, and who wish to include all French Canadians wherever they live, within French Canada.

While the French Canadians' perception of hostility on the part of prairie-based Ukrainians would appear to have been well-founded, it is interesting to consider press reports from Winnipeg of the 1965 meeting of the Quebec Premier, Jean Lesage, with the Dominion executive of the Ukrainian Canadian Committee. Earlier reports had stressed the way in which Lesage's eyes had been opened to the realities of the situation in Western Canada, not only to the degree of genuine anti-French feeling, but also to the lack of domination by "les Anglais". In Lesage's meeting with the Ukrainian Canadian Committee he promised to have the Quebec Minister of Education investigate the advisability of providing classes in the Ukrainian language in Montreal schools where Ukrainians were concentrated; in return the U.C.C. promised to use its influence to secure French-language schools for French Canadians outside of Quebec. Surely this must be an exceptional event—when the elected leader of a provincial government enters publicly into equal-status negotiations (indeed the Canadian Press spoke of an "entente cordiale"[15]) with the leader of a particular ethnic group on a matter which really affects other governmental bodies! It is certainly too soon to predict the outcome of these negotiations—but for our present discussion the outcome is not important. What is significant is that the talks took place. They would seem to give one more example of the contemporary tendency to multiply the divisions within our nation.

Here one should possibly interject that the left-wing Ukrainians, who dominate the "progressive" Canadian Council of National Groups, have given their support to the French claims that Canada is in actuality not only "two cultures" but also "two nations" and have suggested that a new constitution should "recognize and make secure the historically correct status of French Canada as a nation". They see the resolution of French-Canadian aspirations as a necessary prerequisite to the cessation of discriminatory treatment of other national groups and to the achievement by those national groups "as integral parts of English and French Canada" of their "rightful place in Canadian society".[16]

The question still remains—why the Ukrainians? Why are they the ones whose voices have been raised so much louder and so much more frequently than those of any other group? Why have they pressed so vigorously for their own goals, disregarding the growing irritation of other Canadians, including many of the so-called Third Force?

Ukrainian-Canadians are today a highly organized group. Despite the internal conflicts and the large numbers who are not actively affiliated with any Ukrainian organization, it is still probably accurate to state that the public pronouncements of the Ukrainian Canadian Committee and of some of its member organizations on the desired position of Ukrainians in Canadian society would be accepted (or at least not repudiated) by a majority of Ukrainian Canadians. To a certain extent this attitude is a result of the pattern of Ukrainian settlement and subsequent experiences in Canada. However, other ethnic groups with relatively similar settlement and developmental patterns are much less concerned with publicizing their own image and with laying their claims to public recognition and assistance in perpetuating their own cultural values.

For an explanation of the forces which appear to drive the Ukrainian Canadians, we must refer back to the history of Ukrainian nationalism—a history of rebellion against oppressive forces, of struggle to establish and secure recognition of its separate identity, its own language, its own folk arts, its own heroes and other national symbols. Many Ukrainians perceive this national identity to be threatened today by outside forces, in particular by the threat of the Russification of the Ukrainian Soviet Socialist Republic, but also by the general indifference or unwillingness of other nations and other peoples to accept the image of the Ukrainians as a separate people clearly distinct from all others. They feel compelled to counteract this two-fold threat by (a) preserving "in the diaspora" (their own phrase) the language and culture which is threatened with annihilation in the land of their origin and (b) using all possible means to interpret and project their image of Ukrainians. It is my contention that this is the main force which drives many Ukrainian Canadians to press publicly for the attainment of their own goals without taking too much account of the possible impact on Canadian unity.

It was suggested at the beginning of this paper that Ukrainians are not typical of the Third Force. Some of the other minority groups resemble them in certain aspects, others in very few. Nevertheless, at this time of national crisis, when most interest has been focussed on solving the large problem of French-English relations, the effect of such a vocal minority should not be discounted. Two related trends can be observed: regardless of the diversity which may exist among minority ethnic groups, the concept of the Third Force is acquiring wide currency in Canadian political thought and there is an equally wide tendency to perceive the Ukrainians as the spokesmen of this force. If, as a result of these developments, other minority groups should come to regard the Ukrainians as a model of what an ethnic group's position in Canadian society *should* be, then many of them, regardless of their own different history and relationship to their homeland, might come to expect the same type of special treatment as the Ukrainians. In this event, the difficulties involved in coping with the basic problem of Canadian identity might well be intensified.

NOTES

1. For example, cf. articles in *Canadian Slavonic Papers*, vol. VII, 1965.
2. H. R. Trevor-Roper, "Jewish and Other Nationalisms," *Commentary*, vol. 35, (January, 1963.) p. 15.
3. John A. Armstrong, *Ukrainian Nationalism*, 2nd ed., New York, 1965.
4. V. J. Kaye, *Early Ukrainian Settlements in Canada, 1895-1900*, Toronto, 1964.
5. The process was never entirely successful:—there are considerable numbers of individuals who according to certain "objective" criteria could be designated as Ukrainians yet who insist they are "Russians" or "Poles". Also there are small groups who continue to call themselves Ruthenians and categorically deny they are Ukrainians.
6. A. R. M. Lower, "The Growth of Population in Canada", in V. W. Bladen (ed.), *Canadian Population and Northern Colonization*, Toronto, 1962. (R.S.O.), p. 55; Vera Lysenko, *Men in Sheepskin Coats*, Toronto, 1947.
7. cf. C. B. Sissons, *Bilingual Schools in Canada*, Toronto, 1917; S. E. Lang, "History of Education in Manitoba", and Walter C. Murray, "History of Education in Saskatchewan", both in Adam Shortt and Arthur G. Doughty (eds.), *Canada and its Provinces*, Toronto, 1914, vol. XX. pp. 417-447 and 451-474 respectively; J. Skwarok O.S.B.M., "The Ukrainian Settlers and their Schools", M. Ed. thesis, University of Alberta, 1958.

8. Paul Yuzyk, *The Ukrainians in Manitoba: A Social History,* Toronto, 1953, p. 145.

9. Ukrainian National Home Association in Winnipeg, *Propamiatna Knyha Ukrayinskoho Narodnoho Domu u Wynypegu* (Memorial Book of the Ukrainian National Home in Winnipeg), Winnipeg, 1949, p. 61.

10. This dichotomy (however exaggerated the description) was not peculiar to the Ukrainians. Similar deep left-right splits occurred among other ethnic groups— Finns, Hungarians, Poles, etc. However, the Ukrainians were the largest non-British and non-French group and their left-wing halls in many centres became the rallying point for nearly all left-wing activities. The Nationalists, their attention being divided between anti-Communist activities on the local front and preparations for the liberation of the Ukraine, did not attract other groups to the same extent.

11. Will Herberg, *Protestant, Catholic, Jew,* Garden City, rev. ed., 1960; Milton M. Gordon, *Assimilation in American Life,* New York, 1964; Nathan Glazer and Daniel Patrick Moynihan, *Beyond the Melting Pot,* Cambridge, Mass., 1963.

12. But we should note that until very recently the Immigration Branch of the same Department has continued, except when reacting to special outside pressures, to give preference to nationality groups whose cultures are closest to the British on the assumption that this facilitates rapid acculturation.

13. *Winnipeg Free Press,* December 10, 1965.

14. The one large exception appears to be the Italians.

15. *Globe and Mail,* October 4, 1965.

16. *Submissions to the Royal Commission on Bilingualism and Biculturalism by the Canadian Council of National Groups and the Association of United Ukrainian Canadians, passim.*

THE FEDERATION •

federalism, nationalism

and the scope of

public activity in canada • donald smiley

This essay attempts an interpretation of the development of the Canadian political community in terms of the relationship between the sentiments of nationalism, the governmental institutions of federalism and
the scope and nature of public activity. Answers will be sought to these
questions:

First, how did the Confederation settlement deal with nationalism,
federalism and what was then regarded as the appropriate scope of governmental activity, and how was this settlement subsequently sustained?

Second, what is the nature of the present stresses which threaten to
destroy the Canadian federation?

Third, what is the general prescription for the continuing survival of
the Canadian federal system?

In his influential book, Rupert Emerson has said, "This nation is a
community of people who feel that they belong together in the double
sense that they share deeply significant elements of a common heritage
and that they have a common destiny for the future. ... The nation
is today the largest community which, when the chips are down, effectively
commands men's loyalty, overriding the claims both of the lesser communities within it and those which cut across it or potentially enfold it
within a still greater society reaching ultimately to mankind as a whole."[1]
But these questions arise—what are the substantive activities which those
who identify themselves with such terminal communities want to carry

on together? What are the mutual claims which members of nations make upon each other? Under what circumstances have members of nations acted on the assumption that their claims to individual and collective self-fulfilment could be fulfilled through the agency of a sovereign state under their control?

Nationalism cannot reasonably be discussed apart from some consideration of the growing scope and importance of the activities performed by modern governments. An established political community, whether a sovereign state or not, involves the carrying on of a great variety of human interactions within its territorial boundaries. Many of these associational activities relate directly to the competition for or exercise of governmental power. But these political and governmental structures such as political parties, the bureaucracy, the legislature, the law-enforcement and judicial systems and so on, sustain and are sustained by a wide variety of private and quasi-public associations, an increasing number of which are themselves brought into existence by the deliberate action of the public authorities. Even organizations which have little business to do with the state often group themselves as a matter of convenience within political boundaries. A modern political community is thus a very large number of important social interactions within a particular set of territorial limits. There is a complex relation between those activities which are directly involved in wielding or in competing for political power and those which are not, and the number and importance of the latter increase as the scope of government activity expands.

Political nationalism and the politically organized nation are thus significantly different when governments involve themselves in every important aspect of human life than when public activities were more limited in scope. In the contemporary world, nationalism often manifests itself not exclusively as a diffuse sentiment of solidarity or as participation in the ritualistic aspects of national life but also as quite specific demands that nationals as such are entitled to prescribed kinds of treatment in their dealings with each other and with the public authorities; the welfare state and the national bills of rights can in this sense be regarded as the institutional embodiments of nationalist sentiments. Because of the scope and importance of the activities carried on by modern governments, it is less likely than in the past that nations can be induced to live within a political framework other than that of a community possessing the full range of powers of the sovereign state.

The contemporary range of public activities also deeply influences relations between individuals and groups belonging to different nations. For example, the vitality of nationalism in the nineteenth century did not lead to the complex of restrictions on movement across national boundaries with which we are all so familiar today. Contemporary national governments, in accepting widespread and explicit responsibilities for the social and economic welfare of their citizens, must perforce have policies of what Canadians call "selective" immigration.[2] In relations among friendly foreign nations, the traditional concerns of defence and diplomacy are supplemented and in some cases superseded in importance by new functional interactions in respect to such activities as trade and health, cultural matters, economic aid and river-basin development. Even among the most liberal nations, public support of artistic and scholarly activities creates national "immobilities" in relation to these matters and causes members of these international cultural communities to interact with each other, in part at least, as nationals of their respective countries.

Thoroughgoing political nationalism is, of course, incompatible with the maintenance of federal institutions. If, in an established federation, the "terminal community" becomes identified as the region, the federal system is in process of disintegration, although the rituals of federalism may long remain. Conversely, if the federation as such becomes the focus, the influence is toward a unitary state. In the contemporary world the latter trend persists in unicultural countries like the United States and Australia, whereas the multicultural federations, with the exception of Switzerland, find it difficult to comprehend the competing nationalisms within a federal framework. Neither kind of situation can be adequately understood without reference to the functions that are characteristically performed by the public authorities of a contemporary community and the patterns of interaction in the private sphere to which these functions give rise.

THE CONTENT OF THE CONFEDERATION STATEMENT

Among other things, the Confederation settlement, evolved between 1864 and 1867, contained the terms of the new relations between the English- and French-speaking societies. It is significant in the light of later experience that those responsible for this settlement seem not to have found it difficult to agree on a division of legislative powers between the national parliament and the provinces. In terms of the preceding analysis, the highly centralized variant of federalism embodied in the British North America Act of 1867 was believed by those responsible for it to be easily compatible with both the effective discharge of the activities which it was then believed appropriate that government should undertake and the claims of the various "nationalisms" which were influential—the desire of French Canadians to preserve their cultural particularity, the sentiments of solidarity with the British Empire and the aspirations toward Cartier's new "political nationality". The Confederation consensus appears to have included the following elements:

First, the sweeping powers given to the federal government for the expansion and economic integration of British North America were general in application and did not in any way impinge on cultural particularisms. This general point was made in the Confederation Debates by Sir E. P. Taché, George Brown, A. T. Galt and George Etienne Cartier. Cartier was most explicit:

> . . . . He did not entertain the slightest apprehension that Lower Canada's rights were in the least jeopardized by the provision that in the General Legislature the French Canadians of Lower Canada would have a smaller number of representatives than all the other origins combined. It would be seen by the Resolutions that in the questions which would be submitted to the General Parliament there could be no danger to the rights and privileges of either French Canadians, Scotchmen, Englishmen or Irishmen. Questions of commerce, of international communication, and all matters of general interest, would be discussed and determined in the General Legislature; but in the exercise of the functions of the General Government, no one could apprehend that anything could be enacted which would harm or do injustice to persons of any nationality.[3]

Second, the cultural integrity of the French-Canadian majority in Quebec could be effectively safeguarded by conferring on the provinces exclusive jurisdiction over what, according to the perspectives of the day, were a limited number of matters of direct and obvious cultural incidence —education, municipal institutions, the civil law and affairs where the Church was directly involved. In the preface to his recent book on the Confederation period, Professor W. L. Morton has pointed out how the French Canadians defined their situation:

Any author publishing today on the union of British North America must be especially aware of the role played by French Canadians in the formation of the Canadian union. The following narrative, it seems to the writer, makes it clear that the French sense of nationality was as strong in 1867 as in 1837 or in 1964. As a nationality, however, the French accepted the need for union, either with English Canada or with the United States. There was no separatism then, as in 1837 and in 1964. Religion, indeed, rather than nationality was the principal concern of all but the extreme Rouges. Religion, because of the existence of members of the Roman Catholic Church other than the French, made for unity rather than separation. The great concern of both the French as such, and of Roman Catholics as such, was with education rather than with their relative standing in respect to the English or Protestants in either political or economic matters.[4]

Third, there was the expectation that the projected federal government would operate in such a way as to safeguard the rights of the French-Canadian and other minorities. Peter Waite has argued persuasively that the federal principle, so far as the Fathers of Confederation were concerned, did not refer so much to the division of legislative powers between Parliament and the provinces as to the relations between the House of Commons and the Senate.[5] With the constitutional traditions which had developed since 1840 behind them, the Fathers did not expect the institutions of the federal government to work in such a majoritarian way as subsequently happened.

The first two of the expectations of the Fathers of Confederation as I have outlined them were, in a broad sense, fulfilled in the period between 1867 and roughly 1920; the third less so. During this period the major domestic policies of the federal government related to economic development and integration and for the most part French Canadians did not regard the wielding of these powers as a challenge to the ability of their community to preserve its distinctive culture. In a complementary fashion, the conservative policies of successive governments in Quebec had the result of allowing what were perceived to be the necessary measures to safeguard the French-Canadian culture to be undertaken, within the range of matters over which the B.N.A. Act gave the provinces jurisdiction. Although the struggle for provincial autonomy was waged by Quebec administrations from the election of the Mercier government in 1887 onward, most of the dramatic clashes between English and French Canadians in the period prior to 1920 revolved not about this issue, but concerned Canada's external policies and position of the

French-speaking minorities outside Quebec. The bicultural composition and aspirations of the major political parties contributed to keeping the number of such clashes low, but when on a given issue the country did become polarized along cultural lines, it was decisively demonstrated that the English-Canadian majority could and would get its way.

The period between the two World Wars saw a breakdown of the equilibrium which had in a broad sense been established from the Confederation settlement onward, without any clear new directions emerging in the interplay between federalism, the Canadian nationalisms and what was regarded as the appropriate scope of public activity. The major economic objectives of Confederation and the National Policy had by 1914 been achieved and the coming of peace left the country with few important objectives to be pursued through federal leadership. The decade of the 1920's thus saw provincial and regional interests more dominant than at any previous period in the history of the Dominion.[6] The Great Depression demonstrated that this new variant of Canadian federalism was quite inadequate to the demands made upon it, but in the desperate circumstances of the time the reactions of the provincial and federal governments were haphazard and confused, and few clearly-defined objectives to be undertaken through federal leadership emerged.

POST-WAR ENGLISH-CANADIAN NATIONALISM

Recent English-Canadian nationalism has been notoriously devoid of distinctive myths and symbols capable of evoking strong emotional responses. Since the British traditions have lost their power to inspire, almost all English Canadians have at some time felt embarrassed by these deficiencies in the ritualistic manifestations of nationhood. Some persons have portrayed our distinctiveness in terms of the physical environment. Others have tried to parlay their favorite historical characters into folk-heroes. Still more have designed new flags and a few have drafted new constitutional provisions. None of these well-meant efforts has come to much and, because of the absence of the characteristic manifestations of national self-expression so common elsewhere, it has been plausible to assert that the English-Canadian nation did not exist, or, if it did exist, it was something pretty unsubstantial. But this conclusion fails to explain why English Canadians have in very concrete ways continued to act as if there were such a collectivity and have been willing to pay a very considerable price in material and other terms as a consequence of this choice. During the Second World War and the decade following it English Canada became committed to an interrelated set of collective purposes which gave the nation a new sense of direction and which were embodied in a more highly centralized variant of Canadian federalism than had previously existed in peace-time.

The Second World War was for English Canada a deeply unifying national experience. As the conflict went on, federal officials and agencies devoted a very considerable amount of their energies to planning for domestic post-war reconstruction. The results of their work came in the White Paper on Reconstruction presented to Parliament by the government in April, 1945 and in the so-called "Green Book proposals" made to the provinces in August of that year. According to the formulation of national policy presented in these documents, the federal government would undertake the primary responsibilities for guaranteeing a high and stable level of employment and income. It was necessary, therefore, that the federal authorities should have exclusive access to the income tax and succession duty fields. New and far-reaching proposals were made for federal leadership in ensuring higher and more equalized standards of health and welfare services throughout Canada. Housing, urban re-development and planning, natural resource development, vocational training and other matters within provincial jurisdiction were also to be the subjects of federal policies. The federal government was to go further than ever before in ensuring that the provinces had enough revenues at their disposal to discharge their constitutional responsibilities. This, in barest outline, was the federal design for post-war Canada. Although provincial agreement could not be secured at the Conference on Reconstruction, much of what was proposed in 1945 was implemented in piecemeal fashion during the succeeding decade.

There were other dimensions to the new variant of Canadian nationalism than the social and economic ones. At what might be called the "zenith year" of this development, the federal authorities in 1949 took three constitutional decisions of great importance—to admit Newfoundland to Confederation, to make the Supreme Court of Canada the final court of appeal in all Canadian cases and to provide a procedure for amendment of the Constitution; in none of these situations were the provinces consulted. The Report of the Royal Commission on National Development in the Arts, Letters and Sciences, published in 1951, made an eloquent case for federal leadership in support of cultural activities and for federal financial support of the universities, and most of its specific recommendations were implemented in the same decade. Canadian foreign policy in the post-war period also provided for an embodiment of the new-found purposes of the Canadian people. The Canadian Bill of Rights enacted by Parliament in 1960, along with similar legislation in some of the provinces, provided concrete manifestations of the importance of liberal values in Canadian society.

Were the purposes to which the country became committed during and after the Second World War a manifestation of English-Canadian nationalism alone? Certainly no English Canadian a decade ago could have been brought to admit that these purposes embodied the aspirations of only one of the two cultural communities. A French-Canadian Prime Minister was after all in power and other French Canadians both in the federal government and outside had some measure of influence in devising and implementing these objectives. The benefits of the new policies, particularly the benefits of an economic nature, appeared to accrue to all Canadians. In successive federal elections Quebec threw its support to the political party under whose leadership these policies had been undertaken. From the perspective of 1966, however, it is reasonable to assert that the commitment of the Quebec majority to the new directions in which the country was being taken was only apparent and reflected the futility of the traditional Quebec policies of social and economic conservatism in opposing the extension of federal power. The War, whose ending had been the occasion for the new domestic objectives of the federal government, had been for the English-Canadian community a unifying experience. The impact of the conflict on French Canada was much more complex, and seventeen years after its end so perceptive an observer as André Laurendeau could assert that *"During the war, many French Canadians in Quebec felt as if they were living in an occupied country"[7] and that after the hostilities ". . . the French Canadians became more and more ardently attached to the cause of provincial autonomy. Separatism reappeared."[8] The liberal-nationalist individuals and groups who now dominate the public life of Quebec, during this period were subjected to humiliation and frustration. Their ideological

---

* This quotation and all other quotations of French speaking authors in this article have been translated from the original French.

predilections in a broad sense allied them with federal policies. And yet to many, if not most, the stubborn defence of provincial autonomy by the Duplessis government and other conservative forces in the province was a battle for the necessary precondition of French-Canadian cultural survival.

THE NATIONALISM OF THE NEW QUEBEC AND THE CHALLENGE TO CANADIAN FEDERALISM

The élites who have come to dominate Quebec in the 1960's interpret the preconditions of the welfare of French-Canadian society in quite different ways than did their predecessors, and the influence of these new groups has made it more difficult than ever before to comprehend the interests of the two Canadian societies within a common federal system. A decade ago Marcel Rioux saw the three distinguishing features of traditional French-Canadian ideology as "minoritaire, catholique et française".[9] At about the same time in his remarkable survey of French-Canadian thought and institutions, Pierre-Elliott Trudeau asserted, ". . . against an environment which was English, Protestant-democratic, mater-ialistic, commercial and later industrial, our nationalism developed a system of defence in which all the opposite tendencies were emphasized: the French language, Catholicism, authoritarianism, rural life and later the return to the soil."[10] It was inherent in this set of attitudes that government, even that dominated by French Canadians should play a limited and primarily defensive role, and Trudeau went on to say, ". . . in the political domain we had condemned ourselves to a desperate im-potence. For our political conceptions were impregnated with authori-tarian attitudes, and we continued to think of the state as an entity apart from the citizens."[11] There was nothing in this ideological system which would make French Canadians regard their cultural integrity as being challenged by aggressive federal efforts to develop and integrate the Canadian economy; so far as Quebec was concerned, the conditions of cultural survival could be met within the jealously protected sphere of provincial jurisdiction set forth in the British North America Act. In the period after the Second World War, as in the past, the government of Quebec resisted federal intrusions into this sphere, but the efforts of a corrupt and conservative provincial administration were relatively in-effective in the face of the dynamism of the federal authorities and the willingness of the federal political parties to dangle positive material benefits before the Quebec electorate.

The new Quebec speaks, of course, with many voices and there is no single spokesman for the men and influences who have given a new shape and direction to Quebec's nationalism. The most systematic elaboration of left-wing nationalist views which have been influential, if not dominant, in the Lesage government is to be found in an interview given to Jean-Marc Léger of *Le Devoir* by the Honourable Réne Lévesque in July 1963.[12] To Levesque "Our state is that of the entire nation, further, it is the prime instrument of its progress and well-being." The primary ends of government activity should be directed to the economic sphere, "The use of economic force by the State is all the more necessary for us who form in Canada a non-possessing minority . . . (the State), in the economic development and emancipation of Quebec, must be more than a mere participant, it must be a creative agent." Thus ". . . planning, accelerated growth, control of the dynamic sectors, the principal investment decisions, it is above all in Quebec with the appropriate means that all this must be undertaken." To discharge these responsibilities "The State of Quebec . . . needs all the powers, all the instruments which a federal system can bestow on it without ceasing to exist." Lévesque specifically rejected the view that an exclusive concern with education was the solution and said of this "panacea" that, "It is perhaps the most subtle form of obstinate conservatism. For the result would inevitably be the revolt of frustrated talents functioning in a vacuum, where the regime has been stripped of socio-economic power and all the principal levers of power remain beyond their reach." Similarly "biculturalisme" was of secondary importance: ". . . the radiance of the French culture in Canada, respect for the French language, are conditioned in the first place by the vigour, by the economic and political importance of Quebec. It is this which is and must remain by far our chief resource, our dominant and incessant preoccupation."

The "nationalism of growth", as Leon Dion has called it, has led to a number of very specific demands being made by the Lesage administration on the federal government and more generally on the Canadian federal system as such:

First, there is the demand that the provinces acquire a greater share of the direct tax fields. According to the general argument advanced on several occasions by Mr. Lesage, during the war and immediate post-war period the most important needs of Canadians were met by the federal government and in the circumstances of the time there was some justification for a high degree of fiscal centralization. Now the primary social priorities are matters within the jurisdiction of the provinces and a radically new pattern of fiscal sharing is necessary. The very costly nature of the reforms undertaken by the Quebec administration has caused it to be more insistent on this demand than on any other.

Second, the Lesage government has demanded that the federal authorities cease their involvement in matters within the constitutional jurisdiction of the provinces. In circumstances where the other provinces wish this involvement to continue, Quebec has been insistent that neither the provincial administration nor the Quebec people be subjected to financial penalties as a result of their choice.

Third, Quebec has demanded new institutions and procedures by which the federal authorities will consult with the provinces in respect to all matters where provincial interests are directly engaged. Pressure for this reform has been particularly insistent in relation to federal economic policies. Thus at the Federal-Provincial Conference of November 1963, the Quebec delegation presented the argument that because all these national economic policies affected the provinces in one way or another, the provinces should participate in the framing of them through "permanent Federal-Provincial organisms instituted for this purpose" and that these proposed bodies would give the provinces a "voice" in "determining tariff structures, transportation and even the monetary policies of Canada".[13] Although the Quebec government has apparently not pressed this particular demand aggressively, there has been an insistence on more formal and institutionalized procedures of federal-provincial consultation and a predilection in federal-Quebec relations for collaboration "at the summit".

Fourth, the government of Quebec has demanded the right to conclude international agreements in respect to matters within provincial legislative jurisdiction without the involvement of the federal authorities. The Quebec spokesman on this matter, the Honourable Paul Gérin-Lajoie, has argued that such agreements may appropriately be concluded only by the government that has the power to implement them and that the federal authorities cannot give effective expression to the aspirations and interests of the French-speaking culture.[14]

The Lesage government has had a remarkable record of success in pressing its demands. The implementation of contracting-out has seen the federal government withdraw its involvement, so far as Quebec is concerned, from several fields of provincial jurisdiction with compensating fiscal equivalents to that province. A regime of sharing tax sources and the proceeds of taxation much more favourable to the provinces than the previous arrangements has been effected. The federal authorities have proved willing to consult with the provinces more fully and through more institutionalized procedures than ever before in respect to a wide range of matters where the latter's interests are engaged. Ottawa has in no way impeded and has in some cases facilitated the cultural relations between Quebec cultural agencies and those of foreign nations. Despite these successes, the pressures of the Quebec government for a wider range of autonomy seem not to have abated. Prime Minister Lesage in his Labour Day address in 1965 gave notice that when his government's manpower policies were more fully developed, federal activities in this field, including those of the National Employment Service, would have to be adjusted to meet provincial requirements.[15] There have already been sharp conflicts between the federal and provincial authorities in respect to measures for the rehabilitation of chronically depressed areas and it is almost certain that these will become sharper as provincial policies for regional development in Quebec and elsewhere are more explicitly formulated. If present trends continue, it is not unlikely that at some time in the foreseeable future Quebec will wish to integrate all public income-maintenance programmes and will ask that some variant of contracting-out be applied to family allowances and Old Age Security pensions. The increasingly ambitious efforts of the province in economic planning and development may be expected to lead to renewed and more insistent demands than before for provincial participation in federal trade, transportation and monetary policies.

The interventionist directions of the government of the new Quebec and the aggressiveness and sophistication with which it has pressed its demands have created a very new kind of stress on the Canadian federal system. Clifford Geertz has said of the developing nations what is peculiarly appropriate to Quebec at the present time:

> The growth of a modern state within a traditional social context represents ... not merely the shifting or transfer of a fixed quantity of power between groups in such a manner that aggregatively the gains of certain groups or individuals match the losses of others, but rather the creation of a new and

more efficient machine for the production of power itself, and thus an increase in the general political capacity of the society. This is a much more
genuinely "revolutionary" phenomenon than a mere redistribution, however
radical, of power within a given system.[16]

The mobilization of the social resources of Quebec by its government has
been directed largely, though by no means wholly, toward a wider sphere
of autonomy for the provincial authorities. If these demands for autonomy
continue to be met as fully as they have been in the period since the
federal general election of 1963, the effective range of independent federal
discretion, at least so far as the people and affairs of Quebec are concerned, will become a very narrow one. In its other dimension, the
result of the present trends is to eliminate the "presence" of the federal
government in most matters involving the daily experience of the residents of Quebec and the relations among these citizens. In this way the
federal authorities may come to be mediated through the provincial
administration. Under such circumstances the government of Canada
becomes, in fact, as well as in the mythology of French-Canadian nationalism, a "foreign" power.

The pressures of the new Quebec for a wider range of freedom of
action in governmental affairs are paralleled by strains along cultural
lines in several important non-public organizations. In the cases of the
Junior Chambers of Commerce, the Canadian Federation of Mayors and
Municipalities and the Canadian Union of Students, the French-speaking
groups have withdrawn from country-wide organizations. Some of the
Learned Societies now have autonomous or semi-autonomous French-
speaking chapters. There is scattered evidence among such élite groups
as the journalists and the Junior Chambers of Commerce that the at-
tenuation of ties with the English-Canadian associations has been succeeded by closer identification with counterpart organizations in the
French cultural tradition outside Canada. It is reasonable to suppose
that a viable political union must under modern circumstances sustain
and be sustained by a wide variety of private and quasi-public interactions. The Canadian social and political system seems to be failing to
meet this requirement.

CANADIAN FEDERALISM: PRESCRIPTION FOR SURVIVAL

The dynamism of the new Quebec and the confused and undiscriminating responses of the rest of the country to its demands have resulted in a situation where Canadians as such are not agreed on pursuing a common set of important purposes together, either through their common federal government, or through country-wide associations in the private sphere. Some such consensus must be created in the foreseeable future if Confederation is to survive in recognizable form. Because Canadians are not united by their adherence to a national mythology and symbolism, they can perforce be united, if at all, only by their agreement to achieve significant and concrete objectives together. Such circumstances prevailed in the fulfilment of the National Policy enunciated in 1878, the mobilization of human and material resources in the two World Wars, and the pursuit of the policies of social and economic reconstruction to which the country was committed at the end of the second conflict. In all these cases Quebec was at most a quiescent partner of English Canada, a partner whose continuing preoccupation was a stubborn defence of her cultural particularity. This kind of option is not now open. Quebec is passing from a traditional society to a secular, industrial and modernized one, from a preoccupation with "survivance" to a drive for "épanouissement", from a conservative defence of historic ways and institutions through the exercise of a limited range of public powers to the aggressive and sophisticated prosecution of cultural aspirations and interests by the agency of a government determined to exercise leadership in almost every significant aspect of human life. In these new circumstances, whatever new objectives Canadians can agree to pursue together must involve the commitment of the dominant men and movements in Quebec in the most positive and fundamental way.

It would be foolhardy to try to specify in any detailed way the kinds of purposes which could inform the "new political nationality" which those who continue to believe in Confederation might strive to create. Our recent external orientations have been focused far too exclusively on our relations with the English-speaking democracies and the emergent nations formerly under British rule. Rich opportunities await us in the development of the "arts, letters and sciences" within the framework of our bicultural heritage and our evolving traditions of public support for these activities. The fact that Mr. Diefenbaker propagated the "vision" should not deter us from being receptive to the possibility that the intelligent and aggressive development of the Northland could provide a focus for the imagination of Canadians everywhere. There are undoubtedly steps that the two cultural communities can take together in their common interest in retaining a significant degree of independence from the United States in those areas of life where this is believed to be desirable and feasible.

The new conditions for the survival of Confederation require not only an agreement between the members of "the two founding races" to pursue important common purposes together, but also agreement that in respect to these matters there be a sphere of autonomous federal discretion. The directions in which the theory and practice of co-operative federalism are taking us deny this autonomy. There can of course be no return to the old "classical federalism", when each level discharged the responsibilities assigned to it by the constitution in relative isolation of the other; the present circumstances of federal-provincial interdependence clearly make ingenious and widely-used techniques of collaboration necessary. However, the present directions have seen the provinces both roll back the federal authorities from their involvement in matters of provincial jurisdiction and give the provincial administrations an influential voice in affairs which are, under the law and practice of the constitution, assigned to the federal government. Under these circumstances, the provinces become the primary expression of the aspirations and interests of the Canadian people in respect to most matters of importance. In Quebec, where these directions have gone further than elsewhere, the implicit assumptions of provincial policy deny the legitimacy of the French-Canadian members of the Parliament of Canada as representative of important French-Canadian interests.

The modifications in Canadian institutions and in Canadian behaviour which must be made, if we are to make federalism compatible not only with the creative nationalism of the new Quebec but also with the effective exercise of public powers in the face of the challenges that confront us, need to be mentioned only briefly. The acid test of English-Canadian willingness to accept the reality of equal partnership can be demonstrated only by the sharing of power with their compatriots at the crucial decision-points of Canadian society, both public and private. New institutions and procedures are needed to safeguard the French-Canadian community in federal matters of direct and obvious incidence and to better protect the French-speaking minorities outside Quebec. But it is not inconceivable that such an offer of partnership will be refused by those dominant in Quebec, who may find in the governmental and other institutions of that province an exclusive focus for their individual and collective aspirations. Eugene Forsey has better than anyone else stated a reasonable hope for the future:

> A Canadian Anglo-French partnership was the vision of Cartier and Macdonald. It is not obsolete. In the contemporary world of developing internationalism, it is even more necessary than in the nineteenth century world of triumphant nationalism. For Canadian can be not a dividing, but a uniting nationalism. I say, "can be". The Fathers wrought well, and laid our foundations deep and strong. But the building is still unfinished, and parts of it have suffered some damage through the years. It does not need a bombing squad or a wrecking crew. But it does need alterations, repairs, additions, the expansion of certain rooms; and all of us must be made to feel at home in it. We will have to work out some new terms of the Anglo-French partnership in Canada. This will call for mutual respect, mutual understanding, wisdom, justice, generosity; for patience and skill, tact and forbearance, sympathy, and imagination. The results are bound to be less than ideal. But they will be a great deal better than anything else we can hope for in this world, and they will enable us to play our part in the world, to make our contribution to its survival and progress, as we can do in no other way.[17]

NOTES

1. Rupert Emerson, *From Empire to Nation*, Cambridge, 1960, p. 95.
2. The restrictions on West Indian immigration recently imposed by the British Labour government are, of course, an example of one of the dilemmas of liberal nationalism.
3. *Parliamentary Debates on Confederation of The British North American Provinces, 1865*, p. 55.
4. W. L. Morton, *The Critical Years: The Union of British North America, 1857-1873*, Canadian Centenary Series, Toronto, 1964, p. xi.
5. Peter Waite, *The Life and Times of Confederation 1864-1867*, Toronto, 1962, Chapter VIII.
6. *The Report of the Royal Commission of Inquiry on Constitutional Problems*, presented to the Government of Quebec in 1956, tended to see the 1920's as the golden age of Canadian federalism. See Vol. I, First Part, Chapter IX.
7. Andre Laurendeau, *La Crise de la Conscription*, Montreal, 1962, p. 156.
8. Andre Laurendeau, as cited, p. 8.
9. Marcel Rioux, "Ideologie et crise de conscience du Canada français," 14 *Cite Libre* (December, 1955), pp. 9-10.
10. Pierre-Elliott Trudeau, (ed.) , *La Grève de l'amiante*, Montreal, 1956, p. 12.
11. Pierre-Elliott Trudeau, as cited, p. 22. See also Trudeau's article, "Some Obstacles to Democracy in Quebec", *Canadian Journal of Economics and Political Science* vol. XXIV (Aug. 1958) , pp. 297-311.

12. *Le Devoir*, July 5, 1963.
13. *Proceedings*, (Ottawa, 1964), p. 46.
14. *Address to Montreal Consular Corps*, April 12, 1965, Department of Education Information Service, Quebec.
15. Mimeo, pp. 1-2.
16. "The Integrative Revolution" in *Old Societies and New States*, Clifford Geertz, ed., New York, 1963, p. 121 ff.
17. "Canada: Two Nations or One?", *Canadian Journal of Economics and Political Science*, Vol. XXVIII, (Nov. 1962) p. 501.

the decline of

confederation and

the new nationalism* • alfred dubuc

Nationalism is not a homogeneous historical phenomenon and cannot
easily be subjected to a general explanatory theory. Sometimes nationalism is bound to traditional values which slow down the pace of social
change; at other times, on the contrary, it may be the motivating force of
progress. Nationalism must receive its particular explanation according
to the historical moment of its rise and the social groups which use it as a
weapon of comgat. Thus the nationalist explosion in Quebec of the
1960's is an original phenomenon which could not adequately be explained by a simple reference to preceding movements.

Yet, nationalism is but one aspect of a total political phenomenon.
Whenever there is an upsurge of nationalism it is due to the fact that the
entire social reality is undergoing profound changes. For nationalism becomes a specific weapon of combat, among others, whenever social change
in a polyethnic community affects its political structure.

That is why, in order to understand Quebec nationalism today, it is
necessary to analyze the changes which have been taking place in the
infrastructure of Quebec society and of Canadian society in general.
These changes affect the very basis of the most important political institutions and, more especially, the manner of Quebec society's integration into the Canadian community.

* Translated by Peter C. Moes, Dept. of French, Scarborough College, University of
Toronto.

The profound imbalance of Canadian political life is evident to all observers. From every direction demands are heard which shake the solidarity of established relations among the different branches of Canadian society. It may be stated that the objective conditions for a modification of the Canadian constitution already exist: they form the general context within which Quebec nationalism manifests itself.

This paper is based on the fundamental hypothesis that a constitution is more than a simple legal document to be referred to or ignored, to be modified at will or kept in oblivion if, by chance, discussion on a purely political level is preferred. On the contrary, a constitution is a political institution which mirrors an entire society; it is the outgrowth of that society at a given moment in its historical evolution. At a certain moment which normally marks a turning point in its history, a political collectivity is endowed with a constitution. This constitution contains, in a sense, the community's destiny by setting out a well-defined framework of norms to be respected—it is the product of a confrontation of different forces; it is a peace treaty.

Thus, to claim, as is often done in Canada today, that the constitution is a legal document of no importance, that the real problems are solved directly through political confrontation at federal-provincial or interprovincial conferences or by extortion pure and simple of a right or qualification of the other party without reference to the constitutional document, all this is to recognize implicitly that the constitution no longer has any foundation in the underlying social reality. Considered as a simple legal text which no longer inspires respect, a constitutional act is no longer an effective basis for the organization of government.

In this essay we shall develop this hypothesis in two stages: in the first we shall analyze the economic and socio-political foundations of the British North America Act; in the second we shall trace the profound transformations which Canadian society has undergone since the end of the nineteenth century and which are the central factors in explaining the upsurge of nationalism which Quebec is now experiencing.

I.

THE FOUNDATIONS OF THE CONSTITUTION OF 1867

Canadian Confederation can only be understood as a response to the problems confronted by the British colonies of North America in the mid-nineteenth century. These colonies had reached a very precise stage in their political and economic development and inevitably the solutions they arrived at were characteristic of the institutions and policies which such societies could envisage. The dominant social groups had a view of the world, a culture and an ideology capable of inspiring new social structures. Confederation, worked out immediately after the Union Act of 1840 which had united Upper and Lower Canada, was to seek inspiration in this Act both as a model to be imitated and as an experiment to be improved upon. In short, in the perspective of its historical context, the constitutional act of 1867 is capable of an interpretation which takes into account its economic and socio-political foundations.

ECONOMIC FOUNDATIONS

In economic terms Confederation was essentially an instrument of public finance whose object it was to make available to those responsible for effecting investment, the resources necessary for the unified economic development of the British colonies in North America. It was based on a fundamental project of economic growth: the opening up of new regions to agriculture and forestry; the development of national industry protected by tariffs from foreign competition; the development of an abundant work force through a vigorous immigration policy; and the intense cultivation of commercial relations with the British Empire.

To the extent that all those involved were convinced that these economic functions were closely related to each other and that all the geographic regions of Canada, because of their resources and special advantages, complemented each other, it was assumed that one economic sector could be nurtured for the benefit of all and that in this way all the regions of Canada could develop harmoniously along parallel lines. In short, it was to be what we would now-a-days call a project of balanced growth.

The privileged sector was to be that of the railroads. It was precisely the interest groups associated with the railroads which inspired Confederation. Alexander Tilloch Galt and George Etienne Cartier were at the same time administrators of the Grand Trunk Railway Company and members of the Canadian cabinet. In England, Watkin, president of the Grand Trunk, and Baring, banker to both the Grand Trunk and the Canadian government, became instrumental in working out with the Imperial government the political institutions capable of facilitating their investments. It was this same banker, Baring, who had financed the union of the two Canadas in 1840 as well as the great investments in the St. Lawrence waterway from 1842 to 1848. Confederation, like the Union, was also an answer to the problems of public finance confronting the British colonies of North America. The colonies' difficulties stemmed from their inability to borrow in the London bond market which had been closed to them. This had forced them to have recourse to short term loans from Canadian and English banks at interest rates of up to 8%. The solution was found by following the Act of Union of the two Canadas of 1840: by consolidating debts and populations, the ability to borrow was increased and the economy was given new life through investment in transportation.

The immediate economic advantages of this new union were numerous: it allowed each colony to come out of its isolation; it created a greater power with which to face the United States; it lightened the public debt burden of each, and increased the credit rating of the whole in the international capital market. Furthermore, Union permitted the elaboration of an economic policy of development pivoting on the financial interests of Montreal and the railway companies. The economic crisis of 1873-1879, the "great depression" as it was called, forced a more detailed elaboration of this policy, turning this time more on tariff protection with the purpose of stimulating industrialization. This was to be the famous "National Policy" of the Macdonald government which came to power in the elections of 1878.

The Confederation of 1867 granted the federal government all those powers required to stimulate economic development. The fixed capital of all the colonies was transferred to the central government together with all their debts; legislative power in all sectors responsible for development including waterways, railways, telegraph, interprovincial communications, international trade, banking, credit, money and bankruptcy were conferred upon the central government; in conjunction with the provinces, it was to have responsibility for agriculture and immigration. All important sources of fiscal revenue were surrendered to Ottawa. The provinces retained not even enough sources of revenue to meet their own needs; the federal government was to make up the difference by annual subsidies.

There can be no doubt that the first concern of the Canadian constitution was economic: to draw off a portion of the entire country's savings in order to invest it in economic development, that is, principally in the railways, because these were to carry with them all the other sectors. It was through the railways that new regions would become accessible and that agricultural and forestry products could be taken from them; export of these products to Europe and more particularly to England would increase the capacity to import desired consumer goods from the Mother Country, machinery necessary for production, large numbers of workers, and capital funds. The railways would constitute a pole of industrial development, encouraging investment in iron-smelting, metallurgy and mining and, by extension, in all the other sectors of production. Tariff protection of the market would constitute a sufficient enticement to induce contractors to invest in numerous areas of national production. And henceforth each region of Canada would be able to specialize in its productive activity; the railroads would facilitate transportation of the factors of production, semi-finished products, consumer goods and equipment by linking all the regions together *"A mari usque ad mare"*. In this way the Canadian economy would become an integrated economy. But in order to realize this great project of economic development, based on the railroads linking together all regions, the regions had to be, before all else and of necessity, united politically. *Confederation would be the political institution necessary for the pursuit of an economic project.*

Such were the economic aspects of Confederation. Now it must be realized that this project was conceived in the middle of the nineteenth century in an atmosphere of general optimism, at a time when the theory of the liberal state, of maximum laissez-faire, of free competition, of pure individualism, reigned supreme in all governments. And so one should not be surprised, as certain authors have emphasized, that there was no provision whatever for full employment and social security, nor that public education, still poorly developed, did not go beyond the primary and secondary levels and remained a municipal responsibility. Quite the contrary, what is surprising for the period, in this constitutional law, is the enormous responsibility granted the federal government in policies of economic development. Even so, it should be noted that this intervention of the state in economic life did not in any way interfere with the primacy of private enterprise. The state did levy taxes in various forms on the wealth of citizens, but much of this revenue returned to private enterprise in the form of generous subsidies. In this way the state directed investment towards certain sectors, but did not recognize its obligation to prevent economic waste and over-investment.

As to the natural resources of the country, their full extent and variety were not yet known. There was even strong scepticism in England concerning the possibility of growing wheat on the prairies. Nor was there even any question with regard to the sharing of responsibilities between federal and provincial governments in this area.

Thus, in spite of gaps which today appear large, Confederation had as its goal the creation of adequate institutions for the pursuit of a centralized policy of long-term economic development.

SOCIO-POLITICAL FOUNDATIONS

The failure of the Rebellions of 1837 in Upper and Lower Canada had removed from the political scene a social class which, through its demands and its popular origins, could have prevented the formation of a capitalist and bourgeois state. The lower middle class, consisting of small local tradesmen and professional people, inspired by the great republican and democratic principles of the American and French Revolutions, the class which defined the values and spoke for the common people, was completely crushed by the reprisals taken to put down the Rebellions of 1837.

Contrary to what has been repeated in Canadian historiography ever since Lord Durham's Report, this lower middle class was inspired by profound economic motives. If it protested with so much vigour against fraudulent transactions involving public funds, against speculation by highly placed functionaries with public lands, against the appropriation of public monies beyond Parliamentary control, against ministerial irresponsibility, and finally, in Lower Canada, against nomination to the Legislative Council based on privilege, it is because, above all, it wanted, through democratic parliamentary procedure in a responsible legislature, to achieve a rational policy of public investment in the parcelling out of lands and an efficient organization of public administration.

Immediately following the Rebellions a new constitution had united the two colonies of Upper and Lower Canada. But the Union Act of 1840 presented a number of punitive features against the French population. In his Report, Durham had recommended that a policy of assimilation, of Anglicization, be pursued with greater intensity. French as an official language was done away with until 1849 and, under the pretext of a confederative type of union, representation in the legislative assembly was based on an equal number of deputies for each province. The pretext was only valid until the time when the population of Canada East became smaller than that of Canada West; as of 1852, when the English-speaking province held the majority, proportional representation was demanded in the name of the constitutional democracy.

The new constitution also had, as has been said, all the characteristics of "a bankers' constitution" and the financial objectives were quite as much against the economic interests of the lower valley of the St. Lawrence. The small debt of Lower Canada was consolidated with the large debt of Upper Canada so as to avoid bankruptcy for the latter and the construction of the St. Lawrence waterway was undertaken with purely public funds, contrary to the interests of agriculture and commerce in Canada East. The London banker Baring played the same role on behalf of the Union as he was to play 25 years later in connection with Confederation. The canals were for the Union what the railroads would be for Confederation: the banker was the same for both ventures.

The constitution of 1841 had the additional effect of removing from the Assembly individuals "unworthy" of becoming representatives, that is to say, those whose level of wealth was not sufficiently high. Henceforth, in order to be a representative a candidate had to own property worth at least 500 pounds sterling, a condition which denied representation to elements of society which, before the Rebellion, had shown themselves to be the most radically democratic and republican. Considering also that the distribution of income was far from similar among the two ethnic groups, this social discrimination resulted in ethnic discrimination, greatly favouring the Anglo-Saxons.

Union, established on such foundations, could not fail to provoke very strong opposition, ethnic in nature, between the two provinces of Canada. Political finesse during the first decade of the new constitution would consist in an attempt to provoke the formation of interest groups which would create a diversion from the main dividing line. Governor Elgin saw that the critical factor in overcoming the ethnic cleavage was the formation of major political parties based on a coalition of interest groups from the two provinces; competition between these political parties was designed to obscure the opposition of the two provinces. It is necessary to see clearly the basis for this strategy's success, for the political parties which were designed to obscure cleavage were the ones which continued to exist throughout the next hundred years of Confederation.

Basically, this strategy could not be valid unless the French-Canadian lower middle class which had just been crushed in the rebellion, was excluded from the political scene. French-Canadian representatives in Parliament would have to find their place within a sphere of influence different from that to which they belonged before the rebellion: basically the sphere of grand imperial commerce, construction of canals and railroads, and Canadian banking. This new sphere was itself defined in ethnic terms; it was essentially Anglo-Saxon. Only by finding a place within this sphere could French Canadians henceforth hope to participate in Canadian political life.

This strategy of Lord Elgin's was politically valid so long as this new equilibrium was respected. The eventual appearance of a French-Canadian middle class, aspiring to define itself by its own ethnic values and anxious to work out a system of indigenous financial relationships, would risk calling everything into question again. The Canadian state was to be a bourgeois and capitalist state; through their lobbies the great financial institutions and the great industrial enterprises would dominate the political parties as much as the various ministries. In the British North America Act no place was reserved for the middle and working classes. Their demands were impossible: these classes had been put down in the rebellions. From this point of view, Confederation, in the form it took, was made possible through the domination of the financial and commercial upper middle class over the lower middle class.

Given this political background to the colonial debates on Confederation, it is not surprising that they failed to arouse a strenuous opposition in French Canada. Certainly, the opposition parties attempted to demonstrate to the nation that Confederation was what it really was, that is, a project of centralization, repeating for all the British North American colonies in difficult financial circumstances what had been done in the Union of the two Canadas. The reply from the party in power was to try to show the French Canadians that, thanks to Confederation, Quebec broke off its too close union with Ontario. Thus, for Quebec, according to official opinion, Confederation began by an act of separation.

Such were the foundations of Confederation. Beyond a simple legal document, the Canadian constitution was a social institution which reorganized all the aspects of the collective activities and aspirations of the country. It was worked out at a precise moment of historical development. It reflected the society of the period and it constituted the basic project which would serve as a model for all the political institutions that this society might henceforth propose for the pursuit of its development. This project was based on a social structure and on values commonly accepted by all those groups who had been granted the right to express themselves; this project was also based on a generally accepted method of allocating resources for economic growth. Finally, the Canadian constitution was a peace treaty between the dominant political groups, an equilibrium of forces of varying strength. It tried to give permanence to this equilibrium in a legal structure that might be respected as long as possible. The constitution as a political institution would last as long as this equilibrium could be maintained.

With some minor adaptations, Confederation has now lasted a hundred years. But now it may be asked whether, in the light of the political difficulties which Canada faces today, the equilibrium of forces on which the constitution was based has not been disturbed. In any case the hypothesis may be advanced—and that is what will inspire the analysis which follows—that, if the Canadian constitution has not been considered for the past twenty years as anything more than a legal document of no importance, it is because it no longer rests on its fundamental socioeconomic base, that it no longer has anything but a merely formal existence. Such an hypothesis would explain the formation of internal tensions, of strong opposing interests, of particularism and, in Quebec, of nationalism. In addition, it would enable one to understand the inability of the present structure of decision-making powers to provide original and dynamic policies of social change and of economic growth through the full employment of human and physical resources.

II

THE EQUILIBRIUM OF FORCES IN THE 20TH CENTURY

The socio-economic infrastructure which inspired Confederation has completely changed in a hundred years. The Canadian economy is not at all the same any more; Canadian society has adopted new values and its stratification is different; new political forces have been born which demand new strategies.

ECONOMIC STRUCTURE

It is sufficient to mention very briefly the new fields of economic activity which have opened up in Canada since 1867 to demonstrate the growing importance of the provinces in economic activity and the relative withdrawal of the federal government from a programme of economic development. First, the discovery of extensive mineral resources has led to a considerable expansion of the domains and territory subject to provincial jurisdictions. Second, population growth and urbanization have caused expenditures on urban development to rise rapidly. Third, in the sector of primary activities, agriculture has yielded pride of place to mining. Fourth, a technological revolution, utilizing two great sources of energy, electricity and the internal combustion engine, has ushered in vast projects of dam construction and road development. Fifth, within the tertiary sector, the sector which has undergone the greatest development in the 20th century, there has been a continuous evolution of services in the fields of education, public health and social security. Here, then, are five new sectors of economic activity which, as they developed, enabled the provinces to assume an increasingly important role in economic policy.

Just as decisive was the exhaustion or erosion of the national economic policy which had been so closely linked with Confederation in 1867. It is necessary to itemize the ineffectiveness of this policy for the hundred years during which it was in force. The project of harmonious, integrated economic growth has not been realized and the centralized policy of economic development has been revealed as ineffective in achieving the established objectives. Certainly Canada has been able to achieve, among the industrialized nations, one of the highest standards of living, but this evolution is largely the result of American investment in Canada— an eventuality that had not been foreseen, and which a discriminatory tariff policy had even attempted to avoid. It is, then, in spite of Confederation that this development took place. But even so, we must evaluate its cost, see clearly the waste of resources which it involved and raise the question of who has paid and is still paying this cost.

First, the most obvious sign of this waste is Canada's chronic inability to retain its population, to provide it with work and a livelihood. Waves of immigration have been followed by waves of emigration, the cost of training a producer and the making of a citizen often representing a waste of resources to the profit of the American economy.

Secondly, the policy of subsidizing the railway companies has resulted in over-investment in the railway network and permitted irrational allocation of resources which could have been used in the development of other sectors. Besides, on a more general level of analysis, we should note that the failure to take into account the social cost of economic development has often permitted private enterprise to claim an arbitrarily high level of capital productivity by counting only the immediate short range economic cost. While such a system permitted a generous distribution of returns to stockholders and a high evaluation of shares by forcing the state to make unplanned social investments, it encouraged entirely irrational development projects. Investment capital, that is to say, national and foreign funds for investment, were endowed with a mobility that was purely artificial. The federal government, incapable of assuming the responsibilities of development which it had accepted at the time of Confederation, left the burden of working out the projects of Canadian economic development to the administrative departments of financial institutions. The rationality of the calculations made in this milieu was not likely to insure efficacious investment for the whole of the nation.

Thirdly, financial institutions have become increasingly important in economic activity. With a higher national income and the ever-broadening quest for social security amongst the population, funds have accumulated in ever greater volume in insurance companies, investment and trust companies, annuity funds, mutual funds, and banks. These financial institutions grouped in very narrowly defined spheres of influence have become more and more responsible for the direction of investment. They have encouraged the concentration of industrial and commercial enterprises and, in moments of economic crisis, have decided which ventures should disappear in bankruptcy and which should receive support. This situation has meant that economic crises have not always had the theoretical advantage of forcing technically marginal enterprises to disappear. Whether enterprises went bankrupt in a crisis has very often depended on whether or not they were supported by a network of powerful financial institutions.

Fourthly, as the economy has grown, financial institutions have come to play a significant role in the accumulation of investment funds. Now, it was for the most part through public debt that the federal government financed great public works in times of depression and the cost of national defence during the two world wars. To finance its debt the government called more and more on the financial institutions. The latter transferred to the government private savings which they were no longer prepared to invest themselves in production. By this course, the scheme of national policy was completely reversed: it was no longer for the state alone to transfer part of the income of citizens obtained through taxation to production enterprises, but to drain off private funds accumulated by financial institutions.

Fifthly, the principle of tariff protection, on which the policy of national industrial development was based, has not brought about the hoped-for results. In the first place, primary production has retained a considerable importance in exports; the Canadian economy must continue to import large quantities of finished products. In the second place, because the protected sectors of the economy have developed haphazardly, sometimes through over-investment, at other times as a result of the failure to innovate, such enterprises have imposed the burden of low wages on the shoulders of the workers and that of high prices on the shoulders of the consumer. In the third place, because other industrial sectors developed outside those for whom the National Policy reserved a protected market, a few highly specialized producers have assumed great dimensions in order to supply the increasing demand of foreign markets. Canadian exports are no longer solely made up of food products and raw materials.

All this has created profound difficulties for the elaboration of Canada's commercial policy. Those regions that specialize in the production of export goods have always thought that they were penalized by a policy which, favouring industrialized regions, raised the prices of finished products. Then, too, for Canadian industry tariff protection is no longer as obviously imperative today as it was formerly. On the contrary, inasmuch as the structure of Canadian industry is being transformed profoundly, a free market for certain economic sectors where productivity is highest appears to be a prerequisite for growth. The ambivalence and contradictions in Canada's tariff policy can be explained by the pressures which divergent interest groups have brought to bear on the federal government and by the difficulties which the latter has encountered in following a coherent commercial policy.

Sixthly, historical evolution has contradicted the National Policy's aim of giving preferential treatment to close economic ties with England. Since the beginning of the twentieth century the Canadian economy has been orienting its commercial relations towards the United States. That is where it sends the biggest share of its exports; that is by far the most important source of its imports and foreign investment. Furthermore, it is the Americans who provide Canadians with their technology, their scientific and technical competence, their consumption patterns and way of life. In the process of development, American investment in Canada has taken the form of direct investment in subsidiaries, from which Canadian participation is largely excluded. As a result, these American subsidiaries by accumulating their profits and generating their own sources of finance have produced a certain rigidity in the Canadian financial market and have been responsible for investments whose rationality is based solely on criteria valid for American industry but which might not necessarily be valid for the Canadian economy. Also, the export policy of these firms has had the tendency of excluding competition with the parent companies in the United States.

The federal government, particularly when the Liberal Party has been in power—which has been the case for most of the last 40 years—has shown little concern about this alien source of economic decision-making and the role it might play in determining the criteria for social investment in Canada. Indeed, since the second World War several of the federal government's social investments have consisted of imposing the social overhead cost of American economic investments on Canadian citizens.

Seventhly, the cultivation of close economic relations with the United States has undermined the context of the original National Policy in yet another way. The intense development of north-south lines of trade across the border separating the two countries restored to geographic determinism its constraining influence on the east-west integration of the Canadian economy. But the consequent regionalization of the Canadian economy redounded to the advantage of certain regions to the detriment of other less favoured ones. That the process of long-term growth was not uniformly effective in time and space became apparent in the series of extremely profound economic crises. These revealed that the economic instability of the whole affected certain regions much more seriously than others and that the cost of developing the latter fell more heavily on the shoulders of the populations of the former. Capital and labour necessary for the development of the richer regions were drained from the poorer ones. This, without any doubt, has given rise to a structural problem of major proportions. The political consequences of this problem are now beginning to make themselves felt ever more acutely. Once again it becomes evident that the economic problems of Confederation are the mainspring of its political difficulties.

Finally, the federal government, following the example of all western countries, even the most ferociously capitalistic, was convinced by the growing magnitude of instability associated with the economic crises of the last three decades of the 19th century and the first decades of the 20th century that it should intervene in economic activity in order to control fluctuations in aggregate demand. The crisis of 1929 and the long depression of the thirties threatened finally to destroy the capitalist system. This threat demonstrated that private enterprise was incapable of maintaining an adequate level of investment and that the absence of a rational distribution of wealth prevented effective demand from being maintained at a balanced level with production. Social troubles and political pressures forced the federal government to intervene by exercising control over the buying power of consumers through fiscal policy, monetary policy and a policy of public investment. But this equilibrium of national income demands *ad hoc* policies and does not insure full employment. That is why short-term policies may be incompatible with the pursuit of long-term objectives of development. Since the forties the federal government has concentrated its attention, relatively effectively, on the short-term requirements of equilibrium; it has tended to neglect the responsibility of long-term economic development which Confederation recognized as properly its own. The latter responsibility now seems less urgent to it with the soaring scale of development activities under provincial auspices.

The balance sheet on the results of the National Policy is completely negative: in each of the points we have explored the federal government has failed to realize the promise of Confederation. After the analysis which has just been set forth, it is difficult to resist the conclusion that Canadian Confederation has lost its economic foundations. As a reflection of a society, the Constitution of 1867 was the product of the values and interests of 19th century capitalism. It gave preference to private enterprise; it put its faith in self-regulating market forces as the means of ensuring economic development; it failed totally to provide for the social cost of economic development and gave no voice to the working class. No wonder that the ineffectiveness of this Constitution has developed parallel to the inability of the capitalist system to provide for full employment and harmonious economic growth. But the capitalist system at least *has* evolved in the sense of increased socialization and collectivization of decisions concerning the allocation of resources. The legal document, however, has not evolved as far, even if the interpretations of it may have fluctuated. Today this document no longer serves as the principal guide to the elaboration of central economic policies. The new realities of the twentieth century simply can not be guided by its light.

NEW SOCIAL FORCES

In the middle of the twentieth century the structure of Canadian society is fundamentally different from that of 1860. The dominance of the upper middle class has been modified and new social classes have made their appearance on the political stage: the working class and the lower middle class.

Industrialization has decisively altered the composition of the upper middle class of entrepreneurs. No longer is it based essentially on the great merchants of imperial commerce. The high degree of capitalization of industrial production and its ever-increasing recourse to investment capital for the production of tools and equipment, together with the concentration of investment funds in the hands of financial institutions, conferred on the upper middle class of finance the highest social prestige, the most effective economic power and the dominant role in society.

Yet this great upper middle class of finance is no longer as "Canadian" as it could have been at the time of Confederation. To the extent that the great financial institutions are, in large part, dominated by American corporations, this upper middle class has became the instrument of these interests which seek ever more to dominate Canadian policy.

With the general rise in the standard of living, the rising level of technical knowledge and productivity of skilled and professional workers, the multiplying of activities in the tertiary sector of the economy, more particularly in that of the service trades, another social class developed: the lower middle class, the largest of all social classes. Until recently, it would have been difficult to call this section of the population a "social class". For it had neither the collective consciousness which would have allowed it to define itself by its own characteristic features, nor did it have the will to work out a line of action for the defence of its own interests, as opposed to those of other social classes in society. But this consciousness and this desire for action exist today. For the lower middle class is becoming aware of the fact that it is being exploited, not so much in terms of the level of income it receives, but through the system of taxation. Because of the relatively high level and vulnerability of its income, it is this group that pays the largest part of the income tax; because of its great size and the considerable volume of its consumption, it is this group which is most deeply affected by the sales tax and various other indirect taxes. On the other hand, its relatively high standard of living has not been sufficient to satisfy its aspirations: within industrial, commercial and financial enterprises, in the civil service, in various institutions, even in unions, the rank and file today express their demand for participation and democracy. Moreover, this new class, consisting of an ever greater number of salaried people, is discarding forms of behaviour characteristic of independent small craftsmen and professionals, and its members more and more tend to band together to assert their demands collectively: in Quebec they use trade-unions and collective bargaining.

The working class has also undergone a significant transformation. In the society of the mid-nineteenth century the working class had no voice. It had begun, no doubt, to make certain of its demands heard. But the low degree of industrialization, the refusal to confer legal status on the unions, the affirmation of the individual employment contract as the only valid one and the rejection of collective bargaining, all testify to the fact that the working class had not yet carved out for itself a recognized place in society.

In the course of heroic struggles against the established order, in strikes and street demonstrations facing the army and police of various jurisdictions, achieving collective awareness of itself and, through its unions, pressing forward its demands, it finally won a place in the Canadian society of the twentieth century. With the twin weapons of union recognition and the acceptance of collective bargaining, its two most significant victories, the working class succeeded in reducing the unfair burden of the social cost of economic development which in the past it had had to bear.

As the working class acquired a more acute awareness of the shortcomings of an economic system in which the allocation of resources was governed by the blind mechanism of free competition, it became more inclined to demand responsible policies of economic development, not only at the level of the individual enterprise, but increasingly through collective agencies. However, what had until this moment consisted of an exploitation of the worker as producer was little by little transformed into an exploitation of the wage-earner as consumer. The exigencies of the economy of affluence were imposed on Canada along with every other characteristic of the American way of life. By inducing the low income group to consume more, a way was found to exploit it by means of high interest rates for credit buying. In this way, those formerly alienated in their employment became subject to an additional level of alienation in their activities as consumers. But the effort of uniting the consumer, undertaken by the labour unions, runs the risk of breaking down the most powerful rampart of the established system, the financial institutions.

Henceforth, no long-term project of economic development can ignore provision for the social cost of development. It is in the interest of the working class that the dominant institutions of the old order be replaced by new institutions which respect both the dignity of the working class and rationality in the allocation of resources.

Thus the structure of Canadian society has been considerably modified in the twentieth century. New demands are voiced by new groups which will no longer uncritically accede to the financial burdens of economic development. There can be no doubt that these demands will increasingly emerge on the political level.

EVOLUTION OF THE POLITICAL ORDER

For some decades Canada's Constitution has been considered a legal document of little importance. The courts' decisions concerning the division of powers have come to play a less and less significant role in determining the most important disputes. All major confrontations are carried out on the political level and are settled either by the strongest party's monopolization of power, or by a federal-provincial agreement, painfully negotiated, which takes on the appearance of a temporary truce, a truce constantly to be drawn into question again. The Constitution has lost its economic and social bases; it can no longer prevent political chaos. Since the second World War, the federal government has shown itself incapable of assuring long-term economic development and full employment. Furthermore, the short-term balance of national income does not have the effect of necessarily assuring full employment and short-term economic policies are not always compatible with long-term objectives.

During this period, the regionalization of the Canadian economy continued to grow, provincial governments taking a more and more active part in the development of natural resources and the financing of education and social security. While this interior friction was going on, the international status of Canada was gradually modified, England finally granting its former colony, after successive stages, total *de facto* independence.

From 1947 on, the London parliament no longer recognized its right to modify the Constitution of Canada. In fact, one may say that the Canadian Constitution was repatriated as of that time, even if it remains an Act of the British Parliament. In 1949 the Judicial Committee of the Privy Council lost its jurisdiction over the Canadian Constitution; the Supreme Court of Canada became the highest court of appeal in constitutional matters. The federal nature of this tribunal and the nomination of its judges by the government in Ottawa has given rise to numerous doubts about the political impartiality of its decisions in constitutional matters. Recently the Prime Minister of Quebec threatened to ignore the Supreme Court's verdict if it ruled in favour of the federal government in a case concerning natural resources and territorial waters. The Constitution of Canada is no longer respected; the constitutional jurisdiction of the Supreme Court is seriously challenged.

The federal-provincial and interprovincial conferences at the political level now fulfil the function formerly carried out at the juridical level by the Constitution and the courts. These new mechanisms have the advantage of rapidly evolving Canadian Confederation. But they have a major drawback: they interfere with the prerogatives of parliament and, more generally, of democracy. These conferences, generally held behind closed doors, are between technocrats representing a social order supported by the powers that be, and they exclude certain important social and economic groups. Thus the labour unions are generally not invited to these meetings. These conferences, then, by doing away with the juridical mechanisms for the solution of the division of powers, interfere at one and the same time with the parliamentary system and with democracy. The disappearance of the economic and social foundations of the political institutions brings chaos into the relationships which this institutional structure was intended to regulate.

The recognition of unions and of collective bargaining also poses new political problems. Collective bargaining has for some years increasingly gone beyond the level of the individaul enterprise and in numerous instances has extended to the level of an entire economic sector. Confrontation on this level can have immediate effects on the entire balance of prices, production costs and income, reaching indeed to the whole national economy. At the same time, the intervention of the state in economic activity in the three-fold capacity as protector of the consumer, as producer and as planner, places it in an ambiguous position to the extent that the objectives of these three functions are not necessarily compatible with each other: it is impossible to be both judge and participant in a litigation. That is why the participation of labour unions in various political organizations does not prevent them from retaining their principal function of making economic demands even against the state.

This attitude may seem paradoxical, but it imposes a two-fold conclusion: labour unions are going to retain their role of claimant, and for this reason political institutions will have to recognize the mechanisms of collective bargaining; furthermore, the labour unions will demand increasingly closer participation in the formulation of economic policies.

The regionalization of the Canadian economy and the considerable responsibilities which the provinces have assumed explain the demands of provincial governments for explicit recognition of a new division of powers. It is here that the real reason lies for the tensions which have brought about the dislocation of the equilibrium on which the Confederation of 1867 was based.

The desire for a more rational approach to policies of economic development and full employment has undermined the old beliefs concerning the automatic adjustment of market mechanisms through the intermediary of individual decisions of economic agents acting in competition with one another. Certain political forces now demand that the principal decisions relating to the allocation of resources be decided collectively according to the popular will, democratically expressed, by equitably allocating the whole of the social costs and by evenly distributing economic wealth. These decisions and these calculations can only be formulated within a global policy of economic planning.

From this point of view, the fundamental political problem in the division of powers is that of knowing what is to be the adminstrative unit of decision-making in the planned allocation of resources: the federal government or the provincial governments. No matter which position is maintained, this problem requires that the principles and values of the Constitution should be challenged; the inability to resolve this problem prolongs the chaos which today shakes Canadian political life. It is particularly important to keep in mind that, in the elaboration of a new constitutional formula and of a policy of economic and social development, social groups which had been removed from the preliminary deliberations of the Confederation of 1867 and whose opinion in matters of political economy has not often been taken into account, must be consulted.

Confederation was much more than the enactment of a simple legal document: it established an institutional fabric deeply rooted in the economic, social and political structure of Canadian society in the middle of the nineteenth century. During the hundred years which separated that society from that of the Conquest, it was the fifth constitution which Canada had established. The Confederation settlement endured a hundred years, but in the course of that century Canadian society has been profoundly transformed. Its economic structure is now that of an industrialized country, its social classes are more clearly defined and its aspirations for democracy are increasingly heard. The Canadian Constitution is now too far removed from the basic structure and values of that society to remain the touchstone for the division of powers amongst the various jurisdictions. That is why for several decades the B.N.A. Act has been referred to less and less, and why important disputes are no longer brought before the courts. Today the most important conflicts are settled on the political level and become confrontations of power; these are the conditions of political chaos.

For some time this chaos has become more manifest: the disintegration of the national economic system has destroyed the base of the national system of political parties. Since the last two or three federal elections, the Canadian electorate has been divided into regional groups. The political equilibrium based on the strategy of eliminating regional and ethnic divisions by establishing lines of political competition between parties embracing all major social groups is now broken.

But regional division once again nurtures ethnic confrontation. The society of Quebec also is learning to define itself in accordance with new values and to create political institutions more in conformity with its aspirations: that is what nurtures its nationalism.

a programme

for binational

development •   stephen clarkson

Is it to confuse the issue of generating reform policies in Canada that the University League for Social Reform devotes a volume of studies to the problem of nationalism? At first glance this would appear to be so, for to talk of "Canadian nationalism" surely begs the first vital question, whether in fact there is *a* Canadian nation. There are clearly within the geographical bounds of the Canadian federation a multiplicity of cultural groups of varying size, homogeneity and distinctiveness. Not just the French Canadians and the rest, as Anglo-Saxon Canadians like to imagine; for "the rest" is itself a congeries of immigrant groups who have, since the arrival of the United Empire Loyalists, crossed the ocean in irregular spurts—the Irish famine emigrants, the Central European prairie colonizers, the post-war "New Canadians", to count but the most obvious. While it would be abusive to talk of Canada as a multi-national state in the same terms as we do of the Soviet Union or India, it would be equally delusive to minimize the crisis of national identity that Canada's population is experiencing. The French Canadians' most energetic elements will no longer tolerate the disparity between their cultural personality and their state identity; even many Canadians of British extraction are finding, as the flag debate showed, that the reassuring assumption of complete correspondence between their own personality and that of the state is threatened by the New Canadians' claim for a place in the democratic sun; as for these "ethnic" elements,[1] they are apparently

defying the gastronomic inevitability of the melting pot theory by retaining their subcultures distinct from their new environment.

If there is, then, neither a single Canadian nationality nor a consensus
by the component elements of Canada's population about what their
group's relationship to the federal state should be, is an inquiry into
Canadian nationalism condemned to sterility? It is if we fall into the
trap of the professional pessimists who, in lamenting the demise of the
old Canadian colony, deny the possibility of creating a new Canadian
state. But such a self-annihilating attitude is not only unacceptable, it
is obsolete. In bewailing the good old days, it does not come to grips
with our current population problem; furthermore, it is paralyzing because it underestimates the power of constructive policy-making to create
new situations.

If, on the other hand, we look at ourselves as a developing nation, not
in the sense of having to overcome a grinding poverty, but as having
certain problems in common with the ex-colonies of the "third world",
we can gain a new perspective from which to look at our own future.
Like many developing countries, we have a heterogeneous population
requiring a sense of national identity strong enough to offset the centrifugal forces of ethnic division. Like the developing nations, too, we can
harness that potent force of twentieth century politics, nationalism, to
provide the necessary stimulus for Canada's continuing existence as a
federal state.

Much of our current nationalism is piously meaningless: we are provided at school with an ambiguous anti-Americanism to counterbalance
our underlying sense of inferiority; we are cajoled at elections to vote for
the party that will preserve national unity. But this is hardly the kind
of nationalism which can support the programme of nation-building we
must achieve if we are to survive as an integral state. It is the purpose of
this paper to suggest that, by thinking of Canada not as an old, fading
country, but as a new, developing state, Canadian nationalism can acquire
a dynamic role as an instrument to inspire and sustain workable policies
that can complete the construction of a durable state.

If such a state does not yet exist, what then is the national situation in
Canada today? What type of development can realistically be envisaged
for it? It is only when we have answered these two basic questions that
we can go on to propose examples of practical policies, which, based on
the situation of today, can lead us to the state of affairs we desire for
tomorrow.

THE STATE OF THE NATIONS

Perhaps our greatest obstacle in looking at the national situation in Canada is a semantic confusion. "Nation" in English tends to mean a people identified with a state, which, once created, sails serene and stable down the stream of history. The principle of national self-determination also serves to reinforce the idea that nations are pre-existing historical and cultural entities whose destiny is fulfilled when a state apparatus is erected on their cultural boundaries. On closer examination, however, it is clear that the pure nation-state whose ethnically homogeneous population exists entirely within one political system is a concept belonging less to the realm of political reality than to that of political science fiction. The national composition of the great majority of states is highly complex. Even those model nation-states, Great Britain and France, have Celtic subcultures that are not completely assimilated into the dominant culture. Nations must also be thought of as evolving with the passage of time in the course of social and economic development. The process of modernization may act to absorb ethnic subcultures into the surrounding state. The opposite can also occur, modernization arousing the self-awareness of cultural groups that suddenly claim to be separate nationalities and press for autonomy. The problem for the social scientist and politician is to determine, in the one case, how the assimilation process can be encouraged or whether, in the second, the degree of national consciousness has reached the point beyond which the best integrating policy is to allow the constituent nationalities considerable freedom for individual development within the greater state.

The analytical and predictive techniques available to the observer are disconcertingly rudimentary. Nevertheless, the concepts of "national identity" and "political culture" do provide useful headings under which we can look at developing states to determine what stage has been reached in the process of integration or disintegration of their national subcultures and to assess what possibilities are open for their political evolution.

The most obvious place to start in looking at Canada under this light is Quebec, for it is *Québécois* who present the most homogeneous picture as a cultural and linguistic entity. Historically, they can trace their origins back to France and recount over three centuries of collective existence in New France and British North America. Culturally and socially they have been united by a distinctive language and protective church. While one million French Canadians live outside Quebec in varying degrees of cultural and legal precariousness, the other four million have the additional support of Quebec's geographical and political existence as a province in the Canadian federation. The combined effect of these factors is the existence in the Dominion of a linguistically distinct and cohesive nationality whose assimilation by the non-French population is simply out of the question.

While the French Canadians have a definite collective personality, it would be too optimistic to say that this sense of identity is without its psychological blemishes. Their historical position as a conquered, then minority group in a continent dominated by an apparently hostile English culture continues to be a major source of disturbance. The modernization process—industrialization superimposed on a traditional agrarian society, urbanization of the population, the rise of a lower middle class—has intensified the impression of outside domination by undermining the society's isolation and increasing its vulnerability to outside, mainly Anglo-Saxon pressures. Far from causing assimilation, this process has thus reinforced the French Canadians' self-consciousness, aggravating, for important sections of the population, the awareness of a discrepancy between their separate identity and their political status as one of ten provinces in a federation. Nor in terms of economic power do they feel *"maîtres chez nous"* in Quebec.[2] Whether the identity question can be resolved by practical policies within the bounds of the Canadian federation depends on the nature of the French Canadians' political culture.

This political culture, considered as the system of values, attitudes and beliefs that the public holds about its political system, appears to be dangerously uncertain. While the attitudes necessary for the functioning of parliamentary government have been genuinely absorbed by the present political leaders in Quebec, the authoritarian rule associated with Duplessis' long occupation of the Premier's office did not encourage belief in compromise and open policy-making. The success of protest demonstrations and the formation of new para-political movements with separatist programmes indicate that the formal political process is failing to express within its institutions the claims of all groups in French-speaking Canada. This discordance between the political culture and the actual political structure suggests that any solutions designed to strengthen the feeling of national identity in Quebec must be acceptable to more than just the political élite. If a "solution" is not tolerable for the major non-ruling elements, it might spark further protest movements which could upset, rather than improve, the French-Canadian political culture.

While it is common knowledge that the Quebeckers have an identity problem, it has been less evident (because less newsworthy) that the non-French-speaking Canadians have long been suffering from their own identity crisis. The dominant Anglo-Canadians, whose élites staff the professions and governments, have no difficulty identifying themselves with what they think to be Canada, the "true north, strong and free" extension of the British Empire.[3] But this sense of security is undermined by some gnawing doubts. The U.S.A.'s job attraction, New York and Hollywood's cultural domination, American sway over the communication media and the increasing American control over our "branch-plant economy" all undermine the sense of uniqueness necessary for the ruling social strata to think of themselves as leaders of a genuinely distinct nation.[4] An uncertain international identity is further weakened by internal threats. The French Canadians' challenge to Ottawa is at least geographically distinct, but the "ethnic" problem is more insidious. The accumulation of immigration from continental Europe over the past decades may not have upset the place of English as the charter language outside Quebec, but it is reducing the status of the British North Americans to that of just another immigrant group, although one of longer standing and generally higher status.[5]

The New Canadian groups are themselves beset by the problem of uneven assimilation. Some, especially those from northern Europe, have adopted the new language and values with relative ease; others still attempt to preserve their group's personality rather than assimilate into the surrounding culture. The Hutterite colonies are but an extreme example of the problem that is found in serious proportions in the large ethnic groups whose size permits the perpetuation of the native environment and so of an outsider's mentality. The Italians remaining within the familiar bounds of their Little Italies, the Ukrainians trying to maintain their own uncertain personality,[6] the Jews ever conscious of the gap separating them from the Gentiles: this is the situation that makes it urgent to consider "English" Canada in terms of its national integration.

Still another factor complicates the non-French Canadians' identity problem—their relationship with the federal government. If the élites of Ontario have little difficulty identifying with the Dominion government, the geographical distance separating Ottawa from both the Maritime and Western provinces is increased by a real psychological gap. As Ontario happens to be both the wealthiest province and the home of the capital, Ottawa is regarded with considerable hostility by Easterners and Westerners as the preserve of Toronto's business community. Thus the weaker elements of the federation feel their voice in the national government to be disproportionately small, especially if the provincial government, whether for reasons of party or policy, feels itself alienated from the national leadership.

Though not comparable to French Canada in terms of a coherent national identity, the political culture of English-speaking Canada appears more appropriate to problem-solving than is that of Quebec. Generally accepted egalitarian values promote a pragmatic attitude towards government, which is expected to initiate new policies to meet changing conditions. The remnants of a frontier and free enterprise ideology have nevertheless restricted popular expectations of governmental performance to limits that can be satisfied by the parliamentary system. The relative ease with which major social groups have gained access to power or satisfaction for their claims on governmental outputs has created trustful attitudes towards politics. The historical record, which for the French Canadians is a trail of reversals at the hands of the perfidious English is for the non-French a happier tale of increasing participation in the governing process. Even the manifest divisions separating the political parties conceal the fundamental atmosphere of trust which pervades Canadian politics, again with the exception of French-English relations. In addition, the basic spirit of inter-party toleration symbolized by the title "loyal opposition" allows the political process itself to be an integrative force.

What the English-Canadian political culture boasts in stability it lacks in content. Long established nationalities have a tradition in which folklore, architecture and literature combine to create an identifiable civilization absorbed by each new child from his family and his school. Even the developing countries are reviving (or manufacturing) an ancestral tradition which the new leadership can use as the emotive basis for nation-building. But the corollary of being a country of immigrants is to be a land with little common civilization apart from the technology of industrialization and the political process itself. The lack of a unifying tradition might be less serious if the political structure were more rigid, imposing a common behaviour pattern on the citizenry. Yet the very flexibility of the political system and our empirical attitudes to conflicts exclude the acceptance of a common ideology that could form the basis of a solid English-speaking national identity. The failure of Marxism-Leninism to strike roots in the country and the transmutation of the C.C.F. into the N.D.P. are clear proofs of the inhospitality of Canadian culture to Left ideologies; as for the Right, the insignificance of fascist movements and the "progressive" aspects of Canadian conservatism provide further proof that political ideologies offer English-speaking Canada no substitute for identity.

We have, then, as the "given" in Canada's national situation two basic groups. On the one side, the homogeneous French-speaking Canadians who, because of their minority position and rapid modernization, suffer from a relatively volatile political culture. On the other, the non-French part of the population is highly heterogeneous, lacking, for all its stable political values, the civilization or ideology capable of giving it a satisfactory sense of national identity. Finally, at the state level, the federal government is viewed in different ways by the various elements of the citizenry: with general hostility by the French-Canadian, with moderate distrust by Maritimer and Westerner, with possessiveness by the Central Canadian. Granted that Canada is so obviously not a simple nation-state, is it possible to think of the future in terms of national development?

THE BINATIONAL PROSPECT

The nature of Canada's nationality dictates the type of solutions compatible with the peaceful consolidation of a durable Canadian identity. To be peaceful, policies must be acceptable to the various elements of the population; to be durable, they must be anchored in a realistic assessment of what kind of development is possible. I would submit that this development must be *binational,* and this in two senses. "Binational" in the sense that the two basic groups in our system—the French-speaking and the English-speaking—must be encouraged to consolidate their national personalities and perfect their political cultures in terms of their linguistic identity. The French-speaking personality must achieve confidence in both its cultural security and its economic equality, not only within Quebec but in Canada as a whole. Acceptance by the English-speaking Canadians of their French-speaking compatriots' permanence as an equal national component will in itself reduce the latter's fear of persecution and increase their identification with the federation. Whereas the "traditional" French-speaking culture must be encouraged to modernize its value-system, the "modern" English-speaking culture must be given a "traditional" sense of common identity through a fusion of its many immigrant components.

Since this development of the two linguistic cultures must proceed primarily at the regional level, Canada's development must be "binational" in a second sense. On the federal level, the Canadian government can play a "binational" role that expresses the two linguistic cultures' separate personalities. A genuinely binational federal government can give to each culture the sense of statehood which reflects both its own identity and that of the other culture in such a way that each adds strength to the other. This situation exists in Switzerland, where the linguistic cultures maintain their separate French, German or Italian existence locally but form at the federal level the multinational Swiss state.

This is not a call for a revolutionary overthrow of the existing state of affairs. It is rather an attempt to recognize our nationality problem for what it is, so that policies can be generated explicitly to complete the process of national integration. The plea for a binational state is, then, both a call for realism in observing the particular dilemmas of the French- and English-speaking Canadians and a call for constructive nation-building policies on the local and federal levels. It is at this point that the relevance of nationalism becomes clear.

While nationalism has been exploited as a barbarous tool for the manipulation of mass emotion, there is no reason why the emotion of national pride should not be used to supply the impetus necessary to mould a coherent, binational state out of ethnically diverse components. As in the newly liberated ex-colonies, where nationalism serves the positive end of nation-building, so in Canada nationalism, or rather "Canadianism",[7] can supply the emotional drive necessary to sustain a series of policies designed to strengthen a Canadian binational identity. Conceived correctly and implemented wisely, these policies can create a binational political environment such that every citizen can genuinely belong to one of the two major cultures at his regional level at the same time as he feels himself to be a member of the binational federation.

STRENGTHENING THE LINGUISTIC CULTURES

If the Canadian nationality question must be viewed on the two levels of the individual political cultures and the federal state, the policies appropriate to encouraging the formation of this binational identity must also be worked out on these different planes.

The problem of policy-making to strengthen the French-Canadian political culture will not be considered here. It would be presumptuous for a *maudit Anglais* to offer proposals for what should be done in Quebec. In any case, the Quebec government is already launched on a Quiet Revolution of provincial development designed both to make the *Québécois* masters in their own house and to modernize the socio-economic system. It can be expected that the successful pursuit of these objectives will have the important by-product of increasing French-Canadian self-confidence and reducing the fear of oppression from the outside. As the French-speaking Canadians find that their own provincial system is translating their demands into policies of local development and as the rural society adopts an urban industrial value system, their political culture will, hopefully, become internally more harmonious and externally more tolerant of the federal state.

In the case of the English-speaking Canadians, one cannot talk of policies to improve their cultural cohesion in the same way that one can propose tax reforms or social welfare schemes. The process of creating a linguistic culture with an identity of its own from the diverse elements composing non-French Canada has been going on in fits and starts, partly as a result of conscious assimilation policies (English-language schools, language tests for employment or citizenship), partly as an effort of the more adaptive new arrivals to make progress in their new society. In some instances definite policies may be needed to overcome a particular barrier. The settlement of landed immigrants into their new environment through permanent programmes of language training, technical education and community activities is an area where adequately financed governmental action can make the difference between successful acclimatization and incurable alienation.

Generally speaking, however, we are dealing with a modernized society with a social welfare system, an advanced educational network, and an economy operating on modern efficiency criteria. The social machinery that can achieve the absorption of the population's different elements into the new society is thus already operating at the local level. But it will not function effectively without a desire by all the actors involved to achieve the specific aim of creating not a "mosaic" but an integrated society of English-speaking Canadians.

To use the sociologists' jargon, the basic problem in the creation of a new culture is "acculturation", the identification with and acceptance of the values of the new society. In the eyes of the original British Canadians, these values were the social and political culture of Great Britain transplanted in the new frontier of *British* North America. When immigrants arrived from lands other than the United Kingdom, there was no question that English was the language of intercourse. But will not the "ethnic" groups feel that, so long as the British Canadians require the new immigrants fully to accept the social values of the Anglo-Saxon, they are being subjected to unfair conditions of entrance? After all, those of British stock represent only 63% of the non-French population in Canada. Does order of arrival give the British group priority of place on the social and psychological ladder?

It is not my aim to make judgments that can only be the result of extensive empirical research into the various immigrant groups. I would, however, submit the hypothesis that a genuinely integrated English-speaking culture will not exist so long as the "ethnic" immigrants feel under-privileged *vis-à-vis* the British immigrant groups of longer standing. Élite recruitment, for instance, must operate with equal benefit for those of non-British as of British origins. The universities, most important of our élite-training institutions, must play the critical role in recruiting students not just from all social strata, but from all ethnic groups, especially those that do not have a tradition of high intellectual attainment. These groups will consider themselves inferior and hence alienated from the culture of their adoption if their most promising sons and daughters do not rise in status. This is not simply a question of elementary or sentimental social justice; it is also one of crucial national interest. Seen negatively, a group unable to realize its ambitions within the country's social institutions is liable to express its frustration by anti-social activity that will undermine the culture's precarious cohesion. But positively, the talk of a new English-speaking culture will be meaningless unless all the ethnic components of non-French Canada can make their contribution to our society on a footing of real equality

—first as "ethnic" Canadians, but ultimately just as Canadian citizens.

Like the university system, the various professions must also open their ranks to all our ethnic groups. If Canada accepts immigrants from India and Pakistan, these new citizens must be allowed to attempt entry into any profession they choose, including medicine. For, in the context of an immigrant society, "careers open to talent" implies not just social democracy or the most efficient use of manpower in an advanced economy but the integration of all elements of the population into a cohesive entity.

It would be authoritarian to envisage the homogenization of Canada's English-speaking citizenry into 15 million Average Canadians, each with the mellow accent of a CBC announcer and a physique corresponding to chart 4 of the 5–BX plan. Such "ethnic" institutions as the Polish National Union and the Chinese Community Centre, the Primrose Club and the Rosedale Golf Club, will no doubt continue to provide a basic sense of identity for the country's component elements. It would also be illusory to expect the inevitable decline of the ethnic groups as such. Continuous immigration serves to replenish the stock of nationality groups, while improved communications through the mass media and travel increase their sense of special identity.

Under a totalitarian system, the means to combat centrifugal forces are simple: the dispersion, not to say extermination, of nationalities considered to be incompatible with the post-revolutionary society, although even in the U.S.S.R. many national minorities have maintained their identity. For a democracy, the ethnic groupings should rather be considered socially desirable to the extent that they help the immigrant affirm his personality in his new country by providing meaningful small groups with which he can relate. On the other hand, it is essential that the channels for expression and reconciliation of interests in the political arena are not drawn along ethnic boundaries. For the same reason that élite recruitment must absorb the most energetic members of the various immigrant groups without discrimination, the specialized organizations set up to defend professional interests must be supra-ethnic so that political conflicts develop along lines of policy problems rather than in terms of ethnic interests. If a Hungarian pastry-maker can have his professional interests satisfied through the activities of the Bakers Association of Square Root, Ont., he will become more identified with the whole

English-speaking culture than if he finds himself forced to rally all the Hungarians of Square Root to defend his interests as a *Hungarian.*

Just as the expression of interests must be encouraged by occupational, non-ethnic pressure groups, so is the satisfaction of these demands for political action best handled by national parties. If our parties appeal to all regions for support and recruit candidates from all social and ethnic groups, they can play a vital role in aggregating the society's various interests and viewpoints into compromise programmes. Being non-ideological and pragmatic, aiming to embrace the interests of all significant groups, they can contribute to cultural integration by opening channels between the ethnic groups and the political arena.

The acculturation process has been going on irregularly ever since British North America became the Dominion of Canada. Effective action to facilitate and complete this process must now be based on public consciousness of the problem involved. It would be presumptuous for a political scientist to offer policy proposals in an area that is the preserve of the social psychologist and social worker. He can but urge that intensive research, such as that of Elizabeth Wangenheim, be pursued to promote greater knowledge of the particular difficulties of the various immigrant groups. The most important objective of all is to achieve a popular acceptance of a vision of the "English" Canada we wish to build —one in which all the ethnic elements can form, on the basis of social and economic equality, an English-speaking culture no longer dominated by explicitly Anglo-Saxon values.

Effective action to consolidate two relatively homogeneous and stable linguistic cultures can best be conceived at the regional, municipal and community level, for it is in his immediate environment that the new arrival experiences his acceptance or rejection by his adopted society. If, in addition, we wish to make of these two major cultures an effective state filling the present boundaries of Canada, it will be necessary to articulate a genuinely binational identity that is meaningful to both French- and English-speaking Canadians. It is here that the force of "Canadianism" must be called on to inspire nation-building policies that transcend the regionalism of the linguistic cultures.

POLICIES TO BUILD A BINATIONAL STATE

The legitimacy of a state—the degree to which it satisfies the public that it is the rightful executor of their collective will—can be thought of in three lights: (a) the extent to which the constitution provides satisfactory political institutions able to cope with the demands placed on them; (b) the extent to which national symbols express and reinforce the identity of the state; (c) the effectiveness of the state's policies in reaffirming the national identity. It is in these areas that I would like to propose examples of the policies that can be generated, under the guidance of binationalism, to strengthen the binational identity of Canada.

(a) The Constitution. In looking at the cultural identities of French- and English-speaking Canadians, we saw that the federal government is regarded with varying degrees of hostility by Quebec, the West and the Maritimes, whereas the people of Ontario tend to consider Ottawa as a political extension of the provincial government. These attitudes are symptomatic of the uneven degree of legitimacy of our federal institutions, for, if the system itself is viewed as discriminating against certain areas of the country, it will hardly be able to satisfy these regions when major policy issues are being debated. Concrete evidence of this constitutional maladjustment is the increasing resort to *ad hoc* channels of communication between Ottawa and the provincial capitals. Dominion-provincial conferences now have to be called whenever a policy issue of national importance has to be resolved.

If these dominion-provincial consultations have developed in answer to a real need for negotiation and communication between the federal and regional governments, it would appear desirable to institutionalize them through an appropriate constitutional amendment. Given that the second house is a traditional expression of federalism, one solution would be to turn the Senate into a genuinely federal institution representing the provinces in Ottawa on the pattern of the West German *Bundesrat*. The *Bundesrat* provides the *Laender* governments of the Federal Republic with direct representation and control in the national legislative process. Each *Land's* delegation is composed of ministers from the provincial cabinet, although in actual practice provincial civil servants carry out the bulk of their ministers' committee work. In areas of concurrent federal and provincial competence, the *Bundesrat* can refuse sanction to a law, call for mediation and thus gain some satisfaction. It has powers of appointment of some of the Constitutional Court judges. Most important of all, representation of the *Laender* is not proportional to population, but weighted to counterbalance the numerical weakness of the smaller and culturally most sensitive provinces that feel swamped in the lower house.

The applications of such a second house to Canada's binational federalism are appealing. It would regularize an existing but largely clandestine system of consultation. At the same time it would give the provincial governments direct access to the national legislative process, a particularly important advantage when the federal government cannot be counted on to be of the same political composition as the provincial governments. By counterbalancing the preponderance of Ontario in the House of Commons and by giving Quebec a representation greater than its numbers alone would merit, such a second house would help reduce the alienation of Quebec.[8] By having the prairie and maritime provinces vote in blocs, their own regional solidarity might be further encouraged. The very great success of the *Bundesrat* in Germany does call for a serious consideration of how its positive features can be incorporated in the constitutional revision which must soon be enacted if the federal institutions are to strengthen the cohesion of binational Canada.

(b) National Symbols. The role symbolism plays in reinforcing a state's cohesion is as evident as it is difficult to quantify. For symbols properly to express the national identity, they must be coincident within the entire state and more than a reflection of a particular element of its culture. The Liberal party showed itself aware that the red ensign was rapidly becoming more a divisive than a cohesive symbol in the country. The adoption of the maple leaf as the symbol for a national flag may have been the most effective act of national integration performed by the last Parliament. Policymakers must also examine our other national symbols with critical attention. It can be wondered whether playing "God Save the Queen" in the nation's movie temples and concert halls increases the non-British Canadians' patriotic glow; the use of "O Canada" would be more likely to do so. The domicile of the Constitution in Canada is an elementary but important step that would make the nation's symbolism correspond to her claim to sovereignty.

Besides these outright signposts of nationhood, a whole series of measures—cultural, historical, literary and artistic—can be used to reaffirm the existence of a binational state of which the citizen can be proud. The French veneration of their carefully restored historical monuments, all explained for the citizen-tourist by the Michelin guide, and their exquisite postage stamps that proclaim the wealth of their artistic tradition indicate how cultural promotion can also counterbalance social divisions within a society. It is in this light that the celebration of the B.N.A. Act's centennial is so important, less because we can boast of one hundred years of independence (a dubious historical claim) than for the impression it will give the Canadian public of belonging to a nation with roots in the past.

More active, and potentially far more effective, as symbols strengthening our sense of national identity are the institutions of mass communication. The nature of the Canadian Broadcasting Corporation, as Frank Peers indicates,[9] is inextricably linked with the role of national integration. As for our journalism, Canadian Press does little more than provide an internal wire service. For our foreign reporting we rely predominantly on the American, British and even French news services. At relatively small expense, a Crown Corporation could provide the technical organization and steady employment that would support a team of Canadian correspondents abroad, ready to provide independent reporting on international crises.

There are more active ways in which the state's symbolism can be used to identify the population with its binational state. On the level of the individual Canadian, the institution of citizenship should be used to perform the vital function of dramatizing the new citizen's commitment to his new state. The granting of citizenship need not be merely a ceremony according the right to vote to the landed immigrant of five years' standing. Obtaining citizenship should, of course, be of special significance to the recent arrival as proof of his mastery of one of the country's official languages and his acceptance of his adopted country's basic values. It should also be generalized as a solemn initiation into civil society for every young person when he becomes eligible to vote, identifying him explicitly with the binational state and formally committing him to the state's bicultural and democratic ideals.

More actively still, an extended Company of Young Canadians in which all youth are encouraged to spend one year in community service could be used as a means of citizenship training. Civil rather than military in spirit, such a service corps could be used to provide an outlet for the new generation's constructive energy, give the country's youth a chance to get to know their fellows across the land and thus provide a self-perpetuating stimulant for national cohesion.

The group that, second to the nation's politicians, is most closely related to our binational identity is the federal civil service. If the French-speaking culture is to be recognized on a basis of equality with the English, then the summit of our governmental process must reflect this bicultural reality. No argument for technical efficiency can surely outweigh the symbolic importance of a bilingual federal civil service—at least to the extent that every administrative officer at the federal level be able to understand the other national language when written and spoken. The disastrous effects of a subconscious English cultural racism have become amply evident in the last few years' *séparatisme*. Even when observed from a non-French-Canadian viewpoint, charges of élitism indicate that the federal administration tends to be more Anglo-Saxon than English-Canadian. Modelling itself on the English civil service, the civil service personnel policy has been more oriented toward recruiting the talented who have proven their capacity in graduate school than assuring that the federal service reflects the various sections of the population. Once again the criterion of efficiency has won out over the basic aim of nation-building.

There are alternatives. If one accepts the importance of the federal bureaucracy as a force creating the binational identity of the state, then recruitment must be encouraged from all of the country's ethnic groupings for men and women with an acceptable intellectual ability, but not necessarily the social or financial means to have completed graduate school. As in France, specialized training could be provided *after* recruitment. In the French National School of Administration, the future administrative élite is given both a training and an *esprit de corps*: rigorous instruction in practical public administration plus education in the power of public policy to promote national development, a faith that George Grant accuses our administrative "old boys" of lacking.[10] A Canadian Civil Service Institute would have the further very practical function of training our future professional politicians in their other national language.

It is by means such as these that Canadianism can suggest policies to reinforce Canada's binational symbolism.

(c) Government Policy. At first glance it would appear superfluous to insist on governmental output as a means of nation-building. Since the first cabinet of Sir John A. Macdonald, federal policy has of necessity been primarily directed towards national construction and conciliation.

In the 1965 election campaign, political leaders of all parties used their propaganda to stress that they would do more to build a more unified Canada than their opponents. The success of federal policy can in fact be measured in the survival of the Canadian state for the first 100 years. Without denigrating the contributions of politicians past and present, it is nevertheless possible to see how binationalism could be used as a guiding light to design or at least better exploit policies to reinforce the public's impression of belonging to a binational state.

Foreign policy is a classic means for reinforcing the sentiment of national identity. This does not imply that we need launch a policy of arctic imperialism or provoke a war of nerves with Greenland. It does, however, seem clear that the muted partner approach to diplomacy has little meaning for the general public. We are told that our diplomats play a useful part oiling the machinery of international relations by their mediations between the Americans and the British, the Americans and the Brazilians, and so on. Can we really believe that the State Department is incapable of treating directly with the interested powers? Is it even a particularly flattering view of our own international policy to consider it as some secret formula lubricating agent for American diplomacy? Whatever may be thought of the wisdom of this policy in itself, our recent diplomacy has certainly failed to convince the public that Canada plays an independent role in the world arena.

If it is agreed that the basic aim of foreign policy is to further the national interest and if Canada's most urgent interest is to create a strong sense of identity, it follows that our diplomacy should be directed towards convincing the Canadian people that its binational state exists internationally. Rather than pretending to be a major Atlantic power, bringing up the rearguard of the advanced nations, we might better identify ourselves with the developing nations and sincerely take the van in espousing solutions for their pressing problems. It is not a question of directing our diplomacy solely to prove our policy different from the Americans'. Nor is it a matter of misleading the public: it is a question of informing them. It is remarkable that the huge reporting chain, represented by our embassies' daily despatches to Ottawa, furnishes so little information to the communications media about Canada's separate role in the world. That this role can itself be binational is a point that Ottawa is tardily recognizing. The recent increase in our aid programme to the French-speaking African countries and the new cultural agreements with

France are the first steps to providing Canada a "special relationship" with the French-speaking world.

Through its economic policy the federal government must convince the public that it is possible to establish satisfactory political control over our satellite economy. As in foreign, so in economic policy we might more profitably identify ourselves with the developing nations than with the economically dominating powers. As we suffer from many of the vicious circles of the developing economies—foreign capital domination of the economy, yet need for more foreign capital to finance growth; huge deficits on current account, yet a trade structure that perpetuates this weakness—we might well take initiatives towards establishing world standards for a just return for capital invested abroad and towards stabilizing world commodity prices. Our attitude towards outside capital should not be one of irresponsible hostility; on the contrary, it should be welcomed on condition that it respect laws we have designed to promote healthy national development.

It is not only demoralizing that pessimists should bewail the death of the Canadian nation; it is profoundly to misunderstand the power of politics to control the economic structure. If the Canadian people, and more especially its politicians, wish to control their economy, directing it in the interests of the binational state, they have only to design appropriate policies and have the will to implement them. Projects such as the Canada Development Corporation, using the state's prestige to harness Canadian savings for economic development, can have a real psychological impact on public self-confidence. Genuine long-term planning would also allow the Canadian business community to participate with more assurance and less risk in the effort to expand our secondary manufacturing, thus reducing our dependence on raw material exports. The point of this paper is not to defend these economic policies on their own merits, but to argue their importance as a major instrument in continually emphasizing the Canadian sense of identity.

Seen in this light, the relevance of all social policy in reinforcing the citizen's identification with the state becomes apparent. Whether it be family allowances, hospital plans or pension schemes, the Government can very concretely identify the individual citizen with the Canadian state.

An immigration programme should have a prime place in a general scheme of nation-building policies. Assuming the agreed need to expand our population faster than the birth rate would allow, our immigration policy should be conceived and propagated as an essential element in our national policy. We should not simply be told we need to increase the work force or consumer demand by x% per annum; immigration policy, both in its recruitment abroad and in its care for the adjustment of New Canadians to their environment, should explicitly keep alive the ideal of Canada, the nation of immigrants come to build a new society. The binational implications of an avowedly nationalist immigration policy are especially clear. Efforts must be made to recruit more French-speaking immigrants and so bring new blood and moral support to Quebec. By policies in the foreign, economic, social and immigration fields, the federal government still has the chance to make the *Québécois* feel that their interests are protected and espoused.

This essay has not attempted to suggest a complete programme of policies for governmental action. I have rather argued that a frank acceptance of the bicultural nature of the country and the binational character of the federal government is essential for the next stage of our nation-building process. The illustrations were provided to justify the claim that a redefined nationalism can be a lodestar for conceiving policies to strengthen the two major cultures and the binational state.

It is always easy to trump up Orwellian charges against policy suggestions that entail increased state action. But the claim that new state policies are needed to encourage the national integration process is not authoritarian. It does not imply that minority differences can or should be obliterated, just as it does not maintain that family loyalties must be eliminated as a prerequisite for national solidarity. In a nation of immigrants social stability may even be increased if each citizen remembers what are his ancestral origins. But as social man needs societal associations, so does political man need to belong to a meaningful political structure. In multi-ethnic, bicultural Canada, this means participating in one of the two major linguistic cultures and owing allegiance to the binational state.

This has not been an "ideological" argument insisting that national salvation can only come from more or less collectivism or individualism. If attitudes towards national integration split in terms of Left and Right, national integration will be all the more difficult to achieve. Nor is this a moral argument of the type that Canada can become a better country than any other. My thesis to establish a constructive nationalism is an argument of national interest. Nationalism is not an end in itself, but a guiding idea to provide coherence and a rationale for policy-making. It is a plea to substitute for a wistful death-wish of an obsolete cultural fragment or for a negative anti-Americanism a positive view of what is possible at every level of political life—the municipal, the provincial and the federal. It is, I feel, possible to construct a national identity firmly based on two linguistic cultures so that when in 1985 *Time* magazine devotes a cover story to the new Canadian Prime Minister, it will not say, as it did for Shastri's India in 1965, that Canada "is more a notion than a nation".

NOTES

1. The Oxford dictionary would have us believe that "ethnic" means "pertaining to nations not Christian or Jewish; Gentile, heathen, pagan". All readers of the Toronto press know, however, that the Canadian connotation of this concept expresses no narrowly religious prejudice—it simply means "non-WASP".
2. See above, Michel Brunet, "French Canada's Search for a Fatherland", pp. 56-60.
3. See above, Carl Berger, "The True North Strong and Free", p. 3ff.
4. As Maurice Careless points out in his article on "Nationalism and Metropolitanism", failure to react to American "metropolitanism" implies the absorption of the Canadian regions. See below, pp. 281-283.
5. See John Porter's study of "Ethnicity and Social Class" in his *Vertical Mosaic*, Toronto, 1965, pp. 60-103.
6. See above, Elizabeth Wangenheim, "The Ukrainians: A Case Study of 'The Third Force' ", pp. 83-90.
7. See John Holmes' similar view of what must be the binational character of Canadian nationalism in the field of foreign policy in his "Nationalism in Canadian Foreign Policy", below, pp. 214-219.
8. D. Kwavnik, in "The Roots of French-Canadian Discontent" *Canadian Journal of Economics and Political Science* XXXI No. 4, (Nov. 1965) argues that to treat Quebec as the province of the French Canadians, is to lead to piecemeal separation. But, like it or not, Quebec is not "a province like any other" (p. 519). The vocal French Canadians are in Quebec and it was Lesage's provincial government that expressed their extremely dynamic nationalism. That this national fervour could lead to separation would be unrealistic to deny. But pretending to treat Quebec as if it were Prince Edward Island would be the best way to hasten its secession. While it is always possible that Canada will follow the Austro-Hungarian path, it is much more probable that the responsible leaders of Quebec will continue to feel better able to realize their destiny within the bounds of an adjusted Canadian federation.
9. See below, Frank Peers, "The Nationalist Dilemma in Canadian Broadcasting", pp. 262-265.
10. George Grant, *Lament for a Nation*, Toronto, 1965, p. 49.

POLICY •

the nationalism

of the national policy • craig brown

Debating nationalism is the great Canadian national pastime. Since
Confederation it has been the pre-eminent preoccupation of politicians,
journalists, scholars and plain ordinary citizens. All have wrestled dili-
gently with the problem that Canadian nationalism—if such there be—
does not fit any of the classic definitions of nationalism. Common language, religion and ethnic origin must obviously be rejected. Except for
the disciples of Harold Adams Innis, geography provided few satisfactory
clues to the Canadian identity. And a common historical tradition, in the
words of Mill, "the possession of a national history and consequent community of recollections, collective pride and humiliation, pleasure and
regret, connected with the same incidents in the past," raises more questions about a Canadian "nationality" than it answers. There is no great
national hero who cut down a maple tree, threw a silver dollar across the
St. Lawrence and then proceeded to lead a revolution and govern the
victorious nation wisely and judiciously. There are no great Canadian
charters of freedom or independence expressing the collective will of the
people. But the search goes on. Historians and retired Governors General laboriously attempt to define "the Canadian identity" or "being
Canadian". Many nations have manifested their nationalism through
great public acts; Canada has asserted its nationalism by looking for it.

Yet there is abundant evidence that Canadians have both thought and

155

acted like contemporary nationalists in other countries. As Mr. Berger's paper in this volume makes clear, much, though by no means all, of the evidence is provided by the politicians.[1] The evidence is mundane, for seldom have Canadian politicians been political theorists or philosophers. Rather, their concerns have been with everyday problems of government. But within this framework their thoughts and acts have been decidedly nationalist in character. A brief look at the men who implemented and carried out the National Policy may serve to illustrate the point.

Writing to a Conservative editor in 1872, Sir John A. Macdonald noted in a postscript that "the paper must go in for a National policy in Tariff matters, and while avoiding the word 'protection' must advocate a readjustment of the tariff in such a manner as incidentally to aid our manufacturing and industrial interest."[2] In this obvious afterthought at the conclusion of a letter devoted to the necessity for finding an appropriate label for Macdonald's party, is the origin of the National Policy. The context is significant. Macdonald was looking for a policy that would attract, at one and the same time, voters and dollars to his party, and the National Policy would do both. The manufacturers would contribute to the party war-chest and the simplicity of the title and concept of the National Policy would appeal to an electorate looking to fulfill the promise of Confederation. Moreover, as a transcontinental railway, immigration and opening of the Northwest were added to the tariff as items in the National Policy, it took on a strikingly familiar complexion that added to its political attractiveness. It was in most respects a duplication of a similar "national policy" designed for continental expansion in the United States. It was, as Professor Dales points out, "a materialistic policy of Bigness"[3] in an age when expansionism appealed to nationalist sentiment. Canadians could take pride in their ability to compete with their neighbours in the conquest of the continent.

The National Policy was equally attractive because a policy of tariff protection meant another step in the long path from colony to nation within the Empire. As early as 1859 Galt argued for protection less on its economic merits than on the grounds that tariff autonomy was implicit in responsible government. Referring to Imperial objections to the Cayley-Galt tariff of that year, the crux of Galt's argument was that "self-government would be utterly annihilated if the views of the Imperial Government were to be preferred to those of the people of Canada."[4] With tariff autonomy not only achieved but emphasized by protection, in 1911 the ardent nationalist John S. Ewart proudly summed up the elements of "Canadian Independence" by pointing first to the fact that "we are fiscally independent". "By that I mean that we make our own tariffs; that we frame them as we wish; that we tax British, and other goods as we please; and that neither the Colonial Office nor the British Parliament has any right whatever to interfere."[5]

That the National Policy was politically attractive is, then, evident. By 1886 the Liberal party had been driven so far into a "me too" position that Blake in essence declared his party's policy to be, to borrow a phrase, the National Policy if necessary, but not necessarily the National Policy. It is true that in 1891, with a new leader and the new policy of Unrestricted Reciprocity with the United States, the Liberals came closer to victory than they had at any time since 1874. But within two years the Liberals had again revised their policy to "freer trade" and in 1897 the Liberal Government admitted the futility of attempting to destroy Macdonald's brainchild. "I not only would not retire from the Government because they refused to eliminate the principle of protection from the tariff, but I would not remain in the Government if they did eliminate the principle of protection entirely from the tariff", wrote Clifford Sifton. He added that "the introduction of a tariff from which the principle of protection would be entirely eliminated would be fraught with results that would be most disastrous to the whole Canadian people."[6] In 1911, Sifton and 17 other "revolting" Liberals issued their manifesto against reciprocity "believing as we do that Canadian nationality is now threatened with a more serious blow than any it has heretofore met with."[7] Robert Borden simply added that "we must decide whether the spirit of Canadianism or of Continentalism shall prevail on the northern half of this continent."[8]

In short, the idea of protection embodied in the tariff became equated with the Canadian nation itself. The National Policy, by stressing that Canadians should no longer be "hewers of wood and drawers of water" for the United States, as Tilley put it, recalled and reinforced that basic impulse of survival as a separate entity on this continent that had been born of the American Revolution, made explicit in Confederation, and remained the primary objective of Canadian nationalists. Protection and the National Policy, then, took on a much larger meaning than mere tinkering with customs schedules.

The same idea was evident in the building of the Canadian Pacific

Railway and the opening of the Northwest. The Northwest was the key
to the future of both the National Policy and the nation, and an expensive and partially unproductive railway through Canadian territory was
the price Canada had to pay to "protect" it from American penetration
and absorption. It was to be the great market for Canadian industry and
the foundation of a "Canadian economy". Emphasizing that building the
railway was "a great national question", Sir Charles Tupper remarked
that "under the National Policy that Canada has adopted we must look
forward not only to building up thriving centres of industry and enterprises all over this portion of the country, but to obtaining a market for
these industries after they have been established; and I say where is there
a greater market than that magnificent granary of the North-west?"[9] He
added that upon the success of the venture "the rapid progress and prosperity of our common country depends".

The United States played an interesting role in the National Policy
that emphasized its nationalistic assumptions. Fundamental to the thinking of the framers of the policy was the idea that the United States was
much less a friendly neighbour than an aggressive competitor power
waiting for a suitable opportunity to fulfill its destiny of the complete
conquest of North America. The National Policy was intended to be the
first line of defence against American ambitions. And this, I think, is
the reason any Canadian alternative to it was unsuccessful. It was the
"national" implications of the National Policy that hindered the Liberals
in their attempt to formulate an opposition policy before 1896. They
could not accept Commercial Union because it meant the total surrender
of tariff autonomy. Unrestricted Reciprocity was adopted as a compromise
that retained autonomy. But its distinction from Commercial Union was
too subtle for much of the electorate to grasp and left the party open to
skillful exploitation by Macdonald's "loyalty" cry. More important, the
very indefiniteness of what the Liberals meant by Unrestricted Reciprocity
caused confusion and disruption in party ranks and eventually led to the
revelation that Unrestricted Reciprocity did not mean the complete free
interchange of all Canadian and American products after all. Rather,
most Liberals simply wanted a more extensive reciprocity agreement with
the United States than the Conservatives. Or, to put it another way, the
Liberals were only interested in somewhat less protection from American
competition than their opponents. W. S. Fielding's budget speech in 1897
had a very familiar ring to Canadian ears: "If our American friends wish

to make a treaty with us, we are willing to meet them and treat on fair and equitable terms. If it shall not please them to do that, we shall in one way regret the fact, but shall nevertheless go on our way rejoicing, and find other markets to build up the prosperity of Canada independent of the American people."[10]

Other problems in Canadian-American relations in the latter part of the nineteenth century were related to the nationalism of the National Policy. With the abrogation of the fishery articles of the Treaty of Washington by the United States, Canada was forced to adopt what can properly be called a "protectionist" policy for her inshore fisheries. The fisheries and the commercial privileges extended to Americans by the treaty were considered a national asset by Canadians. The object of their Government was to use that asset for the benefit of the whole of Canada, not simply the Maritime Provinces. It was for this reason that from 1871 on the fishery question was always related to reciprocity. On each occasion when Canada participated in negotiations the policy was always the same: Canada's exclusive and undoubted rights in the inshore fisheries would be bargained for the free exchange of natural products.

A different and more complex problem was presented by the Behring Sea dispute arising out of the seizure of Canadian pelagic sealers by United States revenue cruisers. The central problem was one of international law involving the doctrines of freedom of the seas and *mare clausum*. And because the Canadian vessels were of British registry, the British Government assumed a much more active negotiating role than was the case in some other disputes. But Canadian participation was far from negligible, and Sir Charles Hibbert Tupper and Sir Louis Davies made a point of protecting Canadian interests. Significantly, they argued that despite the legal technicalities, it was a Canadian industry that was threatened with destruction by the illegal acts of the United States Government and that the Mother Country had a clear duty to protect that industry.

The Alaska Boundary question also illustrated the relationship between the National Policy and Canada's relations with the United States. All of the evidence available suggests that the Canadian case was hopelessly weak and members of the Canadian Government (Laurier and Sifton) as much as admitted it both privately and in public. Why, then, was the case pressed with such vigour? Part of the answer, it seems to me, is that when the Alaska Boundary question became important for Canadians after the Yukon gold rush began, those responsible for Canadian policy, led by Clifford Sifton, regarded the question less as one of boundary definition than of commercial competition with the United States. Definition of the boundary was important because it was related to control of the growing Yukon trade. The intricate legal details of the boundary dispute were generally ignored by the Canadian Government. Writing during the meetings of the Joint High Commission in 1898, Lord Herschell complained to Lord Salisbury that "I found that the question had not been thoroughly studied or thought out by any Canadian official."[11] The urgent and ill-considered introduction of the Yukon Railway Bill of 1898 providing for a "Canadian" route to the Yukon—a route which was dependent upon trans-shipment privileges at the American customs port at Fort Wrangel and on navigation rights on the American portion of the Stikine River—illustrates the same point. The "imperative reason for immediate action" was that the Yukon trade was at stake, as the Minister of Railways and Canals explained to the House of Commons: "The importance of securing that trade and preserving it to Canada becomes a national question of the greatest interest. . . . It is ours, it is within our own borders and of right belongs to us, if, by any legitimate or proper means we can secure it for the people of our own country."[12]

Again, in the negotiations at the Joint High Commission of 1898-99 the Canadians insisted that if the boundary question went to arbitration, Pyramid Harbour should be reserved for Canada to match American insistence that Dyea and Skagway be reserved for the United States. While both sides thus rejected an unqualified and impartial arbitration, it must be admitted that Dyea and Skagway were established and settled communities under American control; Canada could make no such claim regarding Pyramid Harbour. Pyramid Harbour, as a Canadian outlet to the sea with a corresponding Canadian land corridor to the interior, had not arisen in negotiations until the meetings of the Joint High Commission and, as before, the Canadian claim was based primarily on the desire to secure control of the Yukon trade.

Ultimately, of course, Canadian indignation knew no bounds when Lord Alverstone reportedly suddenly changed his mind and awarded Pearse and Wales Islands to the United States in 1903. The settlement of 1903 was unquestionably diplomatic rather than "judicial". Theodore Roosevelt's pressure tactics before and during the meeting of the so-called "judicial tribunal" were certainly deplorable and these factors, combined with the apparent sacrifice of Canadian interests by Great Britain, have supplied grist for the mills of Canadian nationalists ever since. But too often the emphasis in Canadian historiography on this point has been misplaced by concentrating solely on the alleged British sellout. The more interesting point in all the clamour surrounding the Alaska Boundary decision is that, once again, National Policy interests were considered to be threatened by the decision. Alverstone's agreement with Lodge and Root, that Pearse and Wales Islands belonged to the United States, threatened the Laurier Government's first venture in transcontinental railway building. The projected terminus of the Grand Trunk Pacific, chartered just a few short months before, was Port Simpson on Observatory Inlet; Pearse and Wales Islands, which the Canadians believed could be armed by the United States, commanded the shipping lanes into Port Simpson. Thus, though the Yukon trade had drastically declined in value by 1903, from first serious consideration of the problem to final settlement the National Policy—an "all Canadian" trade route to the Yukon or a secure terminus for a new Pacific railway—dominated Canadian consideration of the Alaska Boundary dispute.

I have tried to suggest that the National Policy was a manifestation of Canadian national sentiment. Its basic assumptions, protection against the United States, the need for a "Canadian economy" with a strong industrial base and secure markets, and the implicit assumption of achieving greater automony within the Empire all crystallized that ill-defined, but deeply felt, sense of difference that set Canadians apart from both their neighbours to the south and the mother country. But why did this desire to proclaim a national identity take its form in economic terms?

Perhaps a part of the answer rests in the dilemma posed at the beginning of this paper. Appeals to a common language, a common cultural tradition or a common religion were simply impossible for Canadians and when they were attempted they were rightly regarded by French Canadians as a violation of their understanding of Confederation. Most Canadians, especially those who built or paid for the building of the transcontinental railways, argued that the Canadian nation would have to be built in spite of its geography and regarded their efforts as "the price of being Canadian". Appeals to national history could also be a divisive rather than a unifying factor for, as often as not, the two ethnic groups disagreed as to what, in their historical tradition, was a matter of pride or of humiliation. What was necessary, then, as Cartier put it in the Confederation debates, was to "form a political nationality". And it is not at all surprising that the political nationalism of the early decades of Confederation was expressed in terms of railways and tariffs.

It is a commonplace to equate the politics of North America in the latter part of the nineteenth century with self-seeking capitalism. But we might remind ourselves that the age of Darwinism and of industrialism was also a great age of nationalism. The nationalism of the large assertive states of the age, the United States, Germany and Great Britain, was assuredly economic in its emphasis. In the United States, in particular, nationalism was equated with the problems of industrialism and industrial expansion. In keeping with Darwinian assumptions, bigness was a virtue for a nation state, and industrialism was the key to bigness. At the very time their own nation was being born, Canadians reasoned that industrialism was the determining factor in the victory of the North in the Civil War and in the apparent reunification of the United States. Industrialism meant power: power to withstand the pressures from the south and power to expand and consolidate the Canadian nation. And a political programme that emphasized expansion and industrialism had the added advantage of ignoring the potentially divisive issues that would disrupt a "political nationality".

In sum, then, the National Policy, a policy for a "Canadian economy" and a "Big Canada", a materialistic policy for a materialistic age, was the obvious policy to give expression to Canadian national sentiment. That policy was adopted in 1878 and accepted by the Liberal party in 1896. Three years later J. I. Tarte urged Laurier to do more than simply accept the National Policy, to expand upon it with more railways, canals and harbour improvements (and presumably with higher tariffs). "Voilà", he observed, "le programme le plus national et le plus populaire que nous puissons offrir au pays".[13]

NOTES
1. See above, Carl Berger, "The True North Strong and Free", p. 3ff.
2. *Macdonald Papers*, (P.A.C.) Macdonald to T. C. Patteson, February 27, 1872.
3. See below, John Dales, "Protection, Immigration and Canadian Nationalism", pp. 167-170.
4. A. B. Keith, *Selected Speeches and Documents on British Colonial Policy, 1763-1917*, London, 1953, p. 60.

5. J. S. Ewart, *The Kingdom Papers*, Vol. 1, Ottawa, 1912, p. 3.
6. *Sifton Papers*, (P.A.C.) Sifton to James Fleming, March 13, 1897.
7. *Manifesto of Eighteen Toronto Liberals on Reciprocity*, February 20, 1911; cited, *Canadian Annual Review*, Toronto, 1911, p. 49.
8. Henry Borden (ed.) *Robert Laird Borden: His Memoirs*, Vol. 1, Toronto, 1938, p. 327.
9. *House of Commons Debates*, April 15, 1880, pp. 1424-5.
10. *House of Commons Debates*, April 22, 1897.
11. Cited in R. C. Brown, *Canada's National Policy, 1883-1900*, Princeton, 1964, p. 379.
12. *House of Commons Debates*, February 8, 1898, pp. 191-2.
13. *Laurier Papers* (P.A.C.), Tarte to Laurier, April 3, 1899.

protection, immigration and

canadian nationalism* •　　john dales

The use of the term "national policies" by Canadians to describe certain governmental policies designed to promote economic growth in Canada suggests, and is perhaps often meant to suggest, that these policies also tend to promote nationalist sentiments among the citizenry. In what follows I take a particular case—our long-standing policy of tariff protection for manufacturing—and ask whether its probable economic effects (which are themselves a matter for dispute) are likely to have promoted Canadians' pride in their country. An analysis of protection is thus my major theme, but this inquiry leads to the subject of immigration, and in a final section of this paper I offer a brief and inadequate commentary on Canadian immigration policy, another of our historic "national policies".

I have a very unsophisticated understanding of nationalism, and define it simply as the pride that the citizens of a country take in their own and their fellow citizens' achievements in all aspects of life—social, political, cultural, technological and economic. National pride, I think, can be *affected* by economic policies. But I want to stress at the outset that I do not believe that growth policies can *create* a nation. I feel obliged to

* The first two parts of this article are a slightly revised version of an earlier paper delivered to the Sixth Annual Seminar on Canadian-American Relations held at the University of Windsor in December, 1964, and published in the Proceedings of that conference. The third part is published here for the first time.

164

make this curious confession because Canadian historians, politicians and journalists almost always get carried away when they are discussing Canada's "national policies" and end up by leaving the impression that without them there would be no Canada, and therefore no nationalism to discuss. I reject this view. I am prepared to believe that the existence of Canada may be explained on the basis of geography, political decisions, military events, or historical evolution—on almost any basis, indeed, *except* economic policy. My own view is that the community we now call Canada was founded in 1608 by Champlain and has had a continuous existence distinct from other communities on this continent ever since; in this I take it that I am being conservative, since most histories of Canada start with Cabot in 1497, and some with Lief the Lucky four or five hundred years earlier. In brief, I take the *existence* of Canada and Canadian nationalism to be independent of Canada's economic policies. My procedure is to try to identify the economic effects of Canadian tariff and immigration policies, and then to ask whether these effects are such as to enhance or to detract from Canadians' pride in their social, political and cultural achievements.

THE TARIFF

I begin with protectionism and ask the straightforward question: How has Canada's tariff policy, now eighty years old, affected Canadian economic development? The answer to that question certainly lies buried somewhere in the historical record; the trick is to find it.

It seems sensible to begin our search by consulting a typical example of each of two types of intellectual guidebooks: those written by Trade Theorists, and those written by Economic Historians. Both guides, we find, give us explicit instructions about how to approach our problem and how to track down the answer to it: indeed both take us into their confidence and tell us what the answer is, so that our own quest at first seems superfluous. When we begin to compare the two books, however, we soon find that each gives a rather different version of where we should look for our answer, how we should go about finding it, and what it will look like when we do find it. Like other guide books, we reflect, these have their mystifying aspects; indeed it is hard to believe that their authors are describing the same tour, and difficult to suppress the suspicion that neither of them has actually made the trip himself.

The Trade Theorist's *Guide* is very elegantly written. We are told, first, to find a country that exchanges goods with other countries on a regular basis, but that never allows either immigrants or emigrants to cross its national boundaries, and absolutely prohibits any export or import of capital. This sounds a little strange, and no country that we know of seems quite to meet all the specifications. (The *Guide* seems to anticipate our difficulty, for it adds, not very helpfully, that if we cannot find such a country, we should imagine it.) After this initial difficulty, however, the rest is clear sailing. We are told that without a tariff the country exports goods that it can produce efficiently, that is to say at low cost, and imports goods that it could only produce inefficiently, i.e., at high cost. Let the country now impose a tariff on imports that is sufficiently high to induce some of the labour and capital within the country to give up making things they can produce efficiently and start making things they can produce only inefficiently, namely commodities that used to be imported. The natural result of this system is that the country will experience a decline in its economic well-being. Its National Income will fall, and National Income per head, since the number of heads remains unchanged, will also fall in the same proportion. So there we have our answer! Apparently that old rascal Sir John A. Macdonald reduced both our National Income and our Standard of Living. The astonishing thing is that he somehow managed, at the same time, to win our undying gratitude for what he proudly called his National Policy.

As we lay down the Trade Theorist's *Guide* we are bothered by this last thought. Was Macdonald really the master confidence man that the *Guide* implies him to have been? Can millions of Canadians have been so wrong, for so many years, about their beloved National Policy? After all what country doesn't follow a protectionist policy? Doubts creep in, and indeed on making enquiries of seasoned travellers we find that no one takes the T.T. *Guide* seriously as a practical handbook. Curiously, however, it commands almost universal respect, even reverence. This reverence seems to derive partly from the *Guide's* antiquity—it dates from the eighteenth century—and partly from the fact that no one has ever been able to find any error in it. "It is completely useless, but it is also completely right", say the experienced travellers, "and for that reason ought to be preserved; every young traveller should read it". "Curious reasoning", we reflect, as we turn to the Economic Historian's *Guide*, universally recommended as the most useful book for intending tourists.

"Curious reasoning", we murmur, as we read in the E.H. *Guide* that Canada's National Policy provides dividends for owners of C.P.R. common stock, and protects Canada's territorial integrity—by which the author seems to mean something akin to Canada's virginity. We cannot undertake to unravel these tangled skeins—we are in search of economic effects, not territorial integrity—and we are about to discard the E.H. *Guide* as irrelevant to our purpose when our roving eye picks up the occasional sentence that seems to relate to the argument of the T.T. *Guide*. Indeed the Economic Historians seem to agree with the Trade Theorists that protection has lowered the Standard of Living in Canada, though they seldom stress the point; characteristically, when the reduction in the per capita income *is* mentioned it is identified as "the price of being a Canadian", a phrase which shows that the author is at least aware that virginity involves foregone earnings. We read further and notice with interest that on another point the E.H. *Guide* disagrees violently with the T.T. *Guide*: Macdonald's National Policy, the Historians say, far from reducing Canada's National Income, has greatly increased it. Even though they do not bother to support their view by logical argument, they obviously believe that our glorious (if inefficient) secondary manufacturing industry has been a net addition to, rather than a subtraction from, our other simple-minded activities of hewing logs and hauling water.

This disagreement is indeed very interesting. True, the Economic Historian's case has not been argued; but that doesn't mean it isn't arguable. And then there *was* that mystifying preliminary instruction in the T.T. *Guide* about either finding a very special sort of country or else imagining it. There is room for thought here. Perhaps Macdonald was right after all, and the T.T. *Guide* wrong, which would explain why it is reputed to be completely useless. Or perhaps Macdonald was partly right, and the T.T. *Guide* partly right, and therefore not so useless as the wordly-wise believe.

I have tried elsewhere to provide a reasoned resolution of the main disagreement suggested by the metaphor of the two *Guides*.[1] Let me summarize my position in three points. First, the odd character of the country that the Trade Theorist talks about, results from his assumption that labour and capital are internationally immobile. This assumption, which implies that a protectionist policy can have no effect on a country's supplies of productive factors, is highly unrealistic in the Canadian case, and is probably unrealistic for all countries; it is responsible for the Trade Theorist's conclusion that a tariff reduces *both* a country's National Income *and* its National Income per capita. I think that it is this assumption, and its related conclusion, which more than anything else has discredited trade theory in the eyes of policy-makers. The main purpose of the Canadian tariff, and perhaps most other tariffs, was to increase the number of jobs in the country in order to prevent emigration and promote immigration of both labour and capital. Policy-makers might have paid some attention to a theory that *proved* this result to be impossible, but they quite understandably ignored one that merely *assumed* it to be impossible.

Second, when the extreme assumption of zero factor mobility is replaced by assumptions that are realistic in the Canadian case (and probably in most other cases) the trade model yields the conclusion that a protectionist policy does increase a country's population and its supply of capital, and *does* increase its National Income; in this respect, then, economic analysis that employs a model appropriate to the Canadian case confirms the Economic Historian's view that protected industry in Canada is an addition to, rather than a substraction from, unprotected production.

Third, the conclusion of the authorized trade model that a tariff reduces a country's National Income per capita is also a conclusion of my unauthorized model. A country is bound to reduce the average output of a man-year of work if it insists on producing inefficiently within its national borders what could be procured more cheaply abroad; the strength of a wine is reduced whether you keep its volume constant and substitute water for alcohol, or whether you simply increase its volume by adding water.

My answer to the question of what the National Policy has meant for Canada is therefore that it has *increased* our National Income and *reduced* our Standard of Living. In asking you to accept these conclusions, at least for the purposes of the present discussion, I doubt very much that I am asking you to accept anything that you don't already believe. You know that the prices of manufactured goods in Canada are considerably higher than the prices of the same, or better goods in the United States, and that this burden on your pocket-book could be removed if the Canadian tariff were removed. Moreover, I doubt that anyone here believes that if the tariff were removed all the supplies of labour and capital at present employed in protected industries in Canada would be able to find employment, at incomes they were prepared to accept, in other sectors of the Canadian economy. Yet that is what trade theory asks you to believe. I think that removal of the Canadian tariff would be followed by emigration from Canada (or less immigration to Canada) of both labour and capital— though I doubt that the emigration would be on a large scale. I suspect that you share these views, both as to the direction and the magnitude of the effects of tariff removal.

In my opinion, therefore, the choice between protectionism and free trade is a choice between a larger National Income with a lower Standard of Living on the one hand, and a lower National Income with a higher Standard of Living on the other. I confront you with this choice. It is a hard choice, both in the sense that it has to be made, and in the sense that reasonable men may differ about how it should be made. Our protectionist policy, and most of our other national policies, from Northern Visions to automobile parts, have opted for size at the expense of quality —for a larger National Income at the expense of a higher Standard of Living. In the remainder of this Section, I want to present the case for the other view, the argument that a high Standard of Living is to be preferred to a big National Income.

I opt for a high Standard of Living because I am an economist, and I would not be an economist if I didn't accept the ethical implications of economics. Let me therefore meet head on the oft-repeated charge that the Economic Ethic is a materialistic ethic. Materialism, it seems to me, is more a desire for bigness in total magnitude than in average magnitude —more the pursuit of a Big National Income than of a High Standard of Living. Let me remind you that no proposition in economic science relates to the maximizing of total size. When an economist speaks of "maximizing total profits" or "maximizing total utility", he is using a convenient contraction for the full phrase, "maximizing total profits (utility) that can be derived from a *given quantity of resources*". The goal of the economic game is more clearly described as the maximization of profit (utility) *per unit of resources available*. The point is that economics has nothing whatever to say about maximizing total income by means of increasing "the resources available". (A study of economics is irrelevant for such institutions as churches, political parties and some trade unions, which seek to maximize a total magnitude, i.e. their membership.) The Economic Ethic is an ethic of proportion, not an ethic of size; it lauds the household, or the community, that makes the best use of its talents, not the household, or the community, that owns, or amasses, the most talents. I therefore fling the "Materialist" charge back into the teeth of the self-styled Canadian Nationalists. They, not I, want a Big Canada.

I get no satisfaction whatever from the knowledge that automatic transmissions for automobiles are now produced in Canada. I see our protectionist policy as a materialistic policy of Bigness, and I reject it as such *because* I am an economist.

And now to nationalism. I suggest that at least three effects of our National Policy—two of them economic and the other political—have been seriously detrimental to our national life. First, as we have seen, protectionism in all its forms reduces a nation's National Income per capita, i.e., the Standard of Living of its citizens. Artificially reduced incomes will be unacceptable to people who have high productive capabilities, and who are therefore likely to emigrate; those whose capabilities match the rewards available will have no complaint. In brief, by opting for a *larger* Canadian economy, supporters of the protectionist policy, the professional Nationalists, are opting for a reduction in the *quality* of Canadian economic life. It is hardly astonishing that most observers find Canadians, after almost three generations of protectionism, to be economically less aggressive than Americans.

Second, low incomes lead to low savings per capita and low domestic capital formation per capita. Since protectionism reduces domestic capital formation per capita, we can easily see why the proportion of foreign capital to total capital in Canada is unusually high—a situation which Nationalists publicly deplore in the strongest terms at every opportunity, but which is nevertheless of their own making. More important in my view is the likelihood that low domestic capital formation will show up most obviously in a low per capita level of *social capital*—by which I mean such things as museums, libraries, parks, universities, and public buildings that are show pieces rather than large economy-size boxes. I suggest that if Canadian incomes are some thirty per cent below American levels, the level of social capital per capita in Canada is a good deal more than thirty per cent below American standards. I further suggest that this discrepancy is not unrelated to Canadian protectionism, and is indeed one of the saddest manifestations of that sacrifice of quality for quantity that the National Policy involves.

Finally, there is the political cost of the tariff. It is confidently maintained by all and sundry in Canada, that the tariff has benefited Ontario and Quebec, and hurt all other parts of the country. This contention seems to me to be the utmost economic nonsense—the tariff raises the price of an automobile in Ontario as much as it raises the price of an automobile in Moncton, and if it raises the "National Income" of Ontario relative to that in Saskatchewan this fact is of no interest to me either as an economist or as a resident of Ontario—but the fact that it is economic nonsense, does not mean that it is not political dynamite. It might seem that the tariff, if it raises the population of Ontario and Quebec, would at least give those provinces a political advantage by increasing their representation in Parliament. But it also gives the other provinces a wonderful argument, on grounds of equity, for special compensation. The result is an appalling collection of crutches designed to compensate the alleged losers: freight rate acts; floor prices; transport subventions; gold-mining subsidies; equalization payments; and so on and on. Federal politics in Canada often seems to be a confused game of regional blackmail in which the victims believe they should bribe others to participate in a game in which they, as well as everyone else, are losers. It is no consolation to reflect that the bribe probably hurts the receiver at least as much as it hurts the giver; part of the public license to be inefficient given by the tariff to manufacuring industry in Ontario is used to allow the continuation of an inefficient coal mining industry in Nova Scotia, and Nova Scotia seems to consider this distortion of its production pattern to be partial compensation for the tariff-created distortion of its consumption pattern. The economist must be humble in the face of political complexities. But it does seem that political deals, consummated in the name of equity, add insult to the original injury inflicted by the tariff. At the very least, the arranging of deals designed to equalize the regional burden of the tariff greatly complicates the political process which, especially in a federal state, is complicated enough to begin with. The National Policy, bequeathed to us by Macdonald, ought to be dismantled, if only in the interest of reducing political frictions and simplifying Canadian politics.

IMMIGRATION POLICY

The Canadian tariff, I have argued, has tended to increase Canada's population by promoting net immigration. By lowering the Canadian standard of living, it is true, the tariff has undoubtedly led to emigration from Canada, especially to the emigration of native Canadians who are both skilled and economically aggressive, and therefore highly mobile. This loss, however, has been offset by the immigration to Canada of skilled

and professional Europeans who could not, because of American immigration quotas, emigrate to the United States, and who therefore took
the "second best" alternative of emigrating to Canada. In addition, the
extra jobs created in Canada by the tariff have attracted both skilled and
unskilled workers to the country, so that on balance protectionism has
fostered net immigration.

But of course the tendency of the tariff to increase immigration will
only be effective if Canadian immigration *policy* permits the increase to
occur, and if a supply of immigrants is continuously available. During
most of this century these conditions have been fulfilled. Canada has
persistently sought as large an immigration as possible, subject only to
the condition that the rate of inflow will not create or aggravate domestic
unemployment problems. Policy, therefore, has consisted largely of controlling the *timing* of the inflow—and also of ensuring that the immigrants
come from the "right" countries.[2] Until recently, moreover, the supply
of immigrants available to Canada has normally been in excess of the
numbers that Canada has been willing to admit. Canada has therefore
not lacked for immigrants, despite the fact that Canadian incomes have
been substantially lower than American incomes. During the past forty
years the main explanation for this situation is probably to be found in
American immigration policy, which has prevented large numbers of
Europeans from entering the United States, and thereby deflected them
to Canada.

How has our policy of "all the immigration the labour market can
absorb" affected our economy? "It expands the market and promotes
growth", says the businessman, and since immigrants both eat and work
the case may be granted; immigration certainly increases the National
Income. "It tends to keep down wages", says the union man (to which
the businessman might well reply, *sotto voce,* "so much the better, if
it does"), but this contention cannot be either accepted or rejected out
of hand; because immigration affects *both* the supply *and* demand sides
of the labour market, its effect on National Income per capita remains
in doubt.

So long as a country is expanding geographically and new resources
are being opened up, so that more new job opportunities are being created
than can be filled by the growth of the domestic labour force, immigration cannot be a threat to existing living standards; the alternative to
immigration would simply be unutilized resources. In Canada the end

of this period of "extensive growth" must be dated not later than 1930. Once the "frontier" is closed, economic progress depends primarily on technological advance, and "extensive growth" is replaced by "intensive growth", that is to say, by improved utilization of both natural resources and human resources. Under the conditions of *intensive* growth, an excess demand for labour results not from *more* job opportunities but from *better* job opportunities; in the absence of immigration the excess demand will be extinguished by "upgrading" the existing labour force and increasing incomes to pay for the additional skills. But a policy of "all the immigration the market can absorb" may seriously distort this process and even short-circuit it altogether. Skills may be imported, in which case the domestic labour force will not be upgraded, or upgraded more slowly than it otherwise would have been. Even if the "upgrading" process is not adversely affected by immigration, the competition of skilled immigrants for the better job opportunities that intensive growth creates will tend to keep the domestic *price* of skill low—and thus, incidentally, foster the emigration of those skilled people who are allowed into other countries where a higher remuneration is paid for skill.

I conclude, therefore, that the union man's view is correct. Within a context of intensive growth, economic advance depends primarily on technological improvement, and technological improvement, in order to be translated into economic growth, demands a complementary improvement of the labour force. Large scale immigration tends to be an alternative to the upgrading of the domestic labour force, and also tends to reduce the domestic remuneration for skill, whether domestically produced or imported; on both counts immigration therefore tends to reduce (or rather to slow down the rate of increase in) the standard of living of the domestic labour force.

It turns out, then, that both the businessman and the union man are correct. Immigration does increase National Income, but it also reduces National Income per capita. The conclusion is identical to that reached in the earlier discussion of the tariff. Both our protectionist policy and our immigration policy are "Big Canada" policies; they increase the "quantity" of our economic life (the size of the National Income) at the expense of its "quality" (the level of the National Income per person).

Though I have stated these conclusions dogmatically, I do not hold them dogmatically. I am all too aware of how little we know about the actual effects of our "national policies", despite all that has been written about their intended effects; until social scientists in Canada stop venerating our national policies and begin to analyze them, *any* conclusion about their actual effects must be viewed as tentative and unproved. It is particularly astonishing that so little effort has been made to study the effects of Canada's immigration policy; because immigration policy is the one major area in which Canadian economic policy has differed dramatically from American economic policy, one would have thought that a study of its effects might be expected to throw light on some of the distinctive features and problems of the Canadian economy. Let us hope that our lethargy in this field of research will be dispelled by Professor John Porter's recent volume, *The Vertical Mosaic,* for in this study Porter makes immigration policy a central feature of his analysis of Canadian society. My earlier remarks have drawn heavily on Porter's work, especially on his argument that heavy immigration has retarded the upgrading of our domestic labour force. More generally, Porter suggests that by relying on immigration to provide an important part of our skilled and professional manpower requirements we have tended to let our educational system fall into disrepair; the alarm engendered by this thesis has not been allayed by subsequent publications of the Economic Council of Canada which present statistical evidence of serious shortcomings in our educational performance.

It may be, too, that recent changes in the setting in which our immigration policy has operated during the past half century will force us to pay more attention to the subject in the future. Rapid economic progress in Europe has greatly reduced the incentive for Europeans to move to North America, and in the past few years Canada has experienced great difficulty in attracting skilled labour from Europe. Moreover, the recent revision of American immigration policy, which will become fully effective in 1968, has replaced the old nativity quotas with a list of priorities based on kinship and skill. One result of the new legislation is likely to be a modest increase in total immigration to the United States; another is that skilled and professional people will find it easier than in the past to be admitted to the United States, so that Canada will in the future face stronger competition from the United States for this class of immigrant.[3] In brief, the days when the Department of Immigration could always count on a large supply of European labour anxious to emigrate to Canada are already past, and will probably never return. Faced with the disappearance of the historic basis of our immigration policy, we probably have only two alternatives.

One is to continue our present policy of "as much immigration as we can manage" by switching our source of supply from Europe to the Orient. *The Globe and Mail* has been a strong proponent of this policy: "The bulk of immigration has so far come from Europe, but, with improved living conditions there, this source is showing signs of drying up. Canada, therefore, needs to look elsewhere for immigrants, and the obvious place to look is the Orient."[4] The Ontario Government actively considered the same policy late in 1964 when it offered to create an air-lift for skilled workers from Hong Kong if Ontario companies would guarantee them jobs.[5] Union leaders objected to the scheme, which seems to have been directed primarily to the provision of skilled workers for some parts of the textile industry, and urged instead that in-plant training programmes (for which government grants are available) should be instituted in order to upgrade the existing labour force. The Government airlift did not materialize; and it is doubtful whether any in-plant training (which is still rare in Ontario) resulted directly from the unions' plea. Nevertheless the incident throws into sharp relief the conflict between immigration and investment in education that John Porter has identified as a major feature of Canadian society.

The other alternative, then, is to give up our Big Canada immigration policy, and instead to give first priority to the improvement of our existing labour force. Under this policy, our Immigration Rule would be almost the reverse of the present Rule. No immigration into an occupation would be allowed unless it was proved to the satisfaction of the Minister of Immigration that wages in that occupation were rising considerably more rapidly than wages generally—for example, that wages in the occupation in question had risen 10% or 15% more than wages in all occupations during the previous calendar year. By making such a relative increase in wages a pre-condition for immigration into that occupation we would provide an incentive to upgrade the existing labour force, and prevent immigration from removing that incentive. (In protected industries, incidentally, the requirement that wages rise *relatively* more than general wages *before* immigration would erode the degree of protection afforded protected manufacturers by the tariff, and would therefore reduce the expansion of protected—that is to say, inefficient industry. This is exactly what we want to happen; by reducing the expansion of inefficient industry we increase the productivity of industry generally!)

One result of this policy would be a sharp reduction in immigration. It will be objected that such a policy is illiberal, and that the present policy is liberal and humane because it allows immigrants to Canada to raise their standard of living. But if, as has been argued, the present policy *prevents an increase* in the standard of living of the existing labour force, how can one balance this effect against an *increase* in the standard of living of the immigrants? Since resident and immigrant must count the same, there is no solution to this problem—unless one argues that the immigrant starts from a lower standard of living than the resident and should therefore weigh more heavily than the resident in the scales of justice. This latter argument contends that Canadians, being rich, should share their wealth with those foreigners who emigrate to Canada, but not with those foreigners who stay at home. But there are many "share the wealth" schemes, of which immigration is only one. Another possibility is for present Canadians to maximize their income per capita, and then to tax themselves for foreign aid so as to leave themselves with a standard of living after taxes that is as low as they please. The tax revenues, given as foreign aid, could benefit *all* foreigners—both those who would have emigrated to Canada under the present immigration policy and those who would have stayed at home. In brief, it is not at all clear that the longstanding American policy of severely restricted immigration plus massive foreign aid is necessarily any less "liberal" than the present Canadian policy of massive immigration plus severely restricted foreign aid.

Thus our examination of both tariff and immigration policy, the two major prongs of Canada's historic "national policy" has revealed that in each case Canadians have opted for Bigness, at the expense of the quality of national life. Indeed, it is the crux of the matter that the latter alternative has hardly been considered. Today Big Canada policies remain the quintessence of appeals made by the most vocal Canadian nationalists. It is surely time that this view be questioned by those whose national pride derives from the quality of the national performance, rather than from the mere size of the cast.

NOTES

1. J. H. Dales, "The Cost of Protectionism with High International Mobility of Factors" *The Canadian Journal of Economics and Political Science*, XXX November, 1964 pp. 512-525.

2. Canadian policy has probably been as discriminatory in terms of national origins and colour of skin as the American policy based explicity on nativity. I avoid discussion of the ethics of immigration policy since the topic is irrelevant to the present argument.

3. Canadians who were born abroad and could not in the past be admitted to the United States may now find that they can be admitted. Native-born Canadians who emigrate to the United States are now to be counted in an annual quota of 120,000 immigrants from independent countries of the Western Hemisphere. More important, perhaps, the new law required "that no Western Hemisphere immigrant could be admitted unless the Secretary of Labor determined that he would not replace a worker in the United States and that his employment would not adversely affect the wages and working conditions of individuals in the United States who were similarly employed." *Congressional Quarterly* (Oct. 8, 1965) p. 2037.

4. Editorial page, July 29, 1963. Similar editorials appeared in the issues of May 9, September 25, and November 16, 1963; and March 9, June 26, and September 15, 1964.

5. See *The Globe and Mail*, November 26, 1964, p. 12.

foreign ownership:

villain or scapegoat?* •   ian macdonald

Foreign ownership is neither unique to Canada nor peculiar to our time. Colonial countries have always been torn by contemplating the mixed blessings of foreign capital, while countries such as Australia, and even Britain in post-World War II days, have displayed anxiety about the threat of foreign take-overs for economic self-determination. Concern over possible foreign domination of Canadian economic life is rooted, however, in the very foundations of our nationhood on the North American continent.

Perhaps the potential threat to Canada appears more subtle and pervasive because it emanates from a nation which most Canadians would regard as their closest friend—a nation with which we share a common language, close neighbourhood, and constant communication of an instant culture apparently well-suited to our tastes. We can never ignore the real possibility that Canadian nationhood may be stifled in spite of our neighbour's good intentions. There are some who are disturbed by the very fact of such a high degree of American ownership and control; their objections are founded on various grounds, real and imaginary, concerned with the effects that this control might have on freedom of economic manoeuvre in Canada. Others see an even deeper danger: that Canada may lose all vestige of political independence and sovereignty.

* When this paper was written and presented, the author was still a member of the Department of Political Economy, University of Toronto.

THE SOURCES OF CONCERN

The stress imposed on the workings of Canadian politics by continuing massive injections of foreign capital, principally of American origin, differs both in its origins and in its manifestation from our anxiety about defence policy or cultural influence. In the case of national defence, the principal determinants of our national predicament are the character of North American geography and the economics of modern weaponry; as a consequence, national defence, to the extent that it exists at all, is necessarily part of a continental system. In the realm of culture, the fact that two nations, one large and one small, but with roughly similar standards of living, are thrust together on one continent, naturally produces an over-spill from the larger to the smaller.

Turning to foreign investment, however, we find two significant differences: first, Canadians themselves, pursuing a higher rate of growth for their own country, have catered to American business instincts and facilitated American ownership; and second, it is well within our power to change the degree of foreign investment. At the same time, there is one very good reason why even the most anxious have hesitated before attempting to change the foreign investment position. We have not succeeded in discovering how to have our cake and eat it too, along with the added guarantee that the supply of cake will be adequate to satisfy our expanding appetite.

It is not difficult to understand why policy-makers feel an instinctive and even an emotional concern about this situation. They know that many Canadians are sensitive to American influence and fear domination of their whole way of life. Since the extent of American capital investment in Canada can be measured and demonstrated by statistics, they are tempted to attack our general psychological concern and its political consequences through devices of economic policy aimed at foreign investment. In that process, there has been a total failure to relate the objections to foreign investment to the real economic effects, with resulting confusion between imagined or unimportant economic problems and what, as I shall argue, is a justifiable quest for a national economic identity.

In the absence of any thorough investigation into the consequences, we might well be cautious about designing policy to change the flow of foreign investment. In the past, economic literature has concentrated far greater attention on the influence of foreign investment on the lending country, while, in comparison, analyses of the effects on the borrowing country have been rather sparse. Recently the literature dealing with economic development in underdeveloped countries has begun to take account of the broad impact of foreign borrowing, but unfortunately there has been little consideration of the influence of foreign investment on more mature economies. Even the recent flood of popular literature is scarcely sufficient to contradict the opinion of Jacob Viner:

> Whether the scale and the manner of American business operations in Canada create for Canada a genuine and substantial *economic* problem, and if so what remedial action it is expedient for Canada to take, should receive serious consideration only after extensive and objective research. Since such research has not yet taken place, it seems that the answers to these questions widely circulated in Canada are at least premature.[1]

In Canada, discussion of foreign investment in particular, and of the Canadian-American relationship in general, usually proceeds from a number of accepted axioms: that Canadian sovereignty must be indivisible, that Canadian independence must be inviolable, that the achievement of a national identity is essential, that distinctively Canadian policies are eminently preferable and that Canada's economic interests must not be sacrificed. The analysis of external influences such as non-resident ownership and control is usually based on a ready acceptance of these propositions. Unfortunately, Canadian public opinion often treats these principles, if not as synonymous, at least as symptomatic of the same underlying condition, while policy-makers have too often sought to attain one of them in the name of the other.

I am not suggesting that these are unworthy objectives, but I am pointing to the confusion which arises when they are all lumped together. For it is clear that these objectives are not necessarily mutually dependent: a nation can be sovereign without being independent, it can formulate distinctive policies without producing a national identity, it can have a national identity without being sovereign and it can do all of these things (or not do them) without necessarily damaging the nation's economic interests. It is of primary importance to examine each of these causes of concern with a view to seeing which of them—economic interests, national sovereignty, independence, distinctive policies and national economic identity—have a bearing on the foreign investment issue. Only in this way can we determine what, if anything, foreign investment offends against and, more important, what policies, if any, should be adopted.

THE COSTS AND BENEFITS OF FOREIGN INVESTMENT

The first avenue of investigation leads directly to the problem of how to assess the cost, and benefits of foreign investment. To what extent is foreign investment, compared with domestic investment, responsible for economic growth? How do the carrying charges in the form of interest and dividend payments compare with the economic gains from growth and employment? How do we determine the extent of external economies, and the indirect effects on commercial policy or monetary policy?

At once we must recognize that we have no conclusive evidence about the costs and benefits of foreign investment in the Canadian economy. Perhaps there is no more complex piece of economic research; for example, the work that has been attempted in Australia, New Zealand, and for Argentina, is far from conclusive. We do not have to look far to ascertain why it is impossible to devise more than a rough estimate of the benefits. We need only ask, for example, "To what extent is domestic capital invested in roads or railways responsible for the development of the Canadian system of merchandise distribution compared with trucks or rolling stock manufactured in American-owned factories?"

In 1957, Professor Frank A. Knox of Queen's University warned that: "To estimate the balance of gains and costs to the Canadian economy of the large, non-resident control of our business enterprises is as yet impossible. The evidence is scanty and the most important results may lie in the future."[2] Similarly, H. W. Arndt has been driven to equally restrictive conclusions in the case of Australia, which provides the closest parallel to recent Canadian experience:

> . . . (do) its benefits outweigh its costs? I shall admit at once that I do not know the answer. Indeed, the thesis I want to argue is that a clear-cut answer is virtually impossible. Besides the direct benefits and costs of overseas direct investment in Australia which can be compared relatively easily, there are indirect benefits and costs which may be very important but are almost incapable of quantitative assessment. The trouble is that, while the benefits, even the indirect ones, accrue currently and are widely felt and appreciated, the costs are largely deferred and some of the indirect costs may not even be

suspected. It is in bringing the less obvious costs and benefits to light and broadly assessing their probable weight that theoretical analysis can be of use.[3]

Unlike Arndt, I believe that even "the direct benefits and costs" cannot "be compared relatively easily." Moreover, in the case of long-term direct investment, the benefits do not always accrue currently; indeed, the time-lag before the full benefits are felt may even extend beyond the period when the costs are being borne.

It is possible to analyse the macro-economic costs in terms of the out-flow of interest and dividend payments compared with the inflow of new capital. Professors Knapp, Rosenberg and others have examined the economic history of New Zealand and Argentina to compare capital out-flow and inflow. But even here, that technique is more difficult to apply to Canada where we have such a heavy concentration of direct investment with a tendency for about 50 per cent of the profits to be reinvested and for capital not to be redeemed or called in for repayment.

There are, however, two calculations designed to provide some comfort for Canadians. In the first place, the burden of foreign indebtedness has been declining compared with the aggregate level of Canadian production. In 1926 and 1939, Canada's net foreign indebtedness was approximately equal to the Gross National Product, whereas in 1962 it amounted to only 62 per cent. In the second place, the proportion of the Gross National Product devoted to servicing the foreign debt has been gradually reduced, notwithstanding our heavy borrowing and the burden of interest and dividend payments. In the period 1926-1930, the net cost of servicing the foreign capital invested here was about 4.4 per cent of the Gross National Product compared with 1.4 per cent in 1962.

The suggestion, then, is that we have put our borrowing to good use by increasing our capacity to produce as well as our economic wealth. And even if the benefits cannot be precisely measured, they are real. The story was reported recently of a highly successful Canadian computing firm that was unable to find risk capital in Canada; it is now 70 per cent owned in the United States. Would it really have been better for Canada if that firm had failed (better dead than American)?

Whatever the origins of capital, such firms provide employment and income for Canadians in the same way as any other business. C. D. Howe is reported to have remarked that he never examined the nationality of a dollar bill. Although this may have betrayed an absence of reasonable prudence, his policy was perfectly sound as far as economic growth, employment and income-creation in Canada are concerned. Moreover, as Professor Harry Johnson has argued, Canada receives the additional benefits of taxes paid into the Canadian exchequer: ". . . private investment contributes to economic welfare in two ways: it yields an income to the investor (a private benefit) and a tax revenue to government (a social benefit). If investors invest at home, the country gets both benefits; if they invest abroad, the host country rather than the investing country collects the social benefit."[4]

Sir Donald MacDougall's study of the Australian experience is highly relevant to Canada. He concludes that:

> The most important direct gains to Australia from more rather than less private investment from abroad seem likely to come through higher tax revenue from foreign profits (at least, if the higher investment is not induced by lower tax rates), through economies of scale, and through external economies generally, especially where Australian-owned firms acquire 'know-how' or are forced by foreign competition to adopt more efficient methods.[5]

The implication of the last remark is that foreign capital is far from homogeneous but carries with it research benefits and entrepreneurial skill of direct economic value.

ARE FOREIGN-OWNED FIRMS GOOD CANADIANS?

In the second area of investigation, the behavioural aspects, the issues strike closely at the heart of Canadian sensitivity and produce deeply-rooted psychological reactions. Canadians are conscious not only of the dynamic economic power of foreign capital but also of its social and political consequences. They react strongly to demonstrations of alien indifference or excess. Many of the fears are undoubtedly based on imaginary dangers and cannot be substantiated. In fact, a number of observers believe that there are no problems in this area at all; much of the evidence that has been collected demonstrates that American firms are performing very well by Canadian standards.

Many American-owned firms have performed better in the reinvestment of profits than have their Canadian counterparts. This is certainly one of the principal reasons for the rapid growth of American firms, compared with their Canadian competitors. In the period 1946-1961, $5,626 million of a total $8,980 million of American capital, or 63 per cent, was provided by capital inflow, whereas $3,354 million, or 37 per cent, was provided from the reinvestment of profits. Yet, the very growth and success of foreign firms has only added to our anxiety.

One of the most common assumptions about the behaviour of American-owned firms is a belief that the parent companies interfere with the export freedom of their subsidiaries, with the Canadian economy being the loser. This is a good area in which to demonstrate some of the mythology which has arisen through failure to ascertain the proper facts, for this assumption is not supported by recently published research. In his valuable study, *Industrial Structure in Canada's International Competitive Position,* Dr. H. E. English has reported that in the three large areas of manufacturing which he investigated—the chemical industries, the machinery and equipment industries, and the consumer durables industries —foreign firms had been willing to export when tariff circumstances enabled and encouraged such exports.

In a different type of analysis, Professor A. E. Safarian concluded that the degree of foreign ownership bears little relation to the size of exports by foreign-controlled manufacturing enterprises, and that "problems which inhibit Canadian exports are generally common" to both foreign-owned and Canadian-owned firms.[6] It could even be argued that the growth of exports of Canadian manufactured goods (which has recently become an important item) is largely the result of foreign investment, for it is the foreign-owned industries which have grown so rapidly in the Canadian economy. In many cases, export markets in the United States and overseas have been opened up as a result of the affiliation of Canadian firms with larger international concerns. Since the international corporation is placed in such an advantageous position, Canada should be in a strong position to broaden her exports of manufactured goods.

However, since many Canadians still do not share the sentiments of C. D. Howe and remain distrustful of the behaviour and some of the policies of foreign-owned companies, surely the remedy is not to rid ourselves of these companies but rather it is to urge Americans and American-owned firms to be more sensitive to matters of behaviour in areas which trouble Canadian public opinion. As a rule, what is really required is for American-owned firms to behave as Canadian institutions, with Canadian responsibilities, and to adapt to the Canadian cultural environment, as so many already do. In some instances, compulsion may be required, although the carrot is generally to be preferred to the stick.

In one particular, Canada could go much further by attempting to secure American governmental co-operation for rescinding the application of the American Trading with the Enemy Act to Canadian affiliates of American corporations. This Act prevents some companies from acting as "good Canadian corporate citizens" in export markets and generates fear that American companies in Canada will be used to implement American foreign policy. We might well strive for a change in American law to allow such affiliates to export under the same conditions as Canadian-owned companies, bearing in mind that any such solution must avoid the possibility that American business could thereby use foreign facilities for the deliberate purpose of evading American law.

SOVEREIGNTY AND INDEPENDENCE

The third area of investigation—the prospect that American ownership will lead to control over Canadian business and industry and ultimately to loss of political independence—has been the underlying emotional target of economic policy even though the shots have often been directed at the behavioural considerations. The important considerations are two: whether the control works against our economic interest and whether it gives rise to a serious diminution of political sovereignty.

On the first point, such research as has been done provides no evidence that control or ownership has had adverse effects on the Canadian economy. On the other hand, it does suggest that we require a much fuller answer to the question: what *is* in Canada's interest? Professor Johnson has argued forcefully that:

> What the opponents of foreign take-overs seem completely unable to appreciate are the facts, first, that take-overs are one of the ways by which productive efficiency is improved and wealth and income increased in a market economy, and second, that while preventing or impeding take-overs by foreigners may or may not damage the economic interests of the foreigners in question, it is practically certain to damage both the Canadian owners of real assets or equities and the Canadian economy as a whole.[7]

Of course, economic efficiency and the relative productivity of foreign-owned firms are not the only economic consequences. The degree of concentration of foreign capital in certain areas may give the foreign owners a degree of influence over the economy far beyond their relative size. Concentration of foreign ownership in the manufacturing sector could lead to the exercise of considerable influence over commercial policy through pressure for tariffs and protection or on other governmental policies such as those affecting the location of industry. In a more subtle way it may influence the future course of capital investment of both foreign and domestic origin. Finally, there is the question of whether a "foreign-dominated economy" is really more or less influenced by economic factors that originate in other countries. It has been commonly argued that Canada is highly vulnerable to economic events in the United States. Will such vulnerability be aggravated by a high degree of American ownership? To the extent that these forces can be analysed, once again there is no evidence of serious harm to the Canadian economy.

Sovereignty means final governmental control (shared in this country between the federal and provincial governments) over the territories of the nation, along with complete freedom to alter the nation's laws and policies. In the political sphere, interference with national sovereignty and the institutions of government would present serious and fundamental difficulties, even if such behaviour were consistent with Canadian economic interests. The economic portion of sovereignty applies to the fundamental decision-making processes in areas and activities affecting the economic life of the nation, and such economic sovereignty is ultimately controlled by the laws of the land. As long as non-residents are behaving as good corporate citizens, there is no danger; if they are not, our political sovereignty still leaves us entirely free to control them. American capital has not come into this country as part of an imperialist plot, and Parliament remains sovereign as the appropriate guardian of the public interest should foreign-owned firms behave in a manner that threatens Canadian independence or sovereignty. Indeed, who assumes the greater risk in the process of foreign investment? The fact is that the host country has the power to expropriate at any moment, as countries such as Mexico have done. It is usually the investor and not the borrower who needs fear the threat of arbitrary authority.

To those who are also concerned about independence, the basic answer is surely that no longer does any nation in the modern world enjoy an absolute sense of independence. The very assumption of international responsibilities and participation in international economic affairs must circumscribe the independence of any nation. The experience of the United States provides perhaps the best proof of that proposition: leadership of the free world has greatly reduced the independence of the United States, but it has not stripped the nation of its sovereignty nor denied it a national identity.

No more can any nation presume to follow distinctively national policies, nor need anything short of distinctively national policies prevent it from being a sovereign nation with a national identity. The very course of economic policy in the modern world runs in a counter direction. In Canada, federal-provincial economic relations require greater co-ordination and consistency in policy formulation. The O.E.C.D. is based on the premise that close co-ordination of economic policies in the Atlantic community can only reduce some of the economic strains of the post-war world.

NATIONAL ECONOMIC IDENTITY

National economic identity, although a term much misunderstood, is the key to what Canadians should really be concerned about. Unfortunately, the quest for national identity has too often masqueraded in slogans about sovereignty and independence. But that is not the issue. The real concern should be that foreign investment has made it difficult for us to construct an economy appropriate to our needs and our own best interest. The problem may have two aspects: the first of these is an economic distortion of the industrial structure resulting from the monopolistic character of direct foreign investment; the second is the derivative nature of the actual industries which are established in the branch-plant sector of the economy. It is the latter of these effects which I shall discuss here; Stephen Hymer will analyse the former in the next paper.[8]

In this final area of investigation, we discover a consequence of foreign investment in Canada that is more subtle and elusive than the more commonly discussed grievances and fears, a consequence that goes to the very heart of the Canadian industrial problem. A number of economic problems which have arisen from the shape and structure of Canadian economic development may be attributed to what I would call the "derivative economy", or what Dr. English has described as the "miniature replica effect". The result of foreign investment in Canada has been a tendency to establish not only a greater number of producers in Canadian industries than the market would economically allow, but also firms and industries which are duplicates of the American parent, although producing on a far less efficient scale. External financial resources, so readily available to Canadian branch plants, have provided a deterrent to the competitive rationalization which economical production would demand and which we would have required in a more open economy.

Therefore, although foreign investment in itself may not have imposed special handicaps on the Canadian economy, there are two related features arising from the parent-subsidiary form of investment in Canada which have influenced the basic character of Canadian economic development. First, the existence of American firms as the principal component of Canadian secondary manufacturing has resulted in products similar to those of the parent firms and this, in turn, has retarded the development of a specialized, indigenous Canadian industrial structure. Secondly, and more important, the development of such industry behind the protective tariff has discouraged a dynamic application of the law of comparative advantage, whereby we might have achieved specialized, low-cost manufacturing. Paradoxically, we have not only failed to develop products in which we have a comparative advantage (and which might have a distinctive Canadian flavour), but we have also not attained the independence from foreign influence for which we have yearned. The victim has been the national economic identity that might otherwise have developed.

In the search for the real villain, the process becomes complicated by a realization that these characteristics of Canadian heavy industry are only indirectly the result of foreign investment which, itself, has come into Canada in the form of direct investment largely as a consequence of our tariff policy. While normal entrepreneurial profit-seeking would be sufficient to promote a high level of American investment in Canada, the protective tariff has been primarily responsible for causing much of that investment to take the form of entrepreneurial investment of the subsidiary-firm type rather than investment in distinctive Canadian activities. The consequences of this type of investment must be assessed not so much in terms of its quantitative effects as in terms of the branch-plant pattern of economic life which it has produced. And if we find that this industrial pattern in some respects, such as managerial activity, technological research, marketing technique and product design, has unattractive features, we should acknowledge that these are self-inflicted wounds. As Professor Johnson has put it: "Insofar as there is a problem, it is largely one that Canada has created for itself by its policy of protection of manufacturing: the tariff creates a profit incentive to foreign firms to establish branch plants and subsidiaries in Canada in order to produce in Canada inside the tariff wall instead of exporting to Canada over the tariff wall, and it is inconsistent to say the least to defend protection yet complain of its effects in stimulating foreign investment in the country".[9] The tariff, by encouraging investment of a kind appropriate to a protected market, led to the growth of replica American firms rather than specialized Canadian production appropriate to the world as well as to the domestic market.

Since it is the tariff (the cause) rather than foreign investment (the effect) that has prevented the achievement of a national economic identity, the remedy is not to be found in the process of buying into foreign-owned firms. Rather, we should be adopting policies that will enable these firms to adapt themselves to the Canadian interest of greater specialization. The buying out of foreign firms (far less giving Canadians nominal participation) will not of itself meet our basic difficulties. Such a policy might well add to our troubles by producing two effects of an unwelcome kind. In the first place, while we were buying up the existing enterprises, foreign capital would likely find its way into the new and more profitable ventures. A more damaging possibility is that we might succeed only in discouraging foreign capital from coming to Canada, leaving ourselves without the capacity to finance our future economic development.

The conclusion then is not that we must never adopt policies designed to reduce the extent of American ownership in our economy, but that we should only do so when we are certain that the gains will justify the costs and that we are attacking the proper target. While we would surely have had foreign investment without our long history of tariff protection, at the same time, without the tariff, we might well have produced an industrial structure more competitive and more suited to Canadian capacity and requirements. Instead, we now face the serious problem of how to disentangle ourselves from the miniature replica effect without undue sacrifice of our economic position. It is unsatisfactory to say that, since foreign investment of the type that has created our real economic problem is a consequence of the tariff, the removal of the tariff will immediately solve our foreign investment problem, although I would approve of tariff reductions for a variety of other reasons. It seems to me that the great issue now facing Canadian commercial policy is how best to reshape our industry along the lines of a national economic identity without paying unbearable costs of dislocation, readjustment and rehabilitation.

NOTES

1. Jacob Viner, "The Outlook for the Relationship: An American View", *The United States and Canada*, John Sloan Dickey (ed.) Englewood Cliffs, N.J., 1964, pp. 132-151.
2. Frank A. Knox, "U. S. Investments in Canada", *Proceedings, American Economic Association*, Evanston, Ill., 1957, p. 609.
3. H. W. Arndt, "Overseas Borrowing—The New Model", *Economic Record*, Melbourne, 1957, p. 251.
4. H. G. Johnson, *The Canadian Quandary*, Toronto, 1963, p. xvi.
5. G. D. A. MacDougall, "The Benefits and Costs of Private Investment from Abroad: A Theoretical Approach", *The Economic Record*, vol. XXXVI, no. 73, March 1960, p. 35.
6. A. E. Safarian, "The Exports of American-owned Enterprises in Canada", *American Economic Review*, vol. LIV, no. 3, May 1964, pp. 449-458.
7. Johnson, as cited, pp. xvii-xviii.
8. See below, Stephen Hymer, "Direct Foreign Ownership and the National Economic Interest", p. 191ff.
9. Johnson, as cited, pp. xi-xii.

direct foreign investment

and the national

economic interest • stephen hymer

Does it really make a difference that so high a percentage of Canadian industry is owned by foreign firms? Most Canadian economists seem to answer that it does not.[1] "Foreign investment may create problems from a political point of view," they would argue, "but from an economic point of view, it is a great benefit to the country. A business firm's behaviour is determined by supply and demand, not by its nationality. Whether a firm is American-owned or Canadian-owned, it invests by choosing the most profitable alternative use of its funds, and strives always to maximize profits. Nothing is lost by having Canadian industry controlled from abroad, while much is gained from the capital and technology which the foreigners bring to us. If we wish to place restrictions on foreign investment for political reasons, we shall have to pay for that action by lowering our economic welfare."

While there is much to be said for this line of reasoning, it is not fully convincing. Foreign firms do bring us capital and technology, but in some cases they may charge too high a price. By judicious regulation and restriction, we might be able to lower the price and obtain the happy combination of greater political independence and higher national income. Because I feel that the darker side of direct foreign investment has been neglected in the past by Canadian economists, I will concentrate on it. By exploring some problems associated with direct investment, I

191

will argue a case for closer control than is customarily thought necessary.

THE MOTIVE FOR DIRECT INVESTMENT: IMPERFECT COMPETITION

Political concern about foreign investment centers primarily, and properly so, on the issue of foreign ownership and control. Not all foreign investment, or inflow of capital from abroad, is accompanied by foreign ownership; foreign purchases of bonds and of non-controlling equities are cases in point. Direct investment, on the other hand, refers to those cases where the foreigner, by exporting capital, does acquire control and retains the locus of decision-making.[2]

Now the proper place to begin any discussion of direct investment in Canada is to put the question: what motivates foreign firms to own branch plants and subsidiaries in Canada? It is not simply differences in the cost of capital; though these play a role, they are not crucial determinants. If the rate of return on capital is higher in Canada than in the United States, Americans admittedly will find it profitable to lend money to Canadians. But this does not explain why they choose to invest directly in subsidiaries which they wholly own and control. Other factors must be present to account for this choice of means.

Nor will it suffice to say that an American or British firm acquires a subsidiary in Canada because it needs a raw material found in abundance in Canada, for that fails to answer the question of why it chooses to acquire the raw material through direct investment rather than by some alternative means. It could, for example, buy the raw material from an independent Canadian firm instead of investing large sums of money in direct ownership and control. Similarly, a foreign firm wishing to use its superior technology or its brand name in Canada does not have to invest in a subsidiary in order to do so; it could rent, license, or otherwise sell its advantage to an independent Canadian firm. Why doesn't it?

It can be said with certainty that the foreign firm will choose the alternative that maximizes its own profits. The issue for Canadians, however, is whether that particular alternative is also in the best interest of Canada. Is it to our advantage to have Canadian enterprise directly affiliated to foreign firms, or would we be better off if the Canadian firm was independent? Which form of business organization results in more Canadian production, lower prices for Canadian consumers, and higher prices for Canadian exports? We cannot be sure until we know what it is that the parent firm is trying to achieve through control of its Canadian subsidiary.

Let us consider a number of cases where the motive for direct investment stems from the fact that the relevant industry in the United States is made up of a small number of firms. This oligopolistic market structure, which exists in many industries, is a situation of imperfect competition which lies somewhere between the poles of monopoly of the single firm and pure competition of many firms. Confining our attention to oligopoly means neglecting the full spectrum of possibilities, but this is defensible, for empirical evidence in Canada and elsewhere shows that direct investment tends to be associated with industries where the market share is largely accounted for by a small number of firms.[3] It makes sense to look for causes and evaluate effects in terms of an industrial structure characterized by the small number of firms, or, in the parlance of the economist, high concentration.

HORIZONTAL INTEGRATION

Consider an industry where there are great economies of scale, or advantages from largeness, or where there are other barriers to entry facing potential competitors, with the consequence that there are only a few firms in each country. Since competition tends to lower price and reduce profits, these leading firms will have every incentive to agree amongst themselves to restrain competition. If international trade takes place, agreements with respect to price and market shares must extend across national boundaries to encompass foreign as well as domestic firms. International cartels based on price and market sharing agreements are one device which firms sometimes have used to achieve international collusion. Direct investment to achieve international integration of firms is another means. The integration is horizontal in the sense that it links different firms producing the same product. Direct investment can give a firm in one country control over price and output decisions of an enterprise in another country. To obtain perfect collusion, all of the enterprises in the world producing a given product would have to merge into one large international firm, controlling prices, production and sales in each country, and maximizing global profits. In reality, collusion seldom goes this far, but stops at the point where there are a few large international firms which neither collude completely nor compete fully.

In such industries it is impossible to evaluate the goodness or badness of foreign investment without considering the effect of foreign ownership on the degree of competition. The operation of foreign ownership decreases the number of firms in the world and tends to encourage imperfectly competitive behaviour. In general, imperfect competition reduces economic welfare because it decreases the efficiency with which resources (such as scarce labour and capital) are allocated. Prices facing consumers tend to be higher than they would otherwise be and consumers tend to be made worse off. Hence, direct investment which creates horizontal integration tends to have detrimental effects on world income. Within an individual nation, legal procedures exist to evaluate the performance of oligopolistic industries and to effect remedies when deemed appropriate; in principle, if not always in practice, this is the function of anti-combines legislation in Canada. There is a tendency, however, in Canada and elsewhere, to discuss market competition (or its absence) as if it were only of domestic origin, and to discuss foreign investment as if it created international problems unrelated to issues of competitive and oligopolistic behaviour. Seldom are direct investment and anti-combines policy considered together. Direct investment is discussed as if it was a matter of capital and technology alone, while competition is investigated with little attention to direct investment.

In fact, anti-combines legislation designed to compel competitive behaviour should be applied even more stringently in cases where foreign ownership is involved than in wholly domestic industries. For as well as misallocating resources and reducing efficiency, the existence of oligopoly increases the profits of firms, or redistributes income in favour of the oligopolists. In a completely Canadian industry, this redistribution effect takes from one set of Canadians and gives to another set of Canadians. Whether this is good or bad depends on who the givers and takers are, and what each does with his money. If, for example, the gainers tend to reinvest their profits and promote growth, oligopoly may not be such a bad thing after all. But where foreign ownership is involved, the outcome is necessarily different. The gains from oligopoly accrue to foreigners, and the redistribution effect reduces Canada's national income. Insofar as the foreigner gains by being paid for services rendered, there can be no complaint. Under oligopoly, however, some portion of the foreigners' gains may be paid for the disservice of restraining competition and reducing the efficiency of resource allocation.

It is unnecessary to look far to find out why the anti-combines implications of direct investment have been neglected. Firstly, it would mean investigating not only enterprises operating in Canada, but also parent and sister firms operating in other countries beyond Canada's jurisdiction. Secondly, any action taken by Canada would affect not only Canadian industry and welfare, but those of foreign countries as well. Regulation of international oligopoly, therefore, requires cooperation between Canada and other nations. At present, no mechanism for such cooperation exists, nor does its creation seem likely in the near future. There is a serious policy gap here, and room for Canadian initiative. The anti-combines or anti-trust legislation in Canada and in countries which invest in Canada is not adequate for a world in which international trade and international firms play ever more important roles.

VERTICAL INTEGRATION

The complexities of dealing with direct investment can be further illustrated by considering the case of vertical integration, that is, the linking of firms that operate at different stages in the productive process (such as a steel mill and an iron ore mine). Consider an industry with two stages of production, with stage A in Canada producing the raw material and stage B in the United States engaging in further processing. For simplicity, suppose there is only one source of the raw material in Canada and only one firm, a monopolist by definition, producing from that source. Similarly, assume there is only one manufacturer, again a monopolist, doing the processing in the United States. How will the price of the raw material be determined in this case? The answer is important, for the higher the price of the raw material, the more profit accrues at stage A and the less at stage B. The firms cannot rely on competition to determine prices, for each party has no alternative but to deal with the other party. The raw material seller cannot find another outlet and the buyer cannot avail himself of any competing suppliers. The price will depend not on supply and demand in a competitive market, but on trials of strength. If, however, the two firms were owned jointly, the conflict of interest would be removed and the issue of setting a price on the raw material obviated. The vertically integrated firm would simply maximize the total profits of A and B taken together and would not worry about how to distribute them between the two stages.

Faced with a situation of this kind, what should be the government's attitude? The economics of this case are quite different from the preceding one of horizontal integration. Vertical integration, by permitting rationalization in the productive process, normally leads to lower prices and greater output, and is therefore desirable from the point of view of world efficiency. The demonstration of this proposition requires somewhat more technical analysis than is justifiable here, but an intuitive argument may suffice. In the vertical case just outlined, with no integration there were two stages of monopoly—one in the market where the raw material was sold, and one in the market where the product was sold after manufacturing. This sequential monopoly involves a doubling of the distortive influences conventionally attributed to monopoly. When the two stages are integrated under a single firm, one source of distortion, in the raw material market, is removed. Though this is far from an ideal solution, it is nonetheless an improvement, and there is thus a presumption that it is desirable.

Even though this vertical integration may lead to a more efficient allocation of the world's resources, Canada may not benefit. What matters in the latter regard is how the gains are distributed. Part of the gains take the form of lower prices of the final manufactured product to the consumer; here Canada gains only to the extent that these consumers are Canadians. The rest of the gains accrue as profits, and Canada's share will depend on tax policy. For accounting purposes, the (vertically integrated) company sets the price at which it sells the raw material from its stage A raw material wing to its stage B manufacturing wing, computes profits using this price, and endeavours to pay taxes accordingly. But this raw material price is an exceedingly arbitrary one. It does not reflect any economic transaction taking place at arm's length, but is rather a book entry linking a parent and its subsidiary. The company will try to set the price to minimize its total tax bill, but that price may or may not be one that maximizes Canada's share of taxes paid. This problem cannot be solved by resort to the handy device of a free market price, for if there was a free market, the stage B firm would have bought its raw material there and never have acquired direct control of the stage A supplier. Because this is not a competitive situation, there is no "just" (competitive) price. The profits that stem from closer coordination of firms in different countries accrue jointly to all of them and cannot be allocated to any single one by economic criteria. A political solution is necessary to distribute the gains resulting from the improved efficiency of vertical integration. It is possible that at present the benefits in many industries go out of Canada to a considerable extent, for Canadian raw materials are often owned abroad and used abroad. Certainly the Canadian tax authorities should very properly appraise all transactions of this type and strive to maximize the Canadian tax share.

TECHNOLOGY AND ENTREPRENEURSHIP

Direct investment involves the flow not only of capital but also of technology and entrepreneurship. An analysis of market imperfection turns out to be a useful way to approach the complexities that inhere in analyzing these two critical factors in the process of economic growth.

Foreign ownership is frequently based on the foreigner's possession of superior technology. A firm which has a patent—or a unique (differentiated) product, or some other advantage—is a monopolist with respect to that advantage. Why does the firm not sell (or rent) the patent rather than make a direct investment? If there were many buyers, it would be tempted to do so, for it would then be in a strong position to extract maximum rent. But its bargaining position is much weaker if it faces only a few buyers. The small number of buyers tends to offset the company's monopoly power. To bypass this countervailing power, the company, rather than renting or selling its patent, may be induced to invest directly in its own foreign subsidiary. But while the company's position may thereby be improved, this does not mean that direct investment is therefore in Canada's interest. It might be possible for Canada to gain access to the superior technology at a lower cost in a way that yields the foreign firm an even lower return. This is a matter which has hardly been explored, and it is impossible to be specific. It is widely accepted, however, that restrictions should sometimes be placed on the use of patents; certainly special attention should be given to patents which prompt international investment.

The issue of technology can be looked at in terms of three targets. Firstly, we wish to insure the rapid adoption in Canada of the best technology in the world. Secondly, we wish to avoid paying too high a price for this technology. Thirdly, we wish to encourage the formation of entrepreneurial talent in Canada. The analysis of oligopoly showed that too great an anxiety to achieve the first target could endanger the second.

An argument can be made that restrictions on foreign ownership are needed as well in the interest of the third target.

The large volume of foreign investment in Canada seems to suggest a shortage of Canadian entrepreneurs. But which is cause and which is effect? We usually think of foreign investment as a consequence of a shortage of domestic entrepreneurs, but perhaps the former has helped create the latter. Suppose, in the extreme case, Canada forbade all foreign direct investment. This would certainly slow down the flow of technology and create a gap between techniques used in Canada and the best available elsewhere. What would happen then? Through time, the gap would grow and there would be an increasing incentive for Canadians to learn how to breach it. Might this not stimulate a growth of Canadian entrepreneurship? Once over their initial learning period, might not Canadian entrepreneurs be able to stand on their own feet? The shortage of entrepreneurs in Canada might disappear and with it the need for so much foreign investment. Just as there is an infant industry argument for a tariff, there may be an infant entrepreneurship argument for restricting foreign ownership.

It could be argued against this that foreign firms stimulate Canadian entrepreneurs by providing a demonstration effect and that banning direct investment would lead to less rather than more Canadian entrepreneurship. There is some case to be made along these lines, for the presence of firms from abroad certainly keeps already existing Canadian firms on their toes. But has the growth of new Canadian firms been stimulated or inhibited? One of the alarming features of the historical record in Canada is that there is no apparent tendency for the extent of foreign ownership and control to decline through time; the evidence is rather of a remarkable stability over time.[4] Both overall and within industries, foreign firms seem to maintain their market share and not give way to Canadian firms. This is true in many other countries as well. In general, direct investment seems to be self-sustaining, tending to hold its own or expand. The only important cases where foreign investment has given way to domestic investment occurred in the United States during the First and Second World Wars when special circumstances led to the Americanization of British and German subsidiaries. War, as it were, created artificial protection for American firms; perhaps protection is needed for Canadian firms.

ALTERNATIVE SOURCES OF CAPITAL

No attention has been paid so far to capital. The reader may very well feel that we have thrown the baby out with the bathwater. If we try to improve the degree of competition in Canadian industries by restricting direct investment, will we not sacrifice the capital that foreign firms bring us, and will this not mean a net loss in economic welfare?

The first point to be made in this connection is that we are not discussing the *amount* of capital that Canada should borrow from abroad, but rather, the *form* that borrowing should take. If we restrict direct investment, we are still free to borrow as much as is desired in the market for bonds and non-controlling equities. Whether we could get enough of this portfolio investment to replace the lost direct investment would depend on how perfect the capital markets were. Suppose, to take an extreme case, Canada compelled all American firms to divest themselves of their Canadian subsidiaries within a reasonable period of time. Clearly there would be a greatly increased demand for capital in Canada as American firms sought out Canadian buyers. But there would be created simultaneously an extra supply of an exactly equal amount of capital in the United States as the American sellers received the proceeds. In a perfectly functioning capital market, the result would be to lower interest rates in the United States and to raise interest rates in Canada, and to induce a flow of capital back into Canada. American investors would increase their holdings of Canadian bonds and of equity securities in Canadian firms. The end result in a perfect capital market would be about the same level of aggregate American investment in Canada, but in a different form; the investment would be held by American investors without control rather than by American corporations with control.

In the real world, however, capital markets are far from perfect. The loss on direct investment would probably not be completely offset by an increase in portfolio investment. There would, then, be a price to pay, but unless capital markets do not function at all, this price would be far less than the loss of the total amount of direct investment in Canada. Some of it would come back in a new form.

But there is also another argument on the side that no net loss need occur. Forcing American firms to sell their securities might lead to some pleasantly surprising results. One of the important characteristics of direct investment is the insistence of parent firms on nearly complete ownership of their subsidiaries. It has been argued throughout this paper that the motivation of the foreign direct investor is the maximization of global profits. To the extent that these profits rest on monopolistic (or oligopolistic) advantage, they are maximized when they are fully captured by the integrated decision-making unit, and this necessitates full control and wholly-owned subsidiaries. While some price would be high enough to induce the parent firm to sell shares in its Canadian operation to Canadians, a number of factors decrease the likelihood. The local capital market may be thin and prospective buyers may underestimate the profitability of the local operation. The parent firm may fear loss of control, or simply not wish to listen to a minority interest; it is, in any event, accustomed to operating an integrated concern at home and is geared to using the same methods abroad. The firm tends to see itself as a manufacturer, not an investor, and has no desire to be left with surplus funds through permitting local participation. Its view is that potential local shareholders should prefer to buy its shares, for they would then have access to global profits and avoid the risks associated with smaller or more specialized local operations.[5]

The foreign firm's preference for full control of its Canadian subsidiary has meant the exclusion of Canadians from participation in equity securities, except to the extent that they have been willing to buy the shares of the parent. The result may have been to deflect Canadian saving into other investments with lower rates of return. This, in turn, may have reduced total Canadian savings. By forcing foreign owners to sell shares in the Canadian operation in Canada one might raise rates of return to Canadians and elicit the extra savings necessary to finance capital investment in Canada.

The argument is an old one. In nearly every country where direct investment is important, there has been some move to compel the selling of local shares. The customary counter-argument is that this interferes with the efficient operation of the corporations. But what it might do is interfere with their efficient *monopolization* and that type of interference might be a very welcome one. It is interesting to note that though Canada has been a net recipient of foreign investment for a long time, it has not had an overall faster rate of economic growth than the United States. This suggests that either the Canadian propensity to save (for investment) is lower than the American, or that the productivity of capital is lower in Canada than in the United States. It is not beyond reason that the high degree of foreign investment is one cause of the lower Canadian saving propensity and/or the lower productivity of capital. There has been little empirical investigation of this issue in Canada and nothing can be said with certainty except that it deserves more study.

I have tried in this paper to counter the presumption that foreign investment is generally beneficial to the Canadian economic interest and its regulation generally detrimental. To argue against government interference in the working of free markets, economists appeal to Adam Smith's "invisible hand" as insuring that profit-maximizing firms promote the general welfare in attempting to promote their own. This argument, however, depends upon the existence of effective competition in the markets for goods and factors of production. There is empirical evidence to suggest that in many cases of foreign investment markets are highly imperfect. The presumption of the invisible hand is missing, and therefore it may be possible for the government to increase the level of income by interfering with the decisions of private corporations.

To the extent that market imperfections are important, the cost of political nationalism is lower than is usually thought. In fact, from the viewpoint of economic theory, restrictions on direct investment make far more sense than the high wall of tariffs that Canada has erected to stimulate Canadian industry. Most economic analyses suggest that these tariffs are quite detrimental to Canadian interests; Canadian per capita income is one-third lower than in the United States and a good part of this differential may be caused by the Canadian tariff.[6] In the case of foreign investment, however, some of the theoretical arguments suggest that the problem lies in the opposite direction of too little nationalism, rather than too much.

My primary purpose has been to analyze rather than to prescribe, but arguments for specific nationalist policies have flowed from the analysis. In particular, the Canadian authorities should consider the feasibility of the following remedies:

—— use Canadian anti-combines legislation to ensure competitive behaviour by foreign firms
—— cooperate with other nations in the regulation of international oligopoly
—— use tax policy to maximize the Canadian share of taxes paid by international firms with Canadian operations

—— use patent legislation, and other means, to encourage the inflow of foreign technology into Canada without foreign ownership
—— use restrictions on direct investment rather than the tariff to stimulate Canadian industry and entrepreneurship.

NOTES

1. See, for example, Irving Brecher and S. S. Reisman, Royal Commission on Canada's Economic Prospects, *Canada-United States Economic Relations*, Ottawa, 1957; Harry G. Johnson, *The Canadian Quandary*, Toronto, 1963; A. E. Safarian, "Foreign Ownership and Control of Canadian Industry" in Abraham Rotstein (ed.), *The Prospect of Change*, University League for Social Reform, Toronto, 1965.
2. For the official meaning of "direct investment" and "control", see Dominion Bureau of Statistics, *Canada's International Investment Position 1926-1954*, Ottawa, 1956, p. 24. For a discussion of the complexities that inhere in these concepts, see Safarian, as cited, pp. 224-225.
3. For a fuller discussion of the theoretical structure and empirical evidence on which this paper is based, see my "The Theory of Direct Investment", doctoral dissertation, Massachusetts Institute of Technology, 1960.
4. Safarian, as cited, pp. 226-228.
5. This list of factors draws on the responses of American parent firms to a campaign by the Montreal Stock Exchange to increase access of Canadian investors to the equity of Canadian subsidiaries. See Appendix XII of the submission of the Montreal Stock Exchange to the Royal Commission on Banking and Finance. The response was described as "completely negative" by the Hon. Eric W. Kierans in an address to the Toronto Society of Financial Analysts, February 1, 1966.
6. See above, papers by John Dales and H. Ian Macdonald. My paper has ignored the much-discussed phenomenon of the tariff factor, that is, of foreign firms attracted into Canada by the Canadian tariff. This has been done in the interest of focusing on neglected issues, and does not imply that the role of the tarriff in foreign ownership is unimportant.

nationalism in canadian

foreign policy • john holmes

Nationalism is best regarded as neither a blessing nor a curse but a historic fact. The reasons for viewing the phenomenon with scepticism need no reiteration. However, the present prejudice against nationalism is largely a response to recent European experience.[1] It is associated with a linguistic and tribalistic concept of nationalism only partly relevant to the Western Hemisphere or Africa. States on these latter continents, most of which are not, in the European sense, nation-states at all, are products of the vagaries of imperial administration rather than the ethnic assertion of tribes and clans. Nigeria, Colombia or Canada differ from the conventional nation-states of Europe in that they are either multi-tribal or a subdivision of a larger tribe. They are quite capable of exhibiting the malevolent nationalism of the European tradition, but they have special qualities and functions to be taken into consideration when estimating the appropriate role of nationalism in the design for a viable globe.

CANADA'S NATIONALISM

Canada is a very special case. We are a binational state and we use the term nationalism ambivalently. Rather than pursue definitions, I propose to treat both uses as valid. For the most part I am concerned with the nationalism of the entity Canada, which we might call "Canada-ism" or less aptly but more fluently "Canadianism", begging the question whether a binational state is a nation. (One virtue of its nationalism can, of course, be pride in its binationalism.) I shall also touch upon the impact of French-Canadian "nationalism" on our foreign policy. As for English-Canadian nationalism, it is doubtful if it exists at all apart from Canadian nationalism. We ought not, however, to ignore the tribalism of Anglo-Saxon Canadians, associated either with an imperial clan or now more often with the idea of the natural superiority of English-speaking peoples. Either in identification with the Empire or with the United States, it has usually been a counter-national or counter-Canadian force. That fact does not necessarily make it discreditable. In its considerable influence on our foreign relations, however, it has always had more of the sectarian characteristics of "nationalism" than has strictly Canadian nationalism which, whether it is constructive or merely competitive, is normally harmless.

The central problem of pan-Canadian nationalism has been the need to find a reason for the country's existence. The disadvantage of a synthetic state like ours is that it lacks the visceral drive to achievement. Its advantage is that it is more likely, although not predestined, to find a rational reason for existence. Canada was the product of a resistance movement. From 1791 to 1871 the evolution of the Canadian state was a sheltering together of those northerly North Americans who, for varying reasons, did not want to be absorbed into the United States. Some, like the Quebeckers, wanted to preserve their culture. Others, like the British Columbians, wanted to stay in the British Empire. The idea of Canada was to come later. Resistance to the active and passive pressures of the United States was a rational enough foreign policy for the first century or two. However, it has not alone been sufficient since the transformation of Uncle Sam from an ogre into a benign ally and our identification in the past half century of distant devils we know less well and fear more. Our nationalism is not now stimulated by the threat of military aggression. Our anxiety about national survival is attributable to fear of our own failure of will.

In an earlier age we would have needed no more justification for being a state than that we lived on the lands our forefathers had conquered or cultivated, and we proposed to go on doing so. We come of Messianic stock, however; the spirits of John Knox and Jean de Brébeuf haunt us.

Our neighbours have indoctrinated us with the assumption that a nation must be ordained for a benevolent political purpose. We came to nationalism late, after the Europeans had discredited it. In the pseudo-sophistication of our adolescence, many Canadians would rather let the country fall apart than be accused of nationalism, a weakness not only malign but also corny. Some find pride in our having conceived the immaculate non-nation. A majority recognize with satisfaction, but without emotion, the blessings of a country which demands little of them—in service or in conformity. Perhaps it is in our external policies of the past two decades, however, that we have done more to satisfy ourselves and others that our existence as an independent state is fortunate and that our disappearance would be unfortunate—though hardly tragic.

The instinct within us for constructive nationalism is jaundiced by the irascibility of our defensive nationalism. The latter is, in our case, the special peevishness of a lesser power which has required a minimum of heroism in its struggle with all too reasonable great powers. Throughout our national life we have been unhealthily preoccupied with two powerful states: our nationalism has been nourished on resistance to both the United States and Britain. While we resisted the encroachment of the Americans on our frontier, the attention of Canadian governments was directed to securing, by manoeuvre and negotiation, independence from Britain. Not too much independence, however, because Britain had to be a counter-weight to pressures from the south. But when the British showed reluctance to stand up to the Yankees on Canada's behalf, the Canadian Government was moved to take the direction of foreign policy more and more into its own hands.[2] Canada was less a lynchpin than a nuisance in Anglo-American relations. Canadian nationalism early learned to seek security by playing off one great power against another, and the technique still comes naturally, though less successfully. It took a longer time to learn that Canada would have to break out of this isosceles triangle if it was ever to take a respectable place in the international community. Two world wars, NATO and the United Nations sent Canada looking for allies its own size—although Canadians still suffer from a myopic concentration on North Atlantic affairs.

FROM COLONY TO MIDDLE POWER

It was half a century after Confederation and the establishment of the

Canadian idea before control over external relations was seriously sought. Control over things that mattered to a pioneer community, such as commerce and border problems, had been assumed earlier, but Canada lacked the resources and the will to seek a role in world politics. The hallucinations of Jubilee imperialism distracted those few Canadians with enough imagination to notice the world beyond the Triangle.[3] Concern for our external relations was largely directed to questions of status within the Empire. While Canadians emerged from World War I with a heightened sense of their own national identity, they were still ambivalent as to whether the Canadian destiny should be primarily imperial or national. Mackenzie King, who dominated the era, rejected the former, and in so doing absent-mindedly created the Commonwealth of Nations, with himself as its prophet. He was not, however, genuinely interested in his creation. Fortunately he left the scene in time for his successors to recognize in the Commonwealth a useful instrument of Canadian national policy. Unfortunately, however, the legacy of the long argument between unsound but imaginative imperialists and sound but unimaginative nationalists has been a public opinion which, confused by old shibboleths, has lagged behind its government (Liberal or Conservative) in appreciating the Commonwealth as a Canadian sphere of interest.

Up to 1945 English Canadians, when they thought about it, found their justification for existence in a consciousness of moral superiority over the corrupt and (as in 1914 and 1939) cowardly Yankees, in the radiance from Westminster and in being a coveted haven for the poor and oppressed of Europe. French Canadians saw their mission in survival. In the Second World War the frustrations of being the third strongest ally, but with little influence, encouraged a new idea of the Canadian mission. Instead of a country which could see itself only in a mirror, Canada would stand on its own as a "middle power". Being, as it was for a time after the War, the strongest of this newly conceived category of states, Canada fancied itself, along with Australia and a few others, as a spokesman and champion of the middle powers. Thus Canada began to define its international role in the context of a new front which crystallized in 1945 at San Francisco. The idea of a united Commonwealth as an integrated diplomatic unit had been finally rejected in 1944 at the Prime Ministers' Meeting in London. The Commonwealth was soon to begin turning out new middle powers in a pattern which strengthened the new Canadian concept of a hierarchical community of states and Canada's role therein. The United Nations accorded to all powers an equality which, however unreal in terms of power, tempered the significance in diplomacy of the military might of great powers. The front of the great powers was itself dissolved in Cold War.

The shift in the external posture of Canadian nationalism from Mr. King to Mr. St. Laurent was revolutionary. In 1939 Mr. King complained, not without justification, that it was madness to expect Canadians every twenty years to rescue a continent which was unable to manage its own affairs. When Canada was elected to the U.N. Security Council in 1947, Mr. St. Laurent declared that questions having their origins far away from our shores were "of first importance to the future of this country", insofar as they represented factors of world security. Mr. King had acquired for us the right to a national foreign policy and built up the resources to exercise it, but he was more concerned with defending the right than using it. He seemed to think we were too weak and too virtuous to be let loose in a wicked world; he really disliked the world beyond the North Atlantic Triangle. His defensive mentality has not yet been exorcised from the land. Nevertheless, the idea that sovereignty may be extended as well as limited by combination and alliance has largely superseded the old nervousness about commitments. The paradoxes of an alliance role are not always comprehended. There lingers an assumption that we can reject commitments to an alliance like NATO or a brotherhood such as the Commonwealth, and at the same time play a decisive role in determining their policies. On the whole, however, Canadians have accepted the proposition that our nationalism is better served by enlarging our influence through group activity than by standing guard over a sovereignty which leaves us impotent. We have learned what Mr. King apparently failed to sense, that chastity may be noble but it is not very creative.

Canada's position in the world was strengthened, furthermore, by internal factors. The old schizophrenic pull between the imperialists and the continentalists was tranquillized by the new partnership of Britain, France and the United States in NATO. Isolationism was dead in North America. As a result, domestic tensions over Canada's external associations subsided. When Canadians next went overseas to fight—in Korea—there were more volunteers from Quebec than from the other provinces. A strongly entrenched government had for a decade an unprecedented consensus behind it in support of a vigorous Canadian foreign policy.

From the perspective of 1966, the consensus may seem more apparent than real because of the quiescence of French Canada. Yet this foreign policy was designed by English and French Canadians, who together nourished a policy positive enough to appeal to most varieties of Canadian nationalism without offending unduly the susceptibilities and prejudices of either of the major elements in the country. Only fanatical minorities—from the British, French and Slavic communities—were at odds with a policy in which a new Canadian nationalism found its outlet in active internationalism.

The United Nations has been a boon to Canadian nationalists. As an international rather than a supranational organization, it satisfies our predilection for a cautious mixture of pragmatism and idealism and it avoids the principle of collective security of which we have always been sceptical.[4] It has also provided a stage on which Canada could emerge from the shadow of the great powers, which gives it complexes, and establish an unmistakable identity. It has given Canada the chance to prove itself, to gain a reputation in the world. In the past decade it has offered also a congenial military role which has given the country a sense of purpose for its armed forces not so readily felt for the more subordinate role of lesser military allies—important and essential though that role may be. Pride in the mediatory role has given a certain style to Canadian diplomacy. The reputation for objectivity is sought. Comment on world events is muted, and emphasis is placed on maintaining contact even with international malefactors.

Either because of Mr. Dulles' intolerance of gray positions or the imperatives of U.S. leadership, the general tone of Canadian foreign policy has differed considerably from that of the United States, and the very distinctiveness of its style has made that policy particularly congenial to Canadian nationalism. While there is no escape—and for the most part no strong will to escape—from the obligation to solidarity on basic things with the giant ally and neighbour, the difference in category, the variation in the role, is all the more to be welcomed by the nationalist. Restlessness over United States foreign policies is a constant element in Canadian foreign attitudes, both public and governmental. The expression of such sentiments is rationalized as the obligation of the best friend to be the most candid. The rationalization is well justified, but the need to dissent is essential to Canadian mental health.

A FUNCTIONAL THEORY FOR CANADIAN FOREIGN POLICY

This concept of the distinct vocation of states was at the root of the so-called "functional theory" which Canadians advocated at the end of the Second World War. It was a rationalization of the new nationalist approach, an attempt to find a sensible and possible occupation for Canada in a world in which, Canadians fully recognized, the most important thing was that the great powers should combine to keep the peace. As Mr. King defined the theory on July 9, 1943, it was a recognition that in international institutions effective representation could not be restricted to the great powers nor extended to all states. It must be determined on a functional basis, according membership to "those countries, large or small, which have the greatest contribution to make to the particular object in question". Although Canada succeeded in having the principle written into one article of the U.N. Charter,[5] it cannot be said to have dominated world organization ever since. Canada, as one of the three original atomic partners, did become the only non-great power to sit on the U.N. Atomic Energy Commission and, by inheritance, subsequent bodies seeking disarmament. This role as the leading middle power on disarmament questions did much to establish the Canadian position in world affairs and satisfy Canadian nationalism. At the same time it created exaggerated notions of Canada's permanent place in the galaxy of nations. This illusion has led to frustration and at times a self-defeating concern for status rather than function, since our position among middle powers suffered a relative and natural decline because of post-war readjustments. Nevertheless, functionalism has provided Canadian nationalism with a frame of reference which encourages it to seek an impact appropriate to its energy and resources without exhausting its zeal in futile effort and making itself ridiculous by universalist fantasies.

The functionalist habit of mind should enable Canada to avoid the worst dangers of that contemporary rhetoric which comes from those who would tear up our roots in the name of abstractions such as Atlantic unity, the West, the Hemisphere, regionalism or world federalism. The need to find expression for the uniquely Canadian role and to avoid losing our identity encourages the Canadian instinct for practical and suitably untidy international institutions. We prefer a world organization like the United Nations which does not pretend to act like a government but is rather a congeries of councils and agencies each with its function and a constitution and membership suited to that function—dominated perhaps, but not run by the great powers. For us it is better, even regionally, to have NATO for defence and OECD, with a different set of members, for economic development, than a rigid Atlantic federation which we know would not work. Above all, we have been encouraged to strengthen our independence by maintaining overlapping memberships in various clubs: NATO, the Commonwealth, and the shifting alignments of what *The Economist* called the "Sanitavian bloc" in the U.N. Assembly.[6] The acquisition of membership in the Organization of American States would seem to be in accordance with this aspect of the nationalist impetus. It has been in conflict, however, with another nationalist instinct, that of avoiding a situation which might subvert our independence by too close an alignment with our large neighbour and the canny fear of provoking quarrels with the United States on remote issues which might jeopardize our immediate economic interests. This caution looks like the old defensive nationalism, but in our changed circumstances it may reflect a new confidence in our ability to play our part in the Hemisphere without tying our hands.

Our way, however, grows more and more difficult to comprehend because the Alliance is less and less a group experience. The bilateral relationship with the United States has become much more significant than the Alliance whose multilateralism seemed to suit the requirements of our nationalism. The inequality of the relationship is a source of discouragement and intimidation to our self-assurance and our sense of mission. Regarded in another way, however, it may be asked whether this factor loosens the obligation of allies to alignment with the United States. The increasing self-sufficiency of United States power reduces its dependence on its allies, including Canada. The security of the world is now determined not so much by the alignments of the Cold War as by the phenomenon of deterrence. May we not regard the United States less as the great ally to whom we are obligated for protection, than as one end of the colossus along with the Soviet Union, which maintains the nuclear umbrella under which we middle powers, small powers, and great powers can try to keep the world in some kind of order? The United States is busy maintaining a kind of world order that is in its interests and, to a lesser extent, in ours as well; it is not its purpose to do us a favour. Our independence in foreign policy should be conditioned by a sense of good neighbourhood and common interest rather than gratitude. The motive may not seem to matter much, but this clarification of the nature of our responsibility *vis-à-vis* the United States could make our nationalism healthier by removing the sense of indebtedness for protection or of guilt when, for example, we do not send troops to Vietnam or ostracize Castro.

Canada can claim some credit for the recognition of the middle power as a constructive element in world politics. Whether the development of this concept was essentially a rationalization of the needs of Canadian nationalism, or a response to the requirements of international politics, may be argued. Probably it was both. That this can be the basis of our continuing foreign policy is, however, a question which should be constantly under review. The danger is that Canadians will be impelled to seek this kind of fulfilment whether or not it is required; that an aggressive determination to middle powermanship will offend or amuse the international community, thereby dissipating the reputation for sense and judgment on which the success of the role depends.

Relations among powers shift, and the middle power concept could be a passing phase. It has represented, in fact, a deviation from the traditional attitude to lesser powers. Walter Lippmann, in his definition during the last War of his country's aims, said, "We must not, as many do, identify the rights of small nations with their right to have an 'independent' foreign policy, that is to say one which manipulates the balance of power among great states."[7] Before the new day of U.N. diplomacy, the conventional role of lesser powers was exemplified in most minds by Sarajevo, not as, at a later stage, by Suez. Now, however, Canada is urged by influential Americans to preserve its national independence for mediatory purposes.[8] At the same time, lesser power nationalism as an abstraction is under increasing assault. Amalgamation is in the air. Supranationalism is regarded as a higher principle than nationalism; regionalism is looked upon as the wave of the future. Although the federal world state is regarded by few as an imminent solution, we seem driven by the assumption that salvation is to be sought by moving towards the central switchboard, the single global computer. The iron law of economics is believed to be mass production, concentration, centralization. As Melville Watkins argues later in this volume, the development of technology is apt to make national boundaries anachronistic and artificial.[9] But against this it must not be forgotten that nations have resulted not merely from tribal passion but also from the groping of diverse peoples to establish governable units on an uneven and irregular planet. As populations grow and the functions of government multiply, the political and administrative requirement often seems to be for smaller states and decentralized government. Our nationalism and internationalism are confused by these paradoxes.

THE CONTINUING NEED FOR AN INDEPENDENT FOREIGN POLICY

Canada may be caught between political arguments for nationalism on the one hand and economic and strategic arguments for supranationalism on the other. (The argument for internationalism, the cooperation of nations in the common interest, is not questioned.) The obvious political requirement for a stronger Canadianism to enable the confederation to work more effectively runs counter to the anti-nationalism, or rather anationalism, of the business community. There are valid arguments on both sides, but we may get the worst of both worlds—the perpetuation of a political state rendered anaemic by the discouragement of any national feeling. The antagonism to Canadian economic nationalism is abetted by the fashionable prejudice against political nationalism as well as by premature extrapolations from the early successes of the European Common Market. We are also confronted by well-intentioned but dubious arguments for supranationalism by Americans and Europeans seeking a way out of the paradoxes of an unequal alliance. In their anxiety to share the military burdens of the Alliance and to offer at least the appearance of sharing policy decisions, spokesmen of the Washington Administration and noble-voiced citizens pour scorn on "petty nationalism"—other people's nationalism, of course—and proclaim the need to find unity in Atlantic institutions in which we would all sacrifice our nationalism and our sovereignty in a common will. That such a common will is bound to be Washington's should be obvious. The result of this mutual sacrifice would be that, in exchange for a nominal share in policy-making, the rest of us would give up our moral right to differ from the United States. While they possess the decisive power and are committed all over the world, the Americans cannot be asked to surrender the right to decide their foreign policy, although they can be expected to pay more attention to the views and interests of their allies. But we should remain cautious about allowing them, more ingenuously than by design, to rob us of that independence we possess, in the name of supranational institutions.

For Canada the siren song is particularly strong because our nationalism can be made to seem perverse and helpless. The term "community", in the context of "the North American community", is easily borrowed from the entirely different circumstances of a multinational Europe to disguise annexation. There is, of course, a standing argument for annexation. It is not a fate worse than death, but if it is to be chosen, the choice should be calculated. However, if we want to remain a separate entity, it is essential that we have a national foreign policy. To surrender our sovereignty to a genuinely international institution might, in the right circumstances, be a contribution to world order. To hand it over to the United States might bring some advantages to us or the Americans, but it is not likely to make the world a better place for anyone else. It would merely encourage the dangerous world trend towards bipolarization. Nor is it likely to reduce the level of global nationalism. The final achievement by the United States of its manifest destiny on this continent might well be followed by an intensification of American nationalism—of which its new northern citizens would no doubt be the most extravagant advocates after having been liberated from a nationalism which had perforce to worship good sense and moderation. One cannot be sure, of course. A united continent, confident of its power, might turn benign and serene.

The kind of Canadian nationalism which finds its outlet in effective middle power diplomacy may wither because it does not appeal to a restless public. Many people are impatient of its moderation and sobriety and above all the discreetness of "quiet diplomacy". They want to fight real devils, nuclear weapons and segregationists, with which there can be no compromise. Although English- and French-speaking youth are to some extent united by such sentiments, they are separated by the preoccupation of the French Canadians with their own problems and, of the English Canadians with other people's. Politically conscious English Canadians are often obsessed by a humanitarianism which, almost as a matter of principle, removes their attention from the issue which threatens to tear their own country apart; it is as if such concern would be evidence of nationalism and therefore less virtuous than intervention in other countries' problems. Those who demand a strongly nationalist Canadian foreign policy of resistance to the United States over Vietnam or the Caribbean are often not nationally conscious enough to realize that they are foreigners in Alabama. To suggest to them that priority might be given to their own country's problems is rejected as offensive to the brotherhood of man. One is tempted to ask, however, whether involvement in the Canadian issue is less attractive because it requires ratiocination, and possibly sacrifice and commitment, in place of heady emotion and adventure from which withdrawal is easy. One is reminded of what Daniel Webster described as "that wandering and vagrant philanthropy" which heated "the imagination on subjects distant, remote, and uncertain". It is the kind of comfortable internationalism which, warming our hearts with noble sentiments and apocalyptic visions, saves us from our own noisome and intractable problems. It is not in the better tradition of Canadian foreign policy, which has sought to exploit the peculiar advantages of the Canadian position in the general interest.

Nevertheless, this restlessness cannot and should not be dismissed by those who see our role in coolly professional terms. If our foreign policy is to be maintained, it must be popular, a little less immaculate and a little more vulgar than the "mandarins" prefer.[10] It must provide some occasions for shouting and for standing up to be counted. It is childish to defy the Yankees merely in order to demonstrate our own virility, but when there is good cause our independence must be made manifest. As a young Canadian put it, "Our present actions have solid worth in themselves but they appear grey and oh so solid." One of the requisites for Canada's playing any distinctive role, other than that of a satellite, is the maintenance of a considerable degree of independence. The strength and vitality of its nationalism is an important element of its independence. Without a sense of identity, pride, attachment to his own group, the citizen becomes too susceptible to external influences to sustain a national foreign policy. Nationalism itself is, in part, a function of what a nation accomplishes in international society. So the foreign policy of Canada must be so designed as to bolster Canadian nationalism and in so doing to bolster Canadian independence. Otherwise we perish or at least dwindle. However misguided the public restlessness may seem to some, for the most part it represents frustrated idealism which needs an outlet. It is infinitely preferable to the cynicism about the Canadian role in the world which is all too common. If it is too often directed towards telling Washington what to do, that may be because it has not felt able to communicate with Ottawa.

BINATIONALISM AND CANADIAN FOREIGN POLICY

Our national foreign policy is threatened by supranationalism on the one hand and also by binationalism. An urgent question to be faced is

whether the policy I have been describing is compatible with the binationalist approach of the new voices in Quebec. (The separatist argument
can be disregarded, not because it is illogical or unattainable, but because
it is irrelevant to a discussion of the foreign policy of a Canada which,
however organized internally, is considered an entity in the world community.) It seems to me that our now traditional middle power policy
is not incompatible with the French Canadians' consensus on what our
national foreign policy should be, although they might interpret it otherwise. If anything, French Canadians would propel us further in the
direction we have been moving. They would urge us to greater independence, in particular less categorical indentification with the United
States and the Anglo-Saxon community, closer association with Latin
America and the French-speaking world, a more sympathetic relationship
with France but not partnership in Gaullist foreign policy. It is a difference of emphasis rather than alignment, and there is room for compromise. There need be no direct confrontation between French and English
views of Canada's place in the world provided extremists on both sides
do not force us into rigid alignments.

There is already some adjustment taking place in our alignments. An
example has been the effort of the Pearson Government to breach the
formidable gap in world outlook which has kept Ottawa and Paris apart
since the War. This has been an act of deliberate policy—an acknowledg-
ment, as a basic dimension of Canada's international orientation, that
there must be a special relationship with France. It has always been
recognized, of course, that although French Canada would not insist on
being an ally of France, we could never have France as an enemy. (Even
Vichy France had to be treated with circumspection.) Nothing fundamental has changed, but the requirement for more positive relations with
France is acknowledged and the image of Canada as a member of the
Anglo-Saxon fraternity diluted.

This adjustment of relations with one Mother Country may be easier
because of the change which has come over relations with the other Mother
Country with which our association had been closer. The decline of
British power and prestige has reduced the place of Britain in the Canadian scheme of things. Impatience with old forms and symbols has encouraged some Canadians to assert their nationalism against the relics
of British suzerainty—to some extent perhaps as compensation for impo-
tence against the realities of American domination. A souring of the old

relationship, however, has come on the British side, where goodwill has often given way to irritation, hostility or boredom as a result of the Suez crisis, the imbalance of trade, dislike of North America in general, and the malevolence towards the Commonwealth which has accompanied the frustrated infatuation with Europe. The Commonwealth, now emphatically multilateral and multi-racial, is less of a bond between Britain and Canada. It has even become a field of contest between British and Canadian influence, as over the issues of South Africa and Rhodesia and the establishment of a Commonwealth Secretariat. Differences were mitigated by the coming to power of a Labour Government which is less anti- Canadian than the Conservative Government and closer to Canadian thinking on Commonwealth questions. The ghost of British domination has almost certainly been laid. Free of the inhibitions of the past, the two countries may come to recognize more easily that, as the two middle powers with the most vital stake in the American Alliance and close and complementary national interests, they have much to gain from a partnership that would, however, have to be closer to equality than it was in the past. Britain has always played an important part in the dogma of Canadian nationalism, and this changing relationship has considerably altered the nature of the dogma.

The prospect of the engulfment of Britain in a European Union, removing as it would the traditional counter poise, has affected the Canadian will to resist what it is fashionable to consider our regional destiny. The pattern of Canadian nationalist foreign policy is more easily maintained if Britain remains a maritime rather than a narrowly European power, and the Atlantic Community is a flexible fraternity of fifteen or twenty countries rather than cast in stalemate by the dumbbell formula. It would be inadvisable for Canada to oppose the development of the European Economic Community, or Britain's entry into it. We are not required, however, to share the illusion of Washington that the transformation of six nationalisms into one sub-continental nationalism is necessarily going to make the world a healthier place for us.

Here we must beware of contradiction. Our sense of national mission in this world has been encouraged by Lord Acton's famous declaration: "The combinations of different nations in one state is as necessary a condition of civilized life as the combination of men in society." He was, of course, thinking more of the Austo-Hungarian Empire than of Canada. We hope for a better fate than the Hapsburgs, although we shall do well if we have as long a run as they had. Can one be sceptical of the virtues of a multinational state in Europe and proclaim that our own binational state is a higher form of political organism than the nation-state? Lord Acton was perhaps too absolute in his principle. The objection to a West European political union is not that it is offensive in principle but that Europe is not ripe for it, and in federations ripeness is all. A union too tight for the circumstances increases tensions dangerously. It is forced to nourish a common external danger and may turn mean, nasty and aggressive rather than benign, tolerant and generous. A West European federation might be in our interest, of course, if we were reasonably confident that it would provide expanding markets or that it would reduce the danger of conflict in Europe—rather than divide it permanently down the middle. Neither can be taken for granted. In the meantime we might remain neutral, viewing sceptically the apocalyptic vision nourished in Washington, of a world which would be redeemed if only it would follow the "anti-nationalist" example of a Europe united —at least partially—in the spirit of '76.

On the other hand, the one-nationality state is an inadequate model for a world proliferating new states at a dizzy rate. The failure of one of the oldest and most sophisticated multi-national states, Canada, would be discouraging to all the new countries striving to find viable formulae of government to encompass diverse nations and languages. Our Canadian nationalism must be binationalist.[11] Our foreign policy will be effective if we succeed internally. Even if the creation of vast and ineffectual regional federations is an uncertain panacea, there is not much to be said for splintering unions which have been in operation for two centuries. Federation is in itself neither good nor bad.

The strength and flexibility of our foreign policy could, however, be unfortunately affected by certain interpretations of binationalism. In such fields as human rights our voice in international circles has always been muffled by the limitations of the federal system—the fact that the federal government, which must speak for us abroad, cannot commit the provinces on subjects reserved for them. We could probably go quite a long way in allowing provinces the right to deal with foreign governments on subjects within their jurisdiction including, of course, cultural matters. On political, economic or security matters our national foreign policies should rest on a consensus of all Canadians, and French Canadians have a case to argue that their views have had less weight than they merited.

They will, of course, inevitably carry more weight if and when French Canada turns its attention from domestic to international problems. Proposals, however, which imply that there is or should be a separate French-Canadian consensus and that Canadian policies should somehow or other be the product of negotiation between Quebec and Ottawa threaten us with paralysis. There never has been any such thing as an English-Canadian or a French-Canadian view of our foreign relations, although there are, as I have said, identifiable differences in emphasis. There has been no consequential issue of foreign policy since the last War on which the division of opinion within the country has been specifically between English and French. It is not in the national interest to create the machinery or encourage the assumptions which could lead to separate foreign policies. It is not in the interest of French Canada to do so, for the inevitable result would be to surrender the determination of federal foreign policy to the sole control of English Canadians. An effective foreign policy cannot be evolved in a provincial capital because it is divorced from the international life of diplomacy, conference, negotiation, secrets and confidences. French Canada is more likely to play a significant role in world affairs acting through a state of twenty million, than as an independent state of five million people. But effective participation in shaping Canadian foreign policy is possible only if French Canada sees itself as a partner in national policy rather than as an indigestible lump of opposition.

For Canada, unlike the heroic nation-state of old, national survival is not the highest priority of foreign policy. The survival of the world, or at least of our kind of civilization, comes first. There are many things more important for us than resisting our absorption, as a minor but influential entity, into an Atlantic state or even our national extinction through annexation by the United States. If either of these acts was essential to save ourselves and others from nuclear annihilation or totalitarian enslavement, we would undoubtedly accept them. Short of that, we would even give up our national identity, I presume, if it were essential to save us from an unacceptably low standard of living. For the time being at least, none of these reasons has persuaded us to forego the satisfactions and the security we find in our own national life. We rarely say so, but we seem to recognize the tranquil advantage of not being a great power. We are saved by our weakness and our diversity from the temptations of aggressive nationalism. We are not devoid of the pettiness of negative nationalism, but our society is so free, our ethnic origins so varied, and the influences upon us so diverse that we cannot avoid being one of the most international of countries. We have found, therefore, satisfaction for our ego in the construction of international organisms which allow us to keep our identity and help build a world order at the same time. Because our identity is political rather than cultural we must, if we are to exist at all, guard our separate constitutional framework more jealously than the nation-states of Europe or Asia. We are dedicated to maintaining a strong United Nations because it is the kind of international rather than supranational organization which suits us and permits us to flourish. We can assume with reasonable assurance, furthermore, that our independent existence is good for the United Nations and that we should preserve ourselves in the general interest. A threat to the U.N. is a serious threat to our national existence because we are cowed more easily in the alternative world of clashing alliances and the unchallengeable rule of the superpowers.

Let me say in conclusion that I am aware of the fact that my definition of a Canadian foreign policy and my comments on other powers and international bodies is less an analysis of facts than the imposition of a framework and a justification for Canadian nationalism. How otherwise does one devise a foreign policy? We cannot argue that we have a divine or racial mission, that we were created for a predestined purpose. We exist; therefore we think. If what we think up for ourselves to do is good for us and serves our ultimate interest in a peaceful and prosperous world, let us rejoice in it. Even the gloomiest denouncers of nationalism assure us that the phenomenon is not dead. In Canada we can, however, tame and civilize it.

NOTES

1. See below, George Heiman, "The 19th Century Legacy: Nationalism or Patriotism?", pp. 332-337.
2. For a discussion of some of the first manifestations of this tendency see above, Craig Brown, "Nationalism and the National Policy", p. 155ff.
3. This kind of schizoid nationalism is well illustrated by the Nova Scotian bard who wrote:
   "Hail our great Queen in her regalia;
   One foot in Canada, the other in Australia."
4. It has been fashionable since the last War to deride Canada's hostility to the collective security provisions of the League and in particular our volte-face on oil

sanctions against Italy. Our hostility was attributable partly to a neurotic fear of getting involved in a wicked world but also to a shrewd realization that a league which did not embrace all the major nations ought not to pretend that it could enforce collective security.

5. Article 23, which says that in electing the six non-permanent members of the Security Council due regard should be paid in the first instance to the contribution of members to the maintenance of international peace and security.

6. That is, the Scandinavian states, Canada, Ireland and a few others who have constantly pursued compromise solutions or resolutions to reconcile the blocs.

7. Walter Lippmann, *U.S. War Aims*, Boston, 1944, p. 84.

8. See "An Address Prepared for Delivery by Harlan Cleveland, United States Assistant Secretary of State for International Affairs, at the Annual Meeting of the United Nations Association in Canada, June 6, 1965: Member of the Parish", esp. p. 3, or Final Report of the Twenty-fifth American Assembly, *The United States and Canada*, New York, April 23-26, 1964, esp. p. 5.

9. See below, Melville Watkins, "Technology and Nationalism", pp. 289-293.

10. See two articles on Canada's role as a middle power by Lloyd Axworthy in the *Winnipeg Free Press*, September 8, 9, 1965.

11. For a full statement of such a conception of nationalism, see above, Stephen Clarkson, "A Programme for Binational Development", p. 133ff.

nationalism and

canadian science •   james guillet

The juxtaposition of the two words "science" and "nationalism" may at first glance scandalize the purist, for what, after all, can be less national than "science", or conversely less scientific than "nationalism"? One could argue that while there are such things as "Canadian Scientists", the concept of "Canadian Science" makes little sense. It is the thesis of this paper, however, that while there can be little doubt that "Canadian Science", if it has a corporate existence, has contributed very little to Canadian nationalism, the latter has on the other hand had a very considerable effect on the former, and this effect may be expected to become increasingly important in the future.

While one may question the existence of a distinct entity known as "Canadian Science" within the body of world knowledge, there is less reason to question the validity of the term if we include within its context the realm of technology, with which it is closely allied and commonly confused in the public mind.

To the scientist, science is devoted to the pursuit of basic knowledge, primarily about the nature of matter and energy and their relationships. Its objective is a more complete understanding of natural phenomena. Technology, on the other hand, seeks to apply scientific and other knowledge for specific material ends, such as to build a bridge or to cure cancer. Since the distinction is primarily a question of motive, it is asso-

221

ciated with the customary lack of precision involved in defining human conduct.

For the purpose of this paper I will therefore use the term "science" to include both science and technology. Nationalism will be considered to have intruded into scientific matters whenever the course of science is affected by decisions made with special regard to what is considered in the best interests of a restricted community, and since we are dealing here with Canadian nationalism, we will be concerned primarily with public policy as it is established at the federal level in Canada.

NATIONALISM AND SCIENCE: THE HISTORICAL RECORD

Historically, the relations between the scientist and the state, like the course of true love, never did run smooth. Since the days of Archimedes, whose ingenious war machines are said to have delayed the Roman capture of Syracuse for three years, it would seem that the scientist was most esteemed in times of national emergency, and the present century is certainly no exception in this regard. In the absence of such special conditions, however, the scientist from Galileo to Linus Pauling, was more often than not in considerable disfavour with the state because of the conflict of his frequently heretical views with accepted political and religious dogma. The change began in England about the middle of the eighteenth century, when it was discovered that scientific knowledge could be applied to produce the means of wealth. The long search for the "Philosopher's Stone" had indeed paid off in gold, but not in the way the alchemists had expected! Since that time, the importance of science and scientists to the economic health of the state has increased at an accelerating pace.

There are three main areas in which public policy can be considered to affect science—in education, in direct support of scientific research, and in economic policy. Although "nationalist" considerations may well affect the education of scientists through influence on the selection of curricula and text books, provision of scholarships, and other matters of educational policy, it is not the purpose of this article to explore this avenue further. We will therefore concern ourselves principally with the impact of nationalism on scientific research and industrial technology.

In Canada the first major step in the formulation of a national policy towards science was the founding in 1916 of The Honorary Advisory

Council for Scientific and Industrial Research. It is not without significance that this step was taken in the middle of World War I. This organization, which soon became known as The National Research Council
(NRC), was formed to advise the federal government in scientific matters,
to supervise the distribution of research grants to universities and industry,
and to establish post-graduate fellowships in science. In 1925 NRC
undertook to establish its own scientific laboratories, and since that time
more than half of its budget has been designated for this purpose. The
amount of public funds expended by NRC increased from $139,000 in
1925-6 to $5 million in 1939. A large expansion in operation occurred
during World War II which raised the federal government's total scientific research budget to $35 million in 1945, and it continued to increase
to an estimated $222 million in 1963.[1] $35 million of this money was
spent by NRC in 1963, but large amounts were also spent by Atomic
Energy of Canada Limited ($30 million), the Defense Research Board
($33 million), the Department of Agriculture ($25 million), the Department of Mines ($26 million), and the Armed Services ($32 million).
Expenditures by other government departments brought the total to
$222 million.

This rapid growth of expenditure on scientific research reflects a recognition by the government of both the economic benefits to be harvested
from scientific research and the prestige attached to a national scientific
Establishment. But in spite of this expansion, the expenditures on scientific research in Canada remain very low compared with those of other
advanced industrial countries. For example, the Royal Commission on
Government Organization points out that Switzerland, Great Britain
and the United States spend between two and three times as much per
capita as Canada. Perhaps a more serious criticism is the very high proportion of research in Canada actually performed in government laboratories (50% versus 33% for U.K. and 14.5% for U.S.A.). Although there
is possibly room for error in these estimates, it is apparent that in Canada
at least half of all research is done by the federal government in its own
laboratories. This preponderance of government research in Canada has
influenced the entire course of scientific and technical development. It
affects the scientists because, in effect, over half of them must be government employees and subjected to at least some of the limitations in salary
and incentive characteristic of the civil service. The research projects
undertaken are usually of a long-term nature, since there is seldom a

strong competitive pressure to produce practical results. This is not to say that such work is not of vital interest and importance, but only to point out that there is a difference, almost of kind, between this research and the type engaged in by industrial laboratories where the pressure to produce practical results is considerably stronger.

From these statistics a picture of the present state of science and technology in Canada emerges. The major expenditures on scientific research in Canada are made by laboratories of the federal government. A lesser amount is spent by provincial governments in organizations such as the Ontario Research Foundation and Ontario Hydro. Industrial technology is supported primarily by importation of technology by Canadian subsidiaries of large foreign manufacturing concerns. Canadian industry itself spends relatively little on the research and development necessary to develop new technology. Canadian universities properly devote most of their efforts to basic research and to the training of qualified scientists and engineers, and their research budgets at present represent only a relatively small fraction of the amount currently spent on research by the federal government. Apart from staff salaries, the cost of university research is defrayed primarily from research grants from agencies of the federal government such as NRC or the Medical Research Council. An appreciable proportion of these funds also comes from granting agencies outside Canada, such as the Ford Foundation, National Institute of Health (U.S.A.) and the U.S. Armed Forces. These U.S. funds are in imminent danger of being cut off because of U.S. balance of payments problems.[2]

THE UNDERDEVELOPMENT OF CANADIAN TECHNOLOGY

The result of this situation is that "Canadian Science" is heavily biased towards the type of basic research most suited to university and government laboratories. The applied scientist, instead of developing new technology, is often restricted to the adaptation of foreign technology to Canadian requirements. This is particularly frustrating to scientists trained in Canadian universities which tend to place an unusually high evaluation on the virtues of basic or pioneering research. As a result of this, a large proportion of Canadian scientists interested in applied research (and this includes medical research) tend to migrate south of the border where the opportunities for such research are incomparably greater.

It has been argued that the loss of such scientists to the United States is more than made up by the number of scientists emigrating to Canada from abroad. This may be true, if one is concerned only with numbers, not quality, but one could hardly suggest that the country would not be better off if it could retain a greater proportion of the most highly trained segment of its population. In most cases it appears that this loss is not entirely because of the higher salaries in the United States, but because of the greater opportunities for research, particularly in applied fields.

As I have pointed out, the distinction between basic research and applied technology is not often appreciated by laymen, who usually assume that most scientific research has a practical goal. From an economic point of view, the advantages of doing basic research in Canada are of a secondary nature—that is, there is no immediate benefit to the economy other than the provision of a large pool of scientific talent whose knowledge and skill can be brought to bear on practical problems, if and when these are presented to them. It is in the nature of basic research that it is truly international, so that the results become available almost immediately to all countries, regardless of where the discoveries are made. Applied technology, on the other hand, is very much an industrial commodity; it is protected from disclosure to outsiders, and guarded far more jealously than the Crown Jewels. Thus it becomes very important to the economic health of a nation either to have a strong programme to develop industrial technology, or to be prepared to pay a rather high price to purchase it from others. In Canada the price is "economic sovereignty".

In Canada the development of a truly indigenous technology has been inhibited by the nature of our manufacturing industry. It is here that H. I. Macdonald's "derivative economy", or the "miniature replica effect",[3] comes into play. Canadian automotive manufacturers, for example, do not manufacture Canadian automobiles, but American, British, German and even Swedish automobiles in Canada. The technology is primarily foreign, and usually American. With a few exceptions (e.g., pulp and paper) there is no distinctively Canadian technology in any manufacturing industry, and for the same reason—namely the subsidiary nature of the major part of our industries. According to Macdonald, this can be considered to be a direct result of the protectionist policies adopted early in our history by successive Canadian governments. It affected not only the economy, as was intended, but also had far-reaching effects on the progress of scientific and technical research in Canada.

Regardless of what policies one may wish to consider the root of the problem, the fact remains that Canadian industry supports a relatively small portion of total Canadian research and development. In 1959, according to the Glassco Report, industry performed 39% of the total research and development, compared with 58% in Great Britain and 76% in the U.S.A. The difference is even greater when considered as a percentage of the Gross National Product (GNP). These figures indicate that industrial research represented in 1959 (the last year of available statistics) 0.28% of GNP in Canada compared with 1.23% in Britain and 1.96% in the U.S.A., factors of $4\frac{1}{2}$ and 7 respectively.

Why does Canadian industry spend so little on research? The answers are obvious. In a subsidiary economy the subsidiary obtains most of its technology *free* from its parent company. Other technology may be purchased at a nominal rate based on a percentage of sales. The dividends paid by subsidiaries to parents may also be considered as payment for technology. In general, conditions in Canada are not sufficiently different from those in the U.S.A. to require the development of products specially suited to the Canadian market, so that little or no development is required after importation. Further, Canadian industry is often protected by tariff barriers from the type of competition which might force it to develop its own technology. Because the subsidiary firm is usually smaller and possibly less efficient than its parent, it feels it cannot afford the relatively large charges which an extensive research and development programme would make upon a manufacturing operation.

In this environment the establishment of Canadian industrial research facilities made little economic sense, particularly when many Canadian factories were closer to their parent laboratories in the U.S.A. than were American branch plants of the same company. These are probably the reasons why even such research-minded giants of American industry as General Electric and Eastman Kodak have not established research laboratories in Canada. As a result of these considerations, almost until the last decade Canadian industrial research was limited to more or less routine technical services and process improvement on existing Canadian-made or imported products. In the last few years a number of bona fide industrial research laboratories have been established in Canada, but it is perhaps too soon for their effects to be realized.

In considering the relative merits of Canada's historic protectionist policy, the value of this importation of "free technology" is often underestimated. Possibly economists share with most businessmen the reluctance to consider technology as a marketable commodity, with all the associated properties of a commodity, such as, for example, conformance to the laws of supply and demand. If given an appropriate dollar value, and included in such considerations as the economic effects of foreign investment, an entirely different picture might emerge. Without the benefit of such a detailed analysis it is my opinion that the present level of economic prosperity in Canada could not possibly have been attained without this importation of "free technology". However it is equally clear that Canadian industry is now in a position to maintain a much higher level of research activity, and, indeed, will be forced to do so if present trends toward free trade continue.

It seems obvious, for example, that the recent American-Canadian agreement regarding free trade in automobile parts will lead to only a temporary increase in markets for Canadian manufacturers unless they are willing to expend the effort necessary to maintain a technology competitive with that of research-conscious American firms. That the federal government is aware of this problem is indicated by the urgency with which recent programmes to stimulate industrial research have been initiated by NRC and the Department of Industry.

We have seen how "nationalist" considerations have affected the development of science and technology in Canada, resulting in a situation where research in laboratories operated by the federal government accounts for about half of the total Canadian research budget, which itself is much lower than that of many advanced nations. We have seen that, because of the subsidiary nature of Canadian industry, industrial research and the development of an indigenous technology has been inhibited, if not completely suppressed. In order to bring Canadian research expenditures in line with those of our potential competitors for world markets, the amount of industrial research would have to be increased by a factor somewhere between 4 and 10 (the factor of 7 would be required to match U.S. expenditures in 1959 based on GNP).

A further necessary step would be a massive increase in funds available for research in Canadian universities. Even the modest increase in industrial research which has occurred in the last three years as a result of the government incentive programme has led to a shortage of skilled scientists and technicians,[4] and an increase in research of the scale envisaged above would make unprecedented demands on the universities, which at the present level of support could not possibly be met. A recent report by

J.W.T. Spinks[5] recommended a five-fold increase in federal grants for university research over the period 1964-1969, and even this may well be insufficient for the task. The combination of these two measures, along with a modest expansion of the government's own research efforts, would bring the research expenditures as a percentage of GNP up to the level reached in the U.S.A. in 1959.

However this argument by analogy has many defects, and should not be pushed too far. What must be obvious from statistics on research in advanced countries is that a modern nation can well afford to spend at least 2% of its Gross National Product on scientific research, and it may well be that an even higher proportion would be beneficial to the economy. This would amount to a little over $1,000 million based on the present Canadian Gross National Product.

The distribution of such expenditures should be considered, not in the light of what is done in Great Britain or the U.S.A., but of what is required by the unique situation which now exists in Canada. The alternatives seem clear. If Canada is to remain an independent industrial nation in an economic environment tending towards free trade, massive expenditures on industrial research will be required to develop a technology capable of withstanding the cold winds of international competition. On the other hand, if Canada continues to rely on imported "free technology", the economic integration of Canada with the United States appears to me to be inevitable. The desirability of the latter alternative will be evaluated within the context of one's own particular brand of " Canadian nationalism".

A PROPOSAL FOR A NEW NATIONAL SCIENCE POLICY

Assuming that one accepts the arguments of this paper that a massive increase in technological research and development is desirable in Canada, what steps could be taken to see that this comes about?

For example, should the federal government expand its present research budget to the level necessary to bring Canada's total expenditures in line with those of other advanced nations? For the reasons mentioned earlier I feel the answer must be no. Government laboratories have not shown thus far the diversity of interest and the devotion to commercial practicality necessary to supply the entire needs of an advanced industrial technology.

Should the government expand its research assistance to industry by the extent required? It seems to me unlikely that this would have the desired effect. In general, most of the present government assistance has gone to relatively small companies whose business is not sufficiently large to sustain research on a much larger scale than at present. The larger Canadian manufacturing concerns, particularly those already involved with research, have been slow to accept the additional responsibilities of an expanded research programme, even when paid for by government grants. Some of those who might have been expected to have reacted most favourably because of the long and profitable research tradition of their "parents", have accused the government of ill-considered meddling in the economic affairs of the nation.[6]

It seems to me that the only way to stimulate research and development on the scale necessary to keep Canada in the front rank of modern industrial nations is to involve ourselves in a project comparable in magnitude to that accepted willingly by the country in times of national emergency. As experience in World War II has proved, countries can expend a very large part of their industrial effort on non-productive ends and yet emerge, even after severe destruction of existing facilities, in a stronger industrial position with new and advanced technology. Surely it should be possible to provide such stimulation artificially without the necessity for destruction!

As in many other areas, the Russians and Americans have indicated a promising solution. The "Space Race" is surely a project which in each case involves the assignment of a substantial portion of the nation's resources to a programme which can have no direct economic advantage (other than prestige) to either country. However, the scientific "fall-out" has already been striking in terms of the development of new technology, from fuel cells and solar batteries to space medicine.

While it is difficult to suggest a similar project for Canada which might give the needed stimulus to Canadian research, it is easy to list the requirements for such a project or projects.

1. It must involve large expenditures for research and engineering in areas of new technology (i.e., not simply an enlargement of existing technology such as building a larger dam or power station).
2. Research in industry must be encouraged by the award of profitable *manufacturing* contracts to the successful firms.
3. It must appeal in some way to the majority of the population of

the country so that the heavy expenditures of taxpayers' money can be justified in terms of prestige, economic advantage or other forms of national interest.

4. It should involve a wide range of technical and scientific skills and should be supported lavishly, so that if people with the necessary training are not available in Canada, they can be enticed from abroad.

5. It should not be a project already receiving substantial research attention elsewhere.

Some attempts in this direction have already been made. The ill-fated Avro Arrow project was a considerable stimulus to Canadian technology, but it was cancelled before its effects could be fully realized. Further, it failed in at least two requirements, in that it was research already being done elsewhere on a larger scale and, because it was related to armaments, it did not receive the undivided support of the Canadian taxpayer. The Atomic Power project could perhaps have developed into a suitable national goal if it had been supported financially at such a level as to ensure Canadian dominance in the field.

What other projects might be adopted? What about the development of an air-car to replace the family automobile, or the building of climate-controlled cities in subarctic regions? The President of the American Chemical Society has proposed as a U.S. goal the laboratory synthesis of living organisms by the year 2000. What about an intensive study of the nature and mechanism of the human brain? There is surely no lack of suitable projects—only a dearth of imagination and initiative in deliberately seeking out the most appropriate and fruitful ones.

It will be seen that we have come full circle in our discussion. In showing how a rather narrow nationalism has led to a curtailment of scientific endeavour in the realm of applied technology, we end by proposing that the powerful appeal of nationalism be used to foster a vast expansion in research and technology in Canada.

NOTES

1. *Report of the Royal Commission on Government Organization* ("Glassco Report"), Section 23, Scientific Research and Development, Ottawa, 1963.

2. Woods-Gordon Report, *Medical Research in Canada—An Analysis of Immediate and Future Needs,* Ottawa, December 1965, p. 32. See also Royal Commission on Health Services, Vol. II. Ottawa, 1964, p. 106.

3. See above, Ian Macdonald, "Foreign Ownership: Villain or Scapegoat?", pp. 187-190.
4. *Chemistry in Canada*, (November 1963) , p. 31.
5. J. W. T. Spinks, *The National Research Council Forecast of Support Needed for Basic Research in Canadian Universities*, Trans. Roy. Soc. Canada, Vol. II, 1964, p. 13.
6. See for example Herbert L. Lank, President of Dupont of Canada, Address to the Canadian Club of Toronto, March 8, 1965, as reported in *The Globe and Mail*, March 9, 1965.

CULTURE •

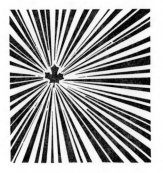

nationalism in

canadian literature • frank watt

This is a topic you can take hold of from several sides, with rather different consequences. Most naturally, perhaps, you would begin by thinking of the extent to which nationalism has been, or is, a motive for the creation of literature, or at least an important factor conditioning the quality of writing in Canada. Obviously this approach requires an historical perspective. On the other hand, an outsider hearing this topic might first of all wonder whether the question was not, to what extent has Canadian literature been a motive for nationalism. An Englishman, I am sure, is all the more an Englishman and proud to be so when he numbers Shakespeare or Keats among his forbears. Anyone who has actually read a fair amount of Canadian literature is unlikely to imagine Canadians being nationalistic in this way out of satisfaction with their literature. Even so, one might conceive of Canadian writing as, in various ways, stimulating national pride and national awareness.

But pride and awareness are not necessarily the same thing. This brings me to a third way of approaching the subject, in which I am not sure whether nationalism, by whatever definition, does not come close to disappearing, leaving us with only Canadian literature, or more barely still, literature, to consider. In this approach we would be seeing nationalism, not as a direct encouragement to writers (one reason for writing), and not as an encouragement for readers (one reason for reading), but as an indirect product or by-product of literature. Literature is then seen as a force which, quite apart from its motives, contributes to the articulation and clarification of Canadians' consciousness of themselves and of the physical, social and moral context in which they live their lives. I say nationalism is an indirect product in this case, because the enlightened and articulate consciousness which literature helps to create might be related in many ways, even the way of outright opposition, to whatever people would generally call nationalism. For example, the poem entitled "From Colony to Nation" shows as strong a national feeling or sense of Canadian nationality as Arthur Lower's book by the same name, but the tone and direction seem to be a little different. Professor Lower hoped "that a careful reading of his pages [would] help Canadians to some of that self-knowledge so necessary if they are to take their rightful place in the world, and still more, if they are to be a happy people, at peace with themselves."[1] For Professor Lower, Canadian history is by and large a success story, and "Canada is a supreme act of faith".[2] For the poet Irving Layton, if Canadians are at peace with themselves their peace is complacency, and if there is a national faith it must be bad faith. This is the conclusion he sees for the triumphal progress from colony to nation:

> A dull people,
> but the rivers of this country
> are wide and beautiful
>
> A dull people
> enamoured of childish games,
> but food is easily come by
> and plentiful
>
> Some with a priest's voice
> in their cage of ribs: but
> on high mountain-tops and in thunderstorms
> the chirping is not heard
>
> Deferring to beadle and censor;
> not ashamed for this,
> but given over to horseplay,
> the making of money
>
> A dull people, without charm or ideas,
> settling into the clean empty look
> of a Mountie or dairy farmer
> as into a legacy.

One can ignore them
(the silences, the vast distances help)
and suppose them at the bottom
of one of the meaner lakes,
their bones not even picked for souvenirs.[3]

A sophisticated reader might of course want to say that here Layton is expressing a very familiar and recognizable variety of Canadian nationalism. But before I go farther into this more attenuated aspect of my subject, the way in which Canadian writers help to bring alive the shared history, limitations, fulfilments, virtues and depravities which make at least some Canadians feel related to each other and to their land, before I go farther in this direction, I must return to and develop the simpler approaches to my subject, nationalism and literature in their historical perspective.

Using the historical approach I can avoid an objection some literary critics and many writers would immediately raise. There are those who are inclined to distrust any approach to literature which emphasizes a close relation with social forces. Both the so-called New Critics who treat poems as self-contained verbal constructions, and artists who have their ears tuned to the Muses, to the subconscious, to the inner voice (or however they choose to describe their inspiration), dislike the suggestion that writing may be conditioned or caused by social forces. They do not always equally dislike the notion that literature has or should have a social function, though they usually object to being directed to any specific function. At one extreme is classical Marxist doctrine—the belief that economic circumstances condition consciousness and artistry. At the other extreme is pure creative imagination theory—that whatever materials he uses the artist brings to them a basic spontaneous freedom of impulse, choice and form which is his essential creativity. Like wave and particle theory in physics, or free will and determinism in philosophy, these theories may seem irreconcilable, yet each explains certain kinds of literary phenomena better than its opposite.

In case this sounds like an excessive academic balancing of one idea against its opposite, I should at once confess my bias towards the romantic position. There does seem to me to be a sort of indeterminacy principle in literature, whatever is true of physics: artistic inspiration, like the most elusive forces in the atom, apparently will not stay still to be charted accurately, and the act of measurement itself can become an alien force distorting the field of investigation. This is true whether you are dealing with the motives of a living writer, or with the meaning of an apparently stable monument of literary history. The approach to both must share some of their own nature, some of their own intuition and inspiration. Marxists, moralists and nationalists are usually reluctant to accept this conclusion.

THE LITERATURE OF NATION-BUILDING

Fortunately these subtleties can be set aside in any study of nineteenth century Canadian literary history. There the practice and theory of literature had a reassuring obviousness, and not much literary tact is required. Most writing in British North America before Confederation was "colonial", in A. J. M. Smith's sense of that word: "Colonialism is a spirit that gratefully accepts a place of subordination, that looks elsewhere for its standards of excellence and is content to imitate with a modest and timid conservatism the products of a parent tradition."[4] The chief fault of this writing, especially the poetry, was a tendency to abstraction, a fault which followed almost inevitably from the attempt to apply literary techniques and language fully formed in Europe to a largely different subject matter in the New World. Writers continued to see their native environment and experience through spectacles developed for a very different kind of world, and, therefore, not to see very clearly or intimately. Some steps, especially in the Maritimes, were being taken towards the acclimatization of the Muses, the founding of an indigenous literature, by the 1860's. But the Confederation movement intervened in this process with a new kind of force which ran, if not counter to, at least across the movement towards a localized and particularized regional literature.

Confederation was bound to have an impact on writing as on other aspects of British North American life; the effect was immediate, however superficial. The cry was raised by new nationalists that literature should serve the new nationality, and vice versa. "Now," H. J. Morgan, the biographer and bibliographer, wrote in 1867, "now more than any other time ought the literary life of the New Dominion develop itself unitedly. It becomes every patriotic subject who claims allegiance to this our new northern nation to extend a fostering care to the native plant, to guard it tenderly, to support and assist it by the warmest countenance and encouragement."[5] Three years earlier E. H. Dewart, the anthologist, had spelled out the social and political demands a Canadian nationality would make on its writers and the service writers would be asked to provide:

> A national literature is an essential element in the formation of a national character. It is not merely the record of a nation's mental progress: it is the expression of its intellectual life, the bond of national unity, and the guide of national energy. It may be fairly questioned, whether the whole range of history presents the spectacle of a people firmly united politically, without the subtle but powerful cement of a patriotic literature. . . . It is to be regretted that the tendency to sectionalism and disintegration, which is the political weakness of Canada, meets no counterpoise in the literature of the country.[6]

Dewart then touched on a larger problem than he realized by adding that although "our French countrymen are more firmly united than the English colonists," "their literature is more French than Canadian, and their bond of union more religious than literary or political."[7] What he might have said more objectively is that French-Canadian writers had different aims from English-Canadian. A French-Canadian nationalism, reacting to the threat of assimilation implicit in the 1840 Union of the two provinces, and inspired by Garneau's historical account of the spiritual greatness of French Canada, was already a strong motive for literature. This nationalism, with its determination to keep pure and alive the language, laws and religion of French Canada, has of course continued to influence Canadian writers in French to the present day. I am unable to say to what extent the new and larger nationalism of Confederation has also been felt, but I would assume comparatively little.

Confederation created a new role for the writer, the role of nation-builder, and since that time few Canadian writers in English have been able to resist at least a few flourishes in this part. The role required enthusiastic involvement in the geography, history and future prospects of Canada. In the 1870's the Canada First Movement had its literary embodiment in Charles Mair, who was called the Keats of Canadian poetry, and who deliberately tried to load every rift of his poetry with Canadian ore. He indicated the programme for nation-building writers in this way: "Our romantic Canadian story is a mine of character and incident for the poet and the novelist, framed, too, in a matchless environment; and the Canadian author who seeks inspiration there is helping to create for a young people that decisive test of its intellectual faculties, an original and distinctive literature—a literature liberal in its range, but, in its highest forms, springing in a large measure from the soil, and 'tasting of the wood'."[8] Mair's historical poem "Tecumseh" was an attempt to follow this programme, and no doubt the plethora of nineteenth century historical novels exploiting the records and legends of early French and British North American life can be accounted for partly in the same way.

By the 1880's one detects a considerable growth in confidence among critics, at least, that the nation-building writer was in fact effectively at work. W. D. Lighthall prefaced his anthology *Songs of the Great Dominion* with spirited claims appropriate to his title: "You shall hear there," he said, "the chants of a new nationality. . . ." "The poets whose songs fill this book," he continued, "are voices cheerful with the consciousness of young might, public wealth, and heroism." Lighthall saw the cultural life of Canada developing a grandeur comparable to that of her physical and political life, and here his enthusiasm was unbounded:

> Canada, Eldest Daughter of the Empire, is the Empire's completest type! She is the full-grown of the family,—the one first come of age and gone into life as a nation. . . . She is Imperial in herself, we sons of her think, as the number, the extent, and the lavish natural wealth of her Provinces, each not less than some empire of Europe, rises in our minds. . . . Her Valley of the Saskatchewan alone, it has been scientifically computed, will support eight hundred millions. In losing the United States, Britain lost the *smaller* half of her American possessions. . . .[9]

It is quite characteristic of writers like Lighthall, who see literature as serving and being nourished by the new nationality, that he should focus his ardour on the physical assets of the country. For of course the difficulties of knowing exactly what the new nation was and where it was heading were as great for the poets as for the politicians. Of the many poets who since 1867 have tried their hand at what might loosely be called the "Confederation ode", almost all have found the tangle of Canadian political involvements and affiliations too complex for simple enthusiasm, even when they were eager to provide it. A bemused poetaster in 1880 began his poem "Canada First" in this way: "Canada first! first, Canada we love! /Next glorious Britain, our most noble sire; /Next, our near neighbour: let us brothers prove. . . .,"[10] and so on. Another chose to spend a briefer time wrestling with political complexities ("Fair land of peace!

to Britain's rule and throne /Adherent still, yet happier than alone. . .") , and went on quickly to the great natural simplicities: "But we who know thee, proudly point the hand /Where thy broad rivers roll serenely grand. . .", etc.[11] Prolonged meditation on Canada's political status and relations with Britain and the U.S. was more likely then, as it is today, to produce perplexity and debate than rapture, and writers aiming to arouse patriotic feeling would do better to dwell on the undeniable depth of the lakes, height of the mountains and breadth of the plains. The one safe common denominator of all nationalistic Canadian writing is the land itself.

During the 1880's and 1890's while Macdonald's National Policy was helping to establish the political and economic basis of the country, anthologists, critics and writers were showing an increasing patriotic interest in the growth of an indigenous literature. Bliss Carman wrote with pride of C. G. D. Roberts, "the acknowledged laureate of this vigorous young nation", and asserted revealingly, if not quite accurately, that "his poetry is in large measure the product of his enthusiasm and his patriotism."[12] In the journals of the day, critics were searching out and rewarding with praise signs of Canadianness among current writers. It would be an exaggeration to say that here we had in operation a *National Policy for literature*. But at least there was a strong awareness that nationalism and literature are intimately related; and in one direction this awareness led to the Canadian Authors' Association of the 1920's with its cultivation of home industries (Buy Canadian Books) , and to the subsidized and protected cultural agencies that are making their contribution to national identity and independence today.

The dilemma of a patriotically conceived National Policy for culture is that only the worst writers seem willing and able to answer direct appeals that literature should serve the national cause, or if good writers respond, they do so with their poorest writing. I doubt if Roberts would have wanted to be remembered by stanzas like this from his poem called "Canada":

> O Child of Nations, giant-limbed,
>   Who stand'st among the nations now
> Unheeded, unadored, unhymned,
>   With unanointed brow. . . .[13]

Looking at Canadian society in the 1880's and 1890's, Archibald Lampman was led to remark that what the country needed most was not panegyric but satire.[14] The only conclusion to be drawn from a study of post-Confederation literature is that the best writers at their best moments have similarly rejected, or simply let go by default, the public role of nation-builder which was created with the advent of Confederation.

INVENTING CANADA

But this brings me to the third and most difficult part of my paper: for nationalism may be influenced by writers who have no apparent interest in it and who would refuse to serve it if invited.

Vladimir Nabokov, in a note appended to his piquant American novel of unrequited love, *Lolita,* tells us how difficult he found it as an outsider in the United States to give his story a satisfactory substance and density. It could not have been the American language which held him up, for he was a master of the language; it must have been the vagueness and indistinctness of the social and atmospheric context, lack of the feel of the country. In order, he says, to write the novel, he had first of all to "invent America". For most readers of Nabokov, the invention of America was highly successful and his new America modifies their old image of the country. Aldous Huxley was obviously thinking along the same lines as Nabokov when he wrote, "Nations are to a very large extent invented by their poets and novelists." Other artists share in the job, as Huxley makes clear in the same discussion:

> How imperfectly did mountains exist before Wordsworth! How dim, before Constable, was English pastoral landscape! Yes, and how dim, for that matter, before the epoch-making discoveries of Falstaff and the Wife of Bath, were even English men and women! . . . The inadequacy of German drama and the German novel perhaps explains the curious uncertainty and artificiality of character displayed by so many of the Germans whom one meets in daily life. Thanks to a long succession of admirable dramatists and novelists, Frenchmen and Englishmen know exactly how they ought to behave. Lacking these, the Germans are at a loss.[15]

It is obvious that if the Germans are at a loss, Canadians are even more so. How should they behave? Should they be calm, urbane and ironical in the tradition of upper-class England, or should they be cheerful, lively and brash like the true North Americans; healthy peasants, or angry young men? Is their country "America's attic, an empty room," or "the big land" with "the big ale"? To what extent have writers succeeded in inventing Canada and Canadians? If one thinks first of all of geography, the physical environment, the Canadian terrain, the answer is that Canada has been very successfully invented, but in a process as long and gradual as that by which this half-continent was explored, settled and mastered, both politically and by technology and communications. It is easy to trace this process through the history of Canadian poetry. Pre-Confederation poetry shows the Canadian terrain as a vast, hostile, dimly seen, unpoetical mass, the poet often struggling ineffectually to catch and express its feeling in imitations of the clear, regular, elegant couplets and poetic diction which Pope and his school bred to civilized perfection in the gardens of England. By the 1880's poets are not any longer bemoaning the inhuman and unpoetical nature of Canadian landscape: they are recording its details and its moods with high fidelity. By the mid-twentieth century poets have gone a stage further: the terrain is no longer merely external, something to be observed closely and described accurately in appropriate language. If it is referred to at all it is used symbolically, or as an extension or manifestation of the human. The country may still appear vast, alien and forbidding at times, but the poet has it under greater imaginative control.

I said that the process of imaginative conquest paralleled that of political and physical conquest. An obvious landmark taken from a late stage in the process is, by a useful coincidence, a modern poem on the building of the transcontinental railway, E. J. Pratt's national epic, "Towards the Last Spike". Pratt has an easy grasp of the physical sweep and immensity of northern North America which would have dazzled his Victorian predecessors, perched precariously on the fringes of their mysterious sprawling wilderness. In this he is helped greatly by a suggestive myth: he sees the northern continental mass as a sort of vast prehistoric monster, a prostrate, somnolent reptile or dragon, and, by an inevitable association, the statesmen and engineers struggling to bridge the continent become dragon-slayers. Because nature for Pratt is not merely external, the dragon of the Canadian terrain becomes a visible manifestation of the monsters of fear and doubt and suspicion that lurked in the minds of many Canadians and nearly prevented them from building their railway and their nation from sea to sea. And because Pratt was a humanist and a Christian the dragon is related, as in most dragon-slaying stories, to the father of all dragons, the Devil, and to the forces of evil and chaos which human societies always struggle to master by imposing human order and civilization on nature. Pratt's poem could be seen as patriotic and nationalistic: it celebrates a central heroic event in Canadian history. But what value the poem has lies in the way it transcends nationalism and presents a national achievement as an instance of the universal archetypal human story. No mere nationalist would go so far in giving the devil or dragon its due as to suggest that the monster might still in the long run win the struggle:

> Some day perhaps when ice began to move,
> Or some convulsion ran fires through her tombs,
> She might stir in her sleep and far below
> The reach of steel and blast of dynamite,
> She'd claim their bones as her possessive right
> And wrap them cold in her pre-Cambrian folds.[16]

The process of inventing the Canadian terrain can also be traced in prose. One chain of examples would begin with Mrs. Frances Brooke's description of the St. Lawrence in the late eighteenth century: "On approaching the coast of America, I felt a kind of religious veneration, on seeing rocks which almost touch'd the clouds, cover'd with tall groves of pines that seemed coeval with the world itself: to which veneration the solemn silence not a little contributed; from Cap Rosières, up the River St. Lawrence, during a course of more than two hundred miles, there is not the least appearance of a human footstep; no objects meet the eye but mountains, woods, and numerous rivers, which seem to roll their waters in vain."[17] The last phrase, "in vain", particularly gives the lie to the conventional protestations of veneration, and points to the underlying baffled vagueness and sense of alienation. A century later William Kirby gives us this description of the St. Lawrence at Quebec: "The broad bay lay before them round as a shield, and glittering like a mirror as the mist blew off its surface. Behind the sunny slopes of Orléans, which the river circled in its arms like a giant lover his fair mistress, rose the bold, dark crests of the Laurentides, lifting their bare summits far away along the course of the ancient river, leaving imagination to wander over the wild scenery in their midst—the woods, glens, unknown lakes and rivers that lay hid from human ken, or known only to rude savages, wild as the beasts of chase they hunted in those strange regions."[18] Here we have the fair mistress—giant lover image indicating an area of control which shades off into vast stretches of wilderness and chaos where the imagination is lost. Though the author's grasp is not entirely firm, there is a good deal of understanding and conviction in his character's enthusiasm for the landscape in general and for Quebec, "God's footstool", in particular.

Of the examples I would choose from the twentieth century, the best is the opening of Hugh MacLennan's *Two Solitudes*, focusing again on the St. Lawrence, but here the imaginative control of the material is assured and the descriptive detail is used to open up the essential subject matter of the novel, the French-Canadian, English-Canadian duality:

> Northwest of Montreal, through a valley always in sight of the low mountains of the Laurentian Shield, the Ottawa River flows out of Protestant Ontario into Catholic Quebec. It comes down broad and ale-coloured and joins the Saint Lawrence, the two streams embrace the pan of Montreal Island, the Ottawa merges and loses itself, and the main-stream moves northeastward a thousand miles to the sea.
>
> Nowhere has nature wasted herself as she has here. There is enough water in the Saint Lawrence alone to irrigate half of Europe, but the river pours right out of the continent into the sea. No amount of water can irrigate stones, and most of Quebec is solid rock. It is as though millions of years back in geologic time a sword had been plunged through the rock from the Atlantic to the Great Lakes and savagely wrenched out again, and the pure water of the continental reservoir, unmuddied and almost useless to farmers, drains untouchably away. In summer the cloud packs pass over it in soft, cumulus, pacific towers, endlessly forming and dissolving to make a welter of movement about the sun. In winter when there is no storm the sky is generally empty, blue and glittering over the ice and snow, and the sun stares out of it like a cyclops' eye.
>
> All the narrow plain between the Saint Lawrence and the hills is worked hard. From the Ontario border down to the beginning of the estuary, the farmland runs in two delicate bands along the shores, with roads like a pair of village main streets a thousand miles long, each parallel to the river. All the good land was broken long ago, occupied and divided among seigneurs and their sons, and then among tenants and their sons. Bleak wooden fences separate each strip of farm from its neighbour, running straight as rulers set at right angles to the river to form long narrow rectangles pointing inland. The ploughed land looks like the course of a gigantic and empty steeplechase where all motion has been frozen. Every inch of it is measured, and brooded over by notaries, and blessed by priests.
>
> You can look north across the plain from the river and see the farms between their fences tilting towards the forest, and beyond them the line of trees crawling shaggily up the slope of the hills. The forest crosses the water-

shed into an evergreen bush that spreads far to the north, lake-dotted and mostly unknown, until it reaches the tundra. The tundra goes to the lower straits of the Arctic Ocean. Nothing lives on it but a few prospectors and hard-rock miners and Mounted Policemen and animals and the flies that brood over the barrens in summer like haze. Winters make it a universe of snow with a terrible wind keening over it, and beyond its horizons the northern lights flare into walls of shifting electric colours that crack and roar like the gods of a dead planet talking to each other out of the dark.

But down in the angle at Montreal, on the island about which the two rivers join, there is little of this sense of new and endless space. Two old races and religions meet here and live their separate legends, side by side. If this sprawling half-continent has a heart, here it is. Its pulse throbs out along the rivers and railroads; slow, reluctant and rarely simple, a double beat, a self-moved reciprocation.[19]

And finally there is Stephen Leacock who, despite his mordant criticism of Canadian life, felt the Canadian terrain to be his home. A misguided Englishman had asked him to go home to England, but he replied, I'll stay in Canada:

It's the great spaces that appeal. To all of us here, the vast unknown country of the North, reaching away to the polar seas, supplies a peculiar mental background. I like to think that in a few short hours in a train or car I can be in the primeval wilderness of the North; that if I like, from my summer home, an hour or two of flight will take me over the divide and down to the mournful shores of James Bay. . . . I never have gone to James Bay; I never go to it; I never shall. But somehow I'd feel lonely without it. . . . No, I don't think I can leave this country. There is something in its distances and its isolation and its climate that appeals forever. Outside my window as I write in the dark of early morning—for I rise like a farm hand—the rotary snow ploughs on the Côte des Neiges Road are whirling in the air the great blanket of snow that buried Montreal last night. To the north, behind the mountain, the Northern Lights blink on a thousand miles of snow-covered forest and frozen rivers. . . . We are 'sitting pretty' here in Canada. East and West are the two oceans far away; we are backed up against the ice cap of the pole; our feet rest on the fender of the American border, warm with a hundred years of friendship. . . . Thank you, Mother England, I don't think I'll 'come home'. I'm 'home' now.[20]

DISCOVERING CANADIANS

So much for the invention of the Canadian terrain. But writers in this country, like painters, have had more success with landscape than with people. If Hugh Kenner is right, no one hearing this will take it amiss: "The surest way to the hearts of a Canadian audience," Kerner says, "is to inform them that their souls are to be identified with rock, rapids, wilderness, and virgin (but exploitable) forest," and, he adds, "this pathological craving for identification with the subhuman may be illustrated in every department of Canadian culture."[21] It is perhaps significant that the only memorable character produced in nineteenth century Canadian literature was an American, T. C. Haliburton's Sam Slick, the Yankee Clockmaker, whose travels through Nova Scotia clearly showed up the natives as apathetic and indistinct nonentities. In nineteenth century Canada there was apparently no actual or potential crystallization of national characteristics comparable to that which manifested itself, for example, in Henry James's *The American*.

By the twentieth century there is some indication that this very indistinctness, apathy, uncertainty of behaviour, this facelessness, is beginning to be recognized as a national characteristic. It is the Canadian type, one could argue, who is seen in Stephen Leacock's "My Financial Career", the confused and embarrassed little man whose efforts to open his first bank account end in ignominious flight.[22] Or he might be seen in a whole run of awkward, self-conscious, uncertain, priggish heroes populating Hugh MacLennan's novels, or in any of the series of helpless, confused, victimized figures created by Morley Callaghan. I sometimes think that Morley Callaghan himself is his most typically Canadian portrait: at a loss how to behave in front of a lukewarm, skeptical Canadian public, sometimes truculently advancing his claims as a great international writer and friend of the famous, and then withdrawing into self-doubts and despair and silence. Or the national type might be seen in the poet Raymond Souster's shadowy Toronto street-figures, standing at night in doorways smoking cigarettes, filled with desire and nostalgia, while the real energy and will of the world go about their business far away.

We might expect the feeling of passivity and helplessness, the sense of being on the periphery, to be part of the consciousness of a people accustomed to living on the fringes of the British and American spheres of power. Millar MacLure claims that this experience is the key to the Canadian sensibility: "this native sensibility, which I define, very badly I know," he says, "as an acute feeling of being at the edge of things, both in the sense of not being in the middle, where moods and modes are generated, but out where they can be felt, but observed tangentially and ironically, and in the other sense of being poised on the narrow line from which one may fall either in the smother of civilization where the mode is satire or into the wilderness where the mode is panegyric."[23] The poetry of George Johnston is full of the same sense of powerless and peripheral life, and he often speaks in similar tones of mild and affectionate irony. Here, for example, is his "War on the Periphery", which for the purposes of my theme I might sub-title, "portrait of the typical Canadian family":

> Around the battlements go by
> Soldier men against the sky,
> Violent lovers, husbands, sons,
> Guarding my peaceful life with guns.
>
> My pleasures, how discreet they are!
> A little booze, a little car,
> Two little children and a wife
> Living a small suburban life.
>
> My little children eat my heart;
> At seven o'clock we kiss and part,
> At seven o'clock we meet again;
> They eat my heart and grow to men.
>
> I watch their tenderness with fear
> While on the battlements I hear
> The violent, obedient ones
> Guarding my family with guns.[24]

But Canada is a growing and changing country. Perhaps we may find clearer, more fully developed, more positive and powerful national types in current and coming literature, in the work of young writers like Mordecai Richler. Duddy Kravitz, for example, surely has an amount of energy unusual for Canadian fictional heroes. But it may be that he is typical in that he has doubts about what to do with it. He eagerly learns whatever his society has to teach him: to fornicate at every opportunity, to cheat anyone, when you can get away with it, and to make as much money as you can. Here Duddy Kravitz comes to share one of the traditional Canadian preoccupations, fascination with the land. Mordecai Richler has a stronger and clearer sense of the Canadian terrain than Mrs. Brooke or William Kirby, and he is more up-to-date than MacLennan. In Richler's novel, Duddy Kravitz gets possession at last of his portion of the Canadian terrain, a potentially valuable piece of resort real estate

in rural Quebec; he visits it in winter and enjoys a brilliantly com-
mercialized and vulgarized version of an old vision:

> He had to walk the last three-quarters of a mile through deep snow. The
> drifts were soft and often, between rocks, he sunk to his knees. But it gave
> him quite a lift to see his land in winter. A thin scalp of ice protected the
> lake and all his fields glittered white and purple and gold under the setting
> sun. All except the pine trees were bare. It must be pretty in autumn, he
> thought, when all the leaves are changing colours. Duddy saw where he would
> put up the hotel and decided that he would not have to clear the wood all
> out in one shot. It's lovely, he thought, and lots of those pine trees I can
> peddle at Christmas-time. . . . He tried the thin ice on the lake with his foot.
> It cracked. He urinated into a snow bank, writing his name. It's my land, he
> thought.[25]

It may seem that I have come a long way from the subject of Nationalism in Canadian Literature, and perhaps I have. The movement has
been from nationalism towards literature. Writing in this country which
is done for the purpose of encouraging and advertising nationalism
seems to me doomed to shallowness or hypocrisy. Canadian writers who
choose to contemplate their country as a national social, political entity
must do so, unless they are inconceivably simple-minded, with a highly
critical eye; with affection and sympathy if they feel it, but strongly
tempered by irony. Otherwise, their fate at best will be the one described
by Mordecai Richler, to be world famous all over Canada. Canadian
writers will go on with the job of inventing Canada, or holding up the
mirror to their society. But a great deal that they create or reflect is likely
to be unpleasing to the pious. They will show Canadians not reverently
worshipping the beauties and mysteries of their vast homeland on God's
footstool, but digging and exploiting and defacing, buying and selling
the land, urinating and writing their names on pieces of real estate. And
they are likely to show, not valiant Companies of Young Canadians ideal-
istically setting out to fulfil a great national destiny, but weary and
bemused intellectuals like Robertson Davies' innocuous young don,
Solly Bridgetower, exasperated at the utter boredom of having to think
about "Amcan. . . , particularly the Can half."

> Why do countries have to have literatures? Why does a country like Canada,
> so late upon the international scene, feel that it must rapidly acquire the
> trappings of older countries—music of its own, pictures of its own, books of
> its own—and why does it fuss and stew, and storm the heavens with its out-

cries when it does not have them? Solly pondered bitterly upon these problems, knowing full well how firmly he was caught in the strong, close mesh of his country's cultural ambitions.[26]

A country's best writers will often seem subversive, and it is a little difficult to know what the modern paternalistic state should do with a class of its citizenry who may at any time, like James Joyce's Stephen, say *non serviam* and fly by the nets of nationality. Perhaps the only answer, as hard for English Canada as for French Canada, is that a vital society is like a generous parent: it gives life to, supports and nourishes its writers as best it can, but it makes no demands and expects nothing in return except that they try to fulfil their potentialities. Its only reward is the chance to live a little more and to know itself better.

NOTES

1. Arthur Lower, *From Colony to Nation*, Toronto, 1946, p. xiii.
2. Arthur Lower, as cited, p. 561.
3. Irving Layton, "From Colony to Nation", *Collected Poems*, Toronto & Montreal, 1965, pp. 159-160, reprinted by permission of McClelland and Stewart Ltd.
4. A. J. M. Smith, *Canadian Historical Association 1943-1944, Report of Annual Meeting*, Toronto, 1944, p. 74.
5. H. J. Morgan, *Bibliotheca Canadiensis*, Ottawa, 1867, p. viii.
6. E. H. Dewart (ed.), *Selection from Canadian Poets*, Montreal, 1864, p. ix-x.
7. E. H. Dewart, as cited, p. x.
8. Charles Mair, *Tecumseh, A Drama, and Canadian Poems*, Toronto, 1901, p. 3.
9. W. D. Lighthall, *Songs of the Great Dominion*, London, 1889, pp. xxi-xxii.
10. "An Appeal to All Canadians by a Toronto Boy", pamphlet published in Toronto.
11. Pamela S. Vining, "Canada" in *Selections from Canadian Poets*, E. H. Dewart (ed.), Montreal, 1864, pp. 101 ff.
12. Quoted by E. M. Pomeroy, *Sir Charles G. D. Roberts*, Toronto, 1943, p. viii.
13. C. G. D. Roberts, "Canada" in *The Book of Canadian Poetry*, A. J. M. Smith (ed.), Toronto, 1957, p. 167.
14. *The Globe*, Toronto, November 19, 1892.
15. Aldous Huxley, *Texts and Pretexts*, New York & London, 1933, p. 52.
16. E. J. Pratt, "Towards the Last Spike" in *Collected Poems*, 2nd edition, Northrop Frye (ed.), Toronto, 1958, p. 379.
17. L. J. Burpee (ed.), *The History of Emily Montague (1769)*, Ottawa, 1931, p. 12.
18. W. Kirby, *The Golden Dog*, Boston, 1896, p. 4.
19. Hugh MacLennan, *Two Solitudes*, Toronto, 1945, pp. 3-4, reprinted by permission of the Author and the Macmillan Company of Canada Ltd.
20. Stephen Leacock, "I Will Stay in Canada" in *Canadian Anthology*, C. F. Klinck & R. E. Watters (eds.), Toronto, 1957, pp. 212-213.
21. Hugh Kenner, "The Case of the Missing Face" in *Our Sense of Identity*, Malcolm Ross (ed.), Toronto, 1954, p. 203.

22. Stephen Leacock, "My Financial Career" in *Literary Lapses*, Montreal, 1910, pp. 5-9.
23. Millar MacLure, "Smith's House of Fame" in *The Tamarak Review, 17,* Toronto, 1960, pp. 64-65.
24. George Johnston, "War on the Periphery" in *The Cruising Auk,* Toronto, 1959, p. 17.
25. Mordecai Richler, *The Apprenticeship of Duddy Kravitz,* London, Ont., 1959, p. 212.
26. Robertson Davies, *Leaven of Malice,* Toronto, 1954, p. 197.

the nationalist dilemma

in canadian broadcasting • frank peers

Two social forces, often in conflict, have in large part determined our broadcasting system. The first is Canadian nationalism; and the second, a belief held in common with some other liberal democracies, especially the United States, that the most natural and democratic system will allow choices to be made by the processes of the free market.

THE NATIONALIST CASE FOR PUBLIC CONTROL

Nationalist sentiment leads toward the insistence upon Canadian ownership and control of stations and networks; upon full coverage for the scattered population of an immense territory; and upon the use of the media to foster national objectives. The national objectives change from time to time; but those most often suggested as aims appropriate for the broadcasting media are national survival, whether of English Canada or French Canada or Canada as a whole; a Canadian sense of identity; national unity; increased understanding between regions and language groups; cultural development; and the serving of Canadian economic interests. In an earlier period, the stated national objectives often included an identification with British or imperial interests. And throughout, the objective has often been stated negatively, as the developing of an identity separate and distinguishable from that of the United States. Seldom was

Regionalism to loose a term - what basis?
geographic? do not communication links
break regional identity? regionalism a product
of imperfect communications technology?
improvements emanate from metropolis as does
communications network -

— common attitudes of all newspapers in U.S. —
aggressive, careless, etc.
Newspapers - split much less evident on a regional
than on party lines - tendency to toe to party
policy regardless of what might appear to be
regional interests - too much to suggest that
parties - + their organs - where ∴ instruments
of nat'l unity - but it is evident that control
of party organs from central Canada & hence
control of communication important here -
newspapers regarded as vital to party interest
+ newspapers of time took their duties seriously
in a sense then central Canada views were
perpetuated but in sense that control of
communication centred there

∴ not say if region attitudes do not exist -
but rather that region, in hist. terms is not
sufficient explanation for them - that they
can be traced to economic, political, social,
even perhaps geograph. influences that are
not inherent to nor unique to the "region" - ex.
progressive movement.

Moscone

Craig —

Thanks —

Damn good book!

Ken

nationalist sentiment precisely articulated, but it was broader than patriotic jingoism and something more ambiguous than national self-interest. In particular, the differing implications or assumptions in French and in English-speaking Canada were left almost unexplored.

In her article, "The Origins of Public Broadcasting in Canada," Margaret Prang has wisely drawn attention to the fact that radio development in the twenties and thirties took place at a time when the postwar generation of Canadian nationalists felt that their efforts to quicken the cultural pace were bringing results. "Ironically, just when an increasing number of Canadians were involved in the activities of flourishing nation-wide enterprises a revolution in communications, possibly as far reaching in its consequences as the change from wood and wind to iron and steam which had done so much to bring about Confederation itself, was threatening the clearer delineation of a Canadian identity."[1] In the early 1920's almost the only public figure who thought in these terms was Sir Henry Thornton, the president of the CNR. "He saw radio as a great unifying force in Canada; to him the political conception transcended the commercial, and he set out consciously to create a sense of nationhood through the medium of the Canadian National radio service."[2] But as the decade wore on, others expressed concern that American commercial interests were about to gain control of Canadian broadcasting. Here is J. S. Woodsworth speaking in the House of Commons on May 31, 1928:

> It is only a comparatively short time before these small broadcasting stations will be bought up by big American companies. I may be afraid of handing power to any one government, but I would rather trust our own Canadian government with the control of broadcasting than trust these highly organized private commercial companies in the United States.[3]

Even before this, the editor of the *Ottawa Citizen*, Charles Bowman, had started a campaign to establish a system of national ownership and national control. Bowman became one of the three members of the royal commission appointed in 1928 to advise the government on the future control of broadcasting. The chairman, Sir John Aird, president of the Canadian Bank of Commerce, was predisposed toward a system of private station ownership and operation but, according to Bowman, upon visiting the headquarters of the American networks in New York, Aird was shocked by their frank assumption that Canada was within the American broadcasting orbit.[4] Although naturally pro-British, Aird had regarded the British Broadcasting Corporation as a "stilted, civil service kind of thing." When the Commission visited London, Aird was impressed with the enterprise shown by the management of the BBC, and especially by Sir John Reith; the engineer who was the third member of the Commission (Dr. Augustin Frigon) was impressed with the technical proficiency of the British Corporation. After their trip abroad, the Commission toured Canada and became convinced, as the Report said, that above all, "Canadian radio listeners want Canadian broadcasting."[5] The Commission concluded that the interests of Canadian listeners and of the Canadian nation could be adequately served only by some form of public ownership, operation, and control "behind which is the national power and prestige of the whole public of the Dominion of Canada."

Following the presentation of the Aird Report in 1929 there was a two and a half year hiatus caused by a federal election campaign, a change of government, and a constitutional dispute between Ottawa and Quebec (supported by Ontario) as to whether broadcasting was under federal or provincial jurisdiction. The group which brought broadcasting again to the fore as a public issue and forced a decision was the Canadian Radio League, under the leadership of Graham Spry, Alan Plaunt, Brooke Claxton, Father St. Denis, E. A. Corbett, Georges Pelletier, and others.[6] Although their central concern was, in short, better broadcasting, they discovered very early that the most powerful public appeal they could exercise was a national one. This was expressed in such tags as "Canadian radio for Canadians " and "The state or the United States", Graham Spry, the first president of the Radio League, explained in 1935 that there were two motives that led to the broadcasting legislation in 1932: "The first of these driving motives was the national motive, and it was predominant. The second motive was the free use of broadcasting by all sections of opinion. The positive aspect of the national motive was the use of broadcasting for the development of Canadian national unity, and the negative aspect was the apprehension of American influences upon Canadian nationality, particularly as it concerned public opinion."[7]

Statements bearing out the nationalist intention of the broadcasting legislation of 1932, 1936 and 1958 can be found in parliamentary debates, in the proceedings of broadcasting committees, and in the royal commissions headed by Vincent Massey and Robert Fowler. The first parliamentary committee on radio in 1932 spoke of broadcasting as a medium for "developing a greater National and Empire consciousness within the

Dominion and the British Commonwealth of Nations", and the "fostering of Canadian ideals and culture, entertainment, news service and publicity of this country and its products."[8] Prime Minister Bennett, introducing the 1932 legislation, said: "This country must be assured of complete Canadian control of broadcasting from Canadian sources, free from foreign interference or influence." Broadcasting must become an agency by which "national consciousness may be fostered and sustained and national unity still further strengthened."[9] The Massey Commission listed three objectives of the national system: "an adequate coverage of the entire population, opportunities for Canadian talent and for Canadian self-expression generally, and successful resistance to the absorption of Canada into the general cultural pattern of the United States."[10] The Fowler Commission in 1957 saw a choice between "a Canadian state-controlled system with some flow of programmes east and west across Canada, with some Canadian content and the development of a Canadian sense of identity, at a substantial public cost, and a privately owned system which the forces of economics will necessarily make predominantly dependent on imported American radio and television programmes."[11]

FREE ENTERPRISE AND THE GROWTH OF PRIVATE BROADCASTING

The second force determining Canadian broadcasting policy is the belief that broadcasting is best carried on as an economic enterprise with the minimum of government interference. Allied to this is the belief that there is a close analogy between the competitive market system and the process of liberal-democratic government. It is felt that the broadcasting system is "democratic" if individuals are allowed to enter the field so far as physical and other conditions permit, with the least possible restraint from any centralized authority; it is even more "democratic" if all other individuals can choose the programmes they receive from a multiplicity of offerings; and it is more "democratic" still if such choices have a direct effect on the ways in which entrepreneurs are rewarded or penalized—that is, through the sale of goods or the maximization of profits. This kind of belief is implicit in a justification of the United States broadcasting system, written by Professor Hettinger in 1935:

> The program service offered by American broadcasting is unusually complete. It is typically American, adapted to national conditions, the broadcaster giving the public those programs which constant research and direct expres-

sion of opinion indicate to be most popular. It is necessary that he do this if he is to build station and network circulation with which to attract advertisers.

The democratic control of programs is by no means a perfect one, though there is probably no better method available. It possesses all the strengths and weaknesses of democracy operating in the social and political fields. Democratic control of programs implies control by the listening majority.[12]

As a more recent analyst of the American broadcasting system has pointed out, the broadcasting patterns produced by the market economy are often represented as "natural and inevitable. . . In the United States, radio quickly became an adjunct to the mass production way of life, accommodating itself quite easily to the requirements and priorities of its developers and promoters."[13]

In Canada few except the broadcasters themselves have been so explicit about the belief that broadcasting is an economic activity, a business, like any other.[14] This belief implies that broadcasting is in reality part of the advertising industry. It was much more difficult to persuade opinion leaders in Canada that broadcasting based on an assumption of this kind was (in Hettinger's words) "adapted to national conditions." Canadian broadcasting began on the same basis as that in the United States, but a drastic modification seemed essential when it was found that such a system did not provide adequate coverage for Canada's population; and that with the establishment of networks and the centralization of programme production, the logical outcome was for Canadian broadcasting to become a mere extension of that centred in New York.

This realization led to a coalition of interests seeking to change the system—educators who felt that the full potential of radio had been unrealized; business men who wanted to prevent American industry from gaining control of the programme and advertising content; newspapers who regarded any form of radio advertising as a threat; labour leaders who were suspicious of business control of stations and networks; farm organizations who were concerned about coverage and a better programme service for rural areas; French Canadians who realized that radio development had been far less rapid in Quebec than in Ontario, and that the growing dominance of American programmes was a threat to their own language and culture. The efforts of these disparate interests were organized and fused by the skilful leadership of the group calling themselves the Canadian Radio League. The result was the Canadian Radio Broadcasting

Act of 1932 which created the Canadian Radio Commission, and the Act of 1936 which abolished the Commission and substituted the Canadian Broadcasting Corporation. Both Acts intended the publicly created authority in the system to be dominant, not only in a regulatory but in an operational sense. Privately owned stations were to continue, but they were to have a strictly local function and they were to be regulated by the Radio Commission or the CBC Board of Governors. Networks could not be formed except by their authority.

Yet the public sector of broadcasting never became as dominant as the founders of the system hoped. Although many battles were fought, the balance between public and private broadcasters remained fairly stable until 1945: the Depression and World War II gave Canadians a live sense of broadcasting as a "public service". But in the period of relaxation following the war, the private broadcasters were able to make more headway. Increasingly, during the last ten years, the private stations have assumed a dominant position. Increases in the power of private radio stations were strictly limited until 1945, when a number of thousand-watt stations received permission to go up to 5,000 watts. In 1949 another hole was punched in the dike when CFRB Toronto was authorized to raise its power to 50,000 watts, thus ending any pretence that private stations were local stations only, with the express function of providing an alternative programme service to their immediate community. The number of private radio stations increased rapidly after 1945. Their total power now far exceeds that of the CBC regional transmitters. The story is the same in television, where there is a private station in each city in which the CBC is established, and many others in cities where the CBC is not operating.

With a new broadcasting Act in 1958, private stations were removed from CBC jurisdiction and placed under another public body, a regulatory board only, the Board of Broadcast Governors. Theoretically the BBG has equal authority over the CBC and the private broadcasters; the intention was that Canada have a single broadcasting system. In fact, there now seems to be a dual system, although the line of demarcation is not clear, as it is in Australia. The CBC has its own board of directors to establish policy and to operate its own network; but the CBC network still depends on private affiliates to distribute commercial and sustaining programmes to the entire country. The other system is made up entirely of private or commercial stations, for whom the regulations of the BBG in practice as well as in theory provide minimum standards. These stations may, by permission of the BBG, join together to form private networks, and one such network (CTV) functions on a continuing basis.

THE NATIONAL SYSTEM IN ECLIPSE

. How has it come about that the system favoured by the Canadian Radio League, given almost unanimous sanction by the House of Commons, translated into legislation by a Conservative and then by a Liberal government, approved and reinforced by numerous parliamentary committees and two royal commissions, lies almost in ruins? Why have the hopes of the founders been so shattered? Graham Spry, the founder of the Canadian Radio League, speaks of "the decline and fall of Canadian broadcasting". He writes: "The Canadian system, except only in the non-commercial, sustaining programs and the network services of the Canadian Broadcasting Corporation, is then essentially an imitation or replica of the American system. . . The dominant part of Canadian broadcasting is the privately owned sector. . . The Canadian audience is a minor part of the American advertising market."[15] The dominant position of the private sector is revealed whether the measurement is by the number and power of stations, size of area covered, audience, or amount of money poured into the system. In fact, the private stations are predominant in every way except in the production of programmes.

The answer to our question "How come?" lies not in terms of the legislation placed upon the statute books, not even in the Act of 1958. A clue to the answer is to be found in our holding two objectives simultaneously that are barely compatible: the objective of a broadcasting system that will serve the ends of the national community, and the objective of a system that will serve private owners and advertising interests. If private owners could produce programmes that could compete on equal terms with programmes from external (that is, American) sources, or even if the industrial sector of the economy were predominantly Canadian, a private system might conceivably be shaped to serve national objectives. But neither condition obtains. The first is not even within the realm of possibility, given the penetration of the Canadian audience by programmes broadcast by our richer and more powerful neighbour. This factor cannot be changed by Canadian fiat.

Tactically, the system has been changed through the unrelenting pressure of interests which stood to benefit directly the more the pendulum swung away from the public authority. Their pressure was not adequately countered by the resistance of other groups which had a less direct interest and exerted themselves only sporadically. Private broadcasters found important allies among business interests (who were tempted to give support not so much out of financial self-interest as out of ideology), local Members of Parliament, and some newspapers (especially those with commercial broadcasting licenses). The private Member of Parliament commonly identified the local station with constituency interests. On the rare occasions when a broadcasting issue was submitted to a vote, he would as a rule vote with his party; but at other times he often supported the interests of a particular station. In parliamentary committees, his voice would be heard asking for more leeway for the private station owner.[16] One searches the parliamentary record in vain to find an example of an M.P. denouncing or even criticizing the local stations in his area.

But more fundamental than the tactics of the private stations in explaining the continued weakening of the public sector in broadcasting is the popular preference for American programmes and acceptance of the advertising rationale which accompanies them. Canadians are not alone in showing a fascination for the product of the American entertainment industries; we find a similar fascination among British and Australian television viewers, and elsewhere in the western world. But because of our adjacency to the United States, the effects are intensified in Canada, and the mixed system we have adopted has left the public sector peculiarly vulnerable. The American television programme is often bound, either contractually or psychologically, to its sponsor. American advertisers may make the programme available on very attractive terms to their Canadian subsidiaries, or, if the programme can be sold to any advertiser, the Canadian network, CBC or CTV, will find other sponsors. Unlike the BBC, the CBC will probably not consider scheduling American entertainment programmes without a sponsor. The Canadian public has grown to accept advertising as an accompaniment to entertainment; tastes are created, and the act of creation does not stop at the Canadian border. The acceptance of an American pattern of programming on the CBC is rationalized as providing a supplementary source of revenue, thus putting more money into the creation of Canadian programmes; as allowing the CBC network to compete with CTV stations and with neighbouring American stations for audience; as enabling Canadian business to compete with American companies; and as a way of securing fuller and more economical distribution for Canadian programmes through the private station affiliates. The perplexing thing is that there is real substance to each of these rationalizations.

FUTURE ALTERNATIVES—THE NEED FOR A SINGLE CANADIAN BROADCASTING SYSTEM

In our mixed system (in which there is public and private ownership, and both commercial and non-commercial elements within the public system) the responsibility for achieving national objectives through broadcasting is placed principally on the CBC. The public recognizes that the managers of private stations and the private network see their primary responsibility as being to their shareholders, whereas the CBC exists to provide a public service. This difference in public expectations makes it even more likely that if we continue a "two-board" set-up, we shall move toward two separate broadcasting systems. This indeed was advocated in a statement submitted to the Secretary of State in 1964 by the then president of the Canadian Association of Broadcasters, Don Jamieson. Parliament must spell out in more detail what is expected of the CBC, but "the local station is in a better position than any regulatory board, or other agency, to determine the needs of its coverage area or 'community'. It makes sense, therefore, to have stations define their responsibilities themselves."[17] The regulatory board would then have the functions of allocating frequencies and seeing that the licensees carried out their intention as stated at the time of application.

Since 1958 the regulatory authority, the BBG, has tried to impose certain social responsibilities on the private stations and networks. But evidence from other countries (and indeed from our own history) suggests that this effort will have very limited success. In Great Britain the Independent Television Authority, a public board set up to regulate private television, has had to deal with only four major programme companies and a small number of regional companies. It has not had conspicuous success. The Pilkington Committee in 1960 concluded that "as independent television is now constituted and organised, the Authority's power to control the companies . . . is illusory and negligible. . . . Because the regulatory function is separated from the creative function of programme planning and production, it is negative and prohibitive. The initiative is held by . . . the four major companies. The positive and creative activity essential for a good service of broadcasting is theirs. This essential cannot be generally compelled by the exercise of regulatory powers. Nor do we believe that a regulatory body, not organically involved in planning and production, can develop a sufficiently perceptive comprehension of the creative aspect."[18]

A regulatory board, in this field as in others, tends to identify with those whom it regulates. J. K. Galbraith observes that after a matter of ten or fifteen years, regulatory boards become (with some exceptions) "either an arm of the industry they are regulating or senile."[19] Even if the Board of Broadcast Governors adheres rigidly to its regulation that there must be at least 55% Canadian content in any television station's programmes, we know that this is unlikely to affect materially the nature or quality of the programme service offered.

Yet with no regulation at all, no attempt to establish national responsibilities for all Canadian stations, private television becomes essentially an outlet for New York and Hollywood, because U.S. network or syndicated programmes are so much cheaper than anything that can be produced locally. If, then, the CBC has to compete not only with American networks but with a carbon copy in each Canadian community as well, the outcome can only be a further weakening of its programming. Unbridled competition for audiences means that profundity of treatment or subject matter, variety and experiment give way to those qualities that quickly produce high ratings—imitativeness, facile entertainment appeal, superficial novelty. The trend is already in evidence on CBC television. Further deterioration will take place if we officially recognize two separate broadcasting systems.

The report of the Fowler Committee in 1965 has the great virtue of recognizing that Canadian broadcasting, despite its private and public sectors, should form *one* system, and should be under the direction and control of a single public agency. It adduces other reasons. In the foreseeable future the CBC cannot secure full distribution for its programmes through CBC facilities alone. Canada cannot yet afford both a complete publicly-owned system (television and radio, English and French) and a duplicate private system entirely separate from the publicly-owned network, with each serving the same audiences, French and English, by AM, FM, and TV—in colour as well as in black and white! The public and private sectors therefore require co-ordination and even a measure of integration. Each must share in the common purposes which Canadians have decided are reasonable objectives for their broadcasting system. Each must in some degree be held accountable in the carrying out of its responsibilities. The Fowler Committee concludes that "jurisdiction of a mixed and inter-related system cannot be divided between two boards without each of them being stultified. A single national purpose will not be achieved by entrusting it to two separate agencies."[20]

We will have to maintain a mixture of public and private station operation, but strengthen public authority and subordinate the private sector once again. A dangerous alternative is sometimes suggested, particularly in academic circles. According to this view, the way to restore standards in Canadian broadcasting is to make the CBC into a self-sufficient network and to remove all advertising from its programme service. This has the virtue of simplicity. It is roughly the system that the Australians have—a publicly-owned, non-commercial system, the Australian Broadcasting Commission, and a system of private stations, under the authority of a regulatory board. What is the result? The standards of the private television stations are even more dubious than ours; there are in fact no "Australian content" regulations. The ABC has a long uphill fight to win audiences. Most surveys agree that in the four large Australian cities, ABC television secures only about 15 per cent of the viewing audience in prime time.[21] This happens in a country which is not adjacent to the United States, where the audience cannot be divided among additional choices provided by two or three American networks. The result of such a "logical" division of programmes between private and public broadcasters would be disastrous in Canada. The CBC's audience would be decimated and money would have to be diverted from production into the provision of more station outlets. The CBC would become rather like the National Film Board, an organization of undoubted worth and prestige, but having about as much influence on the viewing habits of the Canadian public as the Film Board has on the movie-going habits of the average Canadian.

For it is time to say that in spite of the opposition that has been mounted against it, in spite of the continental influences which have weakened the system our governments thought they were establishing, in spite of the CBC's own mistakes and shortcomings, the Corporation has served this country well—never better than in those periods when direction, enlightenment and entertainment were acutely needed. It has given its public—many of whom are immigrants, many of whom have been making the difficult transition from farm to city—a sense of national awareness without glossing over the schisms in Canadian life and without imposing a narrow doctrinaire nationalism. It has provided coverage to sections of the country that would otherwise have been neglected. It has helped in the development of Canadian talent; it has stimulated a wide range of cultural activities, and created new audiences for them. It has provided a forum for the expression of Canadian opinion, drawing on a much larger segment of the population than have the American networks, which ordinarily rely on their own professionals. It has given regions of Canada a chance to know about each other, if not necessarily to like one another better. It has probably heightened a sense of English-Canadian identity; it has without doubt reinforced the sense of French-Canadian identity. It has not been noticeably successful in increasing understanding between French- and English-speaking Canadians, though it is too early to say that it has entirely failed. French and English separatism have too many causes for any communications system to remedy.

To say all this is not to say that most programmes have had a consciously nationalist purpose. Statistically, few programmes show that this has been their intention. I do not agree with Melville Watkins who argues elsewhere in this volume that the broadcasting media have been used "in a largely futile attempt to foster nationalism."[22] Of course nationalism is implicit in all forms of communication; it is a question of what kind of nationalism, or of its quality. There is the nationalism of the United States in a system of free enterprise; there is the nationalism of France or the U.S.S.R., where broadcasting is an instrument of government policies; there is the nationalism of Great Britain, where broadcasting has often reflected class interests. The nationalism of the CBC is still another pattern. It has illustrated the Canadian concern for survival but has not tried to deny that Canadians are part of a North American society. The programmes of the CBC, or some of them, have dealt with Canadian topics and Canadian problems, but not to the exclusion of information or entertainment values that originate elsewhere. The selection of programmes has not been dictated either out of concern for a nationalist ideology or by the simple processes of the market. The nationalism of the CBC has been of a peculiarly pragmatic kind, with all the strengths and weaknesses that implies. But it clearly cannot be depended upon to continue in this fashion unless there is wise and informed public opinion, especially on the nature of "nationalism."

In practice few broadcasters have been made enthusiastic by a nationalist ideal. Most of them are now concerned with concepts that cannot be confined within national boundaries, and they want their programmes to reflect these concepts. It might be argued that more programmes in French Canada have been produced with nationalist ends in view. Even here I suspect that the nationalist tinge comes not so much from ingredients consciously placed in the programmes as from the social milieu.

The differences between French Canada and English Canada have posed particular problems for the national broadcasting system. As media in which language is central, broadcasting has to be organized separately for the two language groups. In the past, some national agencies and government departments have, within their organization and administration, ignored the French-speaking minority, and this fact may have escaped notice for years or generations. The CBC could not do this. French Canadians have always had a prominent place on the Board and in the management of CBC. The programme service centred in Montreal had to provide at least as many hours each week as the service centred in Toronto—usually more. But in spite of long familiarity with the problems created by two languages within a single organization, the CBC is still far from solving them. For many years there have been essentially two production groups, which people in Montreal refer to as "the CBC" and "Radio-Canada". They are both administered by headquarters staff in Ottawa, but almost inevitably the majority in the Ottawa head-office pay more attention to the English networks than they do to the French. In spite of attempts at co-ordination, policies for the two language services differ at least in the way they are interpreted.

A number of French Canadians (some within the CBC) would prefer provincial to federal ownership and control. They are aware of the key role that Radio-Canada has played in the development of their national consciousness, but they think an institution with headquarters in Ottawa cannot be "their own". It is conceivable that a desire for a provincial broadcasting system may develop in Ontario, British Columbia and Alberta. (Most provinces cannot contemplate the public expenditure that a television system would entail.) So far, the regulatory authority has refused to agree to outright provincial ownership of commercial stations. Aside from the unevenness of services that would result from provincial systems substituting for a national system, there are other considerations that should give us pause. The tradition of a non-partisan broadcasting corporation has been hard enough to establish on a federal scale; it would be nearly impossible within our provinces. In most provinces the opposition parties are weak, the provincial assemblies are in session only a short time each year, and the tradition of non-partisan public corporations hardly exists. If the young reformers in Quebec are tempted to support provincial control, they should ask what system they would have with a Duplessis in power.

In fact, there are always dangers in having broadcasting closely allied with government. The temptations for the party in power to attempt to influence the broadcasting authority are very great. One of the best protections for both the regulating board and the programming group is to maintain a close connection with the variety of interests that the service is supposed to reflect and comment on. Such a pluralistic concept does not mean that the broadcaster should abdicate his professional role of planning programmes; much less should he hand a veto power to interest groups. But his programmes will have more relevance and he will communicate better, if he knows his audience. And he will be less likely to give undue attention to those pressure groups which have easiest access— the Government, the Members of Parliament and the press.

Now let us return to what we have called the two dominant forces in shaping the Canadian broadcasting system—nationalism and the belief in the market system. The second, unless it is checked by the first, will clearly lead to a subordination of the Canadian system to the American, if not complete absorption. Nationalism has been a protection, ensuring that the Canadian community will retain some possibility of directing broadcasting in a way that will serve our own particular ends. Yet it is clear that Canadians, individually and collectively, are torn between the objectives of having their own distinct system and of sharing in the values of the system that is dominant on the North American continent. This ambivalence is reflected in our individual choices. On the one hand, Canadians tune in to American programmes in larger numbers than they do to Canadian productions. On the other hand, surveys show that an overwhelming majority of Canadians approve of the goals which they identify with the CBC, and a substantial majority think that the CBC is fulfilling those aims well.[23]

Nationalism has been a potent force in creating a distinctly Canadian broadcasting system, and to some extent in preventing its absorption into the general continental pattern. But nationalism is not in itself a satisfactory objective for broadcasting. Like other media of communication, broadcasting should serve to sharpen people's awareness of their own society (which transcends their national community) and of their needs as human beings. It should facilitate desirable social change. Nationalism is too narrow a sentiment to be at all times compatible with these more universal aims. Yet if we wish broadcasting to have a comprehensive social objective, we must make sure that control is not alienated to a group of powerful individuals in our own country or, even more important, to powerful interests in another country. Canadian broadcasting cannot totally reject the programme and advertising elements that are dominant in American broadcasting; we are too much a part of American society for that. Neither does Canadian broadcasting have to be identical with American. Because the continental forces, especially the economic forces, are so strong, we must consciously make it a national policy to maintain our own broadcasting system. We may even hope (though this is perhaps utopian) that, under wise leadership, Canadians may discard the unworthy concept of broadcasting as primarily a market process, substituting more completely an ideal of communication and public service.

NOTES

1. M. Prang, "The Origins of Public Broadcasting in Canada", *Canadian Historical Review*, 1965, p. 3.
2. D'Arcy Marsh, *The Tragedy of Henry Thornton*, Toronto, 1935, p. 116.
3. *House of Commons Debates*, May 31, 1928, p. 3622.
4. Alan Thomas interview with C. A. Bowman, February 18, 1960. Tape recording on file in CBC Toronto Program Archives.
5. *Report of the Royal Commission on Radio Broadcasting*, Ottawa, 1929, p. 6.
6. The development and tactics of this remarkable organization are traced in a doctoral dissertation by J. E. O'Brien, "A History of the Canadian Radio League", University Microfilms, Ann Arbor, 1964.
7. G. Spry, "Radio Broadcasting and Aspects of Canadian-American Relations", in Carnegie Endowment for International Peace, Conference on Canadian-American Affairs, Canton, N.Y., June 17-22, 1935, McLaren, Corey and Trotter (eds.), *Proceedings*, New York, 1936, p. 107.
8. *House of Commons Debates*, May 9, 1932, p. 2709.
9. *House of Commons Debates*, May 18, 1932, p. 3035.
10. *Report of the Royal Commission on National Development in the Arts, Letters and Sciences*, Ottawa, 1951, pp. 40-41.
11. *Report of the Royal Commission on Broadcasting*, 1957, Ottawa, 1957, p. 10.
12. H. S. Hettinger, *The Annals of the American Academy of Political and Social Science*, Philadelphia, 1935, p. 11.
13. H. I. Schiller, "The Radio Spectrum as an Unexplored Natural Resource for Eco-

nomic Development", a paper delivered before the National Institute of Social and Behavioral Science, Montreal, December 28, 1964; mimeo., pp. 3-4.

14. A fairly explicit statement of this view is contained in testimony before the 1934 broadcasting committee by H. Sedgwick, manager of Station CFRB, Toronto. 1934 Special Committee on the Operations of the Commission under the Canadian Radio Broadcasting Act, 1932 (as amended), *Minutes of Proceedings and Evidence,* Ottawa, 1934, p. 335.

15. G. Spry, "The Decline and Fall of Canadian Broadcasting", *Queen's Quarterly,* Vol. 68, (Summer, 1961) , pp. 213, 214, 216.

16. An exception should be made for the private members belonging to the CCF or (later) the NDP, who have upheld the primacy of the public agency, partly for ideological reasons. But a recent deputy leader of the NDP, Douglas Fisher, takes a different position from his fellows. He believes that the CBC may soon be an unnecessary part of the broadcasting system. Private stations will furnish entertainment, ETV stations will look after "the worthy field of education", and the province of Quebec will assume responsibility for the French network; with these, plus a regulatory board, we will have the essentials of the new system. In other words, nearly an exact copy of the American system. (See his column for July 17, 1965, which appeared in the Toronto *Telegram* under the head, "Educational TV Will Toll CBC Death Bell".)

17. Don Jamieson, "The Role of Broadcasters", mimeographed copy of statement submitted to the Secretary of State, p. 30. Statement was tabled in the House of Commons, May 25, 1964.

18. *Report of the Committee on Broadcasting,* 1960, London, Cmnd. 1753, pp. 166, 168.

19. J. K. Galbraith, *The Great Crash, 1929,* Boston, 1961, p. 171.

20. *Report of the Committee on Broadcasting,* Ottawa, 1965, pp. 97-98.

21. *Measuring Media No. 1* (Research Division of *The Australian Women's Weekly*) , Sydney, 1965, pp. 59-60. Figures for 1964 vary from 8% to 12%. There were two commercial stations and one ABC station in each city.

22. See below, Melville Watkins, "Technology and Nationalism", pp. 291 and 297-8.

23. The most complete survey of public attitudes to the CBC was carried out in 1962 by Canadian Facts Limited on behalf of the CBC Research department. (*What the Canadian Public Thinks of the CBC,* Canadian Broadcasting Corporation, Ottawa, 1963.) About 90 per cent of respondents considered that six objectives listed for the CBC were "important" or "very important". About 93 per cent thought the CBC fulfilled "well" or "very well" the function of letting people know "what's happening in the world today". Of the other five aims, the one which CBC was thought to have filled least well was that of helping French-speaking and English-speaking Canadians to understand and learn about each other.

NEW PERSPECTIVES •

metropolitanism

and nationalism • maurice careless

Nationalism and metropolitanism are two of the most significant phenomena in modern history. The importance of the first admits of no question, and as for the second, wherein large areas and populations are focused on great urban communities, one authority has declared: "The dominance of the economic metropolis is the basic feature of the organization of modern society".[1] But the relations between nationalism and metropolitanism are much a matter of query. This paper will seek to examine some of the aspects of that question, particularly as they relate to Canadian historical experience.

In general, it might be said that there are no simple causal relations to be readily established between nationalism and metropolitanism. Sometimes they seem to work in the same direction, when one promotes the other; sometimes in opposite directions—and, in a sense, even in reaction to each other. Some broad examples might illustrate the point. The rise of English nationalism, for instance, was associated with the rise of the English trading classes and of England's world trading metropolis, London, in the course of the seventeenth century. In France, the organizing, dominating power of Paris, the metropolis, had a good deal to do with the triumph of the French nation over French dynasticism and localism in the eighteenth century. On the other hand, American nationalism was, in part at least, a reaction to the metropolitan dominance, economic

and political, of Great Britain. One might also see the extending, penetrating power of metropolitanism as doing much to awaken nationalism,
in reaction to imperialism, in colonial Africa and Asia in the present
century. Furthermore, the economic nationalism expressed in movements
for protective tariffs in nineteenth-century Canada or Australia may be
considered as a response to the dominance of external metropolitan
centres.

One might merely say, in fact, that the forces of metropolitanism and
nationalism work in conjunction when the metropolitan power falls
within the viable national unit, and in opposition or reaction when the
metropolis acts externally on an area that is a potential national territory
in itself. Yet this notably vague generalization partly begs the question
and partly fails to cover all the aspects of an obviously complicated case.
What, for example, of Germany or Italy? Both produced powerful and
successful movements of national unification without clear evidence of a
dominant metropolitan power. Berlin was Prussia's capital and key city
at the time of unification, but surely not the metropolis of Germany.
Rome came within the Italian nation-state only after the latter's creation.
And it is not easy to link nationalism in vast, sprawling countries like
Russia or China to the emergence of well-organized metropolitan systems.

It may be, of course, that the two concepts fall in categories that are
too divergent for them to be usefully considered together. Nationalism
Hans Kohn has shortly defined as "a state of mind". It is at root a "psycho-
cultural", or better, an emotional and ideological manifestation. On the
other hand, metropolitanism is basically a socio-economic phenomenon.
Can they be effectively related? There are problems, certainly, yet also
cause for trying. In the first place, their fields of reference overlap: while
nationalism has its obvious political, social and economic connotations,
metropolitanism can deal with cultural and ideological factors as well.
In the second place, they have developed so widely and often so coin-
cidentally throughout modern society, that it almost seems unreasonable
not to try to examine them together. The answer, no doubt, is to consider
them first in relation to particular modern societies, that is, in regard to
individual national units. Some general pattern may be developed later,
but with the historian's devotion to the particular I propose in this
paper to discuss them chiefly with reference to but one country—Canada,
of course.

THE SIGNIFICANCE OF METROPOLITANISM

Before proceeding, it is necessary to amplify somewhat on the metropolitan concept, so that we might more readily see the relationship between metropolitan and nationalist development in Canada. This requires a survey of the character of metropolitanism as it has been described and as it appears to me.

Briefly, in N.S.B. Gras' basic formulation, the metropolis is seen as a large city that dominates a wide area, or hinterland, through furnishing that area with market transportation, manufacturing and financial facilities all focused on the metropolis.[2] The consequent metropolitan economy is an organization of mutually dependent producers and consumers, whose wants are chiefly supplied through the paramount city, which is the hub of local trade and the centre of normal relations with the world outside. There may also be numerous lesser, subordinate cities in the hinterland—the region or regions dominated by the metropolis—and these cities may in turn be the dominating centres of their own sub-regions. Indeed, R. D. Mackenzie referred to the metropolitan region *in toto* as a "constellation of centres".[3] This astral analogy may be appropriate in that it suggests a kind of universe of metropolitanism, in which the various star-centres have numerous planets about them, which in turn have satellites, the whole system being organized in patterns of attraction.

But I would prefer a less ethereal and more earthbound historical analogy for metropolitanism: the feudal system. For this especially implies organic interdependent relations. A metropolis may dominate its vassal regional centres which have their own vassals and estates about them, but each remains fundamentally dependent on its subordinate communities. Metropolitan dominance does not mean unilateral influence, as Gras made clear himself. It functions through reciprocal relations, as did feudalism. And incidentally, this latter analogy (which plainly must not be pressed too far) has the further advantage of suggesting not the set, mathematical order of astronomy but the mutable and inexact relationships of human institutions.

Since the basic work of Gras and Mackenzie, economists, sociologists, geographers and others have developed various aspects of the metropolitan concept, in accordance with their own fields of inquiry. Indeed, since the late 1940's the S.M.A. (Standard Metropolitan Area) has been widely applied as a concept in statistical analysis by American government agencies, while on both sides of the Atlantic attention has been given to evolving measures for determining the growth, extent and characteristics of metropolitan organization. But without going into such varied measures of metropolitan dominance as trade and market areas, industrial location, bank-loan distribution or newspaper circulation, I would like to emphasize the critical importance of communications in any consideration of metropolitanism. Here, of course, I build on the work of Harold Innis, who is owed much in this field as in many others.[4]

Metropolitan dominance is, after all, exercised through lines of communication radiating from the chief city to the hinterland by way of sub-centres throughout the pattern. Whatever the importance of capital and labour supply, or the distribution of energy and resources, the emergence of the whole metropolitan system requires the development of a network of effective communications centred on the urban core. What the sea-lanes and the Indiaman meant to London, the Erie canal and barge could mean to New York, and the railroad to Chicago, at various stages in their history. The Roman road carrying the *imperium* and the automotive highway carrying the Imperial might both be deemed vital to the growth and spread of metropolitan power.

Furthermore, lines of communication transmit people and their ideas and customs as well as material goods. In this sense, physical transport must be comprehended within communications, as part of the whole variety of what we have learned to call media. For the sailing craft that carried Puritanism to New England with their cargoes, or the Canadian Pacific that brought twentieth-century technology almost overnight to empty north-western plains, were no less media-instruments than the written papyrus, the printed book, or the television programme. All are, in Marshall McLuhan's terms, extensions of man.[5] All have transmitted influences to reshape the human environment. And that environment, clearly, has both material and non-material aspects, all affected by complexes of communications increasingly organized about metropolitan centres. Viewed in this light, metropolitan dominance is seen as being based on the control of communications, which can influence virtually every aspect of life in the hinterland to a greater or lesser degree.

From this perspective metropolitanism is seen as having attributes far wider than the purely economic. One can speak of a centralized political system as expressing predominant metropolitan power, of Hollywood as a cultural metropolis—defining culture broadly—or, without derogation, of Rome as a spiritual metropolis with a world-wide system of its own. They all exercise their own central dominance through control of radiating means of communication, whether these be constitutional machinery, the motion picture, or the transcendent ties of faith. But this may seem transcendental metropolitanism indeed. All I really need to indicate is that the metropolitan concept, examined in terms of communications, suggests affinities with all sorts of aspects of human life and institutions. And thus it can be the more readily related with that other pervasive element in modern life and institutions—nationalism—even in its "psycho-cultural" sense.

Now at last it is time to turn to Canada directly, and apply this version of the metropolitan concept to the study of Canadian nationalism. I propose to do so, first, in regard to the initial appearance of metropolitanism in French Canada, and next, in regard to its later origin and development in English Canada. What I have to say will inevitably take the form of generalizations. These may leave out accepted facts in one instance and only restate them in another. But I still hope that the result will be a fresh perspective—one that may invite further, more exacting inquiry into the history of metropolitanism in Canada.

THE METROPOLIS IN FRENCH-CANADIAN NATIONALISM

In respect to French Canada, Fernand Ouellet has convincingly refuted the thesis held by some of its leading historians, from traditional providential nationalists like Groulx to social-scientific neo-nationalists like Brunet, that French-Canadian nationalism originated in New France and was moulded in the immediate post-conquest era.[6] Granted, the development of a distinctive French-speaking colony on the St. Lawrence and its transfer to alien British rule created the *potential* for a French-Canadian nationalism; still, national aspirations and incipient national consciousness in French Canada did not really originate until the early nineteenth century. These sentiments were then primarily associated with the emergence of a new middle class lay élite in the two chief Lower Canadian towns, now fast growing—Quebec and Montreal.

Unlike the older seigneurial élite, or the French-Canadian mercantile group in the fur trade (which, as Ouellet demonstrates, did *not* disappear after the Conquest, despite Brunet's claims of "social decapitation"), this newer group was disadvantaged. Educated professional men, they lacked economic vested interest and political influence.

The seigneurs of the country had had their property and position confirmed by imperial policy under the Quebec Act, while rural areas had prospered with the growth of wheat production directed to the British market. The French fur interests were part of a distant hinterland trade that fostered ethnic collaboration, not conflict; the rise of the North West Company, that made the Canadian trade essentially an English-directed enterprise, did not so much destroy, as overtake and pass French mercantile activity. In other words, these older French-Canadian interests had fitted fairly smoothly into the framework of a British metropolitan system based on London.

But the newly emerging French professional group did not. With no place in the system, they reacted against it. In the urban centres they took up a means of communication comparatively little developed in Canada till then, the newspaper. Beginning with *Le Canadien* in 1806, they used it both to support a growing political struggle against metropolitan authority and to spread an increasing French-Canadian self-consciousness outward from the towns. Montreal, more than Quebec, became the centre of this movement, perhaps because the impact of British metropolitanism was greater there. Quebec was the seat of an unaggressive—indeed, defensive—imperial political authority. But Montreal was the dynamic outpost of London business interests, and its own English-speaking business community was fast developing, challenging French Canada's social order with designs for capitalist commercial expansion, costly canal building and the promotion of British immigration.

Soon, the limited radical outburst of the Rebellion of 1837 produced a content of emotional memory and hero-myth for French-Canadian nationalism. The Canadian union of 1840, directly intended to assimilate the French-speaking community, brought instead a decisive national response in French determination to survive. In a real sense, Garneau's eloquent literary celebration of the history of his people was the answer to Lord Durham's espousal of the policy of assimilation, based on his confidence that a small nondescript people in the hinterland had no basis for resisting the inexorable expansion of British metropolitan power and civilization across the world.

Be that as it may, the Rouges' yearnings for a French national republic that developed in the 1840's only moved the response onward to a complete ideological expression of French-Canadian nationalism. By the 1850's a nationalist tradition had been firmly shaped for the future. It might be embellished or variously emphasized in later periods; it might accept working within a union with English Canadians, or look to a separate political existence; but it was always inherently there. How, then, can one assess the interplay of this emergent *Canadien* nationalism with the forces of metropolitanism?

To begin with, it was a reaction of forces within a hinterland region against existing metropolitan dominance. It centred in cities in that region, and made one of them in particular, Montreal, a vigorous centre of its growing pattern of influence. To a degree, French-Canadian nationalism was regionalism as well, striving for its own area of autonomy. Indeed, one might hold that nationalism and regionalism differ more in degree than kind—though the fact that this expression of regionalism in Canada was based on a distinctive language, culture and faith, and engendered an emotional state of mind, no doubt earns it the broader national appellation.

Furthermore, this *Canadien* nationalism was also in part a reaction against the growth of new and alien metropolitan forces in its midst: the rise of Montreal as a metropolis in its own right—though still subordinate to London. And this was an English-speaking metropolis that sought to organize mounting western commerce into the St. Lawrence: a pattern of trade which, in contrast to that of the fur trade days, was no longer to be based on French-English collaboration. The fur trade had left the St. Lawrence in 1821; Lower Canadian agriculture was in deep trouble by the 1840's, thanks to soil exhaustion and repeated infestations. But Upper Canadian wheat-growing was steadily expanding, and Montreal's progress depended much more on providing goods for western farmers and marketing their crops than on the economic development of Lower Canada. As an emerging metropolis it was providing the west with market and financial facilities, striving to improve its transport system westward— virtually passing French Canada by. No wonder, then, there was the clash of ethnic interests, the spreading gulf, the mutual resentments. And no wonder that the rebellion of 1837 focused around Montreal, and that the forces of metropolitanism here stimulated the growth of French-Canadian nationalism in a process of clearcut reaction.

278 · new perspectives

THE METROPOLIS IN ENGLISH-CANADIAN NATIONALISM

The fact that English Canada's nationalism was so much slower to develop may also be related to metropolitanism. There are other obvious factors, of course. For instance, there was not the same basic potential here for distinctive nationalism, since the English-speaking community was of much more recent foundation, was not cut off by conquest, and was largely composed of recent British immigrants, or of people whose strongly anti-American leanings made them regard the imperial tie as essential to security. None the less, it was significant that the colonists' staple grain and wood production fed into a British metropolitan market well protected in the earlier nineteenth century—and the only notable anti-metropolitan reaction from the English-speaking élite came in Montreal in 1849 as a result of the *removal* of the imperial protective system.

Free trade then brought adjustments; but for decades colonial grain and timber moved readily to the imperial market organized on London, while capital and labour to develop the hinterland came back along a sea communications system that functioned with great effectiveness to knit the whole metropolitan system closely together. The returning lumber ships, for example, brought the flood of British immigrants which made English Canada far more British than it had been before. The older, relatively small American loyalist and post-loyalist community did not really absorb this inundation, but was virtually swamped by it instead. This showed its consequence at the time of Confederation. When the new federal union was taking form, the leading politicians of English Canada and its chief newspaper editors were predominantly British immigrants—Macdonald, Brown, Galt, McGee and many others. Union, in fact, as responsible government before it, was achieved under strongly British auspices. Neither produced significant nationalist expressions in English Canada. The emphasis was on British models—on achieving the full glory of the cabinet-parliamentary system in the one case; on producing a monarchical, not a democratic, federal constitution in America on the other. It may even be claimed that these basic Canadian national achievements of self-government and union took the special shape they did because of the efficacy of a British metropolitan system which left the people of the hinterland basically in concord with the power at the centre and not inclined to react drastically against it.

The communications net was being notably improved for Canada in the mid-nineteenth century to reinforce the ties between the metropolis and the hinterland. The coming of transatlantic steamship service meant swifter, surer contact: for one thing, mails on schedule—and mail contracts for the steamship owner who saw that possibility, as did Samuel Cunard of Halifax. On land, the railway brought all-weather communication through to tidewater. By the 1850's the line to Portland had broken inland Canada's winter isolation, and in the 60's the Grand Trunk was conveying continental mails to Rivière du Loup for the short sea route to Britain. Then in 1866 the Atlantic cable brought almost instantaneous contact, when linked with the system of land lines that had spread through Canada in the previous generation. In short, in terms of available communications, the British metropolitan system was being drawn together as never before. And this tended to maintain the sense of English Canadians that they were part of one great British or imperial nationality rather than a separate Canadian one. Thus their newspapers fully reported the events at the centre of the universe, London, reprinted the current English novels in serial form, and paid particular, if often critical, attention to the London press—especially to that oracle of the proud Victorian empire, the *Times*.

Within Canada itself, however, metropolitan development was proceeding further, still largely subordinate to London, but not entirely so. Toronto was emerging between the 1850's and the '90's as a metropolis in its own right. A link in the metropolitan chain to Montreal and London, it had also made connections with the powerful American metropolis, New York. The fact that the products of its own Upper Canadian sub-region could go out to market via the Erie canal, on an American axis, as well as via the St. Lawrence, gave it early scope for economic development autonomous of Montreal's hinterland.

In the 1850's Toronto organized its market and its own transport network, set up the Stock Exchange, built the Northern Railway. Over the next two decades it improved its financial facilities, established the Bank of Commerce to challenge the Bank of Montreal and developed loan and insurance companies like the Canada Permanent and Canada Life. By the 1880's it had emerged as the hub of burgeoning industrial developments centred in the Toronto region. Between 1880 and 1891 its population rose from 82,000 to 186,000, its labour force doubled, as did its industrial output, while the number of Toronto's business enterprises and amount of capital investment tripled. It seemed that either the Great Depression of the latter nineteenth century was not all stultifying or that Toronto was specially blessed for being good.

At the same time, Toronto had developed something like a metropolitan press of its own. While its newspapers circulated widely through the new province of Ontario, shaping and directing regional opinion, it also dominated the region's cultural life. It was the focus of church organization (note that the "Methodist Cathedral" erected in Toronto in the 1870's was the Metropolitan Church!), seat of the provincial university and increasingly influential in literary and publishing activities.

It should be added that the first real literary and intellectual expression of nationalism in English Canada, the 'Canada First' movement, was centred in Toronto. Here in 1874 the *Nation* was established—to Underhill, "the best weekly that has yet been published in Canada"—and the National Club was born.[7] But this nationalism, a youthful flush of enthusiasm for the new Dominion, was not necessarily hostile to Britain, and might well include advocacy of imperial federation. In any case, it was not a major manifestation of Toronto sentiment, which tended far more to downright imperialism. And yet this imperialist feeling, widespread in Ontario by the late 1890's—was it not expressive of a kind of English-Canadian nationalism itself? In its demand for Canadian participation in the Boer War, for instance, there was the desire to move into the larger world and show it what Canada could do. There was maturing consciousness, aggressive confidence—while ardent talk of British blood and loyalty by no means interfered with Ontario support for the protective tariff and hard-eyed economic nationalism.[8] In this, too, one might find a significant connection with the Toronto metropolis that dominated the populous Ontario region: a city thriving, apparently, under the National Policy, full of British declarations from its communications with the older metropolitan system, but no less full of practical proclivities as it developed as an outrider of New York.

One could go on to study that latter development with the expansion of Toronto's hinterland northward in the new century to tap the mineral and pulpwood resources of the Shield. One might note as well the spread of metropolitanism in Canada on a transcontinental scale, along the outthrust communications of the railway, as the west was settled, as Winnipeg arose as the great gathering point for the grain trade, and as Vancouver, the key to Pacific outlet, soon developed links with Far Eastern and Pana-

ma traffic. And one might well relate this whole process of internal metropolitan growth to the upsurge of evident nationalism in Canada under
Laurier or during the era of the First World War. But there is more
than enough here for another full paper. There is space only to suggest
some further areas for examination.

METROPOLITANISM AND CONTINENTALISM

It would be fruitful, for example, to investigate the connections between the rising, organizing cities of the plains and the emerging western
regionalism in Canada. This was sectionalism or regionalism, assuredly,
as expressed in powerful agrarian movements. But no less surely it had
broader national implications, to be displayed in politics by the CCF.
And the fact that Winnipeg became the seat of Dafoe's *Free Press* internationalist nationalism might be usefully illuminated by an examination of that city's metropolitan role—why was it not a northern Chicago,
complete with a closed *Tribune*-land? To give another instance, the study
of national issues in Canadian-American relations in the Far West, from
the Alaska boundary to the Alaska Highway and after, might also be
illumined by further inquiry into Vancouver's contest with American
ports for the Klondike trade, or its competition with Edmonton for communications into the Peace and beyond.

As for still another instance, one might study the effect of new means
of communication on the patterns of metropolitanism in Canada and
their possible relations with its nationalism in the mid-twentieth century.
The spread of automobiles and highways since the 1920's—with their
evergrowing implications for urbanization, the reorganization of regional
traffic systems, and the easy flow of tourism—have all, in the broadest sense,
stressed continental land connections and de-emphasized the older transatlantic sea communications. It is doubtful that air travel, which knows
no land or water barriers, has significantly counteracted this re-orientation
in the communications net. Radio in the '30s, television in the '50s, have
only confirmed the general growth of what one may call cultural continentalism. In this regard, the pervasive Hollywood film, whether on the
big screen or on the little one, has had a similar influence. In short, the
decline for Canada of the old London-based metropolitanism must not be
seen purely as a matter of declining economic power, but also as a loss

of cultural hegemony through a shift in the centres of metropolitan dominance over communications nets.

The lines now, for Canadians, converge on New York, Chicago and Los Angeles; the roads (for the pursuit of happiness) lead to Florida and California. The consequences for Canadian nationalism have inevitably been great. Despite the growth of an interconnected internal metropolitan pattern, the various highly organized metropolitan regions and sub-regions in this country all find places in continental vassal-chains centred below the border. The question still remains whether this broader metropolitanism will work to produce Canadian absorption in a continental American nationality, or may yet induce some basic reaction beyond impotent fears and frustration—so that another phase of Canadian nationalism may follow, stimulated by resistance to an external metropolitan dominance. If, indeed, it is considered as external!

All one may now say is that Canadian history shows developments of both kinds: both identification with and reaction to metropolitan power. The satisfying British metropolitan system produced no strong English-Canadian national reaction, but, in time, a somewhat imperialist nationalist feeling tended to emerge. The spread of metropolitanism within Canada itself, then, seems to have clarified and strengthened that nationalism and identified it far more with the Canadian territorial unit. And the tying of Canada into an American metropolitan system surely seems to have weakened a still not firmly distinctive product. A point to keep in mind, of course, is not only the influence of metropolitan power but also the elements it has to work on in English, as compared to French Canada. Much indeed may always depend on the degree of distinctiveness felt by the communities in the hinterland, and on their sense—at least among their own urban elite—that they are disadvantaged by prevailing patterns of dominance. Is the current situation in Quebec not an example of this?

There is a final point to be made, in any case. Regionalism, which may expand to, or be integrated with nationalism, is a phenomenon which needs much more historical study, especially in a sectionalized country like Canada. It is fundamentally related to the whole question of metropolitanism. The metropolitan system, after all, is an organization of hinterland regions about the great city, and of localities within the regions about their own sub-regional centres. This only indicates the need for another approach than the barely national to our own history.

In fact, I close this discussion of metropolitanism and nationalism in

Canadian history by saying that I think the national approach has now been overdone. Not that it is invalid, but that it has led to too much emphasis on Ottawa-centred history and a comparative neglect of regional study as parochial, antiquarian, or almost un-Canadian. Which is really the more parochial approach in a country such as this? In sum, I would venture to say that instead of another re-working of grand national historical themes in Canada, there may be more of new significance to be learned by studying Port Credit or Swift Current in terms of local, regional and continental history, or even (with no sense of being ludicrous) in terms of the North Atlantic world and Western civilization. These are all valid frames of reference, no less than the national, for Canadian history—as any consideration of metropolitanism inevitably must reveal.

NOTES

1. R. E. Dickinson, *City Region and Regionalism*, London, 1947, p. 14.
2. N. S. B. Gras, *An Introduction to Economic History*, New York, 1922.
3. R. D. Mackenzie, *The Metropolitan Community*, New York, 1933, p. 47.
4. H. A. Innis, *Empire and Communications*, Toronto, 1950; *The Bias of Communications*, Toronto, 1951.
5. H. M. McLuhan, *Understanding Media*, New York, 1964.
6. F. Ouellet, "Le Nationalisme canadienne français: De ses origines à L'insurrection de 1837", *Canadian Historical Review*, XLV, 1964. See also M. Brunet, *La Prisenie Anglaise et les Canadiens*, Montreal 1958.
7. F. H. Underhill, *The Images of Confederation*, Toronto, 1963, p. 18.
8. R. C. Brown, *Canada's National Policy*, 1883-1900, Princeton, 1964, p. 155. See also in this volume his article on "The Nationalism of the National Policy", p. 155ff.

technology

and nationalism • melville watkins

Today technology utterly pervades our private and collective existence; it shapes our values and moulds our institutions. Such statements have become commonplace, and a profound insight has become a cliché to be mouthed and ignored. This paper attempts to redress the balance by examining the relationship between technology and nationalism. The first part considers the usefulness of technology as a unifying theme for the study of nationalism. The second is a cryptic outline of Canadian history around that theme. The concluding section speculates on the proper role of a modern nation-state. *In toto,* the moral of the paper is that the radical character of modern technology, while rendering obsolete both individualism and nationalism, involves man in a diversity of collectivities which may be bound together by nothing more than acceptance of the idea of mankind.

NATIONALISM—THE PRODUCT OF PRINT TECHNOLOGY

A survey of the literature shows a diversity of approaches to nationalism. The historian Louis Snyder[1] defines nationalism by listing five traits, but why there should be exactly five is unclear and, in any event, he adds that there are exceptions to every part of his definition. Karl Deutsch[2] has provided a behavioural and operational approach, which, while it may provide a means of measuring the growth of nationalism in individual countries, does not come to grip with nationalism's more universal and historic sources. Many students of nationalism have attempted classifications. The most interesting, because it is time-bound, is that of Carlton Hayes: humanitarian nationalism, Jacobin nationalism, traditional nationalism, liberal nationalism, and integral nationalism.[3] A very general neo-Marxian classification, again grounded in history, is that of the feudal nation, the bourgeois nation, and the socialist nation.

The difficulties involved in analyzing and explaining nationalism are conceded by Rupert Emerson—one of the most distinguished students of nationalism—when he begins a discussion of the Elements of Nationalism as follows:

> The simplest statement that can be made about a nation is that it is a body of people who feel that they are a nation; and it may be that when all the fine-spun analysis is concluded this will be the ultimate statement as well. To advance beyond it, it is necessary to attempt to take the nation apart and to isolate for separate examination the forces and elements which appear to have been the most influential in bringing about the sense of common identity which lies at its roots, the sense of the existence of a singularly important national 'we' which is distinguished from all others who make up an alien 'they'. This is necessarily an overly mechanical process, for nationalism, like other profound emotions such as love and hate, is more than the sum of the parts which are susceptible of cold and rational analysis.[4]

One way to put Humpty Dumpty back together again is by the application of a unifying theme. A particularly valuable approach may lie in considering the impact of technology, that is, the pervasive consequences of the inherent and varying character of technologies. An economist cannot be unaware of the increasing emphasis on technical change in the literature on economic growth, and of the particular concern, daily voiced, about the economic consequences of automation as symbolic of the new technology. Inasmuch as the nation-state and nationalism are among the most important phenomena of the last few centuries, only a slight leap of the imagination is required to appreciate that the study of "technology and nationalism" merits serious consideration.

To recognize the importance of technology for historical studies is to be compelled simultaneously to admit of its scholarly neglect. Systematic concern with the impact of technology is rare. Among the most important exceptions are the writings of the late Harold Innis and of Marshall Mc-

Luhan.⁵ Their work provides the frame of reference for this paper.

Neither Innis nor McLuhan has written at length about nationalism *per se*. Rather, it is not too much of an exaggeration to say that both have written about everything and anything, and that nationalism has necessarily been included. Their central interest has been in the pervasive effects of technology. A *technology* is regarded as an extension of man, as an externalization of a human organ or sense, as an environment. Created by man, technology then penetrates his life, powerfully and pervasively. The major works of Innis and McLuhan are exercises in the writing of total history around this theme.

A technology can be many things: a natural resource, a staple, a product, a process, a transport system, a communication medium. History is a seamless web formed from the action and interaction of particular technologies, each with its inherent and unique character or structure, and hence its differing effects on the totality of existence. In his early writings Innis was concerned with the role of staple exports in Canadian economic development. In effect, he wrote Canadian history in terms of a "staple approach", or around staple production as the unifying theme. The *physical* character of the staple—the lightness of fur, the perishability of cod, the bulkiness of timber, the variability of wheat harvests, the capital-intensity of mining—became the central theme around which to write the total history of Canada's economic, political, and social institutions:

> Concentration on the production of staples for export to more highly industrialized areas in Europe and later in the United States had broad implications for the Canadian economic, political, and social structure. Each staple in its turn left its stamp, and the shift to new staples invariably produced periods of crises in which adjustments in the old structure were painfully made and a new pattern created in relation to a new staple.⁶

Though staples provided the leading motif for his Canadian studies, the "approach" was not confined to natural resources. There was a generous mixture of references to the peculiar impact of varying modes of transport: rivers, canoes, ships, roads, canals, railways, automobiles, airplanes. Canada as a geographic entity was an extension of the birch bark canoe penetrating outwards from the St. Lawrence for fur. Confederation, the political validation of this extension, provided the base necessary to finance transcontinental railways, which then validated Confederation. Yet higher levels of generalization were reached around the theme of *industrialism* as a technology. The early staples were the "antecedents of industralism", providing the basis for the rise of the "old industrialism" of coal and iron, canals and railways, wheat and tariffs, the nation-state and the price system, but in turn superseded by the "new industrialism" of mining, pulp and paper, hydro-electric power, the limitations of the pricing system, and the economics of disturbance.[7]

When Innis turned to universal history, everything changed but the method. In effect, the medium became the staple. Instead of the great staple trades of Canada, we now find as the unifying theme the great media of history such as stone, papyrus, parchment, paper, print, and radio. The result was a "media approach" to history, an approach that stands in sharp contrast to the conventional "information approach" which studies communication systems in terms of content rather than structure. Innis found the real message of a medium as inherent in its time-space nexus:

> The concepts of time and space reflect the significance of media to civilization. Media which emphasize time are those which are durable in character such as parchment, clay and stone. The heavy materials are suited to the development of architecture and sculpture. Media which emphasize space are apt to be less durable and light in character such as papyrus and paper. The latter are suited to wide areas in administration and trade. The conquest of Egypt by Rome gave access to supplies of papyrus which became the basis of a large administrative empire. Materials which emphasize time favour decentralization and hierarchical types of institutions, while those which emphasize space favour centralization and systems of government less hierarchical in character. Large-scale political organizations, such as empires, must be considered from the standpoint of two dimensions, those of space and time, and persist by overcoming the bias of media which over-emphasize either dimension.[8]

McLuhan has extended Innis' work in a major and substantial fashion. Like the later Innis, he has focused primarily, though far from exclusively, on the media. He has cryptically summed up his approach in the single sentence: "The medium is the message." The real message of any medium as a technology is not its "content"—which is another medium—but "the change of scale or pace or pattern that it introduces into human affairs."[9] "It is the formal characteristics of the medium, recurring in a variety of material situations, and not any particular 'message' which constitutes the efficacy of its historical action."[10] For

McLuhan, the message comes primarily via the impact of the medium or technology on our sense ratios, or patterns of perception, or sensory modalities:

> If a technology is introduced either from within or from without a culture, and if it gives new stress or ascendancy to one or another of our senses, the ratio among all of our senses is altered. We no longer feel the same, nor do our eyes and ears and other senses remain the same.[11]

The import of Innis and McLuhan for present purposes is clear: viewed as an institutional-value complex, nationalism is a symptom of technology and changes its character with each change in technology. Specifically, nationalism as we have known it is a symptom of print, of the Gutenberg press as centre, symbol, and theme of the galaxy of industrialism. Following Emerson and a host of writers, nationalism is regarded as a sense of common identity; following Innis and McLuhan, it is understood as that sense of common identity that flows from the print technology.

In Innis' terms, print destroyed the medieval "equilibrium" or "balance" between the elements of space and time. Print made it possible for men to "see" their vernacular languages, thereby weakening the position of Latin as a universal language and homogenizing dialects within the vernaculars. Nation-states emerged as political entities based on the vernaculars. With print came new techniques of production culminating in the assembly line as the industrial extension of moveable type, more efficient weapons, reduction in the cost and improvements in the speed of transportation and communication. These permitted greater centralization of power and more efficient control of larger spaces. The feudal lord gave way to the king and the king to the national bourgeoisie. At the same time, the power of the Pope gave way to the king and to charismatic and schismatic leaders supported by kings and merchants. Local markets were shattered by vernacular literacy and a common currency and replaced by national markets linked by road and rail and protected by tariffs, with standardized goods sold to a homogenized people.

Along the time dimension, print broke asunder the great time-binding institutions of religion and kinship. The eternal church founded on the rock of Peter gave way to more worldly and nationalistic Protestant sects. The Word of God was nationalized and the nation became sacred. The village based on the extended family gave way to the mobile nuclear family of parents and siblings. Medieval tradition-directed man became liberal inner-directed man. Labour became a commodity and was differentiated and fragmented to produce specialists. Man as a social animal, as a largely unrecognizable entity imbedded in society, gave way to man as "possessive individualist",[12] jealous of his material goods, of his contractual rights, of his political liberty, of his right to communicate with God without the mediation of his priest, of his right to bear arms against tyranny, and, above all, of his right to his private thoughts.

Control over time as well as control over space fell increasingly under the domain of the nation-state. After Gutenberg came both individualism and nationalism. The new technology created a New World, at home and abroad, for the flowering of liberal bourgeois nationalism.

When we examine print, as McLuhan does, in terms of its impact on the sensory modalities, we can see that what it did was to "step up" enormously the visual component of experience. The ear creates acoustical wrap-around space; the intimacy of dialogue and kinship; the confessional box and psychoanalysis; a feeling of involvement; the continuous flow process and do-it-yourself; an emphasis on recitation, memory, myth-making, tradition; drums and tribalism; the village and the globe. The eye creates perspective; the point of view; linear thinking; Renaissance art; conspicuous consumption; the assembly line and replaceable parts; division of labour and specialization; flat, continuous spaces; maps and boundaries; nations and nationalism.

With print technology came the nation. But after the mechanical technology of print came the new technology of electricity; after the book came the newspaper and film as mechanical-electrical hybrids, and radio, television, and communication satellites as electric technology proper. What has this meant for nationalism? As a phenomenon of print, it must inevitably be altered profoundly in the age of post-print. On this Innis and McLuhan agree: changes of a radical nature, fraught with the potential of both opportunity and chaos, have been unleashed by the radical technology of electricity. But on the nature of the alteration, Innis and McLuhan tend to part. As McLuhan makes explicit in his introduction to the new paperback edition of Innis' *The Bias of Communication*, Innis seems generally to have regarded the new electric technology as a further extension of the patterns of the mechanical technology:

After many historical demonstrations of the space-binding power of the eye and the time-binding power of the ear, Innis refrains from applying these structural principles to the action of radio. Suddenly, he shifts the ear world of the radio into the visual orbit, attributing to radio all the centralizing power of the eye and of visual culture. Here Innis was misled by the ordinary consensus of his time. Electric light and power, like all electric media, are profoundly decentralizing and separatist in their psychic and social consequences. (p. xii) . . . whereas the visual power extended by print does indeed extend the means to organize a spatial continuum, the auditory power extended electrically does in effect abolish space and time alike. . . . Visual technology whether by literacy or by industry creates nations as spatially uniform and homogeneous and connected. But electric technology creates not the nation but the tribe—not the superficial association of equals but the cohesive depth pattern of the totally involved kinship group. Visual technology, whether based on papyrus or paper, fosters fragmentation and specialism, armies and empires. Electrical technology favours not the fragmentary but the integral, not the mechanical but the organic. (pp. xiii - xiv)

For McLuhan, the electric technology is tribal, organic, integral, pervasive, and all-embracing. At the same time, it is decentralist, depth-involving, and separatist. Print creates the individual in the lonely crowd. The electric technology makes him seek involvement in depth and crave collective goals in a world that has shrunk to the size of a village and that resonates to the beat of tribal drums. Print creates the nation as an aggregation of possessive individualists, bound together by a common interest that rarely transcends material goals. The electric technology penetrates to deeper layers of love and hate; it casts the inner-directed individual adrift and exposes the superficiality of conventional nationalism. Individualist and nationalist goals are presently being eroded by collective aspirations which sometimes fall short of existing national boundaries and sometimes extend far beyond them. It is no accident that "regionalism" has come to signify the aspirations both of regions within nations and of regional blocs of nations. Both the superficiality and the formality of international relations are seriously threatened. The French in Canada and the negro in the United States no longer tolerate the derogation which each feels he has experienced at the hands of his fellow-citizen—anymore than the African, Asian, or Latin American will longer tolerate imperialism. Traditional concepts of inviolable national sovereignty, secret diplomacy, great power politics, and the legitimacy of war as a last resort are becoming equally untenable and empty. National boundaries defined by vernaculars are as defenceless against information moving with the speed of light as against the inter-continental ballistic missile. The attempt to cram nationalism as content into the new media tends to produce the barbarous and the ludicrous—"Canadian content" rules being a case in point. TV relieved radio of its national burden to show the flag, and freed it to go local and universal; the communications satellite promises to internationalize TV and, in the process, leave national content with nowhere to go.

McLuhan's position—here embellished—is a compelling one. With the advent of the new electric technology, the historic nation-state began to wither away. Since the late nineteenth century, the power of the book to centralize nationally has been weakened by the power of the metropolitan press, and the spread of the corporation as prototype of the modern corporate entity has eroded individualism. The modern world, into which we have been moving for at least a century, is one characterized not by classic nationalism but by new-old tribalism. Nationalism based on the book—the nationalism that is literally nationalism—is obsolete. Man has been compelled to adapt, at enormous social and private cost, to the "global village" of today.

That the new technology has so far worked its ferment largely within the confines of the nation-state is true. The rise of the "welfare state" following the cheap press, of monetary and fiscal policy following radio, and of economic planning and the "war on poverty" following television, has meant the transcending of individualism but, in general, not of established national boundaries. But with instant and all-pervasive communication flows, the nation-state is no longer the sovereign independent entity that it was once believed to be and sometimes was. If one wishes to label as nationalism the new substance within the old form, one must be prepared to recognize that this post-print nationalism differs sharply from the printbound variety. Liberalism now yields to collectivism, and bourgeois values, to socialist values.

The consequences have hardly been uniformly happy. Out of the clash of technologies have emerged the horrors of the twentieth century. Significantly, the worst have been associated with the hybrid of "National Socialism". Print and industrialization liberate peasants and implant great expectations; witness Germany and Japan yesterday, China today. When the world fails to conform to the image, reform can turn to revolution and perversion. The book and the ledger give way to screaming headlines and blaring loudspeakers. The new masses coalesce into a mob. Totalitarianism might be defined as the application of twentieth century commitment and technology to nineteenth century goals. History might be read as signifying that man's salvation lies not in deploring the former but in repudiating the latter. We should remember that the radio created Roosevelt as well as Hitler; TV destroyed Senator McCarthy and enables Senator Fulbright to oppose the war in Vietnam.

The nation-state is the prime collectivity to which, in recent centuries, man has given his loyalty in return for emotional security. Men have more readily laid down their lives for the creed of nationalism than in defence of other faiths and commitments. But the military technology of the electronic age—the most advanced of any part of the new technology—has rendered obsolete nineteenth-century notions of national sovereignty and national independence. The bomb shelter is not a very satisfactory place in which to wave a flag, and fallout shows a fatal lack of respect for national boundaries. Not surprisingly, there has been increasing recognition of the need for disarmament, world law, and a global police force.

It is, in the conventional wisdom, one of the paradoxes of our time that as centralization has appeared to become more feasible and advantageous, centrifugal forces have often tended to prevail. The point may be understandable when allowance is made for the decentralizing tendencies of the new technology. A striking feature of the last generation is the retreat from empire. The capacity of the nation-state to extend its control spatially has clearly declined. From the imperial standpoint, the movement has been from imperialism as the "extension of nation" to "separatism" grounded on ancient tribal and racial groupings. Nor is it surprising that this global decentralization manifests itself at the periphery as "instant nationalism". It is economic growth that is highly valued, and the spread of literacy and vocational specialization, with their concomitant nationalism, remain as preconditions for the adoption of industrial technology with its large mechanical component. In this sense, contemporary Asian and African nationalism is analagous to that of Europe in the nineteenth century. But the insistence of the new nations on involvement in global issues, their capacity to manipulate "great" powers, and their interest in supranational movements and international organizations distinguish the twentieth century from the nineteenth. While the vulnerability of the empire has exceeded that of the nation proper, there is considerable evidence of increasing difficulty in effecting national assimilation within established nation-states. Quebec's separatist propensity is only the most relevant case in point.

Nor would the withering away of the nation-state necessarily be a cause for tears. There is evidence that man, at least in the West, is becoming increasingly involved with collectivities other than the nation. Note such instances as: the revival of the city state as metropolitan area, with urban planning much more acceptable than national economic planning; the centralization of corporate decision-making, with corporate planning the vogue among those who oppose national planning; the evolution of the national corporation into the multi-national corporation, with a world-wide corporate image rather than a national image, and staffed by men of global perspective who allocate resources without respect for national boundaries but who care about local respect and participation; the expansion, albeit slowly, of international agencies and the growing number of supranational civil servants; the evolution of the university as ivory tower into the multiversity as environment, with a staff of modern nomads and a student body that prefers teach-ins to textbooks; the new interest in church union that may heal the schisms that have rent the Catholic church and create a new theology that makes irrelevant the issues on which sects have flourished historically; the return of family life as evidenced by TV-togetherness and the baby boom. It is possible that to list this diversity of collectivities is to begin to map the social web that will be essential for existence in a functioning "global village" of all mankind.

TECHNOLOGY AND THE CANADIAN NATION

Throughout its history, Canada has been a marginal area relative to centres of population, purchasing power, military power, and technological innovation. Technology has been a force emanating abroad, and change, for Canadians, a mostly passive adaptation to external opportunities and pressures. With a majority ethic that reflects liberal-bourgeois origins,[13] the primary goal has been national economic development. The need to provide security for foreign capital—which increases the rate of economic growth both through increasing the supply of savings and by being the carrier of the new technology—underlay the emergence of the nation and has worked since to constrain Canadian nationalism from "excesses" on the left.[14] Historically, the Act of Union of 1840 and Confederation were the political preconditions for continuing access on reasonable terms to the London capital market; in recent years, even the mild restraints on foreign owners such as those proposed by Walter Gordon are labelled left-wing by Bay Street. The ease of emigration has reinforced tendencies to maintain in Canada a reasonable approximation of the American way of life. The feasibility of medicare, for example, hinges on devising arrangements that are sufficiently satisfactory to the doctors as to discourage their emigration to the United States. At the same time, proximity to the world's greatest liberal democracy has complicated the satisfaction that might otherwise have accrued from flag-waving, and has compelled the steady cultivation of a European link as a counterweight to the American fact but at the price of inhibiting Canadian autonomy. Spatial vastness and the French fact have facilitated regionalism and provincialism, just as they have inhibited nationalism even of the liberal variety.

The national history of Canada can be written around the theme of changing technologies, from the river economy of fur to the national economy of wheat to the regional economies of electricity. Except for short periods when fur and wheat were at their peaks, regionalism has been the rule rather than the exception of the Canadian experience, and Canadian nationalism has been largely a conscious strategy of pasting over the cracks. The present boundaries of Canada were defined by the fur trade in the process of retreating in the face of settlement. Areas held by the fur traders tended to be those with limited alternative opportunities for attracting and holding settlers; hence a polity resulting from the exploitation of fur necessarily rested on weak foundations. The new transport technologies of canals and railways created economic and political possibilities that far surpassed those flowing from the canoe. The Act of Union was necessary to build the canals; Confederation and the National Policy were necessary to build all-Canadian railways. The supply of timber to the British Navy was a keystone of Canada's permanent economic development, while the British Navy provided the military power necessary to hold a St. Lawrence polity distinct from the United States.

The persistent difficulties of Canadian book publishers are striking evidence of the limitation of Canada as a nation-state in the Gutenberg environment. The absence of both a single and a unique language has been crippling. The newspaper gave a fresh impetus to urbanization—and hence to new metropolitan centres as foci independent of established centres[15]—but no metropolitan paper in Canada has been able to attain national stature analagous to that of the London *Times* in Britain, or even of the *New York Times* in the United States. In every dimension electricity appears to have weakened an already weak national polity and economy. Hydro-electricity has become the essential ingredient of a host of new staples which find their markets in the United States and fail to utilize the patiently assembled transcontinental transportation system extending from the St. Lawrence. Public ownership, as an expression of the collective will, has had more room to flower at the provincial and metropolitan levels than at the national level. Radio and television have been used, or misused, in a largely futile attempt to foster nationalism, with a consequent failure to exploit adequately the potential of public ownership of the media to offset commercialism and provide free education. The increasing complexity of technology and of life in general has meant an increased insistence on education, or on human capital, as a critical input for economic growth. The limitations of Canada as a nation-state in the age of print are reflected in provincial responsibility for formal education with a consequent absence of national standards and national curricula. The teaching of national history creates national myths which facilitate nationalism—but there are ten versions of Canadian history taught in the schools. As learning becomes continuous in the age of automation, an insistence on national content is likely to be seen as irrelevant to the main challenge of coping with new technologies, community life, and global politics.

The National Policy of the nineteenth century was the ideological content of the new technology of the railway wedded to the old river economy of the St. Lawrence. As a manifestation of nationalism and as an instrument of nation-building, the National Policy was more the commercial imperialism of the St. Lawrence merchants than a broadly based mass movement. National politics were dominated by acrimonious debates about railway subsidies and tariffs. Foreign policy was rigidly determined by the conscious desire to maximize the national *economic* welfare. In a recent study[16] of the major disputes that characterized Canadian-American relations in the years 1883-1900, it becomes painfully obvious that the common element in Canadian policies—from fishing rights in the North Atlantic to the Alaska boundary settlement—was the exclusive concern with national economic benefits. George Hees was in the historic Canadian tradition when, during the 1965 federal election campaign, he drew the attention of his tobacco-growing constituents to the potential gain which the illegal declaration of independence by Rhodesia would bring to them; even racism breeds profits somewhere. Canadian nationalists still take pride in the extent to which national policy lowers individual income while raising national income. To demonstrate, as Professor Dales has done,[17] that it is theoretically possible for the tariff to do this may only strengthen the hand of the economic nationalist. It is not surprising, however, that some find little emotional satisfaction in such a coarsely materialistic conception of what it means to be a Canadian. V. C. Fowke has shown that the old National Policy—high tariffs, railway building, and promotion of mass immigration—was obsolete by 1930;[18] no new national policy has emerged to replace it in spite of frequent appeals by Canadian historians. One can sympathize with Fowke's attempt to find an emerging national policy based on the welfare state, but one is compelled to recognize that as welfare has grown in importance, federal powers have been eroded relative to provincial and municipal powers.

The spread of the railway permitted the U.S. corporation to swell to national proportions. A similar development in Canada was checked by the tendency of American companies to ignore the Canadian-American boundary and to refuse to regard investment in Canada as foreign. As early as the 1850's, U.S. entrepeneurs were investing directly in Canadian lumber mills. The process of foreign control of export-oriented industries based on superior access to technology and markets became cumulative. The imposition of the tariff and the increasing exposure of Canadians to American advertising hastened the spread of American direct investment in Canadian subsidiaries and branches producing for the Canadian market. Wheat as a staple encouraged immigration and by increasing the size of the national market facilitated industrialization based on mass-consumed, mass-produced commodities in which American technology was dominant. A functioning trans-continental economy was revived around wheat in the decade prior to World War I, with considerably more substance than its predecessor based on fur. But within the wheat boom were to be found the nationally corrosive influences of electricity and of the increasing orientation of the Canadian economy, on the import side, to the United States rather than the United Kingdom.

The weakening of the national economy has been paralleled by the increasing strength of both regionalism and continentalism. If the former was highlighted by the election returns of November 8, 1965 (the Liberal power failure), the latter was vividly exposed by the (literal) power failure of November 9. In his *Lament For a Nation*, George Grant argues that because continentalism is inevitable the Canadian nation-state is an impossibility. But Grant reaches his conclusion by dubious means: he assumes that the new technology is simply more of the old centralization and homogenization and that there was in the past a golden age of Canadian nationalism, the disappearance of which is now worth lamenting. Nor is it sufficient to cite, as Grant and others do, the increasing economic interdependence of Canada and the United States, in terms of trade and investment, as convincing evidence of lessening Canadian autonomy. In economic policy, to learn the lesson of Keynes is to appreciate that monetary and fiscal policies, rather than continental automotive industry agreements, are the means preferred by economists to achieve the legitimate goal of national full employment. In foreign policy, a meaningful Canadian approach is denied, in some part at least, by the Ottawa Establishment's preference for secret diplomacy rather than frank and candid public discussion, and for national economic interest rather than global issues as the primary content of Canadian-American relations. It is arguable that the war in Vietnam is as relevant to election campaigns and to Canadian-American relations as where the Chevrolets are produced. Grant's despair—or, more accurately, his whimsical regret—has the curious quality of denying the relevance of the supranational protest and dissent which is now so clearly a part of the electric environment.

In the twentieth century, American periodicals (such as *Time* and *Life*), Hollywood, and radio and TV piping American programmes into Canadian homes, have created mass taste on a continental basis. The Canadian response has been to force the burden of nationalism on to the new media. The CBC is hailed by the Committee on Broadcasting as "the most important single instrument available for the development and maintenance of the unity of Canada"; it is hardly surprising that the Committee then finds the CBC wanting. To charge that the CBC "must awaken Canadians to Canadian realities" invites the countercharge that Canadians should simply be awakened. The banality of Canadian content rules is adequately exposed, albeit inadvertently, by the Committee's remark that, "Religious and educational programs made outside Canada have been a problem."[19] The inherent difficulty involved in effectively wedding conventional nationalism, which has emerged around the printed word, with broadcasting, lends a quality of the absurd to the reports of Commissions and Committees. New nations have the advantage of being able to use the new media, particularly radio, to create nationalism without competition from the historical residue of print.

Canada was only the first to receive the smothering embrace of enveloping U.S. technology as the United States moved to its present position of forming a virtually world-wide environment. American direct investment grew rapidly, for direct investment was *the* efficient medium of communication for the massive information movements required by modern industrial techniques and modern advertising. American television programmes while blanketing the world also awaken it; they may yet turn out to be the most effective technique imaginable for creating anti-Americanism. Canadian nationalism of the type symbolized by Mr. Diefenbaker is, at least in part, a technological backlash analagous to Goldwaterism within the United States. Conversely, nationalism of the type espoused by M. Lévesque reflects, at least in part, the felt need for a collective existence that transcends both individualism and conventional nationalism.

THE FUTURE OF THE NATION-STATE

The most deliberate manner in which to discuss the proper role of the nation-state is by the use of a functional approach, that is, by posing the question: what is the role of the nation-state relative to those of other collectivities such as intra-national regions, extra-national regional blocs, and supra-national authorities? There would be widespread agreement that present military technology already compels supra-national authority. Similarly, the rising revolution of expectations within the poor countries compels a concern with *world* economic welfare and *world* economic growth. Within the nation-state, however, decentralization is feasible. Particularly for Canada, where national goals have been primarily economic, there is no reason to assume that decentralized decision-making must be inferior to centralized decision-making. The provinces already play leading roles in the fields of transportation, education, and welfare, and there is considerable scope for the further decentralization of monetary and fiscal policy. This is not to argue that the nation-state is now obsolete, but rather to suggest that it will survive by recognizing its limitations. Post-print nationalism must grow out of a genuine national society which can support a national government able to perceive and achieve national goals that transcend economic liberalism. There is no task today more urgent than that of recognizing and effecting social goals and aspirations which transcend individualism while avoiding the dead-rot of centralism and bureaucracy.

This is to suggest that, putting conventional political ideology aside, the greatest potential for Canada as a national society may lie in a substantial rejection of the market economy as the cornerstone of the market society and the market mentality. Canadian historiography notwithstanding, national policy has been little more than marginal tinkering with the price system via the tariff and the shoring up of private enterprises until they can stand on their own feet or after they are reeling bankrupt. The history of Canadian railways adequately demonstrates the point. The greater reliance in Canada than in the United States on public ownership and the lesser fanaticism evident in discussion of the virtues of free enterprise are features by which the Canadian way of life can already be reliably differentiated from the American. To downgrade the market might ultimately permit Canadians to rise above that vulgar materialism which has masqueraded as nationalism. The boredom of the young with mere affluence is a heartening sign. The major burden of the tariff is not the extent to which it has lowered the standard of living— real though that is—but rather the extent to which, by monopolizing politics, it has narrowed vision and lowered the quality of national life. To reject the market would significantly differentiate Canada from the United States, thereby lessening the invidious comparisons that have eaten at the soul of Canadian nationalism. It is also possibly the only national policy that can hope to maintain any national commitment within Quebec. Its potential might be thought to be severely constrained by the possibility of a considerable exodus to the United States, though, in the present state of the world's population, emigration could be easily offset by immigration. It has working for it the increasingly unattractive character of American foreign policy.

Advocating the rejection of the market, however, should not be interpreted as simply implying the acceptance of the traditional shibboleths of the Canadian left. Tariffs and the harassment of foreign owners are not endorsed, for their main effect is to protect the Canadian commercial establishment and impede the inflow of the newest technology. A tariff designed to breed infant industries now tends more often to shelter the senile. By encouraging American companies to establish plants in Canada, a tariff deemed necessary to ensure Canadian survival has increased the threat to survival. By encouraging in Canada a "miniature replica" of the American manufacturing system[20], the tariff has nurtured an inefficient industrial structure that needs continuing tariff protection. The history of the Canadian tariff needs to be written around the theme of self-fulfilled prophecies. Adverse effects alleged to result from foreign owership are more obviously attributable to the Canadian tariff and the remedy is tariff reduction. Insofar as monoply power inheres in direct investment —since otherwise the foreigner would not have an advantage over domestic firms—there is a case for some control of foreign investment on economic grounds alone, since otherwise the economic gains for Canadians will not be so large as they might be.[21] But to place significant impediments on foreign ownership and do nothing else risks turning Canada into a technological backwater. More consideration needs to be given to the feasibility of patent and licensing arrangements as alternatives to foreign ownership and, in particular, to the potential for a much more active role for government in encouraging scientific research.[22] The backwardness of Canadian entrepreneurship, on which the foreigners' advantage rests at least in part, could be alleviated by educating top management,[23] increasing social mobility,[24] and increasing the scope for public rather than private entrepreneurship.

There is much to be said, particularly in marginal areas, for accepting the new technology and devoting political energies to its humanization. The electric technology creates a vast potential for improving the environment—for collective action to programme a more meaningful existence. Urban and regional planning is the most obvious case in point. At the national level the greatest potential for Canada almost surely lies in a radical reformation of foreign policy. In this area, Canadian policy has long been guided by the goal of maximizing national economic welfare and, since a foreign policy independent of Britain has been tolerated, by the technique of publicly supporting the United States with any criticisms whispered privately. Secret diplomacy has had its day, and the potential area for disagreement with U.S. foreign policy steadily widens. The crassness and the simplicity of Canadian foreign policy has masked its ultimate innocence and irrelevance. The terror and the chaos loose in the world are too rarely glimpsed and a genuine involvement in the fate of mankind thereby evaded.

But even radical suggestions, so long as they are clothed in the garb of nationalism, are ultimately transcended by the radical message of the new and emerging technologies. As we move into outer space, it is time that we make this planet habitable. What is required is for us to take seriously the idea of mankind as a concept transcending nationalism in any form. Political action is too easily confused with government policy and too rarely understood as the goal-implementation of any collectivity; hence non-national groupings espousing global goals cannot be dismissed as naive if they work outside the formal political structure, for the latter might be regarded as the residue of the old technology. Policy is too easily regarded as the content of government activity and too rarely linked to the collective aspirations of man which transcend momentary institutional arrangements. It would be criminal to stand idly by as spectators applauding the decline of the nation-state. But it would be equally derelict to imagine that nationalism can be an adequate answer to our present discontents. The compelling need for the future is not for national societies in a world community—desirable though such a social system would be today—but rather for a world society fit for a global village.

> To feel one's attachment to a certain region, one's love for a certain group of men, to know that there is always a spot where one's heart will feel at peace—these are many certainties for a single human life. And yet this is not enough. (Albert Camus, "Summer in Algiers")

NOTES

1. Louis L. Snyder, *The Dynamics of Nationalism: Readings in Its Meaning and Development*, Princeton, 1962, p. 2.
2. Karl W. Deutsch, *Nationalism and Social Communication*, New York, 1953.
3. Carlton J. H. Hayes, *The Historical Evolution of Modern Nationalism*, New York, 1931.
4. Rupert Emerson, *From Empire to Nation: The Rise to Self-Assertion of Asian and African Peoples*, Boston, 1962, p. 102.
5. Harold Innis, *Empire and Communications*, London, 1950; *The Bias of Communications*, Toronto, 1951; *Changing Concepts of Time*, Toronto, 1952. Marshall McLuhan, *The Gutenberg Galaxy*, Toronto, 1962; *Understanding Media: The Extensions of Man*, New York, 1964.
6. Harold Innis, *Empire and Communications*, pp. 4-5.
7. On industrialism as a focus for understanding Innis, see W. T. Easterbrook, "Innis and Economics", *Canadian Journal of Economics and Political Science* XIX, August 1953, pp. 291-303.
8. Harold Innis, *Empire and Communications*, p. 7.

9. Marshall McLuhan, *Understanding Media*, p. 8.
10. Marshall McLuhan, "Effects of the Improvements of Communication Media", *Journal of Economic History* XX, December 1960, p. 568.
11. Marshall McLuhan, *The Gutenberg Galaxy*, p. 24.
12. The terminology is from C. B. Macpherson, *The Political Theory of Possessive Individualism*, London, 1962.
13. See Louis Hartz, *The Founding of New Societies*, New York, 1964.
14. For a somewhat different perspective on this theme see above, Alfred Dubuc, "The Decline of Confederation and The New Nationalism". p. xxx.
15. On the relationship between Metropolitanism and Nationalism, see Maurice Careless' paper above, pp. 114-117.
16. Robert Craig Brown, *Canada's National Policy 1883-1900: A Study in Canadian-American Relations*, Princeton, 1964. See also his paper in this volume p. 155ff.
17. See his paper in this volume, and also his "The Cost of Protectionism with High International Mobility of Factors", *Canadian Journal of Economics and Political Science* XXX, November 1964.
18. V. C. Fowke, "The National Policy—Old and New", *Canadian Journal of Economics and Political Science* XVIII, August 1952.
19. Committee on Broadcasting, *Report*, Ottawa, 1965, pp. 12, 17 & 47.
20. H. Edward English, *Industrial Structure in Canada's International Competitive Position: A Study of the Factors Affecting Economies of Scale and Specialization in Canadian Manufacturing*, Montreal, The Canadian Trade Committee of the Private Planning Association of Canada, June 1964. Also, see above, I. Macdonald's article, pp. 187-190.
21. See above, Stephen Hymer "Direct Foreign Investment and the National Economic Interest", pp. 192-197.
22. See above, James Guillet, "Nationalism and Canadian Science", pp. 228-230.
23. On the serious educational deficiencies of top management in Canada, see Economic Council of Canada, *Second Annual Review: Towards Sustained and Balanced Economic Growth*, Ottawa, December 1965.
24. For evidence on the WASPish character of the Canadian élite and the limited extent of upward mobility, see John Porter, *The Vertical Mosaic*, Toronto, 1965.

a psychoanalysis of

nationalist sentiment • charles hanly

The nation is one among a number of human groups. The sentiment of nationalism associated with it is, similarly, only one of a number of group feelings. Nevertheless, its powerful influence upon the political life of mankind has acquired for it a role in history that singles it out from among other members of the species for special consideration. Moreover, at the present juncture in Canadian history, when the continuing existence of Canada is threatened by deep rifts within the country, there are many who feel that a strong injection of national loyalty on all sides would place constitutional, political, social and economic problems in a soluble context. But before such ideas can be accurately assessed, it is necessary to undertake an examination in depth of the sentiment itself. For there are good reasons to believe that all forms of nationalist sentiment derive their force from repressed emotions and that its *extreme* forms are the product of unconscious (because repressed) psychic disturbances.[1] Therefore, it is important first to explore the physic mechanisms involved in the formation of nationalistic feelings, second, to examine some of their manifestations in Canadian national life and, finally, to consider what kind of psychological solutions for the problem of Canadian unity are going to be workable and durable.

NATIONALIST FEELING

An audience in a hockey arena or a theatre stands up ceremonially to

303

sing the national anthem before settling down to enjoy the spectacle. Most of its members experience a mild thrill mingling with their excited anticipation of the game or drama. What is this thrill that passes through each person in the audience? It is nationalist sentiment. But what exactly is nationalist sentiment? What is its genesis? What is its place in the total life of the person? What are its other manifestations? What is the range of its influences upon behaviour, imagination, thought and decision? What is its value in the economy of life apart from the temporary feeling of satisfaction it generates when it is stimulated during ceremonial occasions? Is there a Canadian version of it?

If one tries to answer these questions on the basis of self-awareness and recollection, one encounters only a series of experiences with a somewhat opaque emotion at their centre, around which are clustered memories of similar experiences reaching back into a completely forgotten past. Nowhere in these experiences does there appear a force so powerful that it is able to subsume all other demands and impulses, even the impulse to preserve one's life. This vague enthusiasm scarcely merits the fulsome eulogies or the bitter denunciations that nationalism has received. There must be more here than meets the eye.

Nationalist feeling varies in intensity along a wide spectrum. At one end there is the mild feeling of satisfied pride when a Canadian scores a triumph in the arts, sciences, business or warfare—a pride that is added to the admiration that any unusual accomplishment generates. We admire Crothers for his athletic accomplishments as we admired Snell or Bannister; but when there is added to that admiration a sense of vicarious pride in Crothers' achievements because he is a Canadian we are being nationalistic. Directly proportional to the strength of the pride there will be an equal and opposite tendency to want to disparage the athletic attainments of other nationals. But as nationalist feelings intensify there comes into being the urge to defend the nation against some dangerous internal or external threat (which must be created, if it does not exist) and to defend it heroically by means of physical violence.

The spectrum, then, reveals a transition from mild, life-enhancing feelings to powerful emotions that hold unrecognized dangers. In fact, it is only when the national group is actually in real danger that the most extreme form of nationalist sentiment can appear to be well adapted to the interests of humanity. Now, superficially, it might appear that there is a difference in kind between the emotions that occur at each end of the spectrum. But the difference turns out to be one of degree and not of kind. The psychogenesis of all emotions on the spectrum under consideration is similar. The basis for this conclusion will be elaborated presently, but first it is necessary to describe the mental formation we are considering in more detail.

The nucleus of nationalism is a complex emotion of loving veneration for the nation and hostility toward some other or others. But it also has typical concomitant intellectual, imaginative and moral correlates. Intellectually, there is a vague belief in a national life that transcends the lives of its individual members. It is this life that is thought to be invoked by mass ceremonial occasions. The participant feels himself to be infused with vital energy from outside himself and elevated by self-transcending purposes. Associated with these emotions there are images representing the nature and origins of the national life. These images always answer in the most precise way to the nuclear emotions that exercise a decisive influence over them. On the one hand, there are highly congenial idealized images of the national life; counterbalancing these narcissistically distorted images there are debased images of some alien nation. For example, as Carl Berger has shown in his study,[2] some Canadians have been pleased to trace the origins of our national character to the virile, pure, rugged land and its severe climate, thinking that the land bestows upon its sons its own sterling character. Conversely, many of these Canadian nationalists have imagined the peoples of the Mediterranean and tropical countries to be enervated by effeminacy and a tendency toward epicurean corruption. Finally, there is the moral idea that actions performed for the sake of the preservation or aggrandizement of the national entity are made good *by that very fact*. John Dales has shown the influence that this moral principle has had upon Canadian tariff and immigration policy.[3] The strength of nationalist feeling in a population can be measured by the extent to which it is prepared to make sacrifices of ego satisfactions such as a high standard of living to the demands of national aggrandizement. And by this standard of measurement Dales' conclusions would indicate that Canadians are strongly and crudely nationalistic. Partly because of the vastness of our country, nationalism in Canada has never had to take the form of the German demand for "liebensraum" or living room. But the potential is demonstrated by the enthusiastic response to Diefenbaker's vague yet potent call for a great northern development and expansion programme during the 1958 national election campaign.

306 · new perspectives

PSYCHOANALYTIC POSTULATES

What is the psychogenesis of the emotion that took Canadian volunteers to the Boer War, that makes Canadians willing to sacrifice the quality of their life for the sake of increasing the size of the nation, and carried many of us away in pursuit of the Diefenbaker vision?

Psychoanalysis has shown that the subjectively originated component of nationalistic feeling arises out of the repression of the conflicts generated by spontaneous development in the sexual instinct (the Oedipus complex) during early childhood. By displacing the emotions from their original fixation upon the mother and father onto the more ineffable object (the nation) and the more remote object (the head of state), the individual is able to create the illusion of being cleansed of them.[4] Repression involves one or, desirably, two psychological transformations. The first is the displacement of an emotion originally felt toward one object onto another object (in this case, from the head of the family to a head of state). The second involves the "neutralization" of the feelings themselves so that they no longer promote their original aims, sustaining instead a strong admiration for the national leader—an emotion that serves as the emotional basis for the individual's socio-political attitudes and behaviour. However, neutralization is frequently very imperfectly achieved. In such individuals admiration for the leader is a *psychological necessity* and *not* a response to genuinely superior qualities and achievements in the life of the leader. It will often take the form of an identification with the leader and an idealization of his person. Similarly, love of country, instead of taking the form of a gratitude for whatever natural resources, economic and social opportunities and recreational and cultural facilities the country may have to offer, can become a compulsive preference for all aspects of the national life as such.

For the belief in a transcendent, spiritually nourishing national life is the product of a repressed longing for the infantile symbiotic relation to the mother in whom all things are found. The ego protects itself against what would be a depressing self-realization of continuing immaturity by projecting the yearning for the mother into the nation image, making animate and gratuitously fulfilling an otherwise abstract entity. The childish boast "my mother is better than yours" becomes "my country right or wrong" in the adult. The venerating idealization of the national leader results from the transference of feelings to him that were, in the beginning, fixed upon the father. When these feelings are inadequately neutralized the original ambivalent feelings of loving awe and jealous hatred toward the father are retained in the transference. The idealization of the remote, powerful figure of the leader is a defence against the destructive side of the ambivalence in the led, just as the passionate striving for power and prestige in the leader is often an attempt to overcome and deny his anxiety.[5] By these paths the nation comes to be identified in unconscious emotional life as a super-family. This artificial family has assigned to it the task of resolving emotional conflicts left unresolved by the natural family. It establishes a bond of brotherhood with other members of the nation who manifest in their behaviour the effects of a similar identification.[6] These psychological factors account, in part, for the difficulties some modern societies have encountered in making parliamentary democracy work, as well as the retention, by those that have been successful, of archaic political institutions such as, for example, the British monarchy.

It follows that a basic human fact which we cannot afford to ignore is the *need* which clamours in people to find themselves in a socio-political environment that provides them with objects that will facilitate the projections and transferences described.[7] This need is quite distinct from the rational egoistic needs for co-operative effort to solve common problems, which also act as determinants of social-political organization. And there are some (how many, sociological studies would have to determine), who experience a further desire for national military undertakings that will test filial loyalty to the state. The determining variable is the quantity of emotion still bound to the infantile complexes which is transferred to political experience in the adult.

NATIONALISM AND AGGRESSION

The history of civilization can be viewed from the vantage point offered by psychoanalysis as a series of attempts to resolve the powerful conflicts generated by the instincts. Nationalism is one such attempt. It is now necessary to consider some of its intrinsic weaknesses as a solution for the human problem; for some troubling questions cannot be ignored. Why is animosity toward another human group so often a concomitant of nationalist sentiment? It is baffling to find the most exalted emotions and attitudes, the finest protestations of loyalty and duty connected with suspicion, contempt and destructiveness. Why does nationalist sentiment require a hate object as part of its nature?

Three contributing factors stemming from early childhood experiences are well known. The mother does not and cannot satisfy all the yearnings fixed upon her by the child. Consequently, she comes to have an antithetical nature in the eyes of the child. She is the bountiful source of nourishment and love and also the dark, scrawny, impoverishing source of frustration. Girls experience nightmares of witches; boys fear that their mothers are castrated males. A typical defence against the resulting disturbances is the splitting of the two images, leaving for the time being the good image with the mother, while transferring the evil image to some more or less "appropriate" outsider. The second factor is the intrinsic ambivalence of the Oedipus complex in the male. The son who wants his father's potency will both admire and hate his father because of the father's secure possession and enjoyment of what the son wants. Consequently, the same defence of splitting up the image of the original object into a receptor for the good feelings and a receptor for the evil feelings may be enlisted as a means of resolving the conflict so that unequivocally good feelings can be felt toward the father and the unequivocally bad feelings can be transferred to another object. The result is paranoid fantasies. The third source of destructively organized affect derives from the necessity imposed on most children of having to share parental affection with a sister or brother. A jealous demand that the old relationship be reinstituted is accompanied by a destructive wish to get rid of the intruder. Since neither of these demands can be met in reality, their repression is inevitable. A typical repressive resolution of the feelings consists of the jealous child identifying himself with the person of the brother or sister and becoming moralistically protective of all the interests of the sibling.

The psychic effect in each case is threefold. A pattern for dealing defensively with destructive impulses is set up. Essential to this pattern is the search for debased objects as a means of protecting the idealization of the preferred objects. Onto these debased objects hostility that was originally familial can be projected, thus protecting the hearth from their unwanted influence. A strong flow of destructive affect derivable from all three sources energizes the projections and transferences involved. When political entities and personalities are caught up in this nexus, the idealization of the nation and the debasement of its rivals is the result.

Irrational destructive impulses stemming from intimate personal sources come to invest social and political life.

These psychological factors explain why strong Canadianism is always associated with anti-Americanism or some other "ism." To be sure nationalists can always "find" facts to justify their depreciating attitudes. But the attitude has psychological priority over the facts in three respects. It *motivates* a search for such facts. It *invests* the facts with a special emotional and moral value. It will *invent* facts, if none are to be found. It is this last tendency that is the hallmark of an intense national feeling.

Such a feeling is nicely illustrated by the Canadian chauvinistic idea that the sons of the northern clime enjoy all the benefits of a highly moral character and a virile masculine nature, while southern and tropical countries are inhabited by sly, slothful and effeminate persons.[8] And if that configuration of feeling seems more typical of another generation, then it should be recognized that a quantity of the sum of "concern" that Canadians feel about the American negro problem derives from a need to feel themselves superior to their American neighbours. Or again, the feeling, described by Berger, of rivalrous superiority to the Australians, and New Zealanders, combined with the conviction that there exists a unique relation between Canada and Britain bears a striking structural similarity with the child who, fearing that he will be deprived of his relation to the life-giving, nourishing mother, sets out to get rid of the threatening rivals in fantasy. We argue that this structural similarity is correctly explained in terms of its psychogenetic origin by the development during the childhood of Canadians (who experience this type of national emotion) of a rivalry for special relation to the mother which has to be repressed in childhood but which can, in later life, come to be satisfied in a substitute form through nationalistic fantasies. It is this process that lies at the basis of the "umbilical tie" of Canadians to Great Britain that has been so often mentioned by writers on the Canadian national character.

PSYCHOLOGY OF CANADIAN NATIONALISM

Let us now proceed to explore the contemporary Canadian scene from the perspective provided by the psychoanalytic postulates. To begin, let us take up two questions that must have already occurred to you. How do the feelings analysed above come to be attached to the social, institutional, geographical, cultural and political entity—the nation and national leaders? How does Canadian nationalism differ from German, American, Chinese or other nationalisms? From the psychoanalytic point of view there are two variable factors: the quantity of emotion subject to the repressions that produce nationalistic sentiment and the objects of the emotion.

Our psychoanalytic postulates explain how a set of emotions that resist fixation upon their natural objects come into being by about the age of five or six in the life of the child. It is at this age that religious and social instruction is begun in earnest. An important segment of that education is instinctively designed to facilitate and stimulate the projection of these emotions upon certain selected cultural objects, some of which are national symbols. Thus we require our children at the beginning of their workday to stand solemnly and reverently to celebrate the "majesty" of the queen (and by this very act to fabricate it). American children salute the flag, declare their allegiance to the constitution and sing a hymn of praise to America the Beautiful. These daily exercises are initiation rites in the strictest anthropological sense. Children are gradually "born" into the tribe![9]

The underlying psychic fact of the process is the fixation of the emotions derivative from the repressed infantile conflicts upon these cultural objects. The enactment of the ceremonial by the teacher makes the following ritual non-verbal declaration: "We adults derive our strength and virtue from the queen, flag or nation. We expect you children to form the same allegiance!" The declaration is a magical incantation. The lives of the persons involved are the only real sources of strength or virtue. But the unconscious nature of the projection creates the illusion that the source is external and made available through the ritual act of allegiance itself. The one reality—the improvement of life made possible by co-operative effort—is itself left vague and obscure beyond the illusion of a transcendent group life. It follows that there could be no difference *in kind* between Canadian, American, German, French, Vietnamese, Chinese or British nationalism in so far as psychogenetic roots are concerned. They can vary only in *intensity* and in their symbolic *manifestation*.

As we have already shown, it is not only the nation and its symbolic substitutes (e.g., the queen) that are made the objects of unconscious feelings; the national political leader may also be called upon to serve a similar psychic function. Now nothing stimulates the feeling of awe more easily than the perception of some powerful natural force at work, whether its effect be destructive or beneficial. The same is true of great historic events as well as of men whose decisions and actions appear to shape them. The idea is to be found in its purest anthropomorphic form in Spinoza's idea of God as an infinite power of willing that is a law entirely onto itself. It is just such power that the human unconscious finds especially alluring, because it appears to it as the incarnation of the idealized parent image. Hence, it promises to satisfy an old yearning whose deeper determinants are entirely unconscious. It is for this reason that the political leader who seeks the most devoted following and the most exact obedience must present himself as a man in whom the past history and future destiny of the nation is personified, a man whose fate it is to decide the fate of his people. The charisma of the charismatic leader is made of the stuff of the illusion that the intrinsically unrequitable yearning for the idealized parent can be requited.

The Canadian national scene currently offers the prospect of two political leaders, Diefenbaker and Pearson, whose political styles diverge sharply. Diefenbaker, in his prime, fits well into the category of the charismatic leader. Despite many political setbacks he has declared that at no time since early childhood has his conviction that he was destined for historic national leadership been shaken. Pearson, on the other hand, can still look wistfully upon another life that might have made him the manager of a baseball team, despite his steady progress toward the highest seats of power both international and national. Whereas Diefenbaker, when Prime Minister, preferred to reserve decision-making to himself and enjoyed the prospect of an awaiting world, Pearson initiates an action or a negotiation and allows a decision to emerge often publicly (as in the flag debate) out of the composition of interets that are generated around the issue. Diefenbaker must make it appear that his will exerts a decisive influence over events; for Pearson the political event is part of a history that transcends his person and which he is content to influence, shape and guide. The general lack of enthusiasm for Pearson's political leadership can be seen, then, to be a composition of two types of disappointment. On the one hand, persons may, on the basis of the evidence, believe that Pearson was not decisive enough in dealing with cabinet ministers who had become political liabilities, and that he allowed the flag issue to get out of control. But on the other hand, disenchantment may result from the instinctive realization that Pearson insists on being only a man and refuses to make himself into "the leader" in whom the unconscious yearnings for an idealized father can find a vicarious satisfaction. Setting any objective failures aside, the Pearson style of political leadership stands as an exacting challenge to Canadians to withdraw their fantasy life from national politics. The recurrent journalistic demand for "strong, dynamic leadership" is some indication of the strength of the demand for the "power figure".

But a further point of great importance emerges. An environment may or may not offer objects that facilitate the projection of unconscious feelings onto them. This fact above all others is important in understanding the general "absence" of a strong sentiment of Canadian nationalism.

Here comparison with the United States is instructive. In the U.S., the country, the constitution, the flag, and the President in his ceremonial capacity[10] are widely shared objects of nationalistic feeling. Are there any equally effective Canadian equivalents? Whatever the Governor General might mean to French Canadians, he is to English Canadians only a pale reflection of the British king or queen who is not *of us* in the sense in which the American president is *of them*. We have a flag, after years of avoidance that is called by many English Canadians "the Quebec flag". We have a constitution, the B.N.A. Act, although many Canadians still believe that our constitution is just "the British constitution". It is a constitution, however, that was promulgated by another parliament in another land. It is interpreted by not a few Canadians as a document that guarantees the separate rights of a conquered people, the French settlers and their descendants, against encroachment by settlers from the conquering nation. It is seen by not a few other Canadians as a document that treats a vanquished people with high moral generosity, an act that merits in return a placid loyalty not so much to Canada as to the crown. Consequently, in the psychological sense there is no Canadian nation as there is an American or French nation. There is a legal and geographical entity, but the nation does not exist. For there are no objects that all Canadians share as objects of national feeling.

Nevertheless, this problem can be exaggerated. There is contradicting evidence from very recent history. In 1957, Diefenbaker defeated a French-Canadian Prime Minister and then succeeded in 1958 in making his person and his conception of a greater Canada a focus for the aspirations of many Canadians both French- and English-speaking. The event suggests that French-Canadian nationalist feelings are not so strongly attached to things *Québécois* that they cannot be transferred to objects that can be shared by other Canadians. The Diefenbaker era never materialized. Nevertheless, from the psychological point of view the possibility still remains of forging a strong intra-racial national feeling around a great, bold and imaginative leader whose practical intelligence equals his rhetorical gifts.

But the Diefenbaker era was destined from the outset to fail as a solution for the psychological problem of national unity. The force that would have caused the failure independently of whatever successes the Diefenbaker government might have had is *anglophilia.* In the final analysis it was not a greater Canada that Diefenbaker sought, but a Canada more deeply bound to Great Britain. Diefenbaker, like so many Canadians of his generation, owes his deepest emotional allegiance to Britain and things British in Canada. The signs of this fact are numerous: Canada's intransigent opposition to Britain's entry into the European Common Market (like a pampered self-styled favourite child afraid of the loss of the mother when she shows signs of interest in men of her own generation), the demand for an obvious British symbol on the Canadian flag, etc. The power of the same feeling is demonstrated by the jaundiced hostility aroused by Pearson's role at the U.N. during the Suez crisis. Pearson's action was interpreted in some circles as the work of a communist dupe. The irrationality of this idea is a fair measure of the strength of the "British tie". For it is this emotion that lies at the root of the vague feeling so many Canadians seem to have that Pearson's intervention was an affront to something sacred inspired by modern history's incarnation of the satanic.

It is a long way from the time of the Boer War, when the British lion could pursue her imperial ambitions with her dominion cubs at her side, to the mid-twentieth century, when the Canadian U.N. delegate takes a leading role in applying the leash. Many English Canadians are emotionally incapable of making that transition. Anglophilia represents a major psychological barrier in the way of the formation of a unifying nationalist sentiment in Canada. Many English Canadians have still insisted upon retaining a dependent relation upon *their* country of origin—the British conqueror of Canada. Until English Canadians are able to transfer their basic emotional allegiances to Canada there is little hope for any strong national cohesiveness that could bind together the two racial groups. Until English Canadians are able to abandon Canada as an imitation of an image of Britain and begin the Canadian experiment, we cannot expect French Canadians to feel much solidarity with us.

Now it will be argued that Canadians have worked hard and sacrificed much to preserve Canada's independence of the United States. Surely this points to a strong Canadianism. But the nature of the motive is not directly deducible from the historical fact. Canadian independence of the United States (the delinquent sons who may have now grown big and strong yet do not preserve in their hearts that chaste loyalty to the motherland that is the hallmark of the Canadian!), for many English Canadians, is imposed by the necessity of clinging to Britain. Therefore, the history of Canadian opposition to the U.S. cannot be used to provide evidence of Canadian independence. It is evidence of Canadian dependence on Britain. For many, Canada's *raison d'être* is to be "British North America". Typical of such thinking is George Grant's *Lament for a Nation*. But his anxiety is premature and inappropriate. What he laments is the demise of British North America. And, of course, that conception of Canada must be abandoned, for it should now be clear to everyone that Quebec will not capitulate to its incarnation. It follows that Grant's lament is not for the passing of Canada, but for the passing of an untenable misconception of Canada. The Quebec revolution has made explicit and obvious the latent inadequacies in the thinking of the anglophiles. Instead of mourning the death of Canada we should be rejoicing at the new prospects for growth and maturation.

It is, after all, precisely the transfer of emotional allegiance to Britain that gives rise to the feelings of inferiority that are rightly said to be a characteristic trait of Canadians. For what is the psychological genesis of a sense of inferiority as a national characteristic? The withdrawal of emotional energy from reality-oriented ego life and its distribution to nationalist fantasies always has the effect of enervating ego life to some extent. Usually, however, there is a compensating gain as a result of the buoyant feeling that the national life in which one's own life participates is preferable to others. But this compensation is denied to the Canadian, who, having unconsciously adopted British objects upon which to fix his unconscious life, comes to find that he places a unique value on the British way, with Canadianism as an inferior imitation. British political leaders have something heroic about them; Canadian statesmen are at best mere politicians. The result is a depressing sense of being inferior as a Canadian. A second observable social phenomenon that derives from the same psychological root is the frequency with which rather second-rate English emigrés rise to the top of their chosen field of activity in Canada. They are carried along, in part, by the vicarious veneration they receive as representatives of that land where virtue is of the highest order, customs are impeccable and judgment is infallible.

These considerations shed a new light on the so-called Canadian internationalism. Canadian intellectuals often like to take a special pride in the relative absence of nationalist feeling for Canada in their mentality. It is claimed, perhaps gratuitously, that this state of affairs is the basis for the development of a new international spirit that places the Canadian in the forefront of progress in world history. A more realistic view would have to take into account the extent to which the Canadian's internationalism is merely the product of a failure to find his own identity as a Canadian: a failure that results from his continuing unconscious emotional dependency on Britain. Such an internationalism would best be described as a narcissistic defence against the feelings of inferiority that are produced by the more fundamental dependency. The largeness of the Canadian's international horizon may be the product of a failure to find and accept himself within the political, cultural and economic horizons of his own society.

PROGNOSIS: WILL AMERICA REPLACE GREAT BRITAIN AS OUR NATIONAL IDEAL?

What is the likely fate of the English Canadian's emotional ties to Britain? The tie will probably break down no later than with our children's generation (to-day's public schoolers). We have considered above the factors that influence the object choices made by unconscious feelings, and we cited educational factors along with intrinsic properties of the object. Post-war changes in both factors will probably cause a rapid deterioration in "the British image". History is now made in Washington, Moscow and Peking, not in London. American military, economic and political ascendency in the West is an unavoidable reality. And even though the ego may be governed in its choice of objects by moral and aesthetic predilections, the instincts will fix upon whatever object manifests the greatest power as the object before which they hold the individual in awe. Reinforcing this basic psychological factor is the influence of modern communications media, especially television, which, as Watkins has pointed out[11], provides us with vivid impressions of the American power figures of our time. Reports of the doings of the leaders are supplemented by direct impressions of their persons. This has the effect of rapidly diminishing the contribution that imitations of the British image make to Canadian life.

Further evidence of this tendency is to be found in the *Preliminary Report of the Royal Commission on Bilingualism and Biculturalism*. The Report refers to a prevalent ambivalent attitude toward the United States (pp. 56-59). On the one hand, Canadians tend to seek a strongly unified Canada because of American proximity; on the other hand, they express "a lively awareness of the greater economic development and higher standard of living across the border". It is probable that the second side of the ambivalence is more fundamental than the first. The situation is like that of the Toronto matron who, seeing a corpulent, virile looking Hawaiian, exclaimed, "I wouldn't want to meet him alone on a dark night!" Here the very emphasis of the denial indicates the deeper unconscious wish for just such an event. Similarly, the Canadian preoccupation with retrenchment against American economic and cultural encroachment may be a defensive reaction against something we instinctively admire and to which we are tempted to capitulate.

It follows that Canada stands in real danger of failing to achieve national maturity. Just as the individual can avoid maturation by adopting a series of parent substitutes with the result that his home-leaving is, at the deeper emotional level, a hollow sham, so too the collective sentiments of a people can be transferred from one external group to another —in the case of Canada from Great Britain to the U.S. The tendency is traceable among those academics who collapse into anxious uncertainty if they cannot find a parallel for a new undertaking either in Oxford or Harvard; that is not a frame of mind by which a strong national life is created and sustained.

THERAPY: ALTERNATIVE PATHS TOWARD NATIONAL MATURITY

Having considered a diagnosis and prognosis, what therapy is indicated to maximize the prospects of the growth of a healthy nationalist sentiment in Canada? One alternative, already indicated above, is the emergence of a series of new leaders from our own generation who can stir the interest, imagination and aspirations of all Canadians and so attract the unconscious impulses at the root of nationalist feeling to Canadian objects.

But more than eloquent words and imposing images are necessary to achieve such an objective. Such an approach would require undertakings of a magnitude and consequence akin to the revolution out of which America was born—undertakings which would go far beyond the mere adoption of a distinctive flag or the repatriation of the Constitution. But given Canada's resources, it is extremely difficult to imagine any such magnificent undertakings that would not be retrogressive and foolhardy from other points of view. Canada is not, for example, in a position to take any real initiatives in our own hemisphere to combat some of the reactionary tendencies of U.S. policies. Canada is not politically, economically or militarily in a position to act as a decisive third force that would help to give South Americans an alternative between government by military junta or communist insurrection. For the remainder of the twentieth century at least, Canada's contribution to world history must be a modest one.

There is a second alternative which is consonant with these realities. Canadians can try to learn to accept a national life in which only the mildest forms of nationalist sentiment are sustained. This policy has several things to recommend it. First, the psychoanalysis of nationalist sentiment shows that the intensity of nationalist feeling in an individual is roughly equivalent to the quantity of hostility in his make-up. Consequently, strong nationalist sentiment is intrinsically dangerous. Therefore, moral and rational gains are available to any nation that can tolerate a substantial reduction in its *amour-propre*. One of the constructive tendencies in our generation is the search for a psychic stability and meaningfulness that is independent of ego-inflating national identifications. Instead of affirming with one's life, "I am a Canadian, therefore I am a man" there is a growth toward a way of life that is premised on the converse declaration, "I am a man and I am grateful that I happened to be a Canadian". Secondly, a general acceptance of a diminished national feeling would make possible a more realistic approach to national politics because national policies and leaders would not have to cater to fantasies and irrational demands. Such a course would also enable those Canadians who demand strong group identifications to find them in their respective cultural groups rather than in Canada. Far from weakening national life, as some fear, the effect would be to guarantee its survival in the immediate future and strengthen it over the years. One major difficulty with such a solution is that, if the numbers of Canadians who form cultural group identifications is great and if they distribute a large quantity of feeling to these identifications, our society will be indefinitely troubled by high levels of English Canadian-French Canadian distrust and hostility. Thirdly, the withdrawal of nationalist sentiment from national politics will facilitate Canada's contribution to the growth of world government, international law and global scientific, technological and economic co-operation because unconscious hostilities will not interfere with our perceptions of the needs and resources of other societies. To cease loving one's own nation is also to cease hating other nations.

I am personally persuaded that the latter is the wiser course for Canada. By what paths can it be pursued? The demand for a decision by Canadians to moderate their nationalism is artificial and irrelevant. Being a nationalist is something that happens to a person, not something that he chooses. Furthermore, psychoanalysis has shown that the roots of nationalist feeling go back into inevitable childhood emotions and experiences. Consequently, causal influences have to be brought to bear. Three causal factors are fundamental. The tendencies toward the development of nationalism or some parallel fantasy life is an invariant property of human life. But the tendency need not be realized in the form of nationalism so long as the culture offers satisfactory alternatives. Of the various alternatives, a rich artistic culture is by far the best.[12] The achievement of a rational national political life is contingent upon the growth of a vigorous artistic culture in Canada. But the quality of the artistic culture is important. So far, Canadian art and its official sponsors have been too much preoccupied with efforts to create a juvenile self-conscious Canadianism. Contrary to the romantic view[13], great art is by its very nature international because its essential aim is to express man and only incidentally does it express Canadian man. The second influence is an educational system in the widest sense that is dedicated to exploring reality rather than constructing and nourishing fantasy. But thirdly, the decisive influence must be the lives of the parent generation—our generation. The ability of the next generation to handle successfully the powerful emotions in which nationalist sentiment is rooted will largely depend on our ability to help our children cultivate their lives toward mature intelligence and true humanity. There is an instinctive wisdom in Governor General Vanier's concern to cultivate healthy family life in Canada. For it is in the basic emotional transactions within every Canadian family that the final success or failure of a viable Canadianism will be decided.

NOTES

1. S. Freud: *Group Psychology and the Analysis of the Ego*, Standard Edition, Vol. XVIII, London.
2. See above, Carl Berger, "The True North Strong and Free" p. 358.
3. See above, John Dales, "Protection, Immigration and Canadian Nationalism" pp. 164-168.
4. See also "The Psychodynamic Aspects of Leadership", D. Wilfred Abse and Lucie Jessner, in *Daedalus*, Vol. 90, 1961, p. 694.
5. O. Fenichel, "Character Disorders", in *The Psychoanalytic Theory of Neurosis*, London, 1945.
6. S. Freud: *Group Psychology and the Analysis of the Ego*, Standard Edition, Vol. XVIII, London.
7. Projection and transference are psychological mechanisms that provide defences against unwanted impulses. Projection alienates an impulse from the ego by investing it in an external object which then comes to be an object of fear, e.g., projection handles unconscious homosexual impulses by converting them into a fear of being attacked. When social conditions are right, the fear may take the specific form of an attack upon civilized society by a racial sub-group such as Jews or Negroes. Transference involves an ego-identification with another person who consequently comes to function as an *alter ego* in the way in which the mature personality of the father functions as the ego of the developing personality of the child during his early years. Consequently, moral and aesthetic values as well as life aims are received from the person to whom the transference has been made. The relationship yields to the individual who becomes the object of such transferences a very considerable power over the lives of those who have made the transference—a power limited only by the implicit demand that he create situations in which the unconscious impulses that cause the transference can be gratified.
8. See above, Carl Berger, "The True North Strong and Free" pp. 9-12.
9. For a detailed study of the process see D. Easton and R. D. Hess, "The Child's Political World", paper presented to the World Congress of International Political Science Association, Sept. 1961.
10. For a detailed study of the American child's image of the President see R. D. Hess and D. Easton, "The Child's Changing Image of the President" in the *Public Opinion Quarterly*, Vol. 24, 1960.
11. See above, Melville Watkins, "Technology and Nationalism", pp. 297-298.
12. The importance of the cathartic effect of the arts for the health of the body politic was already appreciated by Aristotle in ancient times.
13. Cf. Isaiah Berlin, "J. G. Herder" in *Encounter*, Vol. XXV, 1965, pp. 42-51.

IDEOLOGY •

the 19th century legacy: nationalism
or patriotism? • george heiman

Of all the modern political phenomena, few are more contentious and
elusive than the concept of nationalism. The term can and does have a
wide range of meanings, implications and manifestations. It is widely and
haphazardly utilized to praise and condemn, to direct and to incite, and
yet the precise meaning of nationalism is hard to arrive at. Canadian
nationalism is no exception. Therefore, before the nature of the latter
notion is examined, it may be prudent to consider the concept of nationalism *per se*.

There is one major reason why nationalism has such a wide variety of
meanings, why it has been called a "secular religion",[1] why it has been
looked upon as a noble and elevating sentiment by some and as an expression of irrationalism[2] leading from humanitarianism to bestiality[3] by
others. The reason: nationalism is essentially a highly subjective and emotionally charged factor. The subjectivism inherent in the concept casts a
shadow over any discussion—a single example will illustrate this contention. It can be argued, for instance, that great deeds have been performed
in the name of nationalism and a prime illustration of this is the way in
which a sense of nationalism contributed to the spiritual strength and cohesion of the English nation in its most perilous days of 1939 and 1940. In
view of the fact that it served to bolster the cause not only of England but
also that of all the Western democracies, one might conclude that national-

ism is a great and desirable force. But there is one fatal pitfall in this line of reasoning: the national socialist and fascist dictatorships against whom England was struggling were also warring in the name of their own particular brand of nationalism. Two or more nationalisms were pitted against one another and the judgement whereby one is found acceptable and the other rejected is, by sheer necessity, quite subjective. Yet such subjectivism is something which a student of nationalism comes to accept. Some of the elements of English nationalism, for instance, are part and parcel of the Canadian political heritage. To most Canadians, then, it is probably safe to say that expressions of English nationalism were much more appealing than those of its enemies. Thus, if this judgement was subjective (indeed, are not all judgements subjective?), then it does not necessarily mean that it had disagreeable or disadvantageous consequences.

But surely it will not do to differentiate simply between nationalism *A* and nationalism *B* and happily declare one to be "good" and the other to be "bad"? For underlying the great variety of nationalisms are a core of common traits and historical forces. Only the nationalist whose zealotry excludes thought could ignore these generic characteristics of nationalism and attempt to grade nationalisms on an absolute, black-and-white basis.

It is the primary purpose of this essay to review the intellectual and material forces which have constituted the common historical root of nationalism. We also wish to trace the alternative ways in which nationalism has manifested itself as a political force in the modern world. Finally, we will suggest the alternative paths which the development of nationalist sentiment might follow in contemporary Canada. Our approach will be built upon an analysis of the historical derivation of the very concept of "nationalism" and its allied terminology. Even though this may at points involve semantics, it is our conviction that this may clarify the issue and encourage Canadians to view their own quest for a sense of nationalism in the larger perspective of Western history.

PATRIOTISM AND NATIONALISM

Derived from the Latin word *patria*, meaning native land, the term "patriotism" denotes the attachment, and indeed love, the individual fosters towards his land of birth or domicile. This is the oldest and perhaps even primeval sentiment connected with the word "nationalism". It is deeply rooted in the psychological structure of man and is closely associated with such concepts as loyalty to the clan or tribe, native hearth, etc. The degree of intensity with which patriotism is active within the individual and his community is, of course, a highly variable factor.

The idea of patriotism can be found in classical literature, particularly in the works dealing with the Greek city-state and republican and (to a lesser degree) imperial Rome. The Middle Ages, on the other hand, showed little tendency towards strong patriotism, for above the native land and the sentiment it commanded there stood the image of universal Christianity. When, however, the unity of Western Christiandom was broken by the Reformation, patriotism emerged again on a religious plane with Luther, and in the strictly political thought of Machiavelli. The Renaissance and the Reformation were succeeded by the Age of Enlightenment, an era of cosmopolitanism where patriotism was considered somewhat *gauche* and quite backward. Yet this attitude too ended by the middle of the eighteenth century, when patriotism and, indeed, what is usually referred to as "modern nationalism"[4] emerged. But more of that later. Suffice it to re-state: patriotism, in our vocabulary, stands for an emotional but also a rational attachment to the native land.

The emotional aspect can be seen in either a terribly simple or excessively complicated light. It is, in a way, "natural" that many would love their land in preference to others, particularly if their experience with the non-native element appears undesirable to them. But the explanation for the existence of patriotism can be excessively complicated or even unsatisfactory because, all psychological arguments with regard to the primacy of groups-consciousness aside, the logical question remains why one man should love one country above all others simply because it has produced him.

At this point, however, the strictly rational aspects of patriotism must be taken into account. A patriot is attached to his country, it can be pointed out, because he has arrived, through a rational process, at the conclusion that his country is the most conducive to his personal political, economic and social aspirations. For instance, appreciation of the Canadian political institutions and political atmosphere need not be one of blind, sentimental devotion. Indeed, it would be irrational to claim that

Canada today, or at any other stage of its political history, is or was the most perfect community. Only blind irrationalism could disregard the deficiencies within the community.

What these deficiencies are is a matter of one's personal convictions. Some would claim that economic inequities make Canada less than perfect. Others would say that centrifugal forces make this country one of ineffectual leadership and insecure domestic coherence. Yet others would criticize the pervasiveness of American cultural factors which, according to these critics, prevents Canada and Canadians from asserting their independence and distinctiveness.

Yet to all these criticisms it could be said that it seems historically hopeless to expect any community to attain perfection in any particular aspect of its existence. It could be argued, moreover, that the failure to achieve a Canadian utopia does not make this country a rationally less acceptable and attractive place to live in. Even when the formidable difficulties of the country are assessed, it is not impossible to point out that the means to alleviate the problems of Canada are available. There is disagreement as to the precedence to be accorded to the problems and as to the solutions to be sought for meeting these problems. But such a condition is natural and essential to a democratic community such as Canada. It is precisely the rational element within patriotism which prevents the demand for improvement from becoming overly one-sided. A patriot's attachment is to the whole community and not only to one of its ethnic, class, party or regional divisions; the patriot is willing to make rational concessions in order to retain some of the fundamental and original features of his country.

Another rational manifestation of patriotism is inherent in the principle of obligation. Today, when the tendency is to hold community, government and society responsible for all the details of individual well-being, this principle is relegated to the background. But it is still possible to detect a trace of that traditional concept of obligation which maintains that it is not only the community which is obliged to care for the individual but that the individual, in return, is obliged to carry out certain duties. The carrying out of these duties does not necessarily have to be done in a spirit of adulating, nationalistic zealotry; it is not a matter of liking or disliking the performance of duties but it is simply a sense of "owing" to the community and paying individual debts by whatever legitimate and rational acts are demanded from the citizen.

Yet another rational aspect of patriotism is expressed in the individual's attitude towards the image of his nation. A realistic appraisal of the virtues and shortcomings of his community are by no means beyond the capacity of the patriot. Once the individual acquiesces in the obvious, the impossibility of obtaining a utopia, he will, precisely because of his rational approach, be a more valuable part of his community. If his country, in today's world, is a relatively small one, then the patriot will not overestimate the stature of his nation in the international power struggle. Having realistically assessed the precise extent of his country's influence, the patriot will refrain from deluding himself and others about him with visions of politically unattainable grandeur.

Finally, and in conjunction with the patriot's attitude towards the external world, his rationalism will prevent him from arriving at the conclusion that it is his country which must perforce, be the very best, the greatest and the most glorious entity on this globe. He remembers, in other words, that his country is best suited for *his* specific political temperament but that it is perfectly possible and rational that patriots of other nations have an identical attitude towards their own communities.

In what manner, then, does patriotism, as seen here, differ from the concept usually referred to as "nationalism"? The essential distinction between the admittedly closely-related notions is to be found in the relationship between citizen and nation. Patriotism, as one psychologist holds,[5] creates demands which lead to nationalist action. Looked at from the other extreme, however, it can also be argued that nationalism sets forth conditions to which the citizen must adhere. The crucial point is to what degree the citizen is obliged to heed not only the legal but also the social rulings of the nation. Or, to put it in other words: nationalism, as opposed to patriotism, commands the ultimate loyalty and devotion to the nation-state. Patriotism, on the other hand, is pluralistic in its inclinations. A patriot can have ties with other associations besides those he has with the nation. He may show loyalty towards a religious group, a political party, a trade union, not to mention the traditional ties of family and kin. These loyalties are not looked upon as being incompatible with the loyalty he shows towards the nation. Where patriotism rather than nationalism prevails, the political structure of the native land, the nation-state, does not encompass or subjugate all of the individual's interests. Rather, the nation-state, or its functioning executive, the government and its organs, keep within certain legal boundaries which prevent them from trespassing into the sphere of private rights and aspirations.

The land and the political atmosphere in which patriotism flourishes are then essentially non-monolithic and liberal. Nationalism, conversely, demands and frequently receives too much of what is the individual's right and prerogative, and shows, moreover, a marked tendency towards authoritarian practices.

Whether the prevalent mood in a political community can be called "patriotism" or "nationalism," depends ultimately upon the power-relations between the state and the citizen. If the demands of the nation-state turn the individual into a totally "public" person, if no room is left for the expression of his "private" rights, then it can be argued that nationalism, if public right is practiced in its name, is prevalent. The argument for a sharp distinction between man as man, and man as citizen has been clearly stated by John Stuart Mill, when he said that "there is a circle around every individual human being, which no government, be it that of one, of a few or of the many, ought to be permitted to overstep: there is a part of the life of every person . . . within which the individuality of that person ought to reign uncontrolled either by any other individual or by the public collectively".[6]

It is this fundamental dualism between patriotism and nationalism that explains the "good" and the "bad", or the liberal and the aggressive faces of what is usually referred to as "nationalism". The duality, as pointed out earlier, has caused innumerable difficulties. Consequently the term "nationalism" has been divided into at least two categories, authoritarian, integral,[7] irrational nationalism or chauvinism[8] on the one side, and humanitarian, constitutional or liberal nationalism on the other. The latter is, for all intents and purposes, the equivalent of what we have called "patriotism" and, for the extent of this essay, we shall retain this distinction. Nor can the bald differentiation between nationalism and patriotism be left standing without pointing to the obvious fact that every nation has its share of nationalists and patriots; hence it is dangerous to strike out and denounce one and praise another. The ultimate judgement can only be based on the political practices of the nation and the demands which its government makes of its individual citizens.

NATION AND NATIONALITY

Definitions of the concept of "nation" have depended to a very large degree on the nature of the sentiment entertained *vis à vis* the nation. The nation can be the subject of worship, as in the case of the German nineteenth-century historian, Heinrich von Treitschke. Or the nation can be looked upon as an organic and somewhat mythical entity, which made Burke declare that "a nation is not an idea only of local extent and individual memory aggregation; but it is an idea of continuity, which extends in time as well as in numbers and in space".[9] On the most empirical level the nation can be viewed as "the ultimate point of reference for political loyalties and actions".[10] In a similar vein but with a slightly different emphasis, a nation has been defined as "a multitude of humans characterized by common and unique cultural factors. This multitude shares in a common historical past and is linked by an awareness of its uniqueness".[11] Finally, in a somewhat whimsical but quite incisive manner, a nation has been defined as "a society united by a common error as to its origins and a common aversion to its neighbours".[12] But whatever the definition one prefers, the most obvious characteristic of the nation is the simple and unalterable fact that it is today the predominant social and political organization. We have come to accept this development though it has been with us only since the end of the eighteenth century.

The nation did not always enjoy such pre-eminence in man's thought and actions. It is equally important to note that today the nation and the state have become one. Until fairly recently the state, that is the governing and administrative machinery of the community in a given geographic area, was thought of as something apart from, beyond or at least distinctly separate from "the people", whoever they may be. It was precisely when "the people", under the urgings of nationalism on the one hand and the democratic upheavals of the eighteenth and nineteenth centuries on the other, turned to thinking of themselves as the "nation", that the union between nation and state came about. Heretofore, the state was personified by the ruler or, in the English case, by parliament or in some German principalities, by the camarilla. Indeed, English political writings are meagre in their discussions of the state and, as a rule, prefer to speak of "government", "cabinet" or, in the Canadian case, of "Ottawa". Yet it would be quite pointless to deny that all modern countries are states based on a national community, in short, that they are nation-states. Futhermore, patriotism and nationalism both need a geographic home, a land upon which the loyalty and affection of its population can focus.

Without a "native country," a "fatherland" or *la patrie*, nationalism and patriotism are abstract notions.

Somewhat less tangible than nation-state and geographic home, but by no means less important to patriotism and nationalism, are such cultural factors as a commonly shared intellectual, artistic and, above all, linguistic heritage. Of these cultural factors, language is the most important and, at the same time, the great devisive factor among nations. Yet there are some notable exceptions. Multi-lingual nations, such as Canada, have shown in the past that the language-barrier is not insurmountable, nor did it preclude the evolution of patriotism in this country.

A nationally-shared religion serving the cause of communal unity is also a somewhat ambiguous factor. It would make our task easier if we could say that patriotism and nationalism are greatly strengthened by the existence of one single religious creed within the nation. Indeed, as in the case of England, we have an example of the unifying role of a national church contributing to cohesion. Similarly, in the case of France, the Roman Catholic Church, as the exclusive spiritual authority, played a large role in the formation of French patriotism. On the other hand, Italy, also predominantly Catholic, knew little unity until the nineteenth century. In the case of Germany, one finds a country strongly divided between a Protestant North and a Catholic South, yet this religious division did not stand in the way of the ultimate unification in 1871. Consequently it can be argued that patriotism and nationalism are not dependent upon one common religion, though the presence of one greatly facilitates the emergence of national unity.

A belief in a common history, a record of a common past, is also an essential ingredient of patriotism and nationalism. The tales of past glories and victories, of great deeds and heroic actions, may be real or highly fictitious. But whether they stand up to close investigation or not, the communal records cast a heavy shadow over the political actions of today. Similarly, a common faith in the future of the nation is of fundamental importance. Indeed, just as the common past binds, in myth and reality, so does a faith in a commonly-shared, preferably glorious future. Education, always a basic concern to patriot and nationalist alike, focuses on the training of coming generations in the unspoken understanding that the national community and its spirit represent a certain historical continuity projected into the future.

Plans vary with regard to their objectives and ambitions. Patriots may content themselves with envisaging their community as prosperous and socially and economically well-balanced. Nationalists, on the other hand, entertain more grandiose and possibly quite different plans. Territorial aggrandizements, conquests and the subjugation of neighbouring peoples are frequently integral to nationalist thought. The promise of collective glory and the temptation of power are great, particularly when there is a strongly illiberal nationalist sentiment prevalent in a community. The presence of such sentiment and such plans, encouraged by nationalist education and utilized by nationalist politicians and demagogues, provide a fertile ground for aggressive schemes.

The foregoing discussion would have been greatly simplified if one could have defined a nation as a *nationality*, possessing a common political structure in a given geographic area, with an awareness of a common past, a confidence in a shared future and bound by sentiments based on this awareness. But the definition would have been quite incorrect.

Nationality, in our discussion, shall denote not a legal or political status but an ethnic and cultural aggregate which has a common language and some commonly shared historical memories. The concept of nationality differs radically from the concept of nation in one major aspect: a nationality is not necessarily organized, it is not always politically autonomous and may not even entertain ideas to this effect. The world has known numerous multi-nationality states and empires, but the growth of nationalism has accelerated the emphasis on those distinctions which are the bases of nationalities. It has, moreover, made nationality an important political force which led to movements for self-determination and the emergence of the many new states since the end of the two world wars. The factors that keep the concept of nationality active are group-consciousness, language and "race". Language is absolutely basic to nationality and to most nationalisms as well, though not necessarily to all nation-states.

The notion of race has haunted nationalism and allied concepts since their inception. But it was not until the nineteenth century that racist features became linked to chauvinist ideology and the concept of nationality. Originally, the word "race" bears no derogatory implications and ultimately it is for the natural scientists to decide whether there can be such a thing as "pure race". (The present consensus is that there is not.) But if nationality is expressly bound to racist features it becomes a highly dubious concept. For "race", if it has any objective validity, must refer to

physical marks of differentiation which are genetically transmitted, whereas nationality embraces cultural characteristics such as language which
result from environmental conditioning.

NATIONALISM AND HISTORY

History and nationalism are intricately bound to one another. Not only
is history a basic ingredient of nationalist thought, but the history of
the concept itself explains a great many of its facets and manifestations.

Until the second half of the eighteenth century, nationalism *per se*
was not really known. Patriotism existed, but with the exception of such
long-established nations as England and France, was of a minor, parochial
nature. National cultures, the breeding ground of European nationalisms,
were subordinated to the cosmopolitan dialogue between the *illuminati*,
who had turned to the French language after Latin had lost its universal
appeal. Intellectual borders, based on political and military boundaries, did not exist. But discontent and intellectual disorientation was
beginning to show from behind the rococo facade of the Age of Enlightenment. And no single man managed to focus on the discontent in a
more poignant and confusing manner than Jean-Jacques Rousseau.

In contradiction to the cosmopolitanism of his own age, Rousseau
argued that "the feeling of humanity evaporates and grows feeble in embracing all mankind." Therefore, "it is proper that our humanity should
confine itself to our fellow-citizens."[13] And elsewhere he laments that
"Our hatred of other nations diminishes but patriotism dies with it."[14]
Rousseau's insistence on the emotional rather than the rational faculties of man, his preference for a small, sharply delimited homogeneous
community, his advocacy of a nationally supervised and nationalistically
directed education and his idea of a civic religion are but the outstanding
examples of his contribution to the growth of nationalism. Equally important is his promulgation of popular sovereignty: it forecasts the ultimate union of the nation with the state which was to take place in the
succeeding century. Collective freedom was confronted by Rousseau with
the individualistic liberty cherished by the rationalists and empiricists
and his decision in favour of collectivist sentiment proved itself prophetic.

Rousseau's theses may have gone unnoticed, however, if a suggestion of
historical developments had not been congenial to his thought. Among

the developments furthering the spread of nationalism, one of the fore-most was the formation of the first national conscript army in modern history. When the new republican government of France found itself threatened by a royalist coalition, it instituted the *levée en masse* in August 1793. The Rousseauian citizen was called upon to defend his country, and defend it he did in a most successful manner.

Nor did the novel creed of nationalism fail to introduce its own set of symbols and rituals. The national flag of France, the stirring national anthem, the Marseillaise, the celebration of new national holidays aided in the growth and spread of the national consciousness. The propagation of this new creed was furthered by a nationalistically oriented system of education which was often more devoted to indoctrination than to scholarly accuracy.

The success of French nationalism could hardly have gone unnoticed in Europe, particularly in those countries that were occupied by Napoleon, the charismatic leader of his transformed nation. In a surprisingly short period, as historical time is measured, the tenor of European politics changed. Patriotism converted into nationalism swept the continent and by 1848 had become the predominant tendency. The results, in retrospect, are far from reassuring.

Initially, the creed of nationalism was closely allied with the libertarian and egalitarian ideas of the French Revolution. Liberty meant a collective liberation of the people of France from absolutist, monarchical rule. This liberation was achieved by uniting a large segment of the population in the name of nationalism. Here, Rousseauian man joined in the General Will, subordinated his particularism to the aims of the whole, the nation, and thereby gained collective freedom as well as a measure of individual liberty.

The sequence of the liberating process is of major importance. In France it meant a thorough and also appallingly bloody overhaul of the ancient political and social order. In the other countries of continental Europe, however, it meant at first liberation from foreign rule, as illustrated by the anti-Napoleonic risings in Spain and Germany. But in these countries the social renovation which took place in France was postponed or never quite attained. Moreover, in their haste to emulate French successes, many central and east European nationalities went to great lengths to create and foster a sense of nationalism based at times on contrived and artificial historical factors. But most significantly, the libertarian ideas originally associated with nationalism were frequently forgotten or ignored in order to subordinate the concept of individual liberty to the interests of the national whole.

The first half of the nineteenth century can be thus remembered for the dissemination and the acceptance of the idea of nationalism. We must also remember that it witnessed the fatal intermingling of liberalism with chauvinism and the latter's victory over the former. The second half of the nineteenth century, on the other hand, can be looked upon as a period of nationalist consolidation. German unification is a prime example and so are the struggles between the European powers for colonial aggrandizement and economic expansion. Not even England, heretofore secure in its orderly patriotism, escaped the outburst of militancy which usually accompanies nationalism. Jingoism, the vision and reality of an empire and even the notion of the racial superiority of the Anglo-Saxon were not unknown to Kipling's England.

Nineteenth century nationalism, it could be argued, culminated neither in 1899 nor in 1914 but with Versailles and the allied peace settlements. These arrangements reflected Woodrow Wilson's desire to see self-determination accorded to those nationalities who, in the past, had been denied autonomy. Yet, though it granted self-determination to some peoples, it denied the same privilege to others. In other words, Wilson's judgment, as all judgments with regard to nationalism, was highly subjective. In effect it promulgated the idea that some nationalisms were "good" and some were "bad", hence punishable. This attitude appeared particularly unjust to the German people who had, since the previous century, fallen prey to a particularly militant form of nationalism.

In its anxiety to match French unity and English power, Germany had grasped the new creed and used it to unify, strengthen and ultimately conquer or attempt to conquer what it considered to be its national territory. While in these ambitions Germany did not differ greatly from the other nation-states, in its devotion to the doctrine of nationalism and the new collectivity, the German nation-state was eventually carried to the extreme. Hitler's rise to power was furthered and facilitated by the smoldering, resentful fires of German nationalism, a manifestation which had taken xenophobia, racism and the distant glories of the past too seriously. What had been dictated by Versailles was to be rectified as of 1939, when a nation-state had fallen prey to totalitarian nationalism and the world suffered for it.

In retrospect and in answer to the perplexed questions on the part of those who fail to see the dangers inherent in nationalism, as distinct from patriotism, some general propositions may be considered.

First, nationalism is both a centripetal as well as a centrifugal force. It is the former, the cohesive power that nationalism exerts, which appeals to its devotees. It consolidates and binds a people and not even the most liberal patriot can afford to overlook the utilitarian functional aspects of collective action. It is obvious, more so now than in any other age, that certain undertakings which are relevant to a nation's political and economic well-being fall, by necessity, under the jurisdiction of the state. If a nation wishes to carry out certain programmes in the field of education, welfare and general economic policies, it is not unreasonable to say that a patriotically united community can do so with more effect than a particularistic one.

At the same time, however, nationalism is a centrifugal influence on a global scale because in its insistence on national interests, national achievements, language, peculiarities and territorial holdings it has sharply divided the world into contending nation-states. Rousseau's observation with regard to the impossibility of encompassing all of mankind in one's humanitarian sentiment is essential to the nationalist ethos. "My country, right or wrong", does not always have the most attractive consequences. But regardless of consequences, the centrifugal tendency of nationalism has proven itself to be a decisive force in shaping the modern world.

Internationalism, the antithesis of modern nationalism, is judging by historical evidence, still in the realm of utopianism and may quite possibly stay there. The idea of a supra-national world-wide authority, the core of internationalist thought, has to this date made little inroad on the centrifugalism of nationalism. The fundamentals of patriotism and nationalism are deeply rooted in human nature. Preference for the native land, the native language and native customs and traditions are not likely to be erased by appeals to a common humanity.

A second corollary concerns nationalism's close association with the rise of the middle class in Europe. That this doctrine should come from this class is not particularly surprising for almost all political thinking emanated from this group in the eighteenth and nineteenth centuries. Intellectual preoccupation was, with some rare and notable exceptions, not the trademark of the aristocracy of the period. The agrarian and the slowly emerging labouring classes, on the other hand, did not have much opportunity to devote time to political speculations until their conditions were improved. Nationalism spread with remarkable speed, not only across Europe but also across class divisions until it encompassed all social and economic groups within the nation.

The third corollary of nationalism is very closely linked to the above point. The industrial revolution had accompanied and, indeed, was at the basis of the rise of the middle class. That revolution had also created a class of labourers whose dire economic circumstances had given birth to the various socialist and communist schools of thought, both on the continent and in England. The Marxists thought along international lines, seeing in the nation-state merely a tool of bourgeois suppression. Their doctrines were directed towards the dispossessed peasant who had drifted into the city and towards the industrial labourer. Both these groups constituted a formless, politically incoherent and legally deprived mass. The individual within this group, torn from his traditional environment of soil and parish and denied access to the economic amenities available to the other classes, was rootless, spiritually and materially disoriented, in short, alienated. The vision of an international brotherhood of individuals in similar circumstances was a tempting one and might have succeeded, if the nature of the nation-state itself had not changed.

Nationalism and patriotism, it has been argued, have a basic emotional appeal. It was more natural for the alienated individual to join with a group of men who shared in his language, customs and history than with men of other nationalities, even though economic circumstances made them similar. If the individual felt himself insignificant, deprived of freedoms and unable to assert himself, then he could find solace in the notions of collective liberty, collective achievement and perhaps even collective glory as extended to him by the patriotism or nationalism of his own country. The nation appealed more strongly to the inherent patriotism of most men and, as an added catalyst towards national unity, contributed to the democratization of the political process. Given then the opportunity to participate, in varying degrees, in the decisions that formulated the nation's actions, alienated man was able to embrace nationalism as a new and secure form of religion. The working-class movements remained international until the demands of their own nations superseded the appeal of supra-national solidarity. Thus the members of the German Social Democratic Party supported the war effort of their country during the First World War and even the most "internationalist" of all left-radical movements, the Bolsheviks, turned eventually to "socialism in one country", when need and necessity demanded such a course.

Patriotism and nationalism, the nation-state and nationality, these basic concepts are dominant when the ultimate thought of social collectivity is considered today. It is quite useless to advocate far-reaching alternatives at the moment. Nor is there any point in lamenting the fact that the historical evolution has taken this direction. To do so would be to express a futile regret over an irreversible development. Not only are nationalism and patriotism, but particularly the latter, deeply-rooted ingredients of human nature but they are also the natural corollaries of the large-scale population growth which accompanied the industrialization of Europe and North America. The appearance of modern technology coupled with modern communications techniques established a more or less nation-wide dialogue. Whether the nation-state is a liberal, constitutional democracy or a totalitarian democracy is, in this instance, of secondary importance. But all rule today is in the name of the "people", regardless of whether the "people" are really consulted or not. But these "people" do, in most instances, speak a common language, share a common geographical home and possess a more or less accurately recorded history. And their dominant political creed is either patriotism or nationalism.

THE CANADIAN PROBLEM

The numerous difficulties which beset the development of a Canadian national spirit are formidable. The existence of two different major nationalities and religious denominations, the federal political structure of the country, in itself an indication of centrifugalism and not only of geographic necessity, the vastness of the land—all these factors present barriers to the emergence of a widely shared sense of national identity. One could also consider the proximity of a huge, militant and cohesive power such as the United States of America as a hindrance to the evolution of the Canadian national sentiment. But such is not necessarily the case. Patriotisms and particularly nationalisms are often fed by a reaction to that which they are not. They depend to varying degrees on the uniqueness, real or imaginary, of their cultural and political identity. Being "non-American", and at times quite pointlessly anti-American, is part and parcel of the Canadian forms of patriotism and nationalism. Such negation is perhaps a somewhat weak basis for a national sentiment to focus on, nevertheless it is integral.

The existence of the two major language groups clearly poses the most prominent problem. While certainly, as we pointed out earlier, multi-nationality states have demonstrated their viability, there is no denying the fact that in Canada difficulties in communications keep the national-ity-question in the foreground. In Switzerland, the classical exceptional example of a multi-nationality and multi-lingual state, Swiss national sentiment has not encountered the kind of stumbling blocks which are typical of Canada. Whether he is of French-Swiss, German-Swiss or Italian-Swiss background, the citizen of that country subscribes to one common political tradition. Such is not the case in Canada.

We have, it may be argued, an all-inclusive Canadian patriotism which, since its inception, attempted to surmount the differences arising out of nationality, language and provincialism. But Canada also contains a form of sentiment which can be classified as nationalism, centered in and on Quebec. It is a nationalism which has been classified as "insular",[15] a sentiment of a relatively small, homogeneous, religiously, culturally and historically conscious nationality which uses its nationalism in the name of communal self-preservation. Surrounded by an English-speaking en-vironment subscribing to a social order more loosely articulated and a great deal more heterogeneous, insular Quebec nationalism is as much a reaction against English-Canadian patriotism as the latter is a reaction against "Americanism".

Quebec political consciousness is and always has been torn between two choices, loyalty to Canada as a whole and supreme loyalty to its own nationality and community. The province has produced prominent men of both convictions, Canadian patriots and Quebec nationalists alike. It is significant and at the same time fortunate for Canada, that the patriots preceded the nationalists. And it is indicative of the changes which have taken place in Quebec since the end of the Second World War that much is heard today of its nationalism. Industrialization, commercialization and urbanization, some of the traditional stimulants of nationalism, are active in the province. Indeed, when the Quebec development is compared to the European examples, the appearance of chauvinism under the guise of separatism is not surprising at all.

To accommodate, assimilate and modify this Quebec sentiment, then, is the difficult task of Canadian patriotism. This task is not made easier by the weakness of many of the prerequisites of patriotism in this country. Perhaps the largest stumbling block is the absence of a specific, widespread and well-articulated national culture. Patriotism, it has been argued, derives from the love of native land. But it is also dependent on a commonly shared and distinctive cultural heritage, a factor which is far from conspicuous in English-speaking Canada. Moreover, the national dialogue is heavily influenced by modern communications and entertainment media, which are not exactly conducive to the strengthening of literature and the arts. Canada is not unique in this respect, but older nations were already equipped with their national cultures before being confronted with the impact of modern communications technology.

Finally, the inevitable question arises—what specific rational, as distinguished from emotional, purpose could Canadian patriotism and/or nationalism serve? Patriotism would indubitably lessen the centrifugal tendencies in the country. It would tone down that provincialism which is by no means Quebec's monopoly. The result would be a more unified country whose national policies could take on a somewhat more efficacious form, freed from both the erosion of local provincialism and the utopian demands of a romantic nationalism.

A heightened sense of nationalism would, on the other hand, be quite undesirable. Indeed, Canada would cease to be the country it is, if an overly-centralized and politically bigoted national authority would replace the current system. Neither the European example of the last and of this century, nor that of some of the currently emerging new nation-states, can be disregarded. Unity at all costs may come at too high a price, particularly if the cry for unity merely serves the political ambitions of one small group of men. Nationalism, moreover, is a delusive emotion and the schemes it produces frequently disregard political reality. A realistic self-awareness must be an essential part of Canadian political thought and action, and it would surely be harmful to the country if realism were drowned in a deluge of Canadian nationalist emotion. Nor is it particularly elating to witness the course of nationalism in Quebec. Legitimate political ambitions can and indeed must be accommodated within the framework of Canada's constitutional system. But a narcissistic self-admiration—incoherent, irrational outbursts of provincial politicians and romantic infantiles playing with homemade bombs are aspects of nationalism which, in view of the existing examples, any community should learn to heed and to avoid.

NOTES

1. C. J. H. Hayes, *Essays on Nationalism,* New York, 1926, p. 101.
2. H. Kohn, *Nationalism, Its Meaning and History,* New York, 1955, p. 71.
3. The Viennese dramatist Franz Grillparzer, quoted in Royal Institute of International Affairs, *Nationalism,* London, 1963, p. viii.
4. C. J. H. Hayes, *The Historical Evolution of Modern Nationalism,* New York, 1931, p. 12.
5. L. W. Doob, *Patriotism and Nationalism,* New Haven, 1964, p. 6.
6. J. S. Mill, *Principles of Political Economy,* Vol. 2, Toronto, 1965, p. 938.
7. The term originated with Charles Maurras, founder of the nationalist *Action Française.* (F. Hertz, *Nationality in History and Politics,* London, 1945, pp. 381-383.)
8. There are two versions as to the origins of the word. One holds that it originated with Nicolas Chauvin, a veteran of Napoleon's *grand armée,* who retained and loudly proclaimed his admiration for the Emperor and the glories of France. The second version attributes the expression to the name of a *dramatis persona* in Cogniard's satire, *La cocarde tricolor,* (1831). The play lampooned French militaristic ventures in North Africa. Sang Chauvin: "I am French, I am Chauvin, I beat down the Bedouin".
9. Edmund Burke, *Works,* Vol. 5, Boston, 1839, p. 405.
10. Hans Morgenthau, *Politics Among Nations,* 3rd edition, New York, 1960, p. 337.
11. Hans Jellinek, *Allgemeine Staatslehre,* 3rd edition, Bad Homburg, 1960, p. 110.
12. Julian Huxley and A. C. Haddon, quoted in B.C. Shafer, *Nationalism, Myth and Reality,* New York, 1955, p. 6.
13. J. J. Rousseau, "A Discourse on Political Economy", *The Social Contract,* London, 1913, p. 246.
14. J. J. Rousseau, "A Discourse on the Moral Effects of the Arts and Sciences", as cited above, p. 123.
15. L. W. Doob, as cited, p. 18.

the 20th century prospect:

nationalism in a

technological society • abraham rotstein

This volume has been devoted largely to the role of nationalism in Canada's past and present. In this final essay it may be fitting to pose the question: Does nationalism have a place in Canada's future?

The future is not entirely indeterminate; it will, in part, be a projection of the past and consequently of many of the themes illuminated in this volume. But the future will take its essential shape within the new social and political landscape that is now emerging. The hallmark of that future is the technological society.

This essay is mainly concerned with the political features of the technological society in so far as we can discern them. The role of nationalism will be examined as only one aspect of the tasks of creative politics in such a society.

Nationalism is usually applied to the sharper, more assertive expressions of national sentiment and national interest in the modern period. But the nation itself has been invoked, more or less directly, during many diverse periods of social change that have swept over society: the restoration of monarchies and their overthrow, the "new Jerusalem in England's green and pleasant land", as well as *Blut und Boden*; the pastoral idyll of nineteenth century Catholicism in Quebec, as well as Russia's "socialism in one country". In this broad context, social movements that have invoked the nation in some way, have been responsible for both virtues and crimes as extensive as those that have been committed, for example, in the name of religion. Sweeping judgments in either case may be pointless.

But today, nationalism, as a self-conscious and direct political force, is with us much more. Indeed, in recent times, it would not be an exaggeration to say that the heightened self-consciousness and intense introspective awareness which accompany nationalism often amount to a virtual *discovery* of the nation.

There is certainly something artificial about this heightened pursuit of national identity, including the deliberate fostering of national culture and national institutions. One might have thought that national existence is, after all, self-evident. Indeed, one might imagine that national existence should be ideally as unselfconscious a matter as walking down a flight of stairs or breathing. Yet it is only when our foot is in pain or when something is amiss in our respiratory system that we suddenly become conscious of every movement in descending a stairway or in breathing. Similarly, when there are serious strains and tensions in a nation's social existence, these manifest themselves in a heightened self-awareness. Thus we may take nationalist assertions of the seemingly self-evident as a symptom or barometer of stress.

This is not to suggest that the laments of nationalists may be brushed aside because they are merely symptomatic. Nationalist programmes are geared to very definite and specific goals, but before we can accept or reject these, it may be appropriate to ask: To what kinds of stress is contemporary nationalism a response, and how do nationalists hope to meet these stresses in a meaningful way within a technological society? This will form the subject of the first part of this essay.

In the second part, we turn to aspects of two dilemmas of nationalism in Canada today—Canadian-American relations and the relation of French to English Canada. In the latter case, we raise the question of the co-existence of two nations within an emerging technological state.

We shall conclude by examining, in the light of our analysis of the technological society, the class philosophical issue of the compatibility of nationalism and freedom. Liberals, who have been consistently suspicious of nationalism and of its policies, have rested their case on the incursions and constraints which nationalism has imposed on individual freedom. This is the level at which the issue must be joined. Can we continue to sustain the liberal view of the world where society consists essentially of distinct atoms—individual human beings contracting to-

gether in the name of their individual self-interest and individual freedom? This essay contends that the pervasive and irreversible manifestations of interdependence, which technology has brought about in modern
society, presume a different view of the individual in his community and
a different view of the nature and possibilities of freedom.

We do not propose to present a rationalization of the traditional concept of the nation. The nation itself is undergoing rapid social change
and the nationalism of the future will be an assertion of the character, the
values and the institutions of the national society of that time, a very
different national society from that of the bourgeois nation in the first
phase of industrialization.

The maturity to which a technological society impels us, if we are to
survive in it, will demand basic revisions of our view of social existence.
This is not to suggest that a reassertion of nationalist values in itself
contains the entire basis for such maturity. But it is to suggest that the
integral character which a human community acquires through the new
technology and the new communications—through ribs of steel and nerves
of electronic impulses—transforms the old slogan of interdependence from
a benign manifestation of individual goodwill into the hard reality of
the new social framework. Nationalists of the left should find themselves
at home in this new society.

I

THROUGH A GRID DARKLY

Jonathan Swift was hardly the prophet of the new technology, yet he
left unwittingly a graphic image of the electric society. Lemuel Gulliver,
while asleep in Lilliput, has been tied to the ground with thousands of
threads by the fearful and industrious Lilliputians. When he awakens,
he discovers that he has been rendered immobile and the struggle to free
himself is in vain.

A society dependent on the pervasive wires for virtually all vital tasks
of daily life—light, heat, food, transport, production, communication and
education—may also be tied down by its electric grid in a way not unlike
that of Lemuel Gulliver. With this vital dependence on electricity, we
ourselves become, in an important sense, plugged into the grid.

The point was brought home in a dramatic fashion on November 9th,

1965, when at the height of the rush hour in the late afternoon, the lights flickered and went out in the eastern half of North America. It was the beginning of the most massive and puzzling blackout that had yet occurred. In the industrial heartland of the United States and Canada, extending over some 80,000 square miles, the daily lives of thirty million people were temporarily disrupted—in some regions for as long as fourteen hours.

The blackout was only a brief moment in the twentieth century, yet it lit up the characteristic shape which existence had taken. We could suddenly 'see' the all-encompassing electric grid. Some imagined that since the grid had become the central nervous system of our society, people might turn to panic and hysteria if it should cease to function. Others wondered whether the blackout was the result of sabotage, and still others wondered whether there would be violence and looting.

None of these fears were warranted. There were no indications of sabotage nor of violence and looting. Instead of panic, quiet camaraderie filled the air. Life suddenly ceased to be harried and frantic. Languid conversations took place in darkened offices. A light-hearted grace flowed everywhere, particularly in the normally rude and belligerent New York City. Those who managed to reach home had dinner by candlelight; many who did not whiled away the hours at a local lounge, not overly concerned with their fate. Businessmen stepped in with relish to direct traffic. Those who were stranded in subways, elevators and railway stations found the blackout less pleasant, but courtesy, calmness and an easy tolerance prevailed everywhere.

A political philosopher might even have been tempted to draw some conclusions about this facsimile "state of nature" of an industrial society. Notwithstanding Thomas Hobbes, people had turned out to be lambs rather than wolves.

We had a brief glimpse of a more benign world, but it was an artificial world and irretrievable. When the towering pylons and the ubiquitous wires sprang to life once more, and we had again donned the technological harness, peculiar questions still remained, not the least of which was the unsolved mystery of what had caused the blackout. There were also other questions: had we any assurances that it would not recur, and what, in any case, was this extensive Canadian-U.S. grid that bound the two countries together like a prolific vine? Thus, together with the questions about the interruption of the grid, there emerged questions about its normal operation. Perhaps in the blackout there lay a paradigm for the evolving technological society, some of whose features flickered briefly in high definition.

For five days following the blackout, hundreds of experts in Canada and the United States were engaged in searching for the cause of the disruption. Once the possibility of sabotage had been ruled out, the assumption became prevalent that some technical or mechanical failure was at the root of the trouble. As matters turned out, the difficulty was not in the malfunctioning of the technology (it worked exactly as was intended) but in the human element. There was, in short, an organizational rather than a technological flaw. The separation of technological and organizational aspects is revealing. Technical constraints and the discovery of flaws bring about a certain kind of organization and reorganization for the more efficient functioning of the system.

One of the conclusions of the investigations that were carried on both in Canada and the United States made it clear that, however unexpected such a massive blackout had been, no reassurance could be given that this event would not recur. The report of the Federal Power Commission in the United States concluded:

> There can be no absolute assurance that outages of the November 9 magnitude will not recur. On the other hand, there is no apparent reason why operating equipment and techniques cannot be improved to the point where the likelihood of recurrence would be so remote that it would not constitute a major worry to either the industry or the public.[1]

In Canada, a statement on the power failure issued by the Minister of Trade and Commerce on December 9, 1965 noted the following:

> There is, however, no such thing as perfect security in power supply, anymore than in any other activity directed by humans. The question is how to achieve the highest practicable degree of security.[2]

In the attempt to achieve the "highest practicable degree of security", as well as economy, two kinds of adjustment had been under way. First, local electrical systems were being integrated in order to provide emergency power to counteract temporary failure of any part of the system. This also allowed power to be shunted from one area to another during peak periods which fell at different times, so as to put the generating capacity to greater use and thus provide cheaper power. These factors were making for larger and larger grids, with a continent-wide grid now being advocated as the next step forward. In the face of these compelling technical and economic advantages, increasing Canadian participation in the American grid had seemed "obvious", and had gone quietly forward with little public awareness or debate in recent years. At the same time there was a shift from private power companies to large governmentally organized power grids operated by administrative boards. This was a shift from market organization to administrative organization, to promote the efficient extension of the system.

But this trend towards greater efficiency and security of the system in the past made the cause of this spectacular failure even more mysterious. As it turned out, the matter was a vestigial element of human oversight. The factors in this situation are worth recounting in some detail, for they may be indicative of the way in which complex technological systems remain vulnerable.

One of the technical problems which confronts electrical transmission systems is the protection of existing equipment from damage in case the system becomes overloaded with electrical power. To meet this particular problem, the device that is used is a circuit breaker, which operates in much the same fashion as a household fuse, namely, it shuts off the system when the power load becomes too great. In 1955, when a circuit breaker failed to operate in the case of a faulty transmission circuit at the Sir Adam Beck Power Station at Niagara Falls, substantial damage was sustained by the equipment. In order to prevent a recurrence, Ontario Hydro installed additional protective devices called secondary relays to make sure that the circuit breakers were triggered in time.

It was one of these relays, known as Q 29—a complex of coils and calibration devices no larger than a loaf of bread—which initiated the blackout. Since the installation of this secondary relay in 1955, it had worked perfectly. In 1963 the relay was set at 375 million watts, the maximum level beyond which the relay was to operate the circuit breaker. This figure included a safety margin over the average power load, but the average had been slowly increasing until the line was carrying a normal level of 356 million watts. When a simple upward fluctuation in the load occurred, the relay operated precisely as was intended, and shut off the circuit. This simple event set the blackout in motion in a grand domino sequence. The power on this particular line was shunted onto five other power lines of Ontario Hydro overloading these in turn, and shutting them down as well. With no other place to go, the electric current normally used by Ontario was sent surging in an electrical torrent through the power system of upper New York state, triggering in turn automatic shut-downs all along the line right through to New York City.[3]

New York City might have been saved from a power failure if it had cut its own electrical system loose from the grid in time. When Edwin J. Nellis, the engineer on duty at Con Edison noticed the dimming of the lights at 5:16 p.m., he thought at first to check the condition of the electrical system of upstate New York. After two short telephone calls, he decided to separate the New York City system from the electric grid of New York State. The decision which he had faced was whether to try to protect the power supply for New York State as a whole, or alternatively, to take no risks and separate New York City from the system. At the end of the second phone call upstate, he had made his decision and stated "I am going to cut you loose". At 5:28 p.m. he began to push a series of eight buttons to separate New York City from the larger electrical system but he was seconds too late. In just 2.5 seconds after that, New York was completely blacked out. Thus when Nellis had been confronted with a significant moral decision and had actually exercised his discretion, it turned out that there had been insufficient time for such a decision to be made.

Other areas such as New Jersey had saved themselves because they had an automatic cut-off device. In the investigation that followed, one of the major considerations was whether the electric grid in the future, as it expanded its connections across the continent, could in fact tolerate these kinds of human decisions at crucial moments.

This example of the relatively insignificant flaw or unforeseen accident which disrupts a complex technological system is repeated frequently in military technology. Instances abound in the U.S. military and space programme—a small plastic disc comes loose to interrupt the fuel supply of a moon rocket; an electrical short circuit sends a space ship far out of orbit; a Strategic Air Command plane with a hydrogen bomb aboard makes a forced landing on American soil and it is discovered that six of the seven protective devices on the bomb have ceased to function; the crash of an American bomber carrying hydrogen bombs in Spain, contaminates Spanish soil, and one of these hydrogen bombs is lost for two months in coastal waters. But military technology is only the herald of the complex technology which will be increasingly widespread in society.

This new characteristic of the complex technological environment has been described as the "fail-safe syndrome". The fail-safe syndrome has wide implications and may become a crucial ingredient of twentieth century politics. "Fail-safe" is a popular term which has thus far been used only with regard to the danger of unintended nuclear war. The main concern has been the possibility that the world would be catapulted into nuclear destruction, not by virtue of a conscious decision of either one of the parties, but by virtue of some technological or human mishap.

THE PRECARIOUS SOCIETY

For the evolving technological society, the "fail-safe" problem may be a portent. For example, in the case of hydro-electricity, the statements of the two governments cited above make it clear that such a system cannot be made foolproof. A vast network of enormous importance to the survival of the entire continent must be regarded as having inherent features of uncertainty, however small this uncertainty may become. Secondly, in attempting to make this system more secure, we are increasingly required to hand over important decisions to automatic devices. Less and less human decision is tolerable because, for example, it cannot be made sufficiently quickly. Important decisions are shaped by technological rather than political considerations. For example, whether the Canadian and U.S. electric grids should be even more closely meshed will increasingly become a technological question.

As integration of technological systems proceeds, the lives of an ever growing number of people will be bound together by the vulnerability of a system that is immensely more disruptive, even though the frequency of breakdowns may be less. In short, the technological grid, including computers, electric circuitry and automatic devices eventually begins to form something resembling an enormous elaborate mobile suspended on thin threads.

In the process, a new political atmosphere or environment is created. The stake we have as a society in such technological systems becomes ever greater. The fears and apprehensions at the back of our mind center, not primarily on the survival of our individual persons, but on social existence itself—the continuity and security of the urban-industrial-machine web. As we become wealthier and the machines and interconnections become more complex, our technological system increasingly becomes an all-or-nothing game with the stakes rising at some enormous rate. The backdrop of our social existence becomes transformed, and becomes, in a sense, the latent emergency. We have been made aware initially of this sense of the latent emergency by the mobilization of the new technology for military purposes. But the main feature of the technological society is the extension of this phenomenon into economic life, as the economy becomes more dependent on integrated, complex technological devices.

While the immediate manifestation of the new technology is the erosion of centers of individual decision-making power within the technological system (through increased automation), this should not blind us to the accompanying development, on another level, of new institutions of political power with entirely different functions. Some will hasten to maintain that technology is, after all, a human artifact and therefore subject to human control so that we need not fear its effects. However, technology is not born naked into the world. It is clothed in human organization which exists in the arrangements to produce, co-ordinate replace and expand the technological system. These organizational or institutional effects are complex. The simplistic assumption which is often made is that the political process of a technological society is coextensive with the technical process, so that as technology pervades ever wider geographic areas, it merely brings with it a political superstructure covering it like a cloak.

But politics is a more volatile, mercurial affair and its functions run in many directions. The attempts to protect man's cultural endowment, his values, the non-economic institutions of his social existence, become as much a feature of political life as the process of making the technological maze more efficient. The nineteenth century is a case in point.

The initial response to the coming of the machine at the time of the industrial revolution was the organization of the market society. Investment in expensive machinery was only possible if adequate supplies of raw materials and factors of production could be assured, as well as reliable outlets for the increased flow of the goods produced. The aim of the market system during its heyday in the nineteenth and early twentieth centuries was the development of markets for genuine commodities and also markets for the factors of production, labour and land. But labour and land involved nothing less than the two constituent elements of society, man on the one hand, and his habitat on the other. Neither were genuine commodities, for they were not produced to be sold.

The social history of that century was encompassed in a double movement: the extension of the market system for genuine commodities was accompanied by its restriction with regard to those "fictitious" ones. In particular, the development of trade unions, industrial codes, building codes, zoning regulations, social welfare legislation, socialism and even protective tariffs and monopolies had the common aim of countering, insulating and mitigating in various ways the operation of an unrestricted market system running on its own independent rules. The 'laws' of supply and demand were inherently unconcerned with underlying human and social consequences, and social existence was embedded in the market. But in a countermovement, new institutions had arisen to protect society.

The collapse of the market system in the 1930's made it clear that society could not be left in the charge of an automatic, supposedly self-equilibrating and unpredictable economic system, the self-regulating market economy. Even though the ideological basis of the market system promised an inherent benevolence and justice, and a specific kind of individual freedom, the spontaneous political reactions to the impersonal forces of the era of laissez-faire were meant precisely to protect society from the disintegrating effects of the industrial technology purveyed by the institutional forms of the market.[4]

While the social necessities of the nineteenth century centered on the institutional constraints of the market and brought forward countervailing political institutions, the focus of concern in our own day has shifted much more to the inherent necessities of technology and technique. Admittedly, the forces and constraints of the new technology to which we are increasingly committed, may pose even more stringent difficulties of social adjustment than those posed by the institutional nature of the market system. Much has been said of the eroding effects of the new technology on our culture, our values and our institutions. Nevertheless, the very experience of the last century should be sufficient to indicate that creative political responses, in part spontaneous and in part deliberate, may form the human and social structure within which we will attempt to contain that technology, to control its rate of change and to distribute its human and social benefits. But cybernetics and self-regulating technical systems, organized and co-ordinated by computers, may present a different and more complex dilemma than the market society, and the solutions may require greater social ingenuity and imagination.

The political climate of the advanced technological society is still barely visible. In particular, we have pointed to the sense of latent emergency or precariousness. An ever more complex and fragile technological web produces latent political responses to protect the continuity of life in such a situation. For example, the intuitive attempt to protect the institutional balance or technological continuity of the precarious society may give rise to conformist pressures against unpopular political positions. In that sense, every technological society has within it the seeds of totalitarianism, insofar as it is prepared to mobilize the resources of the state against even minor threats to the continuity of existence. The stakes become too high and the tolerances too small to permit genuine divergences that threaten the fragile technical-social equilibrium.

Another effect of the new technology is to upgrade economic life to the level of a vital national interest, similar in kind to such potential life and death questions as defence or foreign policy. The importance of the economy in a technological society contrasts sharply with an earlier period where the continuity of small, discrete individual enterprises never posed the same threat to collective existence which the new economic interdependence has created.

In a complex society, the necessity to co-ordinate as well as to humanize the technological maze has given rise to large-scale institutions with immense power to make decisions affecting the entire society. Corporations, trade unions, various levels of government, the military and even the multiversity are examples of the new topography of the political landscape in modern society. Interposed between man and the machine web, we have created new institutions capable of affecting decisively the character of our collective existence.

A discussion of the evolving technological society is necessarily speculative and only some suggestive notions can be offered. But it may be that these fears and apprehensions at the fringe of our mind, generated by the technological society, have found their sharpest expression in our literary imagination. The machine is the child of our own creation, an "extension of man", as Marshall McLuhan would have it, yet we have always been afraid that this child would turn against us and that we would lose control. Starting with simple legends such as *The Sorcerer's Apprentice*, to more ominous tales of Frankenstein, Karel Capek's play *R.U.R.*, Huxley's *Brave New World*, up to the embodiment of our worst fears in the novel *1984*, the advent of the machine, particularly the automated machine, has haunted our imagination. The end result of industrial technology is the progressive extension of man's being and power—a progressive 'outering' of himself to the point where there is loss of control by humans over automatic devices and the fear of the end of human existence as we know it.[5] Literary creations are only suggestive, but they herald our unarticulated fears about the future.

This new political landscape is still evolving but its main features, as far as we can discern them, have been suggested: the fail-safe syndrome or the precariousness of such a society, the escalation of enormous power in the new political institutions, the escalation of anxiety, and the consciousness of interdependence or instant common fate.[6] These are the tendons and nerves of social existence.

THE NATIONALISM OF THE LEFT

The nation-state has assumed in our own day an increasing number of social responsibilities: full employment, economic growth, increasing social welfare, maintenance of stable prices, increased responsibility for education, recreation and communication. Far from becoming obsolete, or being reduced to a sentimental symbol, the nation-state has assumed the vital social tasks of our interdependent existence and we have, consequently, assigned to it enormously increased power, commensurate with its responsibilities. Inherent in these tasks are the present and emerging values of our society: mutual responsibility, greater equality between persons, regions and classes, greater social security and the fostering of education and national cultural life. All of these are the concrete embodiment of the values and aims which have given to the nation a new character and existence in the modern period. In a technological society, the values of efficiency and co-ordination, important as they are, must always be balanced against the tasks of humanization, the preservation of social values, and the democratic division of the benefits of this technology.

These substantial tasks and the fragile character of social existence imply overall control or retention of decision-making power within the national community. Efficiency alone has never been the only consideration, particularly in matters of vital national interest such as defence and foreign affairs. In Canada, for example, the Americans might be able to defend us for half of what it costs us to defend ourselves — they might even do it *gratis*. The British, in turn, have a proven record of being able to run our foreign policy efficiently. Yet in vital matters such as these, criteria of efficiency are secondary to the problem of keeping power within the hands of the nation-state and its citizens. The degree of retention of this power is the measure of our national independence. In a technological society, we see the escalation in importance of other vital national interests which, in turn, bear the same relation to the collective existence of society as a whole, as was once assigned only to defence and foreign affairs. I have in mind, of course, economic life, particularly as it becomes increasingly transformed by modern technology.

The crucial importance for nationalists of the locus of control of the political and economic fate of their society rests on an implicit awareness of the extent to which such decisions affect the vital character of the lives of their community in a technological era. While the economy is the home of the new technology, the nation-state is the home of the new institutions of power.

In an age of the growing interdependence of nations and increased international responsibilities, national autonomy can never be absolute. But only the nation-state, hale within, untroubled and effectively organized, can assume these international tasks and discharge them effectively. It seems almost superfluous to point out that the international community is a community of nations, not of persons.

Our immediate conclusion is that the old view of society, as an atomistic collection of self-seeking individuals concerned with their individual freedom and contracting together to form the institutions of the state, is an obsolete notion in the technological era. The pervasive element of a precarious politics, the accompanying escalation of power as well as anxiety about the use of that power, the growing tasks assigned to the nation-state, the embodiment of society's values and goals within these tasks, point to a new view of existence centering on the indissoluble character of the social framework. This is not a matter of theory, sentiment, or blood, but a matter of collective common interest with regard to the use of the technology on the one hand, and the protection of society through its political institutions on the other. In this new environment, nationalists will feel particularly at home. This is not to say that the twentieth century political landscape is the final vindication of an age-long nationalist myth. Nationalists, however, have always been concerned with the preservation of collective values, have asserted these in times of stress, and within the new political landscape are able to sense the importance of the locus of power and decision-making in the home in which it is located at present, the nation-state.

II

AMERICAN INVESTMENT

A general review of Canadian-American relations from a nationalist viewpoint would be far beyond the scope of this paper. Nevertheless, it may be useful to review certain principles with regard to one of the most troubling aspects of these relations, namely the high degree of American investment in Canadian manufacturing and resource industries. There is a deep ambivalence in this country over American investment and for good reason. American investment forces us to confront various desirable but nevertheless contradictory objectives: technological development and economic growth on the one hand and the more elusive, but none the less crucial, question of political sovereignty on the other.

For economic liberals with an individualist perspective on the world, the feelings of uneasiness with regard to foreign investment seem to be no more than irrational complaints fostered by political opportunists. The record of economic achievement of American capital in this country is very impressive. In terms of the tangible fruits of this investment, Canadians have benefited substantially with regard to employment, taxes, new technology and a higher standard of living. Thus it seems to the economic liberal that complaints about this investment are little more than looking a gift horse in the mouth. It is usually pointed out that Canadian sovereignty vested in the rights of Parliament remains unimpaired, and can be used to restrict or countermand any actions by foreign firms which deviate from the national interest.

"Are Canadian capitalists different from American capitalists?", liberals ask, but they seldom pursue the logic of this question by asking further "Are Canadian workers different from American workers?" Indeed, are any individuals when viewed as factors of production on the market different from any others? The point, of course, is that within the perspective of liberal market economics, political differences have no place except insofar as they affect costs or prices or profits. Non-economic phenomena, such as the nation, fall outside the system except as they aid

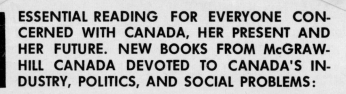

FOREIGN INFLUENCE

Foreign Ownership of Canadian Industry

A. E. Safarian

This book is the first comprehensive survey of the characteristics of
foreign-owned companies in Canada since the 1930's. The degree of
decentralization of decision-making between parent and subsidiary companies, the exports and imports of subsidiary companies, the borrowing
of research and performance of research in the Canadian firm, and
financial policies and practices of the subsidiaries are among the subjects treated in depth. The conclusions of this book, based on a lengthy,
exhaustive study by one of Canada's most informed economists, will
correct many misconceptions about the effects of foreign ownership on
Canadian industry. A. E. Safarian is currently Professor of Economics at
the University of Toronto.

Available in paperback   250 pp   1966
and clothbound editions.

LABOUR

International Unionism In Canada:
A Canadian-American Experiment

John H.G. Crispo

This book embodies a detailed study of the Canadian-American relationship in international unions based on an assessment of the power structure and organization of the unions. In this first truly comprehensive
treatment of the subject, the author discusses the degree of independence and responsibility exercised by the Canadian member within the
international unions. Professor John H. G. Crispo is Director of the
Centre of Industrial Relations, and Professor of Industrial Relations at
the University of Toronto.

400 pp   1966

THE CANADIAN IDENTITY

Nationalism: Canada   Edited by Peter B. Russell

Here is a collection of twenty-two articles by members of the University League for Social Reform — all written specifically for this book and completely up to date. The content has at least three major dimensions: the inquiry into the main determinants of nationalistic thought and sentiment; the effects which nationalistic attitude have had on Canadian policy-making and history; and, finally, all the contributors address themselves to the question of what kind and degree of nationalism is appropriate for Canada.

Available in paperback   380 pp   1966
and clothbound editions.

SOCIAL REFORM

The Prospect of Change: Edited by Abraham Rotstein
Proposals for Canada's Future.

This is the first publication of a group of young University Professors, the University League for Social Reform, who are collectively committed to social reform in Canada. In each of the book's 16 original articles a member of the group discusses an issue of national importance —regional development, social welfare, the arts, education, and foreign investment. Expert, informed thinking is expounded and concrete, practical solutions are advanced. Abraham Rotstein of the University of Toronto is the editor of this incisive work.

                                361 pp   Published

THE GOVERNMENT

Politics: Canada Problems in Canadian Government 2nd. Ed.
Paul W. Fox

This updated version of a popular collection of readings gives the reader a complete inside view of contemporary Canadian government in action. Increased emphasis is given throughout the book to the problems of the Canadian government, the French-Canadian question, and the issue of Co-operative Federalism. Included are the latest discussions on such areas as the Fulton-Favreau formula, and party platforms and the results of the November election. The material used has come from such sources as learned journals, government publications, magazines and newspapers, and scholarly treatises.

Available in paperback   385 pp.   1966
and clothbound editions.

Place your order with your bookseller NOW!

McGRAW-HILL COMPANY OF CANADA LIMITED
330 PROGRESS AVENUE   SCARBOROUGH ONTARIO

or hinder market activity. For economic liberals, the nation is a perverse phenomenon since it frequently interferes with free markets for goods and for capital, through imposing, for example, tariffs and restrictions on foreign investment.

But a society is more than the sum of its market activities and its con-tractual behaviour, and there is no need to accept this limited view of the world. On the other hand, nationalist complaints about foreign invest-ment at the grass-roots level have been little more than an intuitive expression of uneasiness. While these complaints are, I believe, well-founded, they are not a sufficient basis for policy if they remain poorly articulated.

The substance of the complaint is hardly the classical antithesis be-tween spiritual things and material things. There can be no room in a modern nationalist analysis for complaints whose basis is no deeper than the vaguely sentimental, or the vaguely spiritual. The crucial issue in an evolving technological society is the political implications of this economic activity. We use the term "political" in the broadest sense, namely, as referring to the phenomenon of power. In this instance, it is the power to make decisions with regard to our national economic life which is at stake: in the complex and ramified economy of the evolving technological society, the question of the location of decision-making power becomes as essential to the national interest as control in such vital areas as defence and foreign affairs. The *national* economy, we may add, is a fact, defined by currency, commercial policy, price level, employment level and fiscal policy, all of which are national in scope. In the political landscape of precariousness and uncertainty, the locus of decision-making power with regard to the economy is one of vital concern to the nation-state.

In the establishment of American subsidiaries in Canada, the central point is that basic decision-making power is shifted from this country to the boardrooms of New York, Chicago and Washington. Although this shift of power occurs only among individuals—from Canadian citizens to American citizens—the all-pervasive significance of the economy today makes this shift of power no less important than the shift of power on an intergovernmental level, which occurs when we relinquish power in defence and foreign affairs to Washington. Certainly there are differences of degree in this comparison, but these should not obscure the similarity of principle. National independence, of course, is measured by the extent to which decision-making power is contained within the confines of a nation-state. While in the modern world national independence is a matter of degree, these matters of degree are not something to which we can be indifferent. And while, in a legal sense, the sovereignty of the Canadian Parliament over this investment remains, the important point is to exercise not the symbol of our sovereignty but the substance of it. The growth and the importance of large economic institutions which are aggregates of substantial decision-making power require in turn that we sustain control over the decisions made by these institutions.

The implication of this type of political analysis is not necessarily that Canada should follow a restrictionist policy with regard to foreign investment. It is true that foreign American corporations are, on the whole, larger and consequently more powerful than Canadian corporations. But the entry of the Canadian government in a more active way on the economic scene might serve to counterbalance the locus of corporate decision-making power in the economy. In particular, the active use of the Canada Development Corporation may well serve to alter the balance of power in the Canadian economy. Such a corporation might concentrate on the crucial aspect of foreign investment, namely the new technology. It might take the initiative with regard to patent and license agreements, the hiring of management consultants and the channelling of new investment in a more direct way, in order to make this technology available in Canada. It may be useful to note that another corporation, the present Canadian Commerical Corporation, has already acted as an intermediary when direct purchases by foreign governments occurred in Canada. The Canada Development Corporation might well act as a similar intermediary for foreign investment in terms of setting the conditions under which new investment may take place in this country. The Corporation could itself become a partner to such new investment and exercise various regulatory functions as well as mobilizing Canadian capital on its own.

A practical policy which meets legitimate nationalist concern with foreign investment can well avoid either of the extremes that have been put forward. Between the views of Harry Johnson, who claims that there is no problem with regard to foreign investment, and the views of George Grant, who claims that it is already too late, there is a viable middle course.

A policy of government intervention in the economy may not be costless. Yet no one has guaranteed that the world in which we live shall necessarily provide a harmonious conjunction of all our objectives. The simplest

and least costly solution to the political problem posed by foreign investment is to foster greater control for Canadians in the foreign-owned
sphere of the economy, while reducing interference with the free flow of
capital to a minimum.

Capitalists are citizens as well as producers. If any doubt were present
about the possibility of a divergence of national objectives between
Canada and the United States, the recent American Guidelines policy, in-
voking American subsidiaries to purchase more of their materials from
the United States and to return their dividends to the United States at
a greater rate in order to meet the American balance of payments problem,
should be sufficient indication. The possibility of diverging national
objectives makes the political aspect of foreign investment a genuine
matter of concern for Canadians. The interest in retaining national
sovereignty to the maximum practical degree increases as the decisions in
economic life become more momentous.

TWO NATIONS

It has now become commonplace to link the rise of nationalism
in Quebec with the recent progress of industrialization in the province.
This is one more example of the way in which self-protective forces are
mobilized in a society to safeguard cultural values and social institutions
against forces of stress and disintegration. In the process, a new identity
and higher standards of achievement may be established.

At the root of many of the tensions and problems surrounding the
new Quebec is, I believe, a conflict of political values with English
Canada. Quebec's claim that she is not "understood" and English
Canada's demand that Quebec state precisely what she wants refer in
oblique ways to difficulties in articulating the divergent underlying
political values of the two groups.

In English Canada, notions of majority rule, equality of opportunity
and individual freedom are dominant. These are the typical values of the
liberal outlook. Seemingly, the height of political tolerance is expressed
in such phrases as: "It doesn't matter what a man's origin and background
are, all that we care about is his ability". The liberal ethic cannot extend
beyond this level and liberals are thus inherently unable to comprehend
the problems of collective or national survival.

To take a concrete case, from an English-Canadian point of view, the allocation of vice-presidencies in such institutions as the C.N.R. would best be handled by choosing the individual with the highest personal qualifications. For French Canadians, the matter has an entirely different aspect. It involves the view that certain important positions of prestige and power should be filled by able individuals who are French Canadians, and are, in their own persons, representatives of the collectivity of French Canada.

Implicit, therefore, in the tension of English and French Canada are different sets of political values. In the example cited above, each group, while advocating "equality", would have a different definition of the term: individual equality in the one case, and collective equality in the other.

Another instance of divergent views is English Canada's notion of majority rule, which is inconsistent with French Canada's view of minority rights. In the liberal view, only *individuals* have rights.

The federal government has granted substantial concessions to Quebec province under the political pressures of the day, but has never explicitly recognized the *principle* of a special status for Quebec. The recognition of the existence of two nations at a basic political, rather than rhetorical level, would imply not merely a special status for French Canadians, but true equality of the two nations in the collective sense of the term.

The basic distinction of two nations still remains a vital social and cultural fact and if truly recognized through new institutional arrangements would go far to liberating the spirit of this country. What we have inherited up till now is a cold arms-length cordiality which masked the indifference, and even the hypocrisy of both groups. This has resulted in a constriction of the inner freedom of this country as a whole to develop and live up to its tasks and its potentialities.

A nationalist analysis centered on the importance of power in the twentieth century technological society may be able to point out that the redistribution of federal powers is not necessarily inconsistent with the growth of power at both levels, federal and provincial. The fact of the matter is that with the continual growth of new institutions, new power is simultaneously created. A simple test of this proposition can be seen in the fact that the growth of the provincial civil service and its assumption of new tasks does not herald the decline of the civil service at the federal level. The creation of new tasks of social welfare and governmental responsibilities at both levels creates problems of co-ordination, but these are far from insoluble through the use of computer technology and new media of communication.

While minorities who wish to survive are generally inclined to be partisans of a collective ethic, history, tradition and technology have somersaulted French Canada from a pre-liberal to a post-liberal outlook. In a technological era, English Canada too will be jostled by the new environment into a more explicit awareness of the collective dimensions of its own survival and its own identity.

None of the preceding discussion should be taken to mean that we can be complacent about the survival of Canada as the home of two nations. But a technological society, which is aware of the collective dimensions of existence, can more easily make room for diverse collectivities than a society that clings to the liberal view of the world.

III

THE REALITY OF SOCIETY

Premature despair in the face of the new technology has been widespread recently. The erosion of institutions and human values in the face of the stringent artificial requirements of technique cannot be denied. But the proponents of despair too often are unaware of the varied and creative ways in which new institutional forms are interposed between man and his environment to ease the pressure and to safeguard social existence. In these prophecies of despair man usually stands alone, whereas we have pointed to the social history of the market society and the countermovement against the eroding effects of the free market as one instance of the tendency to collective self-protection through new institutional forms.

The essential ingredients of a mature approach to our new environment involve both a fundamental shift in our political values in recognition of the inexorable nature of technological interdependence, and a more conscious and deliberate attempt to protect the human character of our institutional and cultural endowment. No doubt the cost will have to be paid in terms of some technological efficiency.

We cannot be sure of meeting such a challenge, especially when we have hardly staked out the full dimensions of the problem. At issue is the question of freedom in the technological society.

The moral shape of the individual in our society has, as its touchstone, the deep imperatives of individual conscience and their fulfilment. At this level, the commitment to freedom becomes the vindication of the very purpose and meaning of the Western tradition. While the technological era promises in various ways new possibilities for the fulfilment of the individual and a more beneficial material existence, it is at the moral level that the question of the possibility of freedom arises. It is here that the incursions of technology are bound to create substantial limitations.

At bottom, moral and political maturity will require a fundamental recognition of the nature of power in our society. Power, as David Hume once pointed out, rests ultimately on opinion. As long as we have consented to a technological society, we share in the responsibility for the institutions of compulsion and constriction to which it must necessarily give rise. The full promise of freedom rests implicitly on the assumption that the individual may contract out of situations where he participates in creating compulsion and constriction of others, in order that his conscience may not be violated. But it is this very possibility of contracting out which, in a technological society, is in question. The dilemma may not be new in principle, but it is focused more sharply and comes up substantially as a matter of degree in the maze of the complex society. In essence, no one who consents to live in such a society and surely no one who shares in the benefits of this technology can contract out of the pervasive institutional and bureaucratic web.

On one level, we may, through imaginative use of our institutions, create new concrete freedoms: ways of protecting the individual from bureaucratic mismanagement, new ways of providing alternative choices in labour and leisure, new facilities for enhancing the individual's self-development both on an educational and material plane. But at bottom, the technological society will involve the individual morally as a direct consequence of his own aspirations. Compulsion through a ramified bureaucracy is an inevitable consequence of this society and must weigh on the conscience of the individual to constrict the integrity of his absolute freedom. In this indirect fashion, the individual is compelled to compel. In a technological society, the individual has no way of contracting out and may be forced to betray the integrity of his conscience. In this moral sense, his freedom may be suspended.

The road to maturity that follows such awareness must recognize *the reality of society*. Just as we cannot contract out of the institutions of power that have been created, neither can we preserve the goal of the reform of society without recognizing the limits set by the implacable constraints of technology. While the possibility of an absolute moral freedom may thus be suspended, nevertheless the demands of conscience would require us to search for the limits to which such a society can be made more free and more just. These limits are unknown; but without the abiding engagement in such a search, no one can resign himself prematurely to the view that all is lost, that technology triumphant is the foreboding destiny about which nothing can be done.

A moral position which begins with this basic recognition of the reality of society must be accompanied by a commitment to search for its limits. These limits can only be found in action—action in the concrete efforts of social reform.

The passionate moral fervour of "the new left" aims at total reform, disregarding the limitations and irreversible character of technological constraints. Wholesale references to our social difficulties are personified ubiquitously by the term "the Establishment". An absolute freedom is invoked which bypasses the stringencies of the technological environment and its institutional complex, which remain a permanent feature of our social existence. This political philosophy of the "new left" shares to a large extent the neglect and suspicion of power characteristic of liberal political thought in the nineteenth century and exhibited, for example, by the views of Lord Acton.

Virtually all of the aspirations of "the new left" have centered on the preservation of the deepest imperatives of freedom in the technological environment. This criticism of their philosophy bypasses their concrete and inspiring achievements. Yet if we accept our commitment to the new technology as irreversible, we must also accept, at least in principle, the limitation on freedom in ways which we have yet to explore.

The nationalism of the left presumes a different moral position on the possibilities of freedom. The chosen level of action is in the institutional sphere, and the center of concern is the protection of the cultural integrity and political values of the nation. This is a commitment to conservatism only if we fail to recognize the changing character of the nation itself.

The feudal nation was committed to privilege at a time when aristocracy and status considerations were dominant. The bourgeois nation was committed to the preservation of private property, freedom of contract, and to the political values which sustained a market economy. In our own day the nation itself is transformed under the new commitment to greater equality, to measures of social justice already embodied in the evolving welfare state and to a more genuine democracy. The democratic nation increasingly embodies the values and purposes of our present society.

The recognition of the increased responsibilities and changing social character of the modern nation does not limit the possibilities of participating in the growing interdependence of nations. A troubled nation which is the victim of its own conflicts, uncertainties and vacillations is neither in control of its own destiny nor able to fulfill the international tasks which are increasingly placed upon it.

While new technological requirements and new demands for natural resources, including water, will increasingly tie Canada and her economy to a North American framework, the political consequences of these technological developments can by no means be presumed to be congruent, i.e., to follow a mechanistic pattern that simply treads in the footsteps of those technological interconnections. The function of a creative politics has always been to protect society, to ensure order, growth and the flourishing of national life itself. On other continents and in other countries we have seen the way in which the spread of technology has been accompanied by a fierce revival of indigenous cultures, a reassertion of national values and a countermovement to retain national control of decision-making power. The creative response which man has often manifested to processes of rapid social change in the past gives some hope that technological determinism will not set the abiding pattern for future social existence. Of the various political and social responses that have thus far been offered to the challenge of the technological society, the nationalism of the left brings with it some rudimentary insights and values which will permit us to safeguard and to extend those features of social existence which we cherish and hope to preserve from the erosive forces of automation and technology.

NOTES
1. *New York Times,* December 7, 1965, p. 40.
2. Press Release, Department of Trade and Commerce, Ottawa, 90-65.

3. Details are given in the *New York Times,* December 7, 1965, p. 1 and the *Globe and Mail,* Toronto, November 17, 1965, p. 29.
4. This brief reference to the social history of the nineteenth century follows closely Karl Polanyi's *The Great Transformation,* Boston, 1957. The final section of this essay also draws heavily on his work.
5. C.f., Abraham Rotstein and Melville H. Watkins "The Outer Man", *Canadian Forum,* (August, 1965) .
6. Some of these thoughts draw on Douglas Lepan's essay "The Outlook for the Relationship: A Canadian View in *The United States and Canada,* John Sloane Dickey (ed.) , Englewood Cliffs, 1964, pp. 152-169.

conclusion •   peter russell

Are there any common ideas, or at least a common mood that can be detected in these various discussions of nationalism in Canada?

We certainly should not expect these twenty-one authors, being the individualistic academics they are, to deliberately work their way to a common conclusion. But it might be interesting to look back over this collection of essays to see if we can find any marked directions in the authors' opinions or, alternatively, their sharpest points of cleavage. Not, of course, that the thinking of this group could be thought of as mirroring Canadian public opinion—it is far too academic a group for that. But sometimes the movement of ideas in so-called "intellectual circles" can be a harbinger of the broader development of thought and sentiment in society. If this is so, then the prime points of agreement and disagreement in such a group's view on Canadian nationalism could indicate something of the quality and temper of nationalist thought which is emerging in Canada after a century of nationhood.

While this attempt to draw together some of the common strands of thought and debate forms the conclusion to this volume, it does not necessarily represent the contributors' conclusions. In fact, we suspect that where this concluding statement expresses views that are reasonably sharp and clear it is more likely to represent the position which the editor would have liked the authors to have reached, than to express ideas which they could all endorse with equal enthusiasm.

Two old tenets of Canadian nationalism are gone. First, the myth of the land, "The True North Strong and Free", however potent an inspiration it was for the founding generations of the Canadian nation, cannot feed the nationalism of Canadians who by the mid-twentieth century have been freed by industrial technology and urbanization from a real engagement with nature. Secondly, even for Anglo-Saxon Canadians the ideal of *British* North America can no longer provide the rationale for Canada's survival as a distinctive community on this continent.

Carl Berger's opening essays reveals how crucial the North once was to the patriotism of articulate Canadians. But this same revelation exposes to a more scientific generation of Canadians the false inferences, the ridiculous racism, upon which that pride in Canada's climate and terrain depended. In the past those popular theoreticians of Mr. Berger's article, who proclaimed the purifying effects of the Canadian winter and the challenge of its inhospitable soil, could call forth a response from their countrymen because so many Canadians found a real source of identification in the physical character of their land. Indeed, of all the themes which might have given Canadians a common sense of identity, a feeling for the Canadian landscape—its spaciousness, its grandeur and hardiness—probably stood the best chance of success. But this source of identity has been increasingly eroded by the great shift of population from the distinctive Canadian countryside into the relatively undistinguished settings of Canadian cities. This is the central theme of the geographer Cole Harris' essay.

Harris, it is true, sees the Canadian north playing a new role in the life of Canadians—a vacation playground into which the harrassed urbanite can periodically escape from the concrete jungle of the city. However, in this role, the symbolic value of the northern wilderness to nationalist sentiment is greatly reduced; the land—its forests and rocks, rivers and lakes—is no longer the central challenge in the Canadian's daily struggle for survival but, the contrary, more and more it derives its value from the contrast it provides with the normal conditions of the Canadian's work-a-day life.

The withdrawal of the land from the center of the Canadian consciousness is nowhere more evident than in contemporary Canadian art. Frank Watt's discussion of Canadian literature reveals the distance which separates the Confederation school of writers with their dutiful paeans to the Canadian terrain from the modern Canadian writer, whose hero, like

Mordecai Richler's, can best express his relationship to the land by urinating in the Laurentian snow. Carl Berger's retrospective glance at the Group of Seven makes us conscious of a similar tendency among contemporary Canadian painters to break away from their predecessors' almost total reliance on the northern landscape for their inspiration. If Canada is defined at all in the significant writing and painting of the post-war era, it is in terms of the personality and social relations of Canadians rather than their scenic backdrop. Neither Watt, nor surely those artists who have experienced this development, could regard it with any regret; on the contrary, they see it as an emancipating process in which the Canadian artist, released from the parochial duty of idealizing the local scene, aspires to meet international artistic norms and universal human interests.

On the whole it is the man-made environment, the web of institutions and technology with which nature has been tamed, its resources extracted and distributed, rather than the natural geographic setting itself, that our authors now see as the formative influence on the Canadian social character. A number of the papers take up particular phases of the impact of the social environment on Canadian nationality and nationalism. In Maurice Careless' essay, metropolitan centers of economic and political organization are depicted as both stimulating and responding to the growth of nationalism. For Frank Peers, the colossus of the American communications network threatens the very possibility of a Canadian culture and necessitates the establishment of national agencies which can give some national shape to what Canadians can hear and view through the electronic media. Melville Watkins and Abraham Rotstein explore the inter-connections between the technology of an industrialized and electronic era and the shape and substance of nationalism. While they reach rather different conclusions about the specific nature of these relationships, they are at one in insisting that the quality of Canadian nationalism will be thoroughly shaped by the technological fabric of Canadian society. In Alfred Dubuc's essay the failure of Canadian Confederation as a nation-making project is traced to its failure to respond to the new social forces and political demands generated by the transformation of the country's economic structure.

While all of these contributions, and others, testify to the importance of the institutional and technological background as the vital factor in setting the tone and direction of national thought in Canada, they also suggest, in various ways, that this man-made environment has generated powerful influences—communication flows, patterns of trade and investment, political orientations, which, in some sense, detract from or even contradict the national organization of Canadian society. The impulses of metropolitan power, as analyzed by Careless, can stimulate the organization of a region against rival centers of power within the nation or, on a continental scale, may take the form of the cultural imperialism of a New York or a Los Angeles of which Frank Peers is so apprehensive. The technological society of Watkins' and Rotstein's articles clearly facilitates the linking together of people in collectivities which are both larger and smaller than the nation. And in Dubuc's view it is the province or region which appears most prepared to assume the functions of economic management demanded by a post-capitalist society.

In a way, all this may represent the contemporary version of the view which was so prevalent in the past, that if Canada was to exist as a nation it must do so in defiance of its geography. Now it is not the problems of spanning a vast continental space or of overcoming the allegedly north-south contours of the continent's topography which appear to pose the principal challenge to the viability of Canadian nationhood. Instead, it is almost as if the nation-state in general, and the Canadian nation in particular, were viewed as simply one possible configuration of human energies which may or may not be the most appropriate way of handling the various forces and problems created by the modern environment.

We may also note the passing of another classical tenet of Canadian nationalism. None of the authors conceive of Canada's purpose as the preservation of an outpost of British culture on the North American continent. Of course many who have written about Canada in recent years have noticed how much the nationalism of the loyalists and the British colonists has receded from the centre of the Canadian ethos. What is remarkable here is that the members of this group take this so much for granted. They do not share George Grant's lament for the passing of *British* North America;[1] they are much more concerned with the new things the nation might do and become than with the idolization of those fragments of British culture which might be preserved from the colonial past.

Those in the book who attempt to define nationalist goals for English-speaking Canada do not rely on the prescription of distinctively British symbols and institutions. Stephen Clarkson, for one, in advocating the integration of an identifiable English-speaking community to act as a vital partner for the French-speaking community in a "binational" Canada, makes it clear that such an "English" Canada should be English only in the linguistic sense. He insists that this English-speaking culture would have to be one that was no longer dominated by explicitly Anglo-Saxon values or customs. In this way it could provide an attractive cultural focus for the non-French ethnic elements in the Canadian population, such as the Ukrainians who are discussed in Betty Wangenheim's article. While Kenneth McNaught, unlike Clarkson, believes that English-speaking Canadians have already evolved a meaningful national tradition, he sees that tradition as an indigenous one, built upon the historical experience Canadians have derived from the pragmatic adaption of their political and constitutional systems to the stresses and strains of national life. It is a tradition which, as McNaught portrays it, has come to reject a narrowly ethnic conception of Canada, be it in the form of an exclusively Anglo-Saxon nation or a bicultural partnership.

Ironically, it is Michel Brunet, the French-Canadian historian, who records the sharpest impression of Canada as a nation inherently based upon an Anglo-Saxon hegemony. The image of Canada as the British Kingdom of North America which Brunet finds so alien to the nationalist aspirations of French Canadians is also rejected by his English-speaking colleagues in this book. The tragedy may be that his interpretation of English Canada could be close enough to the reality of popular nationalist sentiment among English-speaking Canadians in the past that his own expression of hope for the creation of a homogeneous French-Canadian nation may now represent the delayed, although nonetheless logical response of his French-Canadian compatriots.

Not only is there little evidence of British-oriented nationalism in this volume, but there is also surprisingly little expression of its most prevalent substitute, the negative nationalism of anti-Americanism. Charles Hanly presents a psychoanalytic explanation of the way in which Canadian allegiance to Britain can form the basis of an ardent desire to secure Canada's independence from the United States. The force of Hanly's analysis is to dissuade Canadians, now that they have achieved formal national autonomy, from simply transferring their emotional dependence on the British connection into an equally dependent fear of America.

There would appear to be few traces in this collection of the kind of pathological fear of American threats to Canadian independence which worries Hanly. It is true that both Ian Macdonald and Stephen Hymer evince some concern for the possible detrimental effects which American investment in Canada might have on the Canadian economy, but neither fears the loss of political independence and both would concur with John Dales' view that Canadian protectionism has done much to induce American firms to invest directly in their own Canadian subsidiaries. There is certainly little support here for the new nationalism of the Eric Kierans-Walter Gordon axis which would use the fear of American control of the Canadian economy as the ideological tool for pulling French- and English-speaking Canada together. The only author who may indirectly suggest this possibility is Abraham Rotstein.

But the areas of agreement among our authors are not confined to merely negative themes. In order to reject certain nationalist possibilities they have had to put forward some positive views of their own. While it is considerably more difficult to generalize about these than about the ideas that have been rejected, there are at least two tendencies which nearly all of them appear to share in their approach to nationalism. Most indicate that the kind of nationalism they could subscribe to as Canadians must be both internationalist and pluralist in tone. With some authors these qualities of their nationalism are openly declared. With others they are implicit.

By internationalism we mean, above all, a conception of nationalism which is not motivated by fear of foreign influences or a hostility to other nations but which, on the contrary, is inspired by the hope that Canada might play a constructive and conciliatory role in the community of nations. George Heiman's essay presents the classical analysis of the two-sided nature of nationalist politics: the intense nationalism which can serve as a unifying force within a nation can have equally potent disruptive effects on the international community. Most of the writers seem acutely aware of the dangers of which Heiman warns. Indeed, in expressing their aspiration for a Canadian nationalism which is internationally innocent, they betray at times an image of Canada which comes close to what John Holmes satirically describes as the "immaculate nation".

But more frequently their repudiation of a chauvinistic, negative nationalism takes into account the importance of developing and maintaining in Canada enough national cohesion to enable Canada to act as an effective agent in international affairs. Both John Holmes and Abraham Rotstein remind us of how much Canada's ability to play a significant role in the community of nations depends on its ability to sustain itself as a viable and relatively independent nation-state. Yet it is significant that both these writers emphasize international undertakings as the focus of Canada's national purpose. For Holmes it is the tasks of middle-power diplomacy which provide the key objectives of Canadian foreign policy; for Rotstein it is the harnessing of a technology, international in scope, which provides the rationale for the creation in Canada of effective national agencies.

The other positive characteristic which we have attributed to our authors' nationalist thought—their pluralism—can in a sense be viewed as the domestic application of their internationalism.[2] Just as they would, on the whole, avoid any overtones of a nationalism that threatened to be aggressive or intolerant in relation to other nations, they would similarly repudiate any form of Canadian nationalism which insisted on a highly homogeneous cultural basis for the Canadian nation. They are all pluralists in that they accept multiculturalism as a fundamental axiom of Canadian nationhood.

For some, the multicultural basis of the Canadian nation is conceived of in distinctly bicultural, French-English terms. This is most marked in Stephen Clarkson's programme for a binational nationalism which calls for the development of institutions and policies at the federal level which are equally meaningful and open to French- and English-speaking Canadians, and the integration at the regional level of a homogeneous French language culture in Quebec on the one hand and an equally homogeneous English-language culture in the rest of Canada on the other. In a more negative vein, Elizabeth Wangenheim's article on the Ukrainian Canadians warns of the disintegrative effects on Canadian unity which are likely to ensue if the special claims of the French-speaking minority in Canada are extended to other ethnic minorities. Basic to both Wangenheim's and Clarkson's arguments is the view that the degree of social integration required to sustain Canada as a national society requires that some limit be set to the country's cultural heterogeneity. It is French-English biculturalism which they see as setting the basic boundaries to Canada's cultural diversity.

Several writers, without committing themselves to a thoroughly dualistic view of Canadian nationality, stress the need for national policies which can act as an integrative force by capturing the loyalty and enthusiasm of French- and English-speaking Canadians. Donald Smiley focuses on this requirement of federal programmes in the era of co-operative federalism, when so many of the initiatives in the dynamic areas of government have gravitated to the provinces. John Holmes points to the opportunities in the field of foreign policy for attaching French Canadians' interest to national activities. And Frank Peers urges that the CBC make more substantial efforts to use the national broadcasting system as an instrument for improving communication between the country's two main cultural groups.

In such contributions as these the readers will recognize the now familiar response of English-speaking liberals to Quebec's Quiet Revolution. What this response insists upon is the need for measures of accommodation capable of building a Canada which can provide as satisfactory a homeland for French Canadians as it already provides for English-speaking Canadians. Those who take this stand are sometimes accused of "balkanizing" the country by their willingness to "make concessions" to regional and ethnic demands. But we should notice that their position is a highly nationalist one. Their aim in advocating bicultural policies at the national level is to promote the political integration of the nation. Their strategy in recommending a large measure of autonomy at the local level, particularly for Quebec, is based on the assumption that the loyalty of any part of the nation to the whole can be strengthened by virtue of the freedom the whole provides for the self-expression and self-fulfillment of the part. In a word, the conception of nationalism expressed here is one which sees national unity as the product rather than the victim of the diversification and heterogeneity of Canadian society. They are inclined to accept for Canada the general thesis which the political scientist Lucien Pye has advanced for multi-cultural states in the process of political development that "whenever the pressures of the parochial are too great, as for example in the agitation for linguistic states in India, and parochial interests have had to be accepted into the national political process, the result has usually been a strengthening of the national unity."[3]

This conception of nationalism is not, however, unanimously endorsed by all the book's authors. Indeed there is one, Michel Brunet, who expresses a sharply contrasting kind of nationalist sentiment. Because this contrast provides an interesting insight into the current crisis of Confederation, it is one which we think is worth drawing out in some detail.

The critical point of contrast is not simply that the object of Brunet's nationalist loyalty is Quebec while that of his English-speaking colleagues is Canada. The vital difference is in the very tone or spirit of their nationalisms. Brunet's quest for a French-Canadian fatherland represents the classic nationalism of the nineteenth century. This is the principled nationalism built on the ethic of the self-determination of peoples. It is designed to appeal to a relatively homogeneous people who are thought to possess the characteristics of a distinct nationality, a nationality whose very survival requires its total and exclusive possession of the instrumentalities of statehood. This is the integral nationalism which provoked or inspired various European nationalities in the last century to fight for their political independence so that they might win for themselves a distinct place in the sun.

Beside this brand of nationalist idealism which Brunet articulates for the *Québécois,* the national aspirations which our English-speaking contributors hold out for Canada may look rather meagre. Some might even question whether the latter possess the necessary ingredients for a meaningful sense of nationalism. But they surely do; their nationalism is more relaxed, more cosmopolitan and less ardent than Brunet's, but it is a nationalism nonetheless.

Where Brunet's nationalism is essentially nineteenth-century in its ideological roots, theirs is informed with the quality and tone of the twentieth century. Theirs is the nationalism of individuals who feel part of an urbanized industrialized environment which is larger than the nation. Within that larger environment they conceive of their nation as one way, although not the only way, of organizing human forces to confront the problems and possibilities of that environment. On their agenda of national goals there is no priority for the preservation or the creation of a distinctive indigenous culture by virtue of which Canada might be marked off more sharply from other nations. In this sense they do not seem to be suffering from the identity crisis which is often attributed to Canadians. The national programmes and policies which they advocate are designed not to accentuate the differences between Canadians and other peoples but to engage Canadians in activities which are valid and worthwhile regardless of the ethnic background of the people who undertake them. James Guillet's proposal that Canada take upon itself responsibility for research in one of the major frontier areas of modern technology and Charles Hanly's plea that Canadians find an outlet for their emotions and fantasies in the achievement of significant works of art typify the search for more universal, less parochial national goals.

Again it is remarkable that those writers who deal with the issue of American investment in Canada are more concerned with the way it might diminish the efficiency of the Canadian economy than with any threat it might pose to Canadian independence or identity. Stephen Hymer points to the economic disadvantages to Canada of direct foreign investment which is prompted by the quest for monopoly profits. But there is no peculiar Canadian logic to his argument. In essence his is an international argument designed to alert the international community to the inadequacy of anti-monopoly measures contained within the traditional national framework in an era which is witnessing the proliferation of giant international corporation with near-monopoly positions in their respective industries. While Ian Macdonald is apprehensive about the "miniature replica" effect of direct American investment, it is not American economic imperialism which he blames for this phenomenon, but Canada's own protective tariff. His point in advocating economic identity as a national value is not to make Canadian manufacturing less like American but to promote conditions which direct resources into forms of production where Canada enjoys a comparative advantage over other countries.

The form which economic nationalism takes in these articles is decisively different from the classical nineteenth-century variety with its emphasis on the need for protective walls behind which the domestic economy, sheltered from the destructive gale of international competition, could be nurtured and integrated. In particular, it represents a repudiation of the Canadian version of that nineteenth century economic nationalism which, as Craig Brown's article demonstrates, was the motivating ethos of Sir John A. Macdonald's National Policy. John Dales gives the most explicit statement of the new economic nationalism. His goals are neither bigness nor independence; he does not see independence as an issue, and a mere interest in the magnitude of production he regards as detrimental to a concern for the quality of economic and social activity. It is the latter which he posits as the proper economic goal—the derivation of the maximum utility from the nation's available resources. For him such a goal represents a nationalist cause, for if it is achieved he can take pride in his nation for conducting its economic affairs efficiently. Clearly, this kind of economic nationalism is directed not to the myth of economic grandeur or autarky but to the utopia of economic efficiency.[4]

All this is not to say that the main tenor of nationalist thought which we are attributing to our English-speaking contributors has no myths of its own. The feeling of political innocence which so many authors convey is, in its way, the contemporary counterpart of an earlier generation's belief in their destiny as a virile and pure northerly race. This sense of innocence is, as we have seen, double-edged, containing both the ideal of international goodwill and that of domestic tolerance. As a nationalist myth it provides the image of a nation which, while it is able to enjoy the level of economic and social development achieved by the United States, is at the same time free from both the guilt Americans experience as a consequence of their international power and the arrogance they can assume as the bearers of an idealized way of life.

The potency of this myth is revealed by the shocked sense of disbelief experienced by Anglo-Saxon intellectuals when they are confronted with the kind of charges a contemporary French-Canadian nationalist, such as Brunet, flings at English-speaking Canadians. It is precisely the accusation that English-speaking Canadians have used their majoritarian power within the Canadian dominion to subjugate the French-Canadian nationality which rubs so harshly against their own sense of innocence. They cannot feel responsible for the fact that the larger Canadian society, with all its economic and political opportunities which they wish to share with their French-Canadian countrymen is, right now, a society in which they are more at home than are French Canadians. Nor can they regard their own commitment to a pluralistic, bilingual nation as any less liberal, because bilingualism for them is inevitably a cultural luxury while for French Canadians it is more likely an economic necessity. Our English-speaking authors seem to find no difficulty in identifying their own aspirations with Canada's, no difficulty in thinking of themselves as Canadians and yet on the whole they deny that Canada has a homogeneous cultural base. Perhaps the key to this is that the Canadian environment which they have experienced has become such a natural fit for their own temperament and outlook that they cannot conceive of it as being imbued with its own distinct values which may not be equally congenial to all of their fellow-citizens.

It might appear that if the two kinds of nationalism we have been describing could understand each other and recognize each other's claims it would be relatively easy for them to co-exist within a single nation. Brunet's integral, highly ethnic conception of nationalism is, after all, projected only for Quebec; he leaves open the possibility that such a French-Canadian "nation" might continue to participate as a "nation" in some larger and looser Canadian political union. The nationalist thought of our English-speaking contributors seems flexible and liberal enough to accept a large degree of decentralization within the Canadian federation and of cultural diversification and heterogeneity in Canadian society. Such an analysis may suggest that their respective expectations and demands as nationalists rather than being contradictory are, in fact, complementary.

But the trouble with this prognosis is that it loses sight of the really vital difference which separates the two nationalisms. Brunet's nationalism does not represent simply a more extreme version of provincial rights; *if* his nationalism became the prevailing mood of Quebec's Quiet Revolution, it could neither be fulfilled nor accommodated by simply granting Quebec a greater degree of autonomy within Confederation. For it represents a political philosophy which is fundamentally at odds with the kind of nationalism required for membership in the Canadian federation. Brunet's kind of nationalism requires a political state—Quebec—to which a single ethnic nationality—the *Québécois*—can give its first and highest political loyalty. The minimal nationalism of Canadian federalism must surely insist that the citizen's highest political loyalty is to the federal union, which provides the national framework of a state to which a multitude of (ethnic) nationalities belong. This federal nationalism, at the individual level, eschews any attempt to equate an individual's cultural or ethnic characteristics with his opportunities for citizenship and, at the level of the collectivity, superimposes the claims of the political state over those of any particular cultural unit.[5]

The gulf between these two nationalisms is so wide that if they became the dominant nationalist sentiments of the two main divisions of the Canadian population, these two peoples would surely be better off going their separate ways. To remain together would make it impossible for either to fulfill its highest ideals. Their political cultures would be too far apart to make it possible, let alone profitable, for them to participate in a common citizenship.

While this polarity of nationalist philosophies points to the severance of the Canadian nation as a possibility for the future, there are other signs in the book and of the times that hold out greater promise of convergence. These signs can be detected both in the social and economic environment as well as in certain facets of the political culture.

The transition from a rural and agricultural society to one whose prevailing characteristics are urban and industrial has, as we have seen, had a marked effect on the nationalist thought of many of our authors. Their sense of national identity is far less dependent on blood and soil than was that of the earlier generations explored by Carl Berger. Their national imagery is articulated far more in terms of using the collective powers of their community to direct the new technology to humane purposes than in preserving or cultivating a highly differentiated culture. This process of modernization has been taking place in Quebec, perhaps at a different pace from other parts of Canada, but nonetheless with the same potential for decisively altering the character of that province's socio-economic environment and possibly also the content and direction of its nationalist thought.

It is likely that as the pace of modernization quickens, it diminishes the relevancy of a nationalism which summons people to draw together in defence of an historic cultural tradition, organically linked to a particular linguistic group. Further, the homogenizing impact which both industrialization and urbanization tend to have on working and living conditions should reduce the concrete marks of differentiation between French- and English-speaking Canadians. But none of these trends are likely to promote a closer political union of the two cultures unless they are accompanied by a convergence of political philosophies. We have now seen enough of modernization on a world-scale to realize that while it does generate more uniform patterns of culture and technology, it also stimulates political involvement and heightens political expectations. Unless there is a drawing together at the level of overriding political ideals, modernization may only provide more powerful tools and incentives for cultivating animosities between particular peoples or nationalities.

But we do find some indication here of convergence in what, for the future, is possibly the most important dimension of political thought. It is precisely at the point of intersection between nationalist aspirations and a commitment to social reform that we find the most significant possibility of consensus, not only for our authors but for reformist thought in French- and English-speaking Canada generally. This possibility hinges above all on a common determination to supplant the economic market as the prime agency for distributing social and economic values with collective and democratically organized public agencies.

Alfred Dubuc's contribution to this volume provides a vibrant illustration of this current of thought in contemporary French Canada. For Canadian nationalists the force of Dubuc's analysis of Confederation's past and present is to argue that, if it has a future, it must be in terms of a national organization of political power appropriate for the direction of public affairs in a post-capitalist society. To be relevant to the needs and capacities of this society, such a state must undertake the major responsibility for managing the social consequences of a modern industry and technology and distributing the wealth it makes possible.

This is a concept of national purpose which a large number of our authors could share. Canada's future as a nation may well depend on the degree to which it represents a political idealism in which French- and English-speaking Canadians can make common cause for the whole of Canada.

NOTES

1. George Grant, *Lament for a Nation,* Toronto, 1965.
2. Roy Mathews has recently presented a statement of Canadian nationalism based very much on the twin ideals of internationalism and pluralism in an article entitled, "Canada, 'The International Nation' ", *Queen's Quarterly,* Autumn 1965.
3. Lucien W. Pye, *Aspects of Political Development,* Boston and Toronto, 1966, p. 52.
4. On the distinction between myth and utopia, see above, *Preface,* p. viii.
5. Lord Acton's essay on "Nationality" provides the classic liberal argument against making a single nationality the basis of a political nationhood, *Essays on Freedom and Power,* New York, 1963, p. 141-170. For further discussion of the distinction between nationality and nation, see above, George Heiman, "The 19th Century Legacy: Nationalism or Patriotism?", pp. 328-332.